THE LEPER'S BELL

THE LEPER'S BELL

The Autobiography
of a
Changeling

Norman Maclean

BIRLINN

This edition published in 2010 by
Birlinn Limited
West Newington House
10 Newington Road
Edinburgh
EH9 1QS

www.birlinn.co.uk

First published in 2009 by Birlinn Limited
Reprinted 2011

ISBN: 978 1 84158 891 9

British Library Cataloguing-in-Publication Data
A catalogue record for this book is available from the
British Library

Set in Bembo at Birlinn

Printed and bound in Great Britain by
CPI Cox & Wyman, Reading

For Màiri

CONTENTS

Puedo escribir los versos más tristes esta noche . . .
Tonight I can write the saddest lines . . .
Es tan corte el amor, y es tan largo el olvido . . .
Love is so short, forgetting is so long . . .

Pablo Neruda

ACKNOWLEDGEMENTS

A trio of closet literati encouraged me as I pecked away at my keyboard. Colin Robertson, my former manager, who himself won a prize for a poem he wrote during a long sojourn in an establishment in Angus, was convinced after reading a handful of chapters that the work would rank with that of Ralph Glasser in thirty years' time. Look, Colin is a real hard nut, and, as far as I'm concerned, can say what he likes. Tam McGarvie of GalGael read the second or third draft and described it as 'a magic read'. Brian McGeachan, a freelance journalist friend who is at present writing a stage play called *The Johnny Thomson Story*, praised the odd chapter lavishly. Certainly he was drinking my whisky in my home at the time and – hey, I remember my first drink of beer too. Though I was secretly convinced he was lying, I was able to luxuriate for brief spells in an exaggerated sense of my own importance.

Marion Anderson, the mother of my cousin Norrie Anderson, is an old lady who just likes to read. She was the first human being to devour the first draft, and she claimed that it resembled something by P.G. Wodehouse! The restraint that any reader brings to his or her enjoyment of my writing is not something I am prepared to tamper with.

Reviewing the progress of the work over the past year, I think it would be churlish of me to ignore the very real contribution to my physical survival made by Norrie and his sweet daughter, Sarah. They fetched prescription and other drugs for me; they cooked for me and their frequent visits provided welcome punctuation marks during what were essentially long, boring days. A hundred thousand warm thanks to you guys for keeping me going.

The greatest champion the work ever had, though, a man to whom I shall long be in debt, is Robbie Fraser, as fine a writer and film director as Scotland has produced in the twenty-first century, who wrote a six-page, single-spaced critique of my first draft which imposed coherence on the flashy non-linear, Tarantinoesque even, punchy narrative I had favoured initially. The writer and director of the cult feature film *Gamerz* gave me the motivation and courage to create a new framework for my story. *Mòran taing, 'ille*.

I cannot settle for no acknowledgement of the role of Màiri Mac-Farlane during the last furlong of the story. Advice on phrasing, the presentation of new ideas and, on occasion, the physically typing out of whole passages on to my hard disk provided me with surcease and restored my flagging energy. I wish you luck with your screenwriting career, *a Mhàiri*.

It would be churlish of me to ignore the contributions made by Andrew Simmons and Tom Johnstone of Birlinn Ltd: the former, the company's Commissioning Editor, for discerning merit in the first draft, and the latter whose meticulous attention to the text greatly enhanced the finished article.

AUTHOR'S NOTE

In chapters 15 and 18, due to the intimate nature of their contents, the names Margo McGougain and Greta Macdonald are pseudonyms.

Prologue

The 'Crock-Pot', as my wife Peigi persists in calling this implement of gleaming stainless steel, has finally arrived at my door. It's really a slow-cooker out of Tesco in Oban, and I am about to christen it. A crock-pot for an old crock.

Three gigot chops, a whole onion, two carrots, garlic, one Oxo cube, salt and pepper. Everything ready. Looks simple enough. All I have to do is throw everything into the cooking pan, add two cupfuls of water . . . umh, maybe three . . . I have some macaroni handy, and the pasta, I had been warned, would suck up a lot of liquid.

Now, Norman, I lecture myself. There's no need to get into a frenzy over the preparation of stew. Women all over the Highlands and Lowlands do this every day. Yes, and have been doing so throughout the ages. My late mother, *Peigi Bheag*, Wee Peggy, my various wives and girlfriends, all did this without thinking about it. That is the problem. I have to think about it. Seventy-one years of age, no womenfolk around, and none likely to be either in the immediate future. The shameful truth is: I have never cooked a meal in my entire life.

Firstly, I have to wash and slice the vegetables. This will take some time. A severed nerve in my right forearm has left three fingers of my right hand paralyzed. I know I won't be able to grip the knife firmly. For that matter, I was unable to sign my application for Attendance Allowance last week without using both hands. Not that the left hand is in much better nick. Since the operation last autumn for a broken humerus, when Dr Levi down in the Southern General Hospital had inserted pins in my upper left arm, I haven't been able to raise my left arm above shoulder level. The little consultant confessed to me before I went into the operating theatre that he was having second thoughts about the complexity of the procedure after looking at the X-rays. Since then I've had a hundred thoughts that I ought to have had the operation done in a BUPA hospital. It could be worse, he consoled me afterwards. Although the limb would never be as supple as it was, at least there would be no more pain. With a snout full of morphine, I had to agree with him.

The pain I felt when I took the drunken tumble into a wrought-iron gate was truly excruciating. I had been returning to my tiny 'studio flat' in Lora Drive with a cargo of booze one Sunday evening last summer, when I felt dizzy and thought I'd better take a rest on the steps of a path in the front garden of a neighbour. I never made it. As I pushed the gate open I fell with my arms extended through the vertical iron bars. A bone from my upper left arm was actually protruding from the skin. I felt it in my right arm too: a sharp, stabbing pain in the elbow.

A couple out walking their dog discovered me lying on my stomach on the wet pavement, both arms entwined in the gate's bars. They promptly telephoned for an ambulance. The paramedics administered oxygen on the way to the Accident and Emergency department.

Unfortunately, there was an unprecedented press of patients waiting to go under the knife for hip, knee, foot and arm operations, so that I was confined to bed until a 'window' presented itself. The harrowing ordeal over the next three weeks or so was compounded of morphine, co-codamol and bed rest. There had been perhaps too much of the latter. I developed bed sores. I lusted for tobacco. I was unable to read to pass the weary hours. I had no reading glasses on my person when I fell.

Eventually, the day of the operation dawned. Levi painted a line on my arm where he was going to make an incision. Somebody injected something in the back of my hand. In a short time I passed out.

When I came round, I experienced a warm, drowsy feeling of well-being. Despite having been warned that I'd probably be sick after the general anaesthetic, I hoovered up the toast and Marmite I was offered. Later on, I enjoyed the first deep sleep I'd had in months.

Unfortunately, my appetite severely diminished after that, and by the time I was discharged my weight was down to just over eight stones. For a person of my height – I used to be a six-footer, though I've shrunk with advancing years – this weight loss was a source of worry. My fertile imagination projected all kinds of uninformed diagnoses: cancer, MS, motor-neurone disease.

I was at my GP's only last Friday and I'm just over the ten-stone mark now.

"Well?" I said.

"Well, honestly, Mr Maclean, I'm delighted for you," Dr Russell said.

"Hmmph," I snorted. "I weighed around thirteen stone when I was boxing for the university."

"You're gaining weight, slowly but steadily," young Dr Russell said. "And that's without the use of steroids. Well done." He smiled at me as though awarding me the Dux Medal at Bellahouston Academy, my old secondary school.

I asked him about the severed nerve in my right arm, and he told me that at my age it would take over a year to repair itself. I felt like punching him out.

"Of course, you'll have to continue with the exercises," he said.

The exercises involved raising my right arm to shoulder level and wiggling the fingers of my hand. The last time I had attempted this little manoeuvre was on the aisle seat of the 34 bus going to Govan. Not surprisingly, this prompted two male passengers of dubious sexual orientation to wave back at me. Upon reaching the terminus, my cheeks ablaze, I trapped for the underground station like Dwayne Chambers.

"Yeah," I drawled thoughtfully. "I'll be doing that in the privacy of my home."

The doctor smiled again, but this time rather oddly.

Now, as I stand looking at the foodstuffs on the worktop, my smile is a bit odd too. I suffer a twinge of apprehension as I recall the prodigious obstacle course I had to negotiate in Morrisons to obtain all this gear. Vegetable oil, tortilla wraps, macaroni . . . I had secured the lot. But at enormous psychic cost!

The truth is that I had made these purchases only by exerting almost superhuman will-power. I've known for a long time that I'm allergic to the food aisles in supermarkets. Every time I'd trawl through the shelves of exotic food I would be assailed by a top of the Richter scale panic attack. I always felt the aisles were narrowing in on me, and I would be convinced that I'd never escape to the more sedate pastures of the bakery counter which lay at right angles to the Valley of Hell.

I experienced no such anxiety, of course, when patrolling the fish counter and especially the richly-stocked alcohol shelves. But finding the macaroni in the international food section induced a kind of St Vitus's Dance, in which I leaped from side to side in response to the strange names of the goods on the shelves. As I searched for the macaroni, labels swam into vision. 'Ainsley Harriot Cous Cous', 'Bulgar Wheat', 'Yellow Split Peas' – aarrgh! 'Hearts of Palm', 'Sushi Nori', 'Passata' – eek! 'Pasta Rigate', 'Cavatappi', 'Sun Dried Chillies' – oops! I stagger into a shelf of Penne Tricolore, lose my balance and go down. I am up in a flash, and with a fixed maniacal grin on my face, I grab a packet of macaroni and, cool and dignified, I saunter to the check-out.

Buzz! Inexplicable panic: there's someone at the outside door of my building. Can it be sheriff's officers looking to recover the debt I owe the Halifax Bank of Scotland? Jesus! Why isn't there a resident Free Church minister in this building? I want to repent. I am a sinner!

With my left hand I lift the receiver on the wall with difficulty. "Hi," I gasp. "Yes, this is Norman Maclean . . . who are you? What? . . . a workman. Right, come on up." I press the black button on the console with the paralyzed forefinger of my right hand to release the lock on the outside door.

I open the door to my flat and stand in stocking soles on the concrete landing, looking down. I watch the laborious ascent of an overweight middle-aged man, bulky in luminous parka, as he slowly climbs the two flights of stairs to where I stand. Breathing hard, he scatters mud from his stout work boots behind him.

"Have you got a key for the drying area downstairs, buddy?" he says. "We're going to put some more scaffolding up at the gable end."

"Yeah," I say uninterestedly, retrieving an awl-shaped tool from the hook in the hallway and handing it to him.

"Cheers, mate," he mumbles insincerely. "We'll return it to you when we get back."

"You're leaving the job now?" I say.

"Aye," he says, as though I am some kind of retard who doesn't understand that what he is about to do is the most normal thing in the world in the building trade. "Something's come up." He turns and clatters down the stairs.

Since the fourth of February, this has been happening with baffling frequency. A sole workman with a generator and electric drill will be scrambling along the scaffolding that decorates our building, affixing thermal sheeting to the original walls, which will later be pebble-dashed. The next minute he'll be gone, for no apparent reason.

Shaking my head in disbelief, I return to my spotless kitchen. Part of me is irritated that these ageing goons are taking so long. I recalled an army of Indian tradesmen and labourers, admittedly hundreds of them, erecting a one-hundred-and-thirty-roomed hotel in Muscat in Oman within a week. Another part of me is glad that, because of the lack of organization and native indolence of this Scottish platoon, I won't receive a bill for this work for some time. The Glasgow Housing Association, the building's factor, has informed us all, tenants and house owners, in a self-congratulatory letter sent just before Christmas, that it is their intention to execute a staggering total of 1.2 million repairs city-wide, at the cost of a mammoth £135 million. My share is to be a mere nine-and-a-half thousand pounds. I was assured by letter that the refurbishment would take thirty years off the appearance of the building, and would enhance the value of my home. I thought that unless somebody could refurbish my decrepit old body and enhance my value in the eyes of the manager of the local Bank of Scotland, I would have to consider grabbing a sawn-off shotgun and making an unauthorized withdrawal from another Scottish bank.

Nine and a half thousand pounds! Every cell in my brain and body sagged. I felt symptoms of terminal blood-sweat coming on.

I forced myself to contemplate the ingredients for my stew once more. Nothing else for it. Deep breath. I carefully, even gingerly, place the meat, vegetables and macaroni in the slow cooker. I submerge the lot in nearly a pint of water. And? I pray to Delia and Jamie before switching the apparatus on and turning the dial to 'Automatic'. I am hopeful that something nourishing will emerge in about eight hours' time.

On stiff legs I totter into the living room. Plonking my sagging limbs on the little two-seater sofa, I make a swift inventory of the place. The blazing electric fire to my left, with various pipe and practice chanters propped against the wood surround, reminds me of how my puny savings account is positively haemorrhaging money while I am unable to generate cash. Doing stand-up comedy gigs in the north is simply out of the question because of my poor physical condition. There would be no more playing of the Highland bagpipe for some time, if ever.

About two months ago, I had the notion that I'd accompany a small group of pipers and drummers from Strathclyde Police Pipe Band to Beijing some time in early summer. Once there, the idea was to lay down some backing tapes to which the full band would play at the grand opening of the 2008 Olympic Games. My contribution would have been a minuscule one. In the voice of God I'd declaim some overblown lines I had composed some years earlier as a replacement anthem for 'Flower of Scotland'.

> Side by side we stand together,
> 'Neath the flag of blue and white:
> We salute you now and ever,
> And our souls are filled with pride.
>
> *CHORUS*
>
> In my heart, a flame is burning
> For the land where I belong,
> Thoughts of homeland aye returning,
> Here in Scotland, blood is strong.
>
> *RECITATIVE*
>
> We are neither conquerors nor conquered.
> We prize freedom above all else.
> We offer peace and love to those who share our ideals –
> Harmony, decency and hope to the world from ourselves.

As well as missing out on this jaunt, I'd probably also lose the chance to show off as a member of the Sons of Scotland Pipes and Drums at the World Pipe Band Championship on Glasgow Green in August. I suppose this Winnipeg-based outfit would – how does the locution go? – have to try it without me.

At my feet lies a yellowing press cutting that has been laying siege to my mind for about a fortnight. I pick it up and read slowly. There it is, a full centre-spread with a quarter page of me grinning inanely into the lens.

STORMIN' NORMAN: AN EXCLUSIVE INTERVIEW

GRAEME DONOHOE

Sunday Mail, Friday 10th December 1999

The bizarre life and times of the crazy comic who was . . . Mugged up the Amazon . . . Shanghaied in Bangkok . . . Kidnapped in Michigan . . . Stripped bare in Mexico . . . Blown up in ritzy hotel!

"The last time I was cast in a movie, Bill Forsyth signed me up for a part in *Comfort and Joy* in 1983, but I lasted just three days.

"He made the massive mistake of putting me up in an all-expenses-paid hotel for a weekend – and of course, it had a well-stocked mini-bar.

"I was on the phone straight away to my pals, who were right over to enjoy brandies on the account with me for a full weekend – the bill was about £3000.

"Bill was a really nice guy, but I knew I'd blown it and had no complaints when I was thrown off set."

The Gaelic comic is also currently lining up a series of festive gigs, and has written a new novel, *Keino*.

Norman, sporting a black eye after a boozy session led to him being mugged outside a Glasgow pub, has been off the demon drink for a month.

And the man who wrote and starred in Gaelic soap *Machair*, and boasts Sean Connery and Billy Connolly as fans of his comedy, has vowed to keep it that way.

But he insists he has no regrets – boasting some of the most incredible boozing stories ever.

Amazingly, Norman hit the headlines three years ago after going for a pint in Govan – and waking up in Thailand married to a local girl called PORN!

The funnyman has ligged, gigged and swigged in exotic bars across the globe.

He said: "I started the morning in Govan and got a notion of seeing my daughter in Hong Kong. She then told me I was looking a little pale and booked me a trip to Thailand – it was right up there with launching the *Titanic*, what a mistake!

"The next thing I remember was waking up and finding photos and documents beside my passport that told me I'd got married to a girl called Porn.

"The memory's very hazy, but I can just about remember exchanging rings in a Buddhist temple near Pattaya, with all these baldy men in yellow suits bouncing around. It was like a dream, until Porn turned up with all sorts of documents and made me promise to take her to Scotland.

"The last time I saw her was at Bangkok Airport – I had to call her and explain I had to get divorced, because I was already married. . . ."

Even at home in Scotland barmy Norman has managed to wreak havoc.

On his 1995 Highland tour, blitzed Norman was found snoring in Fort William divorcee Linda MacGillivray's bed, after stumbling into the wrong HOUSE.

Hotels are put on red alert wherever he goes, after he accidentally blew one up and set another on fire. [Not uncharacteristically, in this interview with Graeme I seem to be running along a current of low-voltage humour, as I do to this day, even when describing harrowing events. Old habits, as the English proverb has it, die hard.]

He said, "The time I blew up the hotel, I'd sneaked into the kitchen to make soup, but left the gas on after passing out drunk. Unfortunately, before anyone realized it, another guest had needed a cigarette and had nipped into the kitchen for a crafty drag. But no one was badly hurt, even though the explosion blew the roof off.

"The second time wasn't as bad – it was only my room that was damaged by the flames after I fell asleep while smoking a fag. I'm not proud of pestering firemen for an ashtray while they were trying to put the fire out."

Manic Norman revealed how fans Billy Connolly and Sean Connery warned him alcohol would blight his comic talents. He said: "Billy Connolly was just hitting the big time in 1980 when he asked me to do a gig for him after hearing my tapes.

"He was doing a cycle run from Glasgow to Inverness, and he'd have guest entertainers to join him on tour for gigs along the way. He'd insisted on getting this Teuchter guy from Oban, which was me, to go to Aviemore, and we got on famously . . ."

I crumple this shameful cutting, toss it into the bin by my side and resume my examination of the kitsch before me.

Ahead of me, the Panasonic television receiver, permanently on 'standby', glares red-eyed at me. On top of that my Sony mini-system, the CD element of which went on the fritz three months ago, displays flashing green lights indicating the various electronic marvels it commands: radio, cassette-player, mini-disk player and the CD player which had suffered some kind of nervous breakdown. I rise and go to the cheap ghetto-blaster I had been forced to purchase in Asda, and snap on a CD of Ana Gabriel.

As her depraved voice fills the room with the essential mysteriousness of her native Mexico and the essential bravery of her people, I glance at the cheaply framed photographs and prints that adorn the walls. Topmost is a colour photograph of 'Norman Maclean of Glen Gloy', a pedigree bull for which an Arab syndicate paid an astronomical sum of money at Perth sales about six years ago.

Next to it hangs a music manuscript of a two-four competition pipe march, 'Norman Maclean of Lora', composed by a young lad, Griogair Labhruidh, who wrote the piece in my honour four years ago. Griogair used to come to my place frequently for Gaelic language practice. There is also a rather cheesy watercolour cartoon of me in Highland dress bearing the legend 'Presenting the Tallest Story Competition, "Storming" Norman Maclean'.

On the wooden mantelpiece stands a photograph of my favourite stepson, Martin. Incredibly handsome he looks in morning-dress in Jamaica on the day of his wedding to Dawn.

On top of the television set I see, with unutterable sadness, a photograph of my late mother, *Peigi Bheag*, Wee Peggy, descending the steps of a plane in Benbecula some thirty years ago. (A blown up black-and-white photograph of my father, *Niall Mòr*, Big Neil, looms over me in the bedroom.)

Beside the television stands a photograph of my sister, Lorna, taken around 1961. She was a pretty girl, dressed simply in a sleeveless cotton shift my mother had made for her, glowing with health. It is hard to believe that this smiling, vibrant lassie at the age of seventeen would be taken from us within eight years.

On either side of the doorway to the bedroom there were three framed documents: one, a parchment from the Sony Radio Awards, stating that for my work with Moray Firth Radio in Inverness I had been awarded a bronze – that is, third place – in the sub-category of Short Radio Feature in the Grosvenor Hotel in London in 1991. The second framed image is a watercolour painting of Oban Bay; in the background, the Argyll Mansions and McCaig's Tower. It was in the Mansions that Peigi, my wife, the kids, Kareen, Donald, Martin and I lived happily in the early eighties. Since it was from Oban, the present home of Peigi from whom I'm separated, the 'crock-pot' was sent this morning, my gaze does not linger on that scene.

The third and last decoration to be seen is a photograph, in colour, of Srathan schoolhouse at the head of Loch Arkaig in Inverness-shire.

At the foot of the brae leading downhill from the first school I ever attended, the low-slung outline of Srathan House, my home during the war years, can be seen. In the background the peaks of Streap and Sgurr Thuilm lower. I spend a long time gazing at this photograph.

A plan was forming in my mind, triggered by a chance meeting with a clairvoyant in Leith which I will describe later. I would tell the story of my life – a mixture of monologue and autobiography. Glancing to my right, I knew there would be a darkness coming to my old computer in the corner, a *manadh*, an omen of doom. I would have to record my lifelong history of alcohol abuse, however painful that might prove to be. I determined to make an honest, but not seamless, documentary of my life, which had been rangier than most. I had been aware for some time that somewhere a faint hairline fracture in my sense of belonging had occurred. The thought came to me that my search for the truth of things in the scrambled past was perilously close to folly. I do not know if extradition from Mexico, escape from the Cass Corridor in Detroit, being held up at gun-point in Quebec, or owning a West Highland hotel for all of twenty minutes, all formed threads in a pattern of self-destructive behaviour. But I felt that they did, or, at the very least, that they were more than connective tissue between the start and finish of my days.

I would throw everything onto the hard disc of the processor and hope fervently that something – absolution and insight for me, perhaps, and, hopefully, recognition or diversion for the reader – would emerge . . . in time.

I am going in.

1

Srathan

My intense involvement with the Gaelic language had begun in Srathan House at the head of Loch Arkaig in 1940, when I was three. (Obviously, I must have heard my parents prattling in the language in Glasgow prior to this, but I have no recollection of any time before taking off for the north out of the city.) My mother and I had left Glasgow where I was born – I remember nothing about our departure, which had been prompted by fear of Hitler's bombs – and gone to live with the family of her uncle, James Macdonald, or *Seumas Mòr mac Aonghais 'ic Iain Mhòir*, Big Jimmy, son of Angus, son of Big John.

Children like me were known as 'evacuees', which I thought a romantic term. Not that I was on any official government scheme: kids of Irish descent in the city were being sent to grandparents in Donegal and young Glasgow Gaels made for ancestral homes all over the West Highlands and Islands. James was head shepherd on Cameron of Lochiel's estate, and he and his wife, Mary, and their children, Kenny, Annie, Bella, Nan, Murdo and Christopher, all showed great kindness towards my mother and me during the years spanning World War II. My father, *Niall Mòr mac Iain Eòghainn Ruaidh*, Big Neil, son of John, son of Red-haired Ewan, was serving as bosun on the merchant ships of the Donaldson Line that sailed out of Prince's Dock during this period.

When I was five I joined the rest of the Macdonald clan – Bella, Nan, Murdo and Christopher and two Robertson brothers, whose father, a Skyeman, was the shepherd in Kinlocharkaig – in the little corrugated-iron schoolhouse that stood on the main road three hundred yards up the hill, to be taught the alphabet by a neurotic spinster called Miss MacLean.

On a frosty Saturday I looked across the loch to the slopes of the hill known as *A' Bheinn Bhàn*, The Fair Ben, at a spot beside Muic Burn in the company of my maternal grand-uncle. As the senior shepherd on Lochiel's estate – he would be over sixty then – Seumas Mòr used to rove the estate, with me in tow, repairing bridges and burying dead sheep. I was familiar with every foot of the crooked little road that skirted the north shore of Loch Arkaig, a deep freshwater trench that stretched for thirteen miles from east to west between two crouching ridges. On the slopes on either side, among the birch and rowan trees, great lumps of rock had burst forth from the earth, mere slivers of the planet's ancient bones laid bare by glacial action. It struck me with some force that only a handful of people remained on earth who could put names to the little streams in their eternal dance from the north. Certainly their names were on my lips that morning, and I intoned them softly, again and again, like an invocation before prayer: *Abhainn Ghlinn Dheasairigh*, The Glendessary River, *Abhainn Dhearg an t-Srathain*, The Red River of *Srathan*, *Abhainn Mhurlagain*, Murlagan River, *Allt a' Chùirn Ghil*, The Stream of the White Cairn, *Sruth Chùinnich*, The Burn of the Drying Place, and at the far end, *Allt na Canaich*, The Stream of the Bog-cotton.

Whatever our business, whether heading eastward or returning home to Srathan, we always stopped beside the little waterfall at Muic to allow Rosie, our Clydesdale mare, to come out of the shafts of the cart for a while so that she might get a drink and a bite.

On that morning, with the slopes on the far side a shimmering cascade of red-gold leaves, I asked him what Uist was like, as I had heard from gossip at the dinner table that Miss MacLean would be retiring soon and perhaps the little school would be closed for good. *Peigi Bheag* and I might be moving to Benbecula in the future. He said that Benbecula was so far out in the west that I would be able to see America as clearly as I could the trees on the *Beinn Bhàn*. He told me too that my true father, *Niall Mòr*, Big Neil, would be coming ashore from the sea when the war ended and that we would have a home in Glasgow where my parents and I would live like a normal family.

"Oh, you won't be away for long, Norman," he said in Gaelic. "You'll go on so many trips to America from *Cladach Oighrig Iain Dhoirbh*, the Shoreland of Effie, daughter of Crabbed John, that your father will think you're a Red Indian when you meet up with him in Glasgow." Years afterwards I understood he had been trying to impart a cheerful tone to bad news. He would have known that my father had no intention of coming ashore for some time yet, and that *Peigi*

Bheag, Wee Peggy, and her son would have to go and live among relatives yet again if I was to receive any schooling.

I didn't appreciate it at the time, but I was extremely fortunate to have received such intense pre-school instruction from Seumas. Not only did he teach me practical things like telling the time, using an old, battered alarm clock, along with the most expeditious method of yoking and harnessing Rosie to the cart, but he stimulated and nurtured a lifetime interest in narrative, both fictitious and historical.

"*O, ghràidhein nan daoin'*, Oh, beloved of men," he'd rumble as we proceeded towards Achnacarry at the eastern end of the loch. "Did I ever tell you of the time I went to visit my sister, *Annag* – your grandmother – down yonder in Glasgow? I was shepherding in *Baile nan Cailleach*, Nunton, in Benbecula at the time.

"My mother was still alive in Old Mill. Indifference upon you, boy, I arrived in Queen Street station in Glasgow dressed in my finest *crotal*, russet tweed plus-fours, and with seven working dogs on leather leashes, and after making a lot of enquiries from wee Glaswegians on the streets I made my way to the Govan Road. My sister was living in a house in Mair Street, just off this road.

"Bitter fortune, or perhaps it was what I had in a flask in my jacket pocket," he said "made me miss my stop, and I arrived at Govan Cross before I got myself and the dogs off the tramcar.

"*Uill*, he said, with a heavy sigh. "*Dh'èirich an t-aimhleas orm*, Mischief befell me. I didn't know that the date was the twelfth of July, the day of the Orange Walk. The second thing was, I shouldn't have spent as much time in the ale-house draining glasses of Demerara. You see, Norman, your grandmother was always red-hot against the drink, and I knew that she'd be fumbling against my limbs to find out if I had smuggled any contraband into her house. So, I'm afraid . . .

"I ended up *an grunnd Ifhreann*, in the bowels of Hell," he said, obviously reliving his ordeal. "Somehow me and the dogs joined a flute band. The beasts were terrified of the din made by the big drum and strained at their leashes. I attempted to control them but was being dragged from one side of the main road to the other.

"Then the bombardment started at the corner of Neptune Street, known as the Irish Channel. Men, women and children threw beer and wine bottles at the marchers, but for some reason I was the main target."

I could almost hear this rabble of southern Irish descent retelling this skirmish in the wine shops they frequented.

What? Well, you see, Michael, this big Orange bastard wearing an orange suit and with a herd of wild dogs pulling him about was obviously the main man in this band. So that's why we pelted him with the bottles and bricks. Did we enjoy it?

"No," said Seumas sadly, "I didn't like that experience at all. Fortunately, your uncle James, who's called after me, had been sent out by your granny to find me. And he did, and the dear boy brought me safely home to Mair Street.

"No, I never wore that suit ever again," he concluded, "and I had to destroy the dogs when I got back to Uist. Their nerves were never the same after the attack. They couldn't gather in hens."

But it was not the punchy, humorous personal anecdotes where he was always the victim that entertained me. I was astonished at the amount of history he had in his head about every place he had ever lived in.

"*Shuas an sin aig tuath*, Up there to the north," he'd say, as we trundled in the cart headed for Achnacarry. He waved his left arm as we passed Murlaggan. "Up there lie the Disputed Lands of Loch Arkaig. The great feud of the Camerons with the Mackintoshes over the ownership of the lands of Glenloy and Locharkaig, one of the bitterest feuds in Highland history, continued for three hundred and fifty years.

"The Camerons were a warlike race, whose rallying cry was '*A Chlanna nan con, thigibh an seo, 's gheibh sibh feòil!* Sons of dogs, come hither, and you will get flesh!' Donald Cameron of Lochiel, known as 'The Gentle Lochiel', was a staunch Jacobite. When Prince Charles Edward Stuart landed in Moidart in 1745, without troops, munitions or money, Lochiel was loath to commit his clan, but the Prince persuaded him. Had Lochiel refused to raise his clan, no rising would have been possible. The Camerons fought with great bravery throughout the campaign. After the fatal battle of Culloden, the Prince was hidden in caves and huts near Achnacarry by a band of devoted Camerons.

"Now listen to this, my little hero," Seumas said in a conspiratorial whisper. "On the third of May two French ships, the *Mars* and *Bellona*, arrived in *Loch nan Uamh*. The ships carried arms, money and brandy for the campaign, but the ship's master refused to hand over the money without the proper authority. Three of HM's ships, *Greyhound*, *Baltimore* and *Terror*, arrived in the loch. During the naval action that followed, the cargo was off-loaded by Coll MacDonald of Barrisdale's men, who got drunk on the brandy and accidentally blew up a barrel of gunpowder. During the confusion the gold went missing. The *Mars* and *Bellona* managed to beat off the attack and slipped out to sea, making good their escape to France.

"What happened to the 35,000 *Louis d'or*?" he hissed. "It was buried in several parcels about Loch Arkaig amid much secrecy." He waved his hand in the direction of Allt na Caillich, which we were passing at that moment, and with a wry smile said: "You never know, Norman. Maybe you'll find the equivalent of nearly three million pounds on these shores one day." I was speechless for the rest of the journey to Achnacarry.

Once we reached the Ford of Arkaig, he resumed his history lesson to the rapt small boy. "Here," he intoned, "took place the last confrontation between the Camerons and the Mackintoshes in 1665 when the long feud between the two clans was settled."

Where, I wondered, did get all this stuff? It certainly wasn't from books. He was unable to read, or even speak, English. "No England here," he'd shout at the visiting 'toffs' who'd visit Srathan on their way to the hill to shoot stags.

This was a mystery that was to bedevil me for many a year until I came across a passage about the oral tradition written by John Lorne Campbell of Canna:

> 'It is difficult to make the extent of the Gaelic oral tradi-
> tion . . . credible to persons who have had no contact with
> such a thing. It is not a question of a few people knowing
> some songs or stories by heart and reciting them occasion-
> ally at some party or concert: it is a case of numbers of
> people knowing forty or fifty traditional songs, or scores
> of stories, and not the same songs or stories, but often
> different ones, so that the total runs into thousands of dif-
> ferent songs and many hundreds of different stories . . .
>
> 'Communities where an oral tradition predominates
> are so much out of the experience of the modern West-
> ern world that it is extremely difficult for anyone without
> first-hand knowledge to imagine how a language can be

cultivated without being written to any extent, or what oral history is like, or how it is propagated and added to from generation to generation. The consciousness of the Gaelic mind may be described as possessing historical continuity and religious sense; it may be said to exist in a vertical plane. The consciousness of the modern Western world, on the other hand, may be said to exist in a horizontal plane, possessing breadth and extent, dominated by a scientific materialism and a concern with purely contemporary happenings. There is a profound difference between the two mental attitudes, which represent the different spirits of different ages, and are very much in conflict.'

My initial response as a student in my first year at university was to dismiss this as a load of old tosh. Then I became less sure. There was no doubt that my *prosbaig* or telescope was trained on the vertical plane in both Lochaber and later on in Uist, though it started to waver on the horizontal plane as it embraced what was laughingly called higher education. I'd come to the conclusion that this dual consciousness laid the foundation for the cultural schizophrenia I've suffered all my life, and still suffer from to this day.

I received a premonition of this 'conflict' one dark and stormy night in January 1942. As Christopher and I lay snugly in bed, covered by heaps of blankets, listening to a cold, slanting merciless rain rattling against the windows, we became aware that visitors had arrived at the house. Muffled voices, shuffling feet and unidentifiable bumps downstairs drew us on tiptoe to the living room, where a strange sight greeted our eyes. The room was full of soldiers, maybe a dozen of them, in drenched khaki uniforms covered by ponchos. They were carrying rifles, haversacks and rucksacks which they were in the process of divesting themselves of in full view of the family, and two wide-eyed little boys who stood in the doorway. The flashes on their shoulders proclaimed POLSKA, and the sibilant language they spoke in declared that they came from Eastern Europe. Later I found out that they were trainee commandos from Spean Bridge who had set off on a night exercise, got hopelessly lost in the mist and rain, and had sought shelter from Seumas. How the old man had understood the request was a mystery.

The Polish captain commanded only limited English and Seumas had next to none. Doubtless the numerous bottles of vodka that were crowded on the table and the dresser made communication a little easier. Our old patriarch said they could sleep in the hay shed, but it was early yet and it would be churlish of him to refuse the gifts his very grateful visitors had brought him. The night passed in wild carouse of drinking and music and, not only were the wee interlopers allowed to remain up, but they too were the recipients of gifts from the soldiers. Thick slabs of dark chocolate were taken from emergency ration tins and piled into our laps. As I listened to a young Pole sing to the delight of the Macdonald females, there was the sense that everything that was going on was *right*. The total unexpectedness of the faint revelation that followed set my mind in turmoil. The curvature of the earth, I told myself, promised new people and experiences just beyond the horizon.

Night after night, during the final quarter of the year I spent in the glen, our house would be full of people who used to come *air chèilidh*, visiting. They would come, men and women who knew hardship as they knew the *Shorter Catechism*. Along with members of the Macdonald clan – Seumas, his wife Màiri, three daughters and two sons (Kenny was fighting with the Cameron Highlanders in North Africa), Wee Peggy and I included – there would always be two or three unmarried shepherds, a gamekeeper from Glendessary and a quartet of woodcutters from Achnacarry. With the sour smell of damp wool steadily growing stronger we would find a place to sit as best we could in the glow of the hissing Tilley lamp, which stood on the kitchen table. *Crisdean*, Christopher, the youngest of the Macdonald family, and I would crouch on the linoleum on the floor with our arms around our knees, and more often than not there would be a pair of retired collie dogs lying between us. Between the window seat, or *beingidh*, and the big black 'American' stove, a clumsily-made radio-receiver about the size of a gravestone with a cloth front made of some linen-type material, stood on a pile of cuboid batteries together with an accumulator. My grand-uncle always lolled in the big arm-chair beside the stove, his big piper's hand tightly gripping a mug of strong tea that got constantly topped up by his wife, Màiri, or by his daughters, Anabella and Nan. There was another daughter, *Annag* or Annie, the eldest member of the family now that Kenny had left home, who had contracted tuberculosis in Austria while serving in the

WRAC. But *Seumas Mòr* would never allow her to do anything in the house. My mother, his sister's daughter, always tuned the needle of the radio to somewhere between Hilversum and Prague so that we could hear the news bulletins, and I suspect that she and Annag were the only ones in the room who fully understood the English language of the newsreader.

Certainly, the two youngest sons, Murchadh and Crìsdean, and I did not gather from the clipped gibberish that whined out of the box that the war was coming to an end. Christopher and I would be making preparation for the entertainment to follow.

We would bring out the violin and the practice chanter, a battered old set of Glen bagpipes and a wheezy button-key melodeon with two spoons on the bass end that could only produce hoarse farmyard noises. Annag and some of the lads would descend on the instruments like a pit-stop crew at Monza as soon as the broadcast ended and the old man turned off the radio. "*Chan eil sinn ach a' caitheamh nam bataraidh*, We're only wasting the batteries," he'd mutter darkly. Very soon, loping jigs and fast, lively reels would be heard, to the accompaniment of much hand-clapping and stamping of feet. The adults who were not playing instruments formed partners and with crossed hands swung in circles on the spot, and Seumas Mòr himself would get up, raise his arms aloft and perform rapid heel-toe shuffles in the centre of the room.

When they tired of the dancing everyone took a turn at singing, playing or telling a story. My mother would sing a song about a young girl married to an old man whom she did not love. *Horo chan eil cadal orm*, Horo I am not sleepy, was the first line of it, and as the words swelled in her mouth I could taste some of the great longing that was eating away at her and making her voice so plaintive at that time. It was clear, however, that she was still hopeful; because when she sang the slightly ribald lyrics she would wink and smile. She was always a great hit with the company.

"*Siuthad, a Mhurchaidh, thoir dhuinn òran*, Come on, Murdo, give us a song," Seumas Mòr ordered. Murdo, about twelve or thirteen years of age at the time, would rise, place both hands on the back of a kitchen chair and launch into '*Mo Nighean Donn nam Meall-shùilean*, My Brown-Haired Girl of the Bewitching Eyes'. Crìsdean too would make a contribution. When he shouldered the bagpipe I would feel warmth filling my entire body as he played with thick, clumsy fingers '*Fhir a Dhìreas am Bealach*, You who traverse the Pass'.

You who traverse the pass,
Carry my greetings to the little glen in the north,
And tell my beloved
That my love is steadfast and enduring.
I shall not take another
Nor suffer the mention of one
Until you, love, reject me,
And I'll not accept from others that you hate me.

After I wrote this, I looked up at my favourite photograph. It was now time. I sat rock-steady in my swivel chair. Suddenly the gap between me and the ancient versifier narrowed. My heart was beating more slowly and I felt that my being was no more than another stone in the eternity of the glen. I remembered that beyond Srathan to the west only a rough track snaked between Sgurr na Cìche, The Hill of the Breast, and the Beinn Dhearg, the Red Mountain, until it reached the deserted shores of Loch Nevis and, past that, the Sound of Sleat, and then, much further on, the Atlantic Ocean. I recalled the vast boulders that supported the jetty at the loch's end. These were rocks, dressed by fire and hammer, which battled against choppy wavelets, the very same waters which for all time washed the great continents of the globe. I tried to remember exactly what it was about this loch and its tributary streams that reminded me of my travels to the four red corners of creation.

I made a vow to dive into darkness. I have made Seumas Mòr, my grand-uncle, my guide through the randomness of my life. Old Seumas would guide me in the sad and funny story of a man who failed to fulfil early promise, the story that began at the head of a Highland loch and would surely end in a cosy little flat on the south side of Glasgow. The old man's tongue would tell what happened to young Tormod, Norman, in the years between. It would tell about what happened to the various people who loved him and whom he loved. And I decided to let the old man's voice tell what Tormod did that was so wrong that he became addicted to alcohol. I quoted silently to myself his own words from sixty-five years ago. "Siuthad, a Sheumais, Come on, James, sit forward in your chair! Amuse, amaze and move every one of us."

2
Benbecula

The increasingly eccentric behaviour of Miss MacLean – she used to cycle from her lodgings in Ardechive with her newly washed silk stockings tied to the handlebars to dry – was alarming pupils and parents alike. When she started to issue tin plates and spoons at the beginning of each day and fill them with Creamola pudding. we pupils got worried. She would order us to eat.

"*A-nis, a chlann*, Now, children," she'd say, "listen carefully, please. When you've licked every morsel off your plate I want the boys to undo the top three buttons of their trousers. Everyone will fold arms, boys and girls. Heads down on folded arms, and *sleep!*"

And we did as she ordered. Around mid-afternoon she would put us all on the shake, and as soon as we had slowly come round she'd send us home. This lunatic regime might have lasted for a month or so. One day the father of Myles Robertson asked his son what did he get in school that day. "Oh, just the same old thing," replied the boy. "Creamola pudding and a nice *norrag* [snooze] afterwards." The Skye-man was onto it in a flash. Before long he had notified Seumas Mòr of this madness, and even Lochiel himself was apprised of the situation. One day, when we were in mid-Creamola, the door burst open and three nurses in whites came in, subdued the hysterical teacher and carted her off to Craig Dunain, the psychiatric hospital in Inverness. "*Slàn leibh*, So long," I whispered. I never saw her again. I never put yellow food in my mouth again either.

No replacement teacher could be found and the school was closed. The final step was to transfer Christopher, my mother and myself to Benbecula. My thoughts vacillated between fear and hope in my final days in the glen. Down the north shore of Loch Arkaig we went, the three of us, in the old ramshackle ambulance that served as the estate workers' bus, all the way down from Srathan to Fort William. Onwards then we went to Mallaig on a steam-train. My most vivid memory of that particular lap of our journey was that it was cold tea from an old whisky bottle we drank, and that the scones filled with salt butter and crowdie we ate were in a brown paper parcel tied with white string.

We sailed across to Lochboisdale in the steerage section of the steam packet, the *Lochmòr*, and the clanking of the train and the smell of oatmeal bread gave way to the crash of breaking crockery, the moans of the passengers and the appalling stink of vomit. One thing that stands out about that stormy voyage was the comfort I was offered by an old woman from North Uist, a Mrs Taylor by name, who, without expression, rubbed my bare feet, which were plump and as brown as berries, between her rough hands. There was nothing sexual in the contact. It was performed in an absent-minded way; it was if she demanded physical contact with a young stranger in circumstances that reminded her of her own children many years previously.

The people who lined the pier at Lochboisdale, maybe thirty or forty of them, were dressed differently from the people in Lochaber. Only on the monthly provision runs to Fort William on the estate bus had I seen more folk in one place. The older women were wearing woollen cloth coats, all with self-coloured headscarves the tails of which were flapping furiously in a keen breeze.

The teenaged girls favoured tightly-belted raincoats and went bareheaded, black locks – they were mostly dark of hair and skin, though there were a few blondes among them – streaming back from finely chiselled features. The males formed two distinct sartorial groups. The older men, those above thirty, wore old woollen trousers tucked into Wellingtons below old jackets of dress suits. Glimpses of home-knitted jerseys of Fair Isle and Aran patterns peeped between the jacket buttons. The younger men were altogether more flashy. The pastel suits, bought from the Arab 'bum-boats' in the Gulf or in the Suez Canal, looked as though they were made out of Kleenex. These were the young merchant seamen on whom almost the entire economy of South Uist was founded. They shared one item of apparel with their fathers and uncles: the black beret, very much like the Basque *Boina*, pulled backwards over the head until it stood amost perpendicular to the back of their shirt collars. This was a role-sign I would have to adopt myself if I wanted to assimilate.

The island road north was at the centre of what seemed, if viewed from an airplane, the spine of a long-dead animal. To the west, little roads ran to crofting townships like Askernish, Frobost, Milton, Stiligarry, Ormacleit, Howbeg, Gerinish and Eochar. To the east there was Loch Eynort and the twin peaks of Hecla and Beinn Mhor; leading to Loch Skipport was the track to Oransay and Lochcarnan.

I could see no soil that could be cultivated, and the greenery that had sprouted was only coarse grass, thick clumps of heather and occasional clumps of wind-bent trees. The relentless whistle of the wind and splashes of rain assailed the little bus as it chugged past dark lochans surrounded by reeds and willows. People got off and on the bus at each road end. One young stud stumbled towards the front of the bus to alight, a half-bottle of Martell brandy stuffed carelessly in the hip pocket of a dress suit, the tail of the jacket raised ostentatiously to reveal his cargo. I understood instinctively that this bottle with the wired-rimmed cap was a fashion accessory, and I knew that I too, when I reached my teens, would be similarly attired.

From Lochboisdale on we headed down north in the little green bus of *Dòmhnall a' Mhuilich*, and a rough rattling we got before we were left at Market Stance in Benbecula. From there we had to walk for another mile along the Griminish road. We came to a rough cart-track that snaked off to the right. Laden with cheap cardboard cases, we stumbled along *Rathad an Acrais*, Hunger Road, on a pitch-dark night, until we reached a long, low building with a thatched roof. This was the home of *Seumas Mhurchaidh*, James son of Murdoch, my mother's first cousin, and his wife *Seonag*, Joann, and their three children, Morag, *Seonag Bheag,* Wee Joann and Kenny. Here I was to spend the next three years of my life.

My first day at Torlum school was an eye-opener. Kenny, my cousin Christopher who was lodging with his mother's uncle, *Crìsdean Mòr MacRath*, Big Christopher MacRae, in Torlum itself, and I were standing around in the school playground nervously shuffling. Kenny wasn't nervous. He had been assigned to Primary Four the previous year and knew what to expect.

A man in his late twenties with an extremely red face and wearing a three-piece suit of Donegal tweed emerged in the school doorway. He commanded us, in Gaelic, to form lines, girls to the right and boys to the left, in classes.

I followed Kenny into a line of about ten boys and dutifully filed into the school.

Once inside the classroom the teacher spoke, inexplicably, for the entire morning solely in English. For the first two weeks or so I understood very little of what he was on about. Gradually, however, after half a year I began to comprehend around eighty per cent of what he was saying and, as the lessons were always conducted by rote, I acquitted myself quite well in the round-the-class spelling bees and recitation of arithmetic tables. My writing on the wooden-framed slate with chalk was always exemplary. (Miss MacLean in Srathan had been a stickler for accuracy in the formation of the letters of the alphabet.) I inhaled the English language readers that were issued to the score or so of my classmates – girls, though strictly segregated, were present – in Primary Four. In what passed for a school library I chanced upon a copy of *Bleak House*, and was allowed to take it home with me to 27 Griminish.

As ever when I have acquired a new language, there existed a gap between comprehension and oral and literary expression. My accent when speaking was pitched in the sing-song cadences and the thick labials and dental fricatives of my native Gaelic, and the idioms I employed when attempting to converse with, say, summer visitors, tended to be dredged from the mother tongue. Instead of saying 'I look forward to seeing you again', I would think in Gaelic and say something like 'I am wearying until I shall see you again'. This was alien to the visitors, but seemed to be effective. As a consequence, however, of my voracious reading of *Oliver Twist*, *Treasure Island* and *Kidnapped* I soon came to realize that expressing myself in my second language had less to do with direct translation and more to do with depressing some kind of cerebral mode button.

Within the classroom I was fast becoming gold-plated. Every question posed by Mr Morrison or by the Rev. John Smith, a native of Lewis who was our parish minister and who visited the school every Monday morning, stimulated me to raise my hand and snap my fingers. (Roman Catholic children, who had a slight majority in the school roll, tediously recited the "Hail Mary" and listened to *Maighstir Calum*, Father Calum MacLellan, who came from Eriskay, referring to something called "the Mystery of the Holy Rosary" in a separate classroom. I knew this because I eavesdropped at the closed door of their makeshift chapel on one occasion when I was ostensibly going to the toilets.)

My social radar, however, was picking up a bleep that I was not altogether popular with my classmates because of the promptness of my responses. "*Tha mi coma*, I don't care," I whispered to myself. After all, I knew that my sojourn in Benbecula was a temporary one. Wasn't my father going to whisk my mother and me off down to Glasgow very soon now that the war had ended? And I wasn't shy about gloating over this imminent move in front of the other pupils.

"*Tha sinne a' falbh a Ghlaschu an ùine nach bi fada*, We're off to Glasgow soon," I'd tell the group of slack-jawed pupils surrounding me in the playground. "Yes," I boasted proudly. "Just as soon as my father comes home from sea and collects us, I'll be in the biggest city in Scotland."

This announcement was greeted with total apathy by my audience, except for a waspish interjection by *Ailean Iain*, Allan son of John. This was another lad who attended the chanter practices in the school run by Duncan MacLellan from Kyles Flodda on Tuesday evenings.

"*Nach buidhe dhut!* Aren't you the lucky one!" he said in a voice dripping with scorn, and with his face deformed by a sneering grin. This was the boy with whom I had my first serious fight in the playground. The cause was not serious but trivial in the extreme. During one of the rare and valued periods of recreation, Mr Morrison, the headmaster, had given out paper and coloured crayons. He exhorted us to draw and colour in something – anything, really – while he retired to the staffroom to . . . to tootle on his chanter probably.

Benbecula's answer to Andy Warhol here, me, decided to draw the old thatched cottage in Griminish where I lived. With protruding tongue I laboriously drew the primitive outline and proceeded to colour the door and the window frames purple. I justified this aberration by calling it 'artistic licence'. That's not what Ailean Iain called it when he sauntered over to my desk and disdainfully viewed my masterpiece.

"*Purpaidh!* Purple!" he snorted indignantly. "I've never ever between my two eyes seen purple woodwork on the house of *Seumas Mhurchaidh!*" With that he seized a brown crayon and began to repaint the offending door.

I could not allow such desecration to go unpunished. I smacked his cheek and wagged an admonitory finger in his face. "*Ceart, a mhic na seana ghalla*, Right, you son of an old bitch," I bellowed. "See you at playtime."

The fight, if I dignified the resultant scuffle with the name, was for me almost a non-event. He might have landed a few light punches on my face, but I wrestled him to the ground and with my thighs astride his waist I rained punch after punch on his eyes and mouth. "Nobody, I mean nobody, alters anything I have created for any reason," I panted between blows. "My work is sacrosanct!" I have regretted, it goes almost without saying, those precious words many times in the intervening years.

"*Sguiribh dhen sin sa bhad!* Stop that immediately!" Mr Morrison, practice chanter in fist, roared. His *crunnludh*, the free flow of notes, I thought, must have disappeared on him much in the same way that golfers frequently complain of 'losing their swing'. His face was redder than usual and the psoriasis that disfigured his neck looked radioactive. In short, he was in a filthy mood. He hauled the pair of us into his office, where we were ordered to hold out our hands out, palms uppermost, at waist level, one hand supporting the other. With a flourish he draped silk scarves on our wrists, and with a wind-up worthy of a pro tennis player brought his thick leather tawse with considerable force down upon our trembling hands. Six times for each of us. (This theatrical business with the silk scarf and the elaborate wind-up was something I myself would employ fourteen years down the line.) Neither poor Ailean Iain nor I was able to attend Duncan's chanter classes that Tuesday, such was the sting of the belting we had received.

My years in Benbecula were dominated by three activities: fishing with the worm in *Loch Dhòmhnaill Iain Anndra*, tootling on a rank-smelling practice chanter and perusing with all the intensity of a scholar examining the Rosetta Stone the entire back catalogue of Richmal Crompton's *Just William* stories by the light of a hissing Tilley lamp. I studiously ignored the requests of Morag and Seonag Bheag to join them in a game of chess or dominoes.

When I could tear myself from my compulsive reading I would join Kenny and the girls with their vacuous chatter round the kitchen table and listen to thick 78 records under the aegis of Beltona or His Master's Voice. The singers were mainly Neil Maclean and Archie Grant, the instrumentalist was an accordion player called William Marshall, and unless we were diligent in changing the steel needles in the playing arm of the wind-up device, the crackle and the hiss provided something that was only just recognizably music.

When I arrived in the Hebrides my piping ability was, to put it delicately, limited. Back in Lochaber I had learned from my cousin Crìsdean how to play '*Horo, Mo Nighean Donn Bhòidheach*, Horo, My

Nut-brown Maiden', in the key of C natural, as opposed to the key of D favoured by more orthodox Earth People. My mother's cousin *Aonghas Iain Mhurchaidh*, Angus John Macdonald, newly demobbed from the Argylls and fresh from the tutelage of Pipe Major Ronnie MacCallum of Inveraray, piper to the Duke of Argyll, soon put that nonsense out my head and insisted that I adhere to Received Technique. Three times a week at least he'd visit his brother's house in Griminish and put me through my paces. (I mention this detail because I know that, having embarked on a wrong course in the past, I am always capable of modifying my behaviour. It was ever thus. Once I get locked into an activity I have a tendency to push it as far as I can.)

The result of all this intensive tuition on the practice chanter was that I became pretty slick. While possessing a fair degree of digital fluency on the wee chanter, when it came to shouldering the Great Highland Pipe I was found lacking. I couldn't – godangitty! – tune my own drones. I didn't have to. Doting uncles and scores of neighbours in Benbecula who wanted to be close to my light did that for me. Yes, I was a wee swot at *Cnoc na Mòna,* Torlum School, and you could have read MacBrayne's timetables in the glow of my annual report cards. Accordingly, I was never entirely sure that my pipe was in tune. Of course, I really didn't have the patience for faffing about with drones, battering out tuning notes and resetting the drones again and again. I've always wanted action and heavy breathing, not equivocation. As an adult I've rationalised my backing out of the tuning chore by saying that I've been hoping Andrew Lloyd Webber might want to marry me, because, after all, the dames he courted couldn't sing in tune either.

During all the time I lived in Uist, although I often sat, enduring the rain and wind that battered the island from the Atlantic, in the lee of the ruined house of Oighrig Iain Dhoirbh looking constantly westward, never once did I get a glimpse of America. Then, on a bright day in summer, *Donnchadh Mhurchaidh*, Duncan Macdonald, my mother's first cousin, handed a letter to my mother. My father, Niall Mòr, was coming for us. The lover of jollity had finally decided to leave the sea and was seeking to find work as a dock labourer in Glasgow. Joy unconfined.

The first time I had set eyes on Niall Mòr was on his last leave on the island. Shockingly, the vision of a tall, handsome man in a light blue suit topped by a fedora appeared. He stood, broad in the shoulder, in the middle of the kitchen of Clachan Beag – this was the home of Donnchadh Mhurchaidh, the brother of James – surrounded by a crowd of people.

A bottle of amber-coloured rum from Guyana, the kind of gift seamen used to receive from a skipper at the end of a voyage, had been opened, and Duncan, my mother's cousin, whose house was much larger than the thatched cottage half a mile down the road, was filling little inch-high shot glasses until they overflowed.

The smell of the liquor, ripe and spicy, filled the room. My father spoke in the sibilant accent of the people of Tiree, a dialect full of broken words and glottal stops. "Peggy, love," he said to my mother, "I know the war's been over for a while, but there's no word of the Glasgow job yet. Don't worry, darling, I haven't lost hope yet. All you have to do is be patient." He grinned in an attempt to put my mother in a good mood, and revealed large white teeth below a closely trimmed blond moustache. "Anyway," he said, "the agent will be sending a telegram any day now for this trip to Buenos Aires. That'll be the last, I promise you, Peggy!" Briskly, he went round the grown-ups, and from the tray proffered by Uncle Duncan he gave them all a dram. He gripped the base of his own glass with his thumb and the tips of his fingers, kept his gaze on my mother and proposed a toast for us. It was an attempt at drollery that prompted him to use the tag-line of an old joke, familiar through repetition to everyone present. On this occasion, there was a cruel edge to his voice and nobody laughed. "Here, my dear," he intoned, "*agus, a Dhia, nach tachdadh i thu!* and, God, may it choke you!*"

Horrified, I watched him raise the glass to the cleft in his chin. Concentrating only on the dram in his hand, he slowly inclined his head and clamped his lips and teeth round the entire rim of the glass. Suddenly, he tossed his head backwards and threw both arms wide in one movement. After swallowing the dram, he plucked the glass from his mouth and threw it to the stone kitchen floor where it smashed into smithereens. He shuddered and said in English: "Aaaagh, great stuff that Bass!"

I see the massive vault of a Uist sky, pale and distant, on a long-dead day in summer . . . Crouching in the marram grass I view with wonder the wrestling match which is taking place between my father Niall Mòr and the MacMillans' servant girl Seonag in a sandy hollow below me. Seonag Thormoid 'ic Nill, two

17

years out of Cnoc na Mòna school, the youngest of a family of seven children who live with drunken parents in a shack 'a-muigh sa bheinn', 'out on the moor', straddles my father, their faces and upper bodies touching, while her slender, bare legs, so brown against the smooth white sand, flex and straighten rhythmically as she drives herself back and forth across his thighs. The girl's back is a bow at full stretch. Her hands are clasped behind her neck, and she tilts her face, eyes tightly closed, towards the sun, so that the gasps that come from her gleaming, open mouth ascend to the heavens. The bleached flowing tresses of his partner hide my father's face, but I can see his powerful arms as they envelop the girl's entire back, pushing and pulling her relentlessly. In particular I am fascinated by his thick forearms, and by each ugly, mysterious tattoo that covers them. These hateful images of birds of prey and foundered ships, all in faded shades of green and purple, attract and disgust me.

Slowly I rise to a standing position like someone bewitched. Fully upright now, I gaze upon Big Neil and Seonag in their ancient and abiding rhythm, and I understand that their actions comprise an inherited wont. I sense too, somewhere deep inside my being, that a distant door has opened and that I too will have to enter a luscious emptiness sometime.

The image quickly fades. Suddenly, the reel of my memory unspools. I receive a glimpse of my mother's tearful eyes as she sings a song full of repressed passion in a happier time and place. In a flash I realize that my life has changed so radically that from now on the penalties I shall have to pay if I am to trust another human being will be enormous. Shall I turn my back on the faithlessness of others? An unclear picture shimmers before me. Down at the shoreland of Oighrig Iain Dhoirbh a little fair-haired boy slowly turns away, the weight of a massive stone pressing heavily on his innards. Swiftly, images disappear and thick darkness envelops me . . .

A little later, I am transported to another time . . .

My mother's face is looming close from the other side of the kitchen table in Griminish. Her mouth is opening and closing, but I cannot hear speech at all. I do not need to hear her. I have learned her chant a long time ago. She has been asking me questions for two hours now about the identity of the female who was along with Daddy down by the machair: "Was she young, the woman? What did she look like? Was she pretty? Did you recognize her, Norman? Won't you tell me the truth, love?"

Eventually, thinking it makes no difference anyway, I surrender. I inform my mother that it was Seonag Thormoid 'ic Nìll I saw with Big Neil earlier that afternoon. Now she knows, I think, and I experience some relief. For a short while. Yet, when I see my mother's tears rolling down her cheeks, an intense feeling of anger overwhelms me, one that will not diminish until I breathe my last. Already I have taken the first step away from my parents. . . and perhaps from the rest of mankind.

Good news! The telegram informed us that we were off to *Glaschu Mòr nam Bùithean*, Great Glasgow of the Shops. In truth, my life on Benbecula during my last days on the island was closed and circular. I trod the wheel of habit. My horizons were near and unchanging. Mucking the byre before setting off for school, herding the cattle, cutting and transporting peats, provided no intensity of experience. The chanter practice was bearable because it gave me a chance to show off. In some deep core of myself I felt lonely and depressed.

The pilgrimage to the great city beckoned me invitingly to ever new experiences. After tearful farewells my mother and I took off yet again, once more on the wee green bus, up south to Lochboisdale where we embarked on the *Loch Earn*, bound for Oban. Next day, pressed against the starboard rail of the vessel, I anxiously scanned the crowd lining the pier. There, standing about a head taller than anybody else, was Niall Mòr, my father. He had to weigh at least fifteen stones, and the muscles displayed by the short-sleeved shirt he wore were strung like bridge cables. At the foot of the gangplank he embraced me enthusiastically, and gave Wee Peggy a perfunctory peck on the cheek.

Before I had time to absorb the sights and scents of Oban Bay, the fishing boats rocking gently and tugging at their bowlines, the neat little crescent of hotels and shops all crowned by the miniature Coliseum of McCaig's Tower, we were moving very fast towards a bus stop opposite the entrance to the Railway Pier.

A smart blue and white bus bearing the logo of a bluebird on its curvaceous flanks swept the three of us down to Glasgow, my mother seated up front by herself and my father lolling in an aisle seat by my side. On the route I later came to know quite well – Connel Ferry, Taynuilt, the brooding gloom of the Pass of Brander, Loch Awe, Dalmally and south to Tarbet and Helensburgh – I had plenty of time to view my father more closely. With the build of a heavy-weight boxer, he had the biggest hands I had ever seen. His palms rested on his thighs, and his fingertips, I swear, brushed his shins. I was still fascinated by the ugly, mysterious tattoos that covered his thick forearms.

Nearing our destination he leaned towards me and I caught a whiff of alcohol on his breath.

"*Dè mar a tha a' dol dhut aig a' phìobaireachd*? How are you getting on with your piping?" he said.

"*Tha mi a' sìor fhàs math air an fheadan*, I'm getting pretty good on the practice chanter," I replied.

He informed me that nobody ever won the Gold Medal at the Argyllshire Gathering or the Gold Clasp at the Northern Meeting in Inverness playing a practice chanter. He had plans for me, he went on. Drifting off, I remained silent for the rest of the journey.

Wee Peggy had told me before boarding that I was about to become the big brother of a baby.

3

Tenements

When I think about it, I suppose my first brush with trouble occurred when I arrived in Glasgow at the age of nine. My father, seemingly content in his work as a docker in Prince's Dock, Plantation, and my mother rented what was called a 'room and kitchen' at 191 Brand Street, on the border between Ibrox and Govan. Shortly after our arrival my sister, Lorna Flora, was born.

On my first day out in the back-court of our tenement block, I was exposed to serious culture shock. Surrounded on all four sides by three-storey tenement buildings and dotted with wash houses, middens and air-raid shelters, the back-court was the centre of the universe to the children of the hundred and thirty families who lived in our block. Boys and girls, between the ages of four and ten, played the games of 'Allevio', 'Kick the Can' and 'Statues'. And, of course, football.

Some boys I liked the look of were playing a game of 'Three and In' with a cheap tennis ball and with jackets representing goalposts. I approached them shyly. I must have pressed the wrong mode button. What issued from my smiling mouth was Gaelic. "*Am faod mise cluich cuideachd*, Can I play too?" I enquired sweetly. The boys stopped the football game immediately and began to surround me slowly. One stocky lad, perhaps a couple of years older than I, stepped forward. "Where are you from?" he asked. What he actually said was: "Where urr ye fae?" He could have been speaking Mandarin as far as I was concerned. Wrong button again. I started babbling in direct translation mode. "I should be long in obligation to you if you would allow me the ball to kick," I said. He punched me on the nose.

"Shut up," he said and I began to cry. "Right, Jimmy, whit team dae ye support?" he demanded. I kept talking in Gaelic and the leader of this gang of young toughs kept asking me what team I supported.

"*Chan eil mi gad thuigsinn*, I can't understand you," I said.

"Whit team dae ye support?" he kept saying. (This, of course, is a peculiarly Glaswegian locution employed to establish religious affiliation. If you support Celtic, you're a Catholic; if you support Rangers, you're a Protestant. Another piece of west-central Scotland shorthand used, particularly by journalists, was the insertion of the name of the school attended by the criminal, footballer or pop star they were describing.)

I shook my head and the leader-off hit me again, this time in the mouth. I'd had enough. I broke free and ran home. I sat on my bed, which I shared with my father, immobilized by my own adrenalin, and vowed to learn the language of my attackers.

After a few more beatings on subsequent days when sometimes I gave as good as I got – I once hooked the dreaded leader with a good right-hander and was regarded with some respect – I was speaking Glaswegian like a native.

"Some'hin' the matter wi' yer eyes, ya bam?" I used to enquire aggressively of anybody who as much as looked at me. Another belligerent threat of mine was: "Ah'm gonnae *plunge* ye, shiteface." Please, I have drawn a veil over these linguistic tics.

In a very short time I was a member of this all-Protestant low-echelon little gang. Kicking a little ball around in Midlock Street until very late was our main activity. When a careless clearance by a defender sent the ball bouncing out of the accepted bounds of our nebulous 'pitch', we had no compunction about hailing a passing adult male with the cheeky local request – "Hey, Mister, that ba'?"

Invariably the man would indulge in a little bit of showing off, keeping the ball in the air using foot, thigh and head, before returning it with a mighty kick. "Thanks, Mister," we would shout, as much in appreciation of his rusty skills as in our gratitude for the favour. The relationship between the generations in our neck of the woods was, I think, a healthy one. There wasn't the fragmentation that obtains today. Any adult, male or female, was able to chastise us when needed, and we accepted their right to do so. After all, we ourselves would soon have the same rights and privileges. What imposed homogeneity on our neighbourhood was the fact that none of us was rich and none of us was poor.

After street football, our other pastime was fighting, either among ourselves or against neighbouring rival gangs. When fighting, as we did almost every day, I had adopted a cunning strategy. If I was sure I could get the better of my opponent, I would punch and kick like a Tasmanian Devil. If I suspected that an older or stronger lad might get the better of me, I'd make him laugh with quaint insults derived from the Gaelic. Our leader was Iain Macdonald (whose grandfather came from North Uist, I discovered later), and other members included 'Pudgy' Sutherland, 'Beef' McDonald, Iain and Willie MacKenzie (of Skye descent), Jacky Ramsay and a few affiliate members like Gus Matheson, Ian Sharp and Iain McGibbon. The only Catholic allowed to share in our activities was a boy, my own age, whose parents came from Donegal. His name was Francis Aloysius Carrabine. His uncle, Jimmy Carrabine, played football for Third Lanark, and 'Frannie' himself could play a bit. In addition he attended a boxing club associated with Saint Anthony's Roman Catholic Church down in Govan and had very fast hands. Accordingly, we all considered him an asset.

The favourite pastime of our group was 'Jumping the Dykes' or 'Daein' the Jumps'. This involved leaping from one wash-house to another, or from an air-raid shelter to a midden. The permutations were mind-boggling. These 'jumps' all had quaint names. There was 'The Wee Step', 'The Big Step', 'The Point', 'The Midgie' and, most challenging and dangerous of all, 'The Big Gilly'. We conducted these obsessive-compulsive rituals every night after tea in our own and adjacent back-courts. There was a lot of absurd, macho posturing associated with the Jumps. When it was your turn, for example, to attempt 'The Big Gilly', you had to paw the roof of the building you were on with your 'sannies' or plimsoles. You had to spit a lot in order, as the rest of the gang put it, 'to get your nerve up'. It was thrilling and exhibitionistic. Urban myths about lads impaling themselves on spiked railings, which were often planted down below between the take-off place on a wash-house and the landing-spot on a midden twelve feet away and fully twenty feet below, made your heart beat a little faster before you'd try to emulate the achievements of your fellow gang members who had successfully accomplished the leap. Golly! It was exciting.

At school, Bellahouston Primary on Paisley Road West, attended by all the members of our gang except 'Frannie' – he was a pupil at Saint Saviour's in Govan – I shone as I had done in Benbecula. Whether the desire to excel had its roots in a residual belief that being a 'Teuchter' meant being second-class was probably something not even I would ever know for sure. What I did know, however, was that I was a fairly big fish in a little pond. I certainly gathered a lot of prizes for academic attainment. I loved going to school, and I positively glowed with pride when Miss Wilson, my teacher in Primary Five, would invite me to come out to the front of the classroom and entertain the rest of the kids with one of my wee stories. By this time – I'd be ten or eleven – I was able to speak English fluently. Even so – and I did this deliberately – when I'd be regaling my classmates with the story of *Colann gun Cheann*, The Headless Body, my sentences were infused with that sometimes charmingly eccentric notion of grammar and tense that is forgivable in the newly conversant, and the odd lurch into Gaelic when I couldn't bring the word or expression I was looking for to mind. Yeah, that soft Hebridean lilt I could assume at will worked wonders for my popularity quotient in school.

Sunday was a day for dressing up in one's best clothing and toddling down to Govan, three times a day, to attend Sunday School, English afternoon services and Gaelic evening services in St. Columba's Church of Scotland at the junction of Copland and Govan Roads. Though I sang enthusiastically in a clear soprano voice, drawing admiring glances from the mainly elderly female members of the Rev. Tommy Murchison's congregation, I remember little of his sermons except the simplistic vision of Jean Calvin that humankind was divided into the elect and the damned. I learned large chunks of scripture by heart, but in the words of the Psalmist, '*Mura tog an Tighearna an taigh, gu diomhain saothraichidh a luchd-togail*, Except the Lord build the house, they labour in vain that build it.' *Psalms* 127:1.

Most Sundays, after attending morning service and Sunday school, I'd meet my father at the close mouth and we'd toddle down to a stable in Clifford Lane, a narrow alley that runs between Paisley Road West and Clifford Street. There stood the true object of my father's affections: a grey pony called Mackie. After watching Big Neil hand feeding the horse with clumps of hay, lumps of sugar and occasionally an apple for quarter of an hour or so, we'd march down to Percy Street, cross Paisley Road West into Cessnock Street, then right into Brand Street, making for a tin shed my father had the use of on the Sabbath to perform little splicing jobs for local engineering companies. This was wire splicing. A bench, a vice and huge steel spikes were the tools of the trade – those and enormous hand-strength were all my father needed to manufacture slings, eyes, hooks and other objects whose purposes were unknown to me. I usually sat in a corner and read the *Sunday Post*.

One fair May morning he deviated from our routine. Sure, we visited Mackie, but instead of proceeding to the hut we stopped at the entrance to Cessnock underground station. I watched him take long drags from a cigarette.

"Who are we meeting, Daddy?" I asked.

"You'll see soon enough, *a bhalaich*," he said. And I did. Within a minute a tall, slim, blonde lady skipped up the steps from the subway station, her high-heeled shoes clacking on the pavement. Without hesitation she came up to my father and, with well-practised fluency, slipped her arms round him and kissed him full on the mouth.

"Wait, Daddy!" I shouted. There was a kind of astounded horror in my voice.

Big Neil disengaged himself from the blonde's embrace and smiled at me.

"*Trobhad, a Thormoid*, come here, Norman," he commanded. "I want you to meet a good friend of mine, Mrs . . ." Brisson? Brasson? Bryson? I didn't catch the surname properly, but approached the tall lady shyly.

"Hello, my dear," she cooed. "What a lot of female hearts you're going to break when you're older."

I shook her extended hand firmly.

"Today, *a Thormoid*," my father said, "we're going on a trip."

"Where to?" I asked

"We're going for a sail on the Renfrew Ferry," he replied, obviously relieved on seeing my delighted smile.

So there I was, squashed between the hounds-tooth pleated skirt of Mrs Bryson and my father's worsted grey trousers on a bench seat in the front cabin of a corporation tram car. We were headed down the Govan Road for Renfrew, a place as exotic to as Reykjavik or Rome. What a delightful prospect for a working-class nine year old from Govan!

On the journey, as Mrs Bryson and Big Neil chatted amiably over my head I learned what I considered an arresting piece of biography. It seemed that Mr Bryson, Christian name Andrew, worked full-time for the British Broadcasting Corporation over in Queen Margaret Drive. He provided piano accompaniment for the tenors and sopranos whose recitals were practically a staple on the "wireless" in the First World War years. This woman's husband was a star!

The day went from good to better. In an ice-cream parlour in Renfrew my father ordered a Scotch pie with mushy green peas doused in vinegar, followed by a glorious rainbow of ice-cream scoops served in what looked like a flower vase. This was the splendid Knickerbocker Glory, and I have never tasted anything half as good since. Another mystery confronting me was the ease with which Mrs Bryson purchased a giant bar of Bournville chocolate. Food rationing was still in force, and to buy sweets you had to present coupons to the shopkeeper. No coupons passed between the blonde lady and the Italian proprietor. Nevertheless she made the purchase with all the ease of someone picking up a morning newspaper today, and with an easy smile presented the gift to me.

As my granny would say, "*Bha mi gu dearbh am broilleach nan uais-lean an la'ud*, I was indeed in the bosom of the gentility that day." And I loved it.

My next meeting with the liberal blonde took place a couple of years later. It was a most unpleasant experience and I shall make reference to it in a future chapter. It involved a ghastly tug-of-war between my mother and father for possession of my sister Lorna while Mrs Bryson and I stood and looked on.

It should be clear that I was constantly negotiating between the Highland and Lowland cultures. This dexterity bred distance, if only to mask insecurity. The language of the hearth was still Gaelic, and both my parents were keen that I should become a good piper. My mother enrolled me in the College of Piping, a pretentious name perhaps for a modest institution run by a remarkable man called Seumas MacNeill and his pal, Tommy Pearston. Seumas, a Lecturer in Physics at Glasgow University by day, and I shared a demented sense of humour and a healthy contempt for stupidity. I enjoyed being taught by him. Every Wednesday night I'd happily set off with my practice chanter, notebook and manuscript book ostentatiously on show, and take a tram to the junction of St Vincent Street and Elmbank Street. I'd then toddle northward for about six hundred yards to the College in Pitt Street, which was situated in a suite of dank rooms in a basement. (Soon afterwards, through the good offices of Captain Hepburn, the proprietor of Red Hackle Whisky, we all moved to much grander and more sumptuous premises in Otago Street in Kelvinbridge.)

Though I did well at the College, winning little internal chanter competitions held every month on a fairly regular basis, my father had greater ambitions for me. As a card-carrying member of the Ciamar-a-Tha-Thu club, he'd arranged for me to receive lessons from the South Uist born *Seonaidh Roidein*, Pipe Major John Macdonald of the famous Glasgow Police Pipe Band. At an amateur piping contest in Glasgow's Highlanders' Institute, while chatting with fellow competitors like Kenny Macdonald, Iain MacFadyen, Norrie Gillies, John Graham, Jimmy Jackson, Iain MacKay and others, I delivered myself of the line: "I'm off to Orkney Street Police Station next Monday to get lessons from Pipe Major John Macdonald." I admit I got a real bang out of hearing the pronoun in the first person being used alongside the name of the greatest piper of his generation. Immediately the air was thick with advice. "Don't go, Norman," they implored. "It could be dangerous. They're mad for the drink, these policemen." I ignored them. "Don't go, Norman," begged others. "It could be boring. All that tedious memorising of mad tune titles – *Failte Prince, Failte Oborcarnic, Tarbh Brach Derg, Bidagvoyach, Slum hin an Glan, Stir a phay u* – come on, Norrie, it'll detract from your schoolwork. You'll never pass your Qualifying Exam and you'll have to go to school in a grey bus where the poor kids lick the condensation off the the windows." "Go, Norman," said one voice. "It could be a laugh and maybe you'll learn something." And blow me if that one dissenting voice didn't turn out to be mine.

The night before my appointment with the great one I slept fitfully, got up at six to deliver milk from the local branch of the Co-op to families in neighbouring tenements, went to school and returned home to collect my practice chanter and manuscript book. On my way down the Govan Road I passed several loud groups of children playing street football, 'Rounders', and my own particular favourite, 'Dodgieball'. Though keen, I was hopeless. I'd last about two seconds. It was like, 'Go!' and almost immediately BOOM – the ball would bounce off my rather prominent nose. "Okay," I'd say in an adenoidal whine, "I'm out." Then, as I'd be walking slowly homeward, BOOM again! This time I got bopped on the back of the head. "Hey," I whimpered, "I *said* I was out." BOOM. The ball hit me in the kidneys. "Look," I turned and faced my tormentors, raising my voice, "I'm not even dodging!" BOOM. The ball smacked me in the mouth. I screamed in pain and in anger: "*Girls!*"

Well, I was done playing now. Pipe Major Macdonald was expecting me and I was going to learn the *Ùrlar* or Ground of *Bodaich Dhubha nan Sligean* or The Old Men of the Shells. I was about to find out at first hand what a really rotten time Jesus Christ had on Good Friday. Knowing what I know now, I'd maybe have been better sticking to the Dodgieball.

The great one was waiting for me at the corner of Orkney Street and Govan Road, and we retired to a greasy spoon specialising in indifferent food. The Lyceum Café in Govan Road, all marble tables and watercolours of Sorrento and sepia-tinted photographs of Govan Cross circa 1901, was where we had our power meal. John was handsome, with the long upper lip of the Celt. At the age of fifty he had accumulated the traditional icons of success in the piping world: both gold medals at Oban and Inverness (gained in the same year), a pensionable 'berth' in a respected profession, a majority in the most renowned pipe band on the planet, a magnificent fully silver-mounted set of Henderson bagpipes, commodious lodgings in Clifford Street, Ibrox, and the esteem of every bilingual tartan-head on Clydeside. Indeed, my own grandmother, *Anna Bheag nighean Aonghais 'ic Iain Mhòir 'ic Ruairidh Hoghaigearraidh,* considered *Seonaidh* a paragon of virtue and held him up to her own lascivious sons as an ideal role model. *"Duine còir gasta a th' ann an Seonaidh,* Johnny's a fine upright man," she used to say, *"nach do phòs 's nach do dhìolain riamh,* who never married and never begat illegitimate offspring."

The melting 'McCallum' (vanilla ice cream doused in carmine-red sauce) on my plate, which my host had so masterfully ordered ten minutes previously, looked like a self-portrait by an Expressionist who had been skipping his Lithium. After volunteering my piping credentials – the lessons on *ceòl beag* I had had from Seumas MacNeill, Thomas Pearston and John Garroway at the College of Piping in Pitt Street – the big man clasped massively veined hands before him on the table and smiled. That smile projected qualities of reassurance, confidence and good-humoured mischief. *"Dè mar tha dol dhut san sgoil?* What about your schooling?" he enquired. I needed little prompting, counting off on my fingers my triumphs in what was laughingly called Primary Education at that time. First Prize in Creative Lego, Honourable Mention in Plasticine Sculpture, special classes in Latin, Greek,

French and Mathematics and a bursary to one of the semi-independent schools in Glasgow assured in a couple of years' time.

The great one interrupted my recital of triumphs with a snap of his big fingers. "Norman," he intoned in beautifully modulated South Uist Gaelic, "I will teach you *ceòl mòr*. Allow me to guide you. You may even play my pipe at the competitions and I myself will accompany you to these competitions in order that I may set up and tune the instrument. Can't have you displaying yourself in public with a Cocuswood set of Grainger and Campbell drones, can we?" I found myself in complete agreement with John's generous proposal. I've always believed it's not what you are that matters in public: it's what you wear. Who cares what you really are?

"*Math dh'fhaodte, Thormoid*, Perhaps, Norman," he suggested, "*gun dèan thusa fàbhar dhomhsa*, you could do me a favour." My radar was picking up an unusual vector to the conversation and I grew wary.

"*Dè bhiodh an sin*, What would that be?" I squeaked. John concentrated all his attention on me. When he did this, he reflected only the best impression you had of yourself.

"*'S e gille gu math tapaidh a th' annad*, You're a very intelligent lad," he said earnestly. "*Dh'fhaodadh tu 'na spotaichean' ionnsachadh dhòmhsa*, You could teach me about 'the spots'." I reached out slowly for my spoon and took it in my right hand, which was shaking a little now, along with my other appendages and the rest of the world.

"*Chan eil mi gur tuigsinn, a Mhaighstir 'icDhòmhnaill, dè tha sibh a' ciallachadh*, I don't get it, Mr Macdonald, what do you mean?" I said.

What did this giant want? Could this sixteen-stone teuchter with hands like the roots of an oak tree be a bellowing lunatic pansy? Is this the end of the line . . . the door of some cell in Orkney Street Police Station locked, my mind wrenched . . . thrown to the concrete floor by a poofter teuchter heavyweight? What would my granny think?

"The spots," said John in Gaelic.

"What spots?" I asked in a falsetto voice, imagining this was an oblique reference to some outlandish sexual perversion I didn't know about.

"The exam," Seonaidh explained patiently. "The examination for the rank of sergeant."

"Yeah?" I said doubtfully.

"Yes, the Pipe Major of the Police Band carries the rank and pay of Inspector," he said.

"Yeah?" I said, completely baffled by now.

"Yes, I've got to sit the sergeants' examination . . . again," a doleful Pipe Major Macdonald sighed resignedly.

"Really?" I said, with genuine interest this time.

"I'm beat by the spots every time," Seonaidh said, sadness dripping from his voice.

"Really?" I said for the umpteenth time.

"I reckon with your mathematical ability you could help me," he said, with a hopeful smile creasing his craggy features.

I laughed nervously. "Where do the spots come in, Mr Macdonald?" I asked.

"In the Arithmetic examination," he replied.

"How do the spots come into the Arithmetic test?" I asked.

"Well, they give you addition sums to do," the giant before me said with some diffidence.

"Right," I said brightly, without understanding a word of this crazy exchange.

Seonaidh sat upright and recited examination instructions he had obviously memorized: "CANDIDATES WILL ADD THE FOLLOWING NUMBERS: TWO SPOT FIVE, ONE SPOT SEVEN FIVE, THREE SPOT TWO FIVE AND TWENTY-SEVEN SPOT ONE TWO FIVE."

"You're talking about decimal fractions, sir?" I said with relief.

"That's it, Norman, decimal fractions . . . with the spots," my would-be tutor exclaimed, equally relieved.

"This is unbelievable, Mr Macdonald," I gasped. "Of course I'll help you. Decimals are easy."

"Nothing unbelievable about it," said John. "I've tried that test . . . oh, about seven times, and the spots beat me every time."

I smile, radiating confidence. "Mr Macdonald," I said, "we have a deal."

"*Mòran taing, a Thormoid*, Thanks a lot, Norman," John said.

"My pleasure," I said.

Fractions, not *ceòl mòr*, subsequently dominated our sessions in the police station. We began at 4.30pm and finished at 6.30pm. This was two hours, or a year and a half, after we had started. I used to run out of cigarettes. In fact, I was frequently running out *for* cigarettes, and also to make farewell calls to my mother whom, I was convinced, I would never see again. In more optimistic mood, I used to cancel appointments made for three weeks hence. Most of the time the world of *Bodaich Dhubha nan Sligean* seemed like a big mushy swamp, and playing the *hi-harin, edre, cherede* and *hiharada* movements, changed on a weekly basis, was like trying to sprint through quicksand.

It is small wonder, then, that I didn't exactly set the heather alight initially at the amateur contests I competed in. After a period of adjustment, the phrasing of 'The Old Men' was cauterized on my brain cells, and I began to take pleasure in the classical music of the Highland Bagpipe. The important consequence of this period in my life was that I became a performer. I wasn't an outstandingly good one at first, but I consoled myself by saying to anybody who'd listen, "The ability to attract consumers has nothing to do with the intrinsic value of an artistic statement." I lied. As a singer and, later, a stand-up comedian, my impulse was to give and get pleasure through performing.

The primary need of performers is to make as many people love them as is possible. True: I've spent my life trying to fulfil that need. I've now got to force myself to stop thinking about it.

4

Pursuit of Excellence

In the event, I didn't take up any of the bursaries I qualified for a couple of years later. "I just want to stay with my pals in Bellahouston Academy," I explained to the Depute Head Teacher of the secondary school, and I started to walk. Two seconds later I would have remained in Bellahouston Academy for life. Flora MacIntosh was seated on a bench outside the school office, obviously a new start, crossing and uncrossing impossibly long, tanned legs. Five-foot-seven-inches tall, a hundred and ten pounds, cascading auburn hair, Celtic green eyes, crisp yellow blouse that served up a magnificent pair of breasts with nipples on them like the studs on football boots. I wasn't afraid to admit this. At the age of twelve, I really, really liked big tits.

I still continued to attend the College of Piping. If something was enjoyable to me, I couldn't get enough of it. One of my heroes was Seumas. Every night in Brand Street, after the evening meal, I'd strike up this instrument of torture and totter off, with stoic, knock-kneed baby steps to the laboured strains of 'The Earl of Mansfield'. So physically exhausting was this activity that I had seriously considered (gasp!) giving up the entire learning process. But of course I didn't.

One night, Seumas announced that another young boy, George Robertson from Maryhill, and I would go with him to the studios of BBC Scotland in Queen Margaret Drive. There, Seumas was to be interviewed by a famous radio broadcaster called Jamieson Clarke about the mission statement of the College. I gathered that George was to be the tyro student, which he was, learning on the practice chanter the first part of 'The Earl of Mansfield'. I was supposed to be the finished article, playing the entire tune on the Big Pipe.

The playing went well enough, I suppose. What stuck in my memory was the aplomb and coolness Seumas displayed when responding to the questions read out to him by Jamieson Clarke. With his hands clasped behind his back and swaying slightly on the soles of his feet, he responded to the written questions looking, with his gaunt face and his thin aquiline nose pointing at me like an accusation, like an arrogant aristocrat, or a Sicilian hitman. The man seemed to have a undergone a mood transplant. In response to a question by the broadcaster about the admission policy of the College, he stated that, no, he would not accept stupid people. "I don't like to mock the handicapped," he said, "but I will not attempt to teach someone who doesn't have both oars in the water." He brought me into the conversation. "Norman," he intoned gravely, as though he knew about some life-threatening illness concerning which I had not yet been informed, "you know what they say about village idiots, don't you?"

"No, Mr MacNeill," I crooned as I entered into the spirit of things. "What do they say about village idiots?"

"Too many village idiots," he snapped curtly, "spoil the village."

The mood of the interviewer changed abruptly. "Mr MacNeill," Clarke said, "I think we have enough already to make an excellent programme. You were excellent . . . and so were the boys."

"We thank you most civilly," Seumas said.

"But there's just one thing that bothers me," Clarke said.

"Yes?" Seumas said.

"You don't seem . . . umh, you don't rely on notes, do you?" the famous broadcaster said, a note of puzzlement in his voice.

"No," Seumas said. "Why should I?"

"It's just . . . I don't know," he said. "We in broadcasting would die if we didn't have some kind of *aide-mémoire* before starting to record."

"Really?" Seumas said, with some asperity. "Look, I do this kind of stuff every day of the week. I lecture at the 'yooni'."

The famous interviewer looked hurt. It has since been my experience that people in the media can never understand that the rest of the world doesn't have the same priorities as themselves.

After perfunctory handshakes all round we collected our fees – mine was one guinea – and went back to Otago Street.

It was not the money that excited me. It was the example of the Principal of the College of Piping that made me vow that I too would some day be as fluent, as grammatically correct and as entertaining in my discourse as the example I had just been shown. I would accomplish all this in two languages.

Bilingualism was not a problem for me. With practice I was now correctly hitting the proper mode buttons. This was not the case with big Iain McGibbon. One evening he visited the house and made a kind of confession.

"*Thormoid*, Norman," he said, "'*s ann a tha an t-eagal orm gun dùisg mi latha brèagha air choreigin is bidh mi nam bhalbhan!* I'm afraid I'm going to waken up one morning and I'll be a dummy!"

"What do you mean?" I said.

"You know," he said with the impeccable logic of a ten-year-old, "I go to my granny's in Loch Carnan every summer?"

"Yes," I said.

"Well," he said slowly, "after listening to *Fraochan*, my grandfather, and my aunties all talking in Gaelic for a couple of weeks, I wake up in the bedroom with the V-lining and I can't remember a word of English. Somehow I've lost it."

"And?" I said.

"Well," he said even more slowly, "I come back to Midlock Street to start school again, and inside a week I've lost my Gaelic."

I found this amusing and gave a short laugh.

"It's no laughing matter," he said. "When the same thing happens every year – you know, losing one of my languages? – and it happens so easily, who's to say that I won't waken up some morning and I've lost the lot?"

"You'll keep one or the other, Iain," I consoled him, anxious to get on with my chanter practice. I left him at the door looking very worried. "Is sign language difficult to learn, Norman?" he said in parting. I went back into the room and slogged my way through 'Pretty Marion' in anticipation of my weekly lesson with Pipe Major Macdonald.

But it wasn't all hell being associated with Seonaidh. Indeed, good things started to happen for me, and I became dependant on Pipe Major Macdonald in many different areas of my life. First of all, I became a conscientious trophy-gatherer at amateur competitions. With Seonaidh five paces in front of me, we'd glide into the Assembly Hall of the High School of Glasgow, say, employing what is known in the Uists as *ceum na mòintich*, the gait of the moorland, a slow, long-striding march accompanied by a kind of pimp-roll of the upper body. A massive oak, alone in the garden of eyes, John would divest himself of his tightly-belted trench coat, soft hat, scarf and gloves, and lay them carefully on the seat nearest the judges' table in the front row. I did the same. Picking up the massive wooden pipe-box, which contained, among other things, a handsome full silver-mounted set of Henderson bagpipes, reeds, hemp, and – this discovery fascinated me – a *searrag*, flask of whisky, Seonaidh, with me in tow, would then slow march in his confident, chin-out, I'm-a-winner manner to the tuning room. There, he'd strike up this magnificent instrument and let loose a volley of embellishments, while I massaged my hands in an ostentatious manner. (I hadn't discovered the Bill Livingston trick of sprinkling talcum powder on the fingers yet, but if I had done, I'd surely have employed it.)

The effect on the other people in the room was instantaneous. Suddenly, it was like the stampede that follows a duff performance in a concert hall. Fathers, uncles, tutors and fellow competitors would make a dash for the door.

Modesty and a burden of guilt forbid me from reciting my many triumphs. Suffice it to say I was rarely out of the top three in these events, which took place indoors in venues like the 'old' Highlanders' Institute in Elmbank Street in Glasgow, the College of Piping itself and the Pearce Institute in Govan. Outdoors, I competed at places as distant as Crook of Devon Highland Games, the Cowal Gathering, Inverness, Oban, and the Highland Games in Hosta in North Uist and Askernish in South Uist.

With John at my side footering with the tuning slides of the drones, I would blast out a cascade of 'birls'. (Seonaidh hated these 'birls', describing them as 'Edinburgh tuning notes'. At practice sessions he'd grimace as though his teeth hurt and chant in a monotone 'Edin-boro-boro-boro'.) Finally, John would satisfy himself that the drones were finely tuned. He'd step aside and place an enormous paw on my shoulder, and in a stage whisper that could be heard five hundred yards away intone in a rich baritone: "*Siuthad, 'ill' òig, 's ann dhut a rinneadh an saoghal,* Proceed, lad, the world was made for you." The fix was well and truly in.

This dependency on The Great One, however, had its downside. I'm pretty sure I came across as vain and brattish. It was becoming increasingly difficult for me to divine my true character. I was, outwardly at least, punch-the-air, I'm-definitely-gonna-impress confident. This aping of the older man became so familiar to me that I started to walk, dress and talk like him, even when I was chatting up girls at secondary school dances. I'd be thirteen at this time. My pals would invite girls to share a soft drink with them at the trestle table in the school assembly hall.

I, in contrast, dressed in bullet-proof blue serge suit, white nylon shirt, slightly yellow at the collar, secured at the neck by a tightly knotted club tie beneath a Fair Isle-patterned pullover . . . *tucked into the trousers* . . . would saunter up to Evelyn, Arlene or even Flora, and in a deep brown voice with a heavy Hebridean accent drawl: "Hello, my treasure, do you like to dance?"

Most of the time they'd give me the elbow. Well, what they'd actually say was: "Piss off, you freak!" It wasn't all that pretty, was it? I recovered quickly from rejection, however. When the girl was reluctant to dance with me, I'd shrug as though I didn't care and, wheeling away from her with my arms in the air, I'd perform a rapid back-step on the spot and announce airily over my shoulder: "Darling, as you can see, I *love* to dance." I'd then spin into the general melee of partnered dancers, laughing uproariously. Oh, what a merry wag I was in those days!

I never seemed to learn from experiences of rejection and modify my behaviour. Humour and an air of superiority continued to be my defence weapons. Nevertheless, I continued to pursue Flora McIntosh of the magnificent knockers relentlessly. You'd think that Flora McIntosh was the only thing that interested me during my introduction to *ceòl mòr*. Flora McIntosh *was* pretty much the only thing that interested me during my introduction to *ceòl mòr,* the classical music of the great Highland bagpipe. And no, not just because my hormones were running riot (well, a little, maybe).

One night, in the locked communal toilet of our landing in the tenement building at Ibrox, I experienced a minor epiphany. What better way to combine my sexual and musical obsessions than to encourage Flora to skip afternoon classes and accompany me to Gleniffer Braes? There, I'd regale her with beautiful renditions of *Maol Donn, Bodaich Dhubha nan Sligean* and 'Somebody's Farewell to Somewhere'. Afterwards, physically exhausted, I'd lay my head on her lap and gaze up fondly at the rise and fall of her generous bosom . . . and – Hold it! You've got the general idea.

Well, I floated the first part of my wicked plan past her and she agreed. Okay, she wasn't punching the air in delight at the prospect of going into the woods with a vertically-challenged youth who suffered from terminal acne, but I knew she didn't fancy two periods of Latin

Prose Composition in Miss Forrest's class, and she gave me the green light; sort of. Interesting that. In my endeavours to impress the girl, I spent the best years of my life translating Vergil, Cicero and Ovid, correcting her attempts at scansion, and becoming pretty slick at oral expression in the language of ancient Rome. What a sad confession!

Anyway, for about three weeks before the date I liberally plastered my pustule-ridden face with a repellent pink substance called 'Zap' or 'Zit-Blaster', and ended up with facial skin that had the colour and texture of a Florida orange. My poor wee face looked as if it had been reconformed for the purposes of a witness-protection programme. My father, Niall Mòr, disowned me. "This is not my son," he'd chunter furiously. "This is the son of Frankenstein's monster!"

On the morning of the long-awaited day, during the break, I was having a crafty smoke with some of the older lads in the toilets, and couldn't refrain from telling them what I was going to do that afternoon.

"Remember, Norman," said one of the older boys, "don't forget about foreplay."

"What? What's that?" I said sharply.

"Och," said one of the other lads, "it's just like tuning the drones of your bagpipes before you start to play melodies on the chanter."

"Hang on a minute," I protested. "What do you mean, like tuning the drones of my bagpipes? I can't even tune my pipes. Pipe Major John Macdonald does all that stuff for me. I'm not even fifteen. I'm fourteen. This is like entering me for the Bursary Competition at Glasgow University four years early. This is putting pressure on me. Can't I get a cancellation from Flora and fix up some coaching or something?"

The boys were howling with laughter at my mounting paranoia. I couldn't see a way out of the predicament. I could hardly get on the phone to Govan Police Station to ask Seonaidh if he could possibly come to Glennifer Braes with me and my girlfriend. He would refuse. Quite rightly too. At lunchtime I gave Flora the news.

"Sorry, Flora," I sheepishly said. "Unfortunately my tutor, Pipe Major John Macdonald, has asked me to attend . . ."

"Right," she said grimly. The look she gave me said: "I know your sort, you rat. You stalk me for months and then blame your piping instructor."

I didn't see much of Seonaidh after that. I didn't see Flora *at all* after that.

But that didn't deter me from pursuing the girls. Big Donald MacRitchie and I had discovered a new hunting ground: the Art Gallery and Museum across the river in Partick. This was the hangout of choice for teenagers from Scotstoun, Whiteinch, Partick, Overnewton, Finnieston, Anderston and from a large swathe of the south-west of the city. Hordes of teenage boys and girls would constantly promenade through the brightly lit galleries and neatly tiled corridors. A couple of girls might be admiring Salvador Dali's 'Crucifixion'. Two lads would approach them and elaborate tribal greetings would be exchanged. Big Donald and I got lucky quite a few times. Nothing much happened. We'd separate into two couples and exchange dreams, aspirations and false addresses before going home to a dinner of cold cuts and chips.

Our entire family – mother, father, my young sister, Lorna Flora, and myself – are together in the kitchen of the flat in Ibrox. It is noon on a Sunday, the last day in the life of Niall Mòr. I am seated at the table drinking tea, mother is washing up, Lorna Flora is playing with her dolls on the bed in the recess and my father is crouched in the big chair by the fireplace trying to reassemble the jumbled pages of the Sunday Post *that I have scattered carelessly on the floor after reading them earlier. He is wearing brown moleskin trousers and heavy boots. He will be off shortly to work on a Canadian grain boat moored down at the King George V dock in Shieldhall. I and my big pal, Donald MacRitchie, father from Ness in Lewis and mother from Baleshare in North Uist, are eschewing work in favour of chasing girls over at the Art Gallery and Museum in Partick.*

"Norman,' says my father in English, "why can't you learn yourself to put a newspaper back the way you found it?"

"Daddy," I reply, and when I recall my sarcasm, a tide of filthy water scalds my throat, "if you insist on speaking a language whose grammar will always be problematic to you, please remember that the verb 'learn' is inappropriate before a personal pronoun: 'teach' is the word you ought to have used."

The big man is speechless.

I am unaware of it at the time, but these are the last words I will speak to my father while he is still alive . . .

In the rocket of my mind I sped to a close-mouth in a tenement on Dumbarton Road, on a Sunday afternoon.

The girl is about my own age, fourteen, and is wearing a dark green trench coat, tightly belted to accentuate her breasts. During our restless walk through the Museum, arm in arm, I have been conscious of the pressure of these same breasts against my right forearm. I remember speaking to her without opening my mouth, without altering my expression of feigned interest in the great paintings in their heavy wooden frames: 'Ah, nameless girl, can it be that you are unaware of my arm as it rubs against your bosom? Your insouciance is my almost-pleasure.' Later we stand in the close, face to face, her arms round my waist, mine resting lightly on her shoulders. She stares at me without blinking and poses her question.

"You're not going to be seeing me again, Norman, are you?" she says. I see in her eyes the desperate longing I was to see many times in the future.

"Maybe," I say, and I know now with certainty that this courting game with the girls is easy. Big Donald was right when he whispered to me, before going off with this one's pal: "Norrie, mate, this dame'll do you till you learn the ropes, but you can find better than a plain wee soul from Finnieston who only wants to chuck school as soon as the holidays come round."

I place my hands in the safety of my pockets. "Look, I've got to trap," I mumble. "It's Sunday service on the Underground, and my old man'll be home from the docks by now. . . and I've got, you know, a Latin Ink Exercise to do for school tomorrow."

I cannot leave it like that: I have to finish up with a few lying words. "I'll see you next week at the Art Galleries, all right?" I say, knowing it was all wrong.

There is silence between us for two or three seconds. We both seek the hem of our stories: the clean parting. But we are young and unpractised, and the separation is cloying, without satisfaction.

One night in early December 1951, I left Ibrox Underground Station – we called it Copland Road in those days – and strode proudly up Woodville Street and on to Brand Street. At the close entrance to my home our next-door neighbour, Mr Bankhead, a rigger from Belfast, placed his hand on my chest as I tried to wriggle past him. The words he spoke have been a long time dead, but I am able to mouth them to this day like some familiar litany . . .

"I'd like a word with you, Norman," he said.

"I've got to get up the stairs, Mr Bankhead," I said.

"Not right away, son," he said, with the lengthened vowels of the Ulster-man. "Yer ma asked me to speak to ye."

"So?" I said.

"Yer da's had an accident down at KG Five, son," he announced solemnly.

"What kind of accident – what do you mean, Mr Bankhead?" I say, a shrillness creeping into my voice.

"He's dead, Norman," he said, in funereal tones.

"Where is he?" I enquired.

"He's up the stairs," Bankhead said. "Yer ma's with the body. Yer wee sister's in with us and the boys."

"I'd better go, Mr Bankhead," I said in a hurry.

"Be good to yer ma, Norman," Mr Bankhead said softly.

It turned out that after my priggish lecture on English usage at noon, my father, accompanied by two teuchter fellow-dockers, was walking down Shieldhall Road on his way towards his 'spell' at unloading an iron-ore boat, when he suffered a massive heart attack. (Another version of his death was that he had fallen between the hull of the ship and the quay. Whatever happened, Niall Mòr was finally and irrevocably dead.) He was brought in a taxi – Mr Campbell, a native of Lewis, organized this, I think – to the Co-operative Funeral Home in Kingston. The undertaker did his stuff, and returned to our home with the coffin.

All this was being done while my pal and I whistled and made lewd sucking noises at the backs of likely-looking girls in the Art Gallery and Museum.

None of what followed – the casket in the middle of the room where my father and I slept in a recessed double bed, the three days and nights of psalm singing, the terror of sharing the room with a corpse – was a dream, but it passed like a dream.

Someone, at the funeral service in the back room, pushes me forward towards the casket so that I may kiss my father for the last time. I lean over the open coffin and kiss his brow. I am astonished at the coldness of his skin and how hard the bone beneath it is. In an instant my heart is crushed.

An unwanted thought comes. You never really knew this man, Norman. Now, it's too late. But I knew that he had been unhappy in his marriage. Our 'Sunday treat' with the elegant blonde woman called Mrs Bryson was a constant guilty memory. One night, two years afterwards, he came home with her. For some reason, I am sleeping on a mattress in the kitchen while my mother and Lorna share the matrimonial bed. (I suspect that Wee Peggy knew there was going to be trouble that night.) Wide-eyed, I watch my parents conduct a tug-of-war involving my sister. To my shame I cannot intervene. Eventually, Big Neil and his paramour depart and the three of us somehow endure a sleepless night.

With regard to Lorna, I cannot forget the fact that I slapped her on the cheek one evening when I was in second year at secondary school. I had been wrestling with a piece of Latin prose composition all afternoon, and it was plain that my heart was not in my work. Lorna had been interrupting me 'ben the room' with foolish suggestions.

"Why don't we get a bottle of American cream soda, Norman, and go for a picnic to Plantation Park?"

"No, Lorna," I had said firmly, "I have this ink exercise to hand in to Miss Forrest tomorrow and I've got to beat Neil Alexander." (He was the son of a Primary School Head Teacher and was challenging me for supremacy in the Latin class. I *had* to get a higher mark than Neil the following day.)

"That's okay," said Lorna with indulgent approval. "A bit of fresh air will do you good."

I drew a long rasping breath at her third or fourth interruption. "Let's go out and have a game of rounders with the lassies," she proposed.

I simply had to be strong. These outrageous suggestions had to be stopped. I rose, stepped forward and drew the palm of my right hand hard against her left cheek. I had never been filled with such rage before. The savaged seven-year-old girl burst into tears and fled into the kitchen to complain to my mother. I locked the room door and resumed my studies.

Wee Peigi did not intervene, and I almost convinced myself that the shocking attack never occurred. More fool me. Not a day has gone by in the succeeding fifty-eight years when I have not remembered and bitterly regretted my action. It may sound melodramatic, but often, particularly in the depths of drink-induced depression, I have seriously considered thrusting the offending hand, palm downwards, on the red hot rings of the cooking hob.

No, I was not filled with any great degree of fraternal piety towards my wee sister. I couldn't even watch her die in a grey room in the Western Infirmary. Without kidneys she was kept alive only by dialysis. With a head like a thumb and mouth agape, she was totally unrecognisable to me. With but twenty minutes of life left to her, as it turned out, I looked at my mother and said: "*Gabh mo lethsgeul, ach feumaidh mi dhol dhan taigh bheag*, Excuse me, but I have to go to the toilet." Of course, I didn't. I fled the cursed hospital to which I had driven Lorna dozens of times over the preceding eighteen months, and scurried across Church Street and Byres Road to a pub called The Chancellor. Only after I had fortified myself with several large whiskies was I able to return to the little room, where Peigi Bheag sat weeping on a chair in front of an empty bed.

Though I had tried to raise myself in Lorna's esteem by being particularly attentive to her needs during the last ten months of her complete renal failure, when the curtain came up at her death, or more accurately when it became 'tabs closed', as they say in the theatre, her cowardly big brother was nowhere to be seen.

Bitter remorse has assailed me ever since the summer of 1969.

And everything I did after my father died was feigned. As a dutiful son I wore the black diamond of mourning on the sleeves of every outer garment I possessed. I went from plimsolls to black socks with suspenders round the calf overnight. I was the man of the house now, and though I displayed false filial piety towards my widowed mother, secretly I concealed my anger and embarrassment by adopting a reckless, devil-may-care persona. Away from home, I became an actor.

And, I'm afraid, I remained an actor all my life. There was no clearer evidence of this than my habit of assuming a new character when there was no ostensible reason to do so. If you asked me to buy you a pint in the pub, I would place the order with an indifferent waiter in broad Govanese. If you told me on my return from the bar that you didn't know I was Glaswegian, I would tell you I was from Argentina. If I trusted you, I'd come over as lower middle-class Scottish – maybe. Mine was not a voluntary exercise in deception – it was a reflex that had its genesis in the death of my father. Some events, I realized, come too soon, and others come too late, and by the time a man finds out about them, there is nothing to be done.

5

Summer Holidays

Every summer throughout the nineteen-fifties, between the ages of thirteen and twenty-two, I spent school holidays and part of university vacations in Uist. I never forgot the summer of 1951, the last time my father accompanied me to the train before his death later that year.

This, then:

Niall Mòr is leaning across me in the bedroom of our home in Ibrox. His large hand is on my shoulder and he is gently rocking me into wakefulness. "Dùisg, a bhalaich, Wake up, lad," he says. "That's four o'clock. The Mallaig train leaves at six." It is the first day of the school holidays and I, like hundreds of other children of my background, am being sent 'home' to Uist.

Within half an hour I am washed, fed, and dressed in short trousers, blazer and highly polished brogue shoes. My father picks up the battered leather suitcase that has been packed for a week by the outside door. I carry the much lighter bagpipe case. I enter the kitchen and approach the recessed bed where my mother and sister lie sleeping.

"I'm off, then," I say.

My mother opens her eyes, turns to face me and reaches for something beneath her pillow. She extends an envelope. "Here," she whispers, "take this. Give it to your auntie Seonag."

I accept the envelope and place it in the inside pocket of my jacket. There is a brief silence. "Right," I say. "I'm off."

"Dia bhith timcheall ort, God be round about you," she says in benediction.

"I'll write, mammy," I promise.

"Mind and do that, Norman," she warns.

Soon, in the pre-dawn darkness, my father and I are briskly walking along Brand Street to the tram depot where we will board the tram that will take us into the city centre, or 'up the town' as we Southsiders call it. I marvel at the ease with which Niall Mòr swings the heavy suitcase in his left hand as he puffs a Capstan cigarette he is holding between the fingers of his right. He is a big, strong man, and I would gladly give up all my so-called intelligence and the academic prizes which, I am assured by teachers, await me, if only I could attain stature and presence . . .

At Queen Street Station, at half past five in the morning, islanders – young girls in service, merchant seamen on leave, family men in dark suits and soft hats, fussing mothers and scores of children – swarm through the place. It is the children, may God bless them, I remember most vividly. Clumps of baggage and parcels, guarded over by women in cheap coats and dark headscarves, are scattered all over the concourse. The children, all between the ages of six and thirteen or fourteen, scamper restlessly from group to group. The parents of these kids come from Lewis, Skye, Harris and the Uists, and they have made sure that the Police Force, the Docks, the Clyde Navigation Trust and the Psychiatric Hospitals all belong to them. Their offspring move restlessly from one temporary encampment to another, much in the same way as they themselves at a later date will leave their rented flats in Partick, Overnewton, Govan, Ibrox, Plantation, Kinning Park and Kingston and flee to the suburbs and beyond. These are the children who in twelve years' time, from comfortable homes which they will own in Whitecraigs, Newton Mearns, Clarkston, Kelvinside, Bearsden and Milngavie, will make their assault on Teaching, the Law, Broadcasting, Film, Popular Music, the Theatre, Accountancy and Publishing. And while the patronymics of their blood relatives on the islands who will nourish them over the coming months trip off their tongues fluently this morning, it will not always be so . . .

My father speaks to a woman, Bean Mhìcheil Dhonnchaidh, *the wife of Michael son of Duncan, who comes from South Uist and is accompanying her son and daughter to Lochboisdale. Roddy and Kathleen are about my own age and are near neighbours, but they are unknown to me since they attend a Roman Catholic school, St Margaret's, in Kinning Park. It is likely that daddy has asked the lady to keep an eye on me, particularly on the* Lochmòr, *where opportunities for mishaps abound.*

On the platform, Niall Mòr stands apart from the little clusters of groups who gabble last-minute advice in Gaelic to their excited offspring crowding round the open windows of each carriage. Eventually, he steps forward, easily forcing a path through the other adults, and indicates by lifting his chin smartly that I should approach the window.

The other children in my carriage, awed perhaps by my father's height and upright, silent stance, reluctantly give way and allow me to come forward to the window. The two of us are separated by a foot and we watch each other, as if we are about to back away in different directions.

"Norman," my father says, producing a white ten-pound note from his wallet, "here's some money. A man needs something to rattle in his pocket."

I look at the hand with the note in it, as if memorizing it. Finally: "Thank you," I say, taking the equivalent of two weeks' wages from him.

"Keep up the practice, Norman," he says. "Your uncle Angus John will keep you right."

"Uh-huh," I concur.

"You're my son," he says quietly, "and I want you to be the best you can be."

'I'm not your son,' I silently scream behind clenched teeth. Suddenly I find my voice. "Don't touch me!"

My father has offered his hand, and when he sees that I'm not going to take it he walks away.

Tears sting the corners of my eyes as I take my seat in the corner of the carriage, but I am smiling. I am happy. My father does love me, doesn't he? Please don't walk away. Wait.

I felt anger, shame and resentment at my father's death. Why did he have to mark me out as different from my schoolmates by dying at the comparatively young age of fifty? I would miss the Christmas school dance as a consequence of my obligation to display filial piety and observe the obligatory year-long period of mourning. I experienced corrosive feelings of shame on Monday mornings when I received a *free* dinner-ticket for lunchtime meals up in the old Scout Hall annexe in Jane Street.

I did not feel very pleased with myself and with my self-centred reactions, but, without a thought about my mother's or my sister's emotions, I managed somehow to blame Big Neil for my unhappiness.

What did I have to complain about? It was a good life in Ibrox in the Fifties. There was enough food, plenty of books to read, and a devoted widowed mother and sister. We lived in an extended family group in a room and kitchen with my mother's youngest brother, Colin. For over forty-five years, my mother obeyed my grandmother's admonition to look after my wee uncle, who was – how to put this delicately? – perhaps not the brightest bulb in the chandelier. My mother and sister shared a bed in the kitchen. Colin, another dock labourer, slept beside me in a double bed in the only bedroom. When transient relatives arrived from Lochaber or Uist, I was farmed out to the two-bed roomed flat of *Cailleach 'Tait'*, a native of North Uist and my grandmother's best pal.

I was learning to play the Highland Pipe properly. I was also learning a bit about girls. I have danced with a few pretty girls in secondary school. Betty, Arlene, Sandra. I have fumbled with their underwear in back closes. I know their smell, a combination of cheap perfume, talcum powder, sweat and sex. A clean smell on one level, a dark odour underneath.

Out of a fog of disjointed recollection the outline of a shape begins to appear. It was *Tormod*, aged fifteen, gaining third place in the Ceòl Mòr competition at Hosta, North Uist, in the summer of 1952. There among the dunes I met Donald Morrison from South Uist, who went on to serve as Pipe Major of the Aberdeen City Police Pipes and Drums. Dressed in a lounge suit and a fawn single-breasted raincoat belted at the waist, he approached me, and after congratulating me on my playing in the Pibroch – I think I played 'The Little Spree' – he asked me if he could borrow my bagpipe when it came his turn to play. I felt flattered that this professional piper wanted to compete with the Grainger and Campbell set my late father had bought for me for the equivalent of a month's wages. Donald, who was incapable of playing anything that was not musical, won the event at a canter. But I was bitten by the money bug and relished the cash I received for my effort. During the vacation of the following summer I was awarded first place in the Open March, Strathspey and Reel in Askernish, South Uist. This was achieved against competitors like John D. Burgess, Iain MacFadyen and Jimmy Young.

Suddenly, the reel of my memory unspools and a picture shimmers before me. The year was 1954 and I see, near Griminish crossroads in Benbecula, a lanky youth carefully replacing the chain on an old 'minister's' bicycle, the weight of a massive stone pressing heavily on his innards.

Swiftly, new images appear. The boy, his teeth bared and his shoulders bent over the handlebars, his legs pumping hard, shot out of Griminish road end and onto the main road leading to Creagorry. That summer, like every summer, was spent in the home of Seumas Mhurchaidh, who had built a fine new bungalow for himself and his family nearer the main road. That year I was the nearest thing

Benbecula had to a pony-express rider: every day, rain or shine, I made my rounds on an old rattletrap of a bicycle. I didn't simply move about the island – I revolved. Daily trips to Balivanich to have my pipes set up by *Aonghas Iain Mhurchaidh*, Angus John Macdonald, another of my mother's cousins, were involved.

Cigarettes were bought at the Post Office in Clachan Beag. I adored a girl called Anna MacPherson who worked in *Bùth Nilidh Ruairidh Fhearchair*, Neil MacLennan's shop near the Gym (the local dance hall), and on the slightest pretext I'd make an excuse to visit *taigh Ruairidh Fhearchair*, the house of Roderick son of Farquhar. There, with the roses in my cheeks, I'd watch Anna's slim, tanned limbs and the vibration each way free of her upper body as, barefoot, she scattered sand on the concrete floor and afterwards swept everything up with a stiff broom.

Every morning I'd call at Rose Cottage, where Johnny MacLean resided, and take a modest shopping list to MacIntosh's shop in Cre-agorry. Every afternoon I'd play the practice chanter for an hour or so, and have a shorter blast on the big pipe. The evenings were spent ceilidhing in various houses throughout the island, and my head was filled with music and stories.

Benbecula in the 50s enjoyed the most sophisticated network of communication. Everybody talked, exchanging scandals and celebrations, deals, promises, threats and propositions. Family, clannish networks of reliability and loyalty, linked the people: by their common ground, and by an endless history of past events. These ceilidhs were music-saturated, and a kind of immersion course in local legend and fantasy.

Then there were tales of the supernatural. Bizarre commandments were drummed into us: don't travel in the middle of the road after midnight lest you meet *am Fear Mòr*, the Devil. Do not look back when travelling after midnight: you will see Satan following you. Do not whistle after midnight; if you do, the Devil will come to you.

The South Ford was a dangerous place. Ghosts of people who had been drowned made frequent appearances. They were to be recognized by traces of sand in their hair.

Liniclate too, on the west side of Benbecula, was swarming with spirits after dark. A man in Liniclate, Angus Macneil, had built a new house and was busy digging a potato pit nearby when a neighbour told him that he had better stop as a man was buried there. Angus ignored him and got on with his work. Soon after this, lots of sticks and peats started to be thrown around the house and around the fire. After a while, a shinty stick was administering beatings to the house's inhabitants. That stopped after some time. Then, a small hand would be seen playing with a switch (*stiofag*) and it would come through the boards of the bed. This ghost was known as *Bòcan beag Aonghais 'ic Nìll*, the little ghost of Angus, son of Neil.

Another hazard in the darkness was occasionally encountered at *Loch nan Daod*, which lies to the East of the main Lochboisdale–Lochmaddy road between Torlum and Griminish. This was the dreaded *bean-nighe*, the washerwoman of shrouds. If you heard a slapping sound as though someone or something was pounding a garment on rocks at the edge of the loch, you were about to meet an apparition who was the harbinger of death. She was preparing a shroud for someone, inevitably close to you, who would sleep in, for good, in the immediate future.

Inevitably, at the conclusion of tales about the supernatural, I'd indulge my exhibitionistic streak by offering – nay, insisting on it – to play a few selections on my Grainger and Campbell bagpipe.

A bit like Iain McGibbon who was repeatedly losing one of his languages, I too was amazed that my persona, that of an urban achiever, was so easily shed in this ghost-ridden environment.

The ease with which the names of Joyce, Shakespeare and John Donne slid off my tongue in Paisley Road West was replaced by a stuttering reluctance to retell to younger neighbours the plot of the story about the Devil's claw marks on the pews of *Eaglais a-Staigh*, the Inner Church of Scotland in the village. I had regressed from rational, philosophical student to superstitious peasant. I was afraid of the dark, whether it was because of the horror stories of *Tormod Ruadh*, Red-haired Norman MacMillan, or because I was reminded of the nightmarish wake that preceded my father's burial, I didn't know. It was probably a bit of both.

The evening of the roadside repair on the *Rathad an Iar*, the West Side road, however, was different. I had screwed up my courage to venture forth with love as my motivator. I wore a black beret pulled to the back of my head at an angle of forty-five degrees, then pushed forward slightly so that two Brylcreemed 'waves' adorned my brow. The beret, the Fair Isle pullover, tucked into the trousers, the spring-linked belt with the stars and stripes of America enamelled on the buckle, and the inside of the right trouser-leg cuff tucked into the stocking, spoke of male Hebridean chic. Earlier that evening I had had a brief conversation with the man of the house, Seumas Mhurchaidh.

"*Seadh, ill' òig*," he said.

"*Seadh*," I responded.

"*Cài'l thu a' dol a-nochd*, Where are you off to tonight?" he said.

I lit a cigarette to demonstrate my sophistication. "*Tha mi a' dol suas gu Deas*, I'm going up south," I informed him.

(That's how they talk in Uist. You go 'up' south, and 'down' north. It derives from the method the Celtic peoples employed to establish the points of the compass. Facing the rising sun in the east, on their right hand they had south – the source of all good – and on their left hand, cf. Latin *sinister*, they had north – the source of evil: cold and Norse raiders, for example.)

I was headed for the weekly dance in Eochar village hall, South Uist. *Muinntir an Ìochdair*, the people of Eochar, had a reputation for violence. For the duration of the dance – anything between four and five hours – there would be a kind of tag boxing match taking place outside the hall. 'Biffy', a notorious scrapper from Loch Carnan, would stand in the doorway and issue a general invitation to any male in the place to come outside and fight with him. He had plenty of takers. Accordingly, if you got tired watching couples performing Quadrilles and Lancers, you could go outside and watch a couple of lads knocking lumps out of each other. Quite often, I admit, I was frightened when I went to South Uist – physically frightened that somebody might hurt me. It never happened. On the contrary, I often discovered that the majority of the people attributed to me virtues I didn't have. You see, piping in Uist at that time provided an opportunity within the recondite confines of the local culture to become 'well known'.

Okay, there I was pedalling across the South Causeway, eyes like golf balls and perspiration streaming down my face, which by now was a rather attractive shade of puce. I was about to enter a hidden country. The first indices of differentiation were the roadside shrines dedicated to the Virgin Mary. To a lad of Presbyterian descent, these were scary. Why, then, was I rushing into this strange country?

The truth was that I was making for *taigh Lachlainn Seonsan*, the house of Lachie Johnston, to listen to the piping of one of the daughters of the family, Mary Margaret. If her brothers, George and Ronald, were home on leave from the Queen's Own Cameron

Highlanders and were up for a blast, that would be a bonus. But despite my conviction that George had the best bottom hand I've ever heard, the centre of my attention would be the lovely Mary Margaret.

She was – I faint, I swoon – an older woman. A prison officer in Greenock, she must have been irritated by the fawning adulation of a callow seventeen-year-old. She had black, curly hair, high cheekbones to die for, finely-chiselled full red lips and excellent upright posture. It was her technique on the pipe chanter, however, that fascinated me. Small, thin fingers moved up and down like typewriter keys, accurate, precise and without any unnecessary expenditure of energy. She knew all the heavy competition tunes, and when she played and moved to a Competition March, her slender body swaying at the hips, she could make grown men weep.

Eventually, after frequent stops to replace the slipping bicycle chain, I'd arrive at the Johnston thatched home on rubber legs and with greasy hands. I'd snap a chain and padlock on the rear wheel – this was, after all, Apache territory – and enter the 'porch', turn right, and after knocking politely on the door leading to the living room, enter paradise.

My absorption with Mary Margaret was so intense that it frightened me. At times, her dark beautiful face, framed by a cascade of black curls, a tumbling river of onyx, assumed an Egyptian, not Hebridean, cast.

She glided over the surface of the music, but did not have the macho bravado of, say, her brother George, who was not afraid to vary his technique to suit what he considered the melody demanded. Sometimes he played heavy, at other times light. Mary Margaret, on the other hand, played the way Japanese robot pipers play. Imagine the playing of robots constructed by a famous Japanese electronic engineer who's also a keen piping buff. Iain Macdonald, Pipe Major of the Neilston and District Pipe Band, has told me that these machines play perfectly – pitch, tempi and embellishments are all spot on – and the result is . . . uh, boring.

"*Siuthad, a Mhàiri, a . . . uh, ghràidh*, Come on, Mary, . . . uh, love," I'd mumble with what I hoped was boyish charm, "give us 'Hugh Alexander Lowe of Tiree'." With a sexy little shrug of her shoulders, Mary would hoist the drones onto her left shoulder, place the blowstick between carmine-red lips, and slowly inflate the bag. To me, this was almost the most important part of her recitals. I'd be like a setter dog on point. The delicate fingering was okay, but the white, glistening teeth through which a plump, pink tongue protruded from time to time always set my pulse racing. My opinions on her actual playing were always clouded by a puff or two of steam. The various solo contributions over, George, Ronald and Mary Margaret – I was pointedly excluded from ensemble work – would get together for a 'stramash'. Their renditions of 'Men of Argyll', 'Caledonian Society of London' and 'The Old Ruins' would absolutely soar, and the blazing sonority of drones and pipe chanters would take the music into the high country of exaltation.

I'd thank the *cailleach,* old lady, for the tea and scones, and, flanked by the two girls, I'd saunter proudly westward in the direction of the village hall. Between *taigh Lachlainn*, Lachie's house, and the hall, there was a hazard: the school. The head teacher was one of *clann Sheonaidh*, the children of Johnny, from Gerinish. He was Fred Morrison, father of one of the gods in the present-day pantheon, young Fred Morrison. On dance nights he'd be standing at the living room window of the schoolhouse looking to the east, and when he spotted me he'd beckon me inside. Reluctantly, I'd detach myself from the ladies and, promising to see them later at the *bàl*, dance, I'd trudge up the flagstones leading to the front door of the schoolhouse.

Then, the interrogation would begin. Old Fred wanted to know was . . . well, just about everything about Seonaidh Roidein's settings. "*Dè mar a chluicheadh Seonaidh 'Bodaich Dhubha nan Sligean'*? How did Seonaidh play 'The Old Men of the Shells'?" he'd enquire. And every week I'd assume the locutions and accent of my tutor, and invariably I'd change the phrasing. After all, that's what Seonaidh did. Old Fred's patience would visibly crumple like paper in a fire. Abruptly, he'd dismiss me and I'd gallop off to the dance.

The dance would be a kind of anti-climax. There were numerous rounds of coronary-inducing heavy dances like Quadrilles, Lancers, Eightsome Reels and Highland Schottische with Iain MacLachlan, composer of 'The Dark Island', battering out jigs, reels, 2/4 and 6/8 marches, hornpipes and polkas, accompanied by his father playing two kitchen spoons. There were the usual fights outside the hall. Indeed so frequent were these gladiatorial battles in Eochar it was rumoured that on the morning after a dance or wedding reception, a *bodach*, old man, would pick up all the teeth he could find and collect them in a *crogan silidh*, jam-jar – to what end, nobody knew.

"Fancy that," I said to the guy who provided me with this information.

And of course I did.

After the ball was over, as the old music hall ballad has it, the piping wasn't. With the Johnson girls in tow, clasping their high-heeled shoes to their bosoms and gingerly walking on stocking feet, the two sisters and I would straggle eastwards towards their thatched cottage. When we'd pass the schoolhouse on the left hand side of the road I'd studiously, no, resolutely, turn my eyes to the right.

Once safely inside the Johnston home – this would be about three-thirty in the morning – the girls would make tea and prepare buttered scones with syrup. Eventually, the boys would return from their escort duties and, in order not to disturb the *cailleach*, old woman, they'd whip out practice chanters, and an orgy of pipe tunes would ensue.

We'd take turns on the chanter, and the tunes, old and new, burbled forth in a veritable torrent. Old reels, played 'round' as I recollect, tickled my ears and absolutely enchanted me. I heard George playing '*Mo Shuirgheach Laghach Thu*, You are my Pleasant Wooer', '*Cailleach nan Cearc*, The Old Woman of the Hens', '*Anna Nighean Mhurchaidh*, Anna Daughter of Murdoch', and '*Nighean na Caillich*, The Old Wife's Daughter'. I drowned in this stuff. Ronald would then follow with '*Do Bheatha, Theàrlaich*, Charlie's Welcome', '*Bodachan a' Phinnt Leanna*, The Old Man's Pint of Ale', and '*Dòmhnall Bàn nan Gobhar*, Fair Donald of the Goats'. Technically he was not as proficient as his brother, but it seemed to me that his tunes were derived from the dark roots of Gaelic culture. Mary Margaret would play Gaelic melodies like '*Bealach a' Mhorbhain*, The Pass of Morven', and '*Ceud fàilt' air gach gleann 's air na beanntanan mòr*, A Hundred Welcomes to Every Glen and to the High Bens', and, my own favourite, '*Dh'fhalbh na Gillean Grinn*, The Doughty Soldier Lads Departed from Uist'.

Like every adolescent, I suppose, I had at that time an intense longing to belong. I decided after this musical feast that these were my people. All these sounds, the high-pitched bleating of the chanter, the requests in the mellifluous Gaelic of South Uist for particular tunes and the cries of encouragement and congratulations, all acted like methamphetamine on my nervous system. Man, I was *up, up*. From then on it was free-form until I left.

Parting was such sweet sorrow. As I mounted my bicycle with a theatrical flourish, Mary Margaret, her sister and brothers would stand in the doorway and anxiously call out, "*A bheil thu taght'*, *a Thormoid*, Are you all right, Norman?"

I'd invariably lie. "*Na gabh dragh, a nighean*, Don't worry, girl," I'd always reply, "*bithidh mi taght*', I'll be fine." Talk about Macho Man: I was full of confidence. As soon as I said, 'I'll be fine', it brought to mind the old adage that if you can keep your head when all around are displaying grave concern about your welfare, then you probably haven't grasped the full gravity of the situation. This was certainly true in my case. I was in for a very long trip home.

As we used to chant in Miss Forrest's Latin class in Bellahouston Academy, *Tempora mutantur nos et mutamur in illis*, Times change and we change with them. My transition from studious urban pupil to superstition-ridden rural hick was always fairly rapid, a kind of histori-cal jump-cut.

For a short time, at first, I handled myself pretty well for a boy under threat from *Am Fear Mòr*. It was when the shrine to the Virgin Mary hove into view that the first waves of fear engulfed me. I found myself – a disciple of John Calvin – dismounting and genuflecting. I even mumbled a half forgotten prayer:

> '*A Mhoire, màthair nan naomh,*
> *Beannaich an t-àl 's an crodh-laoigh.*
> Mary, thou mother of saints,
> Bless our flocks and bearing cattle.'

Then I improvised: '*Agus Tormod*. And Norman'. You can't have too much insurance, I reckoned.

At snail's pace I'd cycle along the South Causeway, keeping as far to the left as I could, almost clipping the grass verge at times. Passing-places presented a hazard. If I held my line when I came to one of these, I'd be perilously near – gulp – *the middle of the road*. Now, I just knew the Devil would be measuring my tyre tracks, and if he decided I was travelling in the middle of the road I'd meet a monster that Walt Disney could not have created. It would be awesome. The result would be blood and raw meat. I muttered a few ill-remembered prayers from Sunday School and wobbled into all these passing-places, keeping as far to the left as possible. Inevitably, the chain would come off at some point.

I'd crouch down, looking neither left nor right, but, keeping my unblinking eyes on the Atlantic Ocean to the west, I'd very carefully place the greasy links on the teeth of the sprocket. The sound of waves breaking on the coral strand was truly frightening. WHOOSH. Pause. THUD. Pause. WHOOSH. Pause. THUD.

See, Norman, you're crouched down here, and some guy with sand in his hair comes wading out of the sea, right? You're going to put a few knots in his sandy head with . . . uh, your bicycle pump. You'll blow that sucker away, man.

Sweeping through Creagorry, I caught myself whistling some of the tunes I'd heard earlier. Immediately, I'd clamp my jaws shut. I certainly didn't need the *Fear Mòr* responding to a whistled summons, did I? I'd then content myself by humming the new tunes. Well, it wasn't exactly humming. It was more a series of adenoidal squeaks. I had convinced myself that the Evil One wouldn't be turned on by high-pitched squeaks and squawks punctuated by asthmatic gasps. Questions asserted themselves unbidden, too. What movement did George play in the first bar of '*Calum Fìdhlear, Calum Tàillear,* Malcolm the Fiddler and Malcolm the Tailor'? First beat was High G: down to E: then a grip on E. Or was it a grip? *No . . . the freak played a 'Pele'* – G grace note on E, followed by an F grace note on E, followed by a strike on E.

So, there was this spotty adolescent, emitting high-pitched whines in time with the slowly grinding pedals of an old bike. I was fast losing my grip, folks. *Aww . . . Mama, you were right. 'Whatsoever a man soweth, that he shall also reap.' There were to be no free lunches. It's Physics, fool. If you have a good time and are feeling up, up, the time will surely come when you'll be feeling down, down.*

After Creagorry it was Elvis time – 'It's Now or Never'. At the crossroads I was impaled on the horns of a dilemma. A left turn would take me onto the *Rathad an Iar,* the West Side road, and through Liniclate. A right turn would take me onto *Rathad an Ear,* the East Side road, through Torlum road end and past *Loch nan Daod.* If I took a left for Liniclate, I'd risk getting my precious piper's fingers smashed up by a shinty stick wielded by a demented goblin, *Bòcan beag Aonghais 'ic Nill,* the Little Ghost of Angus, son of Neil. Take a right, and I'd maybe have an unforgettable date with the *bean-nighe,* the washerwoman of the shrouds. Either way, there were no good choices. Head down, I'd charge down one or the other, and though I cycled swiftly to work up a sweat, I'd feel a downdraught from the back room, feel its fetid, chill breath on the single track roads of Benbecula.

I'd make it home to Griminish, somehow. I'd be shaking, and I'd be ashamed of it. I was completely shot. My nerves were frazzled. After a curative cup of tea with a tot of whisky in it, and a calming cigarette, I'd decide to renegotiate my status between the mainstream (Lowland Scottish) and Gaelic cultures. (I did this frequently, and my oscillations proved confusing.) I'd maybe read a few pages of Tacitus, or attempt to solve some quadratic equations. Then I'd retire to my bedroom, and after diligently checking out the bed for little hands carrying switches, I'd lie down and sleep like a stone.

The seeds of cultural schizophrenia had been well and truly sown.

6
Saved by the Bell

I enjoyed my years as a pupil at Bellahouston Academy. This was a pretentious establishment built in the mid-nineteenth century. The buildings were grey-clad neo-gothic piles, turreted and crenellated, and the actual fabric of the place was celebrated in the words of the school song which we were obliged to sing at Monday morning assembly in the main hall.

> O, Bellahouston founders, who in your earlier age
> Set up these walls and turrets to be our heritage;
> To you our thanks we tender, we praise your vision clear
> That planned and raised a structure so stately and austere.

The year was 1954 and I was seventeen and looking forward to the summer holidays. During the final term of my fifth year at Bellahouston Academy, despite netting a respectable group of Highers – English, Mathematics, Latin, French and Lower Geography – I had no clear idea what I wanted to do with my life. I dreamed of becoming a newspaper reporter or a barrister, but didn't know how to go about getting jobs like these. My male relatives were no help. Two of my mother's brothers were dock labourers, another a carpenter with the Clyde Navigation Trust. My late father was a dock labourer too, whose 'badge' or licence to work would pass on to me on my eighteenth birthday. However, I wasn't turning cartwheels at the prospect of going out early doors with the 'hook' entwined in the back of my belt and waiting around each morning for the gaffer to choose me for a shift or a 'spell'. If you weren't chosen you got what was called a 'Duck Egg'. That is, no pay for that day. You went home or repaired to the pool room or the pub and hoped to get picked the following day. No, the rhythm of that life did not appeal to me. My father's brothers weren't in a position to advise me either. Hughie was a labourer at the Granary over on the other side of the Clyde, and uncle John Neil worked in the lower echelons of the Clyde Trust. None of these folk provided suitable role models or influential contacts for a kid who showed fair academic promise. I knew not where my future lay.

Help, or yet another shortcut in my life, was at hand, though. One fine May morning we had to double up classes. (Miss Muir, our French teacher, was unwell.) There we were, about seventy of us, crammed into a classroom designed for thirty pupils, and having to sit three to a double desk. The teacher in charge, unknown to me, was the head Gaelic teacher, Jake MacDonald from the Braes district of Skye. Although Bellahouston Academy was one of only two schools in Glasgow that offered Gaelic as an academic discipline, I really didn't have much truck with the Gaelic people. I suspect that as a would-be Classicist and French scholar, I felt a tad superior to the offspring of Highland folk who wanted their kids to be literate in the old language. These kids had to *learn* Gaelic. My own head was full of it. I didn't need to take it as a subject.

Anyway, for the next forty minutes we had a fun time of it. Jake had brought an old-fashioned reel-to-reel tape recorder into the classroom, and he invited his pupils to entertain us with song and poetry. Some of the girls sang sweetly enough, but the boys were dire. After about thirty minutes of listening to each performance and hearing them all again on playback, predictably, the 'special' pupils – my mob – were becoming restless. "Please, Sir," piped up one of my pals, Neil Alexander, "you should let Norrie Maclean recite a French poem. He's got the most authentic Parisian accent in our class."

"Really?" Jake said. "Come out, boy, and recite into this microphone."

You unthinkingly obeyed Jake MacDonald. He had a rasping voice thick with a dense Skye accent and a fearsome reputation as a disciplinarian. The most disconcerting thing about him, however, was that he was cock-eyed – *sùil gu beinn 's gu baile*, one eye on the mountain, the other on the township. He had soldiered in North Africa and Italy with the 51st Highland Division and he had the bearing of an RSM.

I didn't need any prompting. My narcissistic streak took over and I grabbed the microphone eagerly, to cheers from my classmates. I bowed elaborately in acknowledgement of the applause, and, with nerves like a bank robber, I launched into a French poem.

> *Si tu veux voir une vase au belles formes naître,*
> *Suis moi dans l'atelier jusque cette fenêtre*
> *Ou l'ébaucheur travaille, assis devant le jour . . .*

> If you wish to see a beautiful vase being created,
> Follow me into the studio right up to this window
> Where the potter labours, seated in front of the day . . .

My Gallic effusion went down a storm – with the 'specials' and the Gaelic crowd alike. I greeted their enthusiasm with studied indifference. I was far too good at imitating the likes of Sacha Distel, Gilbert Becaud and Charles Aznavour to be vain about my talent for mimicry.

I was making my way to my desk at the very back of the class, clasped hands aloft in a triumphant boxer's salute, when a bellow issued from Jake's moustached mouth: "Come back here, boy!"

I swaggered back to the front of the class and focused on one of Jake's eyes.

"What's your name, boy?" he said.

"Norman Hector MacKinnon Maclean," I said proudly.

"With a name like that you ought to be singing Gaelic songs," Jake said.

"Oh," I said, real cool, "I can do that too."

Jake was speechless. In the silence I took hold of the mike for the second time, and began to sing an old Gaelic song called *Mo Nighean Donn nam Meall-shùilean*, My Brown-haired Maid of the Bewitching Eyes.

> *Mo nighean donn nam meall-shùilean,*
> *Gur òg thug mi mo ghealladh dhut,*
> *Nam faighinn thu le òrdugh Clèir,*
> *Chan iarrainn sprèidh no fearann leat.*

> My brown haired maid of the bewitching eyes,
> I was only young when I gave you my vow;
> If I should get you under order of the Clergy,
> I should want neither cattle nor land along with you.

I had a good, if untrained, singing voice, and my rendition was met with even greater applause than the cheers for my French poem.

"When the bell goes at the end of the period," Jake said, "I want you to remain behind. *Tha mi airson bruidhinn riut*, I want to talk to you."

When the bell signified the end of the period, I dutifully stood before Jake, who was seated behind his teacher's desk.

We spoke in Gaelic.

"Are you leaving school next month?" Jake said.

"Maybe . . . I don't know," I said.

"Do you have a job to go to?" Jake said.

"No, not really," I said. "I thought I'd write to various newspapers and see if they've got some kind of vacancy for me as a cub reporter . . . or something."

"How did you get on with the Highers?" Jake said.

"Higher English . . . and I won the David Orr prize in that subject; Higher Maths; Higher French; Higher Latin and Lower Geography," I said, I hoped humbly.

"You did Higher Latin?" Jake said.

"Of course," I said simply.

"That's perfect," he purred. He squirmed in his seat in obvious excitement. He leaned forward with his elbows on the desk and spoke earnestly: "Maclean, you're the pupil I've been looking for all my teaching life. You're bright, you're personable, you can speak Gaelic, and you're a fine singer too."

He was giving me the stroking of a lifetime, and it felt . . . great.

"Listen carefully to me," Jake said. "I know what you're going to do."

"Really?" I drawled.

"Yes, really," he said, his voice a hoarse whisper. "You'll come back for a sixth year . . . and you'll do Higher Gaelic. Oh, I know you don't need additional qualifications. You've enough just now to get you a Certificate of Attestation of Fitness, but I have greater plans for you than adding to your total number of Highers." His voice trembled with excitement. "Then," he said, "you'll go to university and you'll study for an Honours degree in Celtic Language and Literature." He paused for a moment. "You'll sit the Bursary Comp. next year, and with Latin one of your subjects you'll be ready for Honours Celtic. You see, one of the conditions of getting into Junior Honours and your final year is that you must have at least a pass at Ordinary level in Latin or, as they say at yooni, Humanities."

I felt relief at his conviction. "What happens when or if I get this Honours degree?" I said.

"The world's your oyster. A job lecturing at one of the universities or colleges, perhaps? Maybe some kind of producer's job over at the BBC in Queen Margaret Drive?"

He smiled. When Jake concentrated his attention on you, he set your self esteem soaring. His voice grew evangelical: "Don't worry about Higher Gaelic. If you have any difficulty, and I don't think you will have, I'm quite prepared to give you private tuition on Saturday mornings, say."

"I can't do Saturday mornings, Sir," I said firmly.

"Why not?" Jake said.

"I play the pipes over at the College of Piping every Saturday morning," I said.

"You're a piper as well?" Jake said, his squinty eyes bulging.

"I've won quite a lot of prizes," I said, as modestly as I could.

"That's marvellous," Jake said. "Oh, I see a glorious future in front of you, Maclean: trips to University College Dublin and St Francis Xavier in Nova Scotia. You'll be an academic star."

"I'll have to think about all this," I lied. I had already made up my mind. I had been going nowhere and here was a ready-made plan for my future. I'd follow it.

"Indeed," Jake said, his moustache quivering and making him look slightly menacing. "Talk to your mother. I'll see you at the end of the week and we'll find out what decision you've reached." He extended his hand and gave my limp hand a crushing shake. "This," he said, "could change your life."

And it did. I did everything he asked me to do. My mother made no objection to my going to university, and indeed seemed proud of my decision. Thereafter, Jake made all my decisions for me, and I sort of drifted along under his tutelage.

I myself was excited and a wee bit apprehensive about going to university. I'd get to wear a smart black blazer with the fourteen-carat gold shield of Glasgow's coat of arms embroidered on the breast pocket. For outdoors I'd wear the dun-coloured duffel coat topped by a multi-striped Arts Faculty scarf. I wondered now how my poor mother was going to afford all this regalia. But of course I knew the answer. It entailed extremely hard work at her Singer sewing machine. All during my adolescence and young manhood the whirring of that electric-powered machine, night and day, was a constant accompaniment to activities in our home. What really turned me on about attempting an Honours degree was that I'd have new audiences to appreciate my mimicry and singing voice.

An interesting development took place during this halcyon period, my sixth year at school. Jake, it seems, had allowed Mrs Kidd, the Head of the Music Department, to hear my little Gaelic song, and she must have been taken by my lyric tenor voice because before I knew it I was singing in quartets, amateur operas like *Così Fan Tutte* and giving solo excerpts from the *Messiah* in various churches in and around Glasgow. I loved it – the buzz and the adulation were heady stuff for a boy from, let's face it, an inward-looking, deprived, even, background.

All in all, my sixth year was a delight. I found the Gaelic students an amiable lot, and I made many friends as I and another Glasgow Highlander of Skye descent, John Finlayson, skipped our way through classes one to four with ease. By Christmas we had joined the eight pupils or so who, along with John and me, would sit the Higher Gaelic examination. I took a real shine to one of the Maclean family, a girl called Catriona, a redhead with a voluptuous figure. The budding romance came to nothing, however. She fancied my good-looking pal, Big Donald MacRitchie. The image of 'Keena', even to this day, has always roused in me parched erotic heat at night.

Academically I did well. I soon got the hang of Gaelic orthographic conventions and cleared the Higher examination with ease. Though I read some Latin and French texts and fiddled with Differential Calculus in preparation for the Bursary Comp., singing was my pastime and my passion. I specialized in arias like '*Una Furtiva Lagrima*', and what we used to call 'Your Tiny Mitt is Frost-bit', '*Che Gelida Manina*'.

One cold Sunday night Donald and I were walking down Carrick Street in Anderston heading for the ferry that would take us to our side of the city, the south side.

Faintly at first, then swelling louder, we heard the strains of an accordion and the rattle of a snare drum issuing from the Hibernian Hall to our left. The music wasn't our kind of dance music, but it *was* dance music, Irish dance music. We inferred that on the blessed Sabbath these Catholics were holding a dance. And where there was dancing we knew there would be girls. We crept up to the double doors and peeked inside through a slight gap where the doors didn't quite meet. There were girls accompanied by boyfriends, and a handsome lot they were too. As they swung their partners in some kind of eightsome reel I was sorely tempted to try to gain admission, but decided against it on the grounds that these atavistic tribesmen from the bogs of Ireland looked as though they could handle strangers.

We turned slowly away.

"GOOD EVENING, BOYS!"

The voice came from over my shoulder.

"Boys! We've been watching you! What do you want?"

I turned to face our questioner, a burly priest in full sacerdotal fig. Just keep walking away from this apparition in black, I told myself, but Donald didn't seem to appreciate the danger and stood where he was. "Were you hoping to join us?" the priest said with a grim smile on his face.

"No," I blurted.

"Yes, indeed," Donald said.

"No, Father," I said glaring at Donald. "We've got to get going . . . to . . . er, to Mass."

"Oh, you're Catholic, are you?" the priest said, still smiling.

"Yes," I lied.

"What's your parish?" he enquired, suddenly nervous.

"St Margaret's," I said quickly.

The priest was still curious. "Who's the priest there now?" he asked.

I shook my head, barely able to speak for a full three seconds. I looked to Donald for assistance, but there was no help there. He was looking longingly at the hall door.

"I believe it's . . . umh, Father Hickey," I stammered, recalling a name frequently mentioned by Francis Aloysius Carrabine many years previously.

The priest leaned towards me and seemed uncomfortable. "Would you mind coming inside with me?" he said, and he wasn't smiling. "There's a few things I want to clear up. The main thing that's confusing me is that Father Hickey passed away five years ago."

The game was up. They had us. With these Catholics the shark ethic prevailed – eat the wounded. We'd be lucky to get down to the ferry alive. I was anxious to leave.

"Good God, Norrie!" Donald said in Gaelic. "Let's go back in with him."

"We're not going anywhere *near* that place," I howled. "That's just what he wants us to do . . . get us trapped in there. They'll beat us with telephone directories while one of these bastards prepares the tar and feathers."

I could almost hear my cowardly monologue:

What? What parish, Father? Well, the thing is we're merchant seamen and we travel all over the globe and perform our duties wherever we put in. The last time I made my confession was in a brand new church in Montevideo, Uruguay. You probably won't believe this, Father, but it was one of these inter-denominational churches. Our Lady of the Mezuzah I think it was called.

So that's why we're a bit confused about our parish, Father. Can you believe that?

No.

"See you later, Father," I snapped. "My friend and I have to go." Then Donald and I were off, sprinting down the incline that led to the ferry landing. We often laughed about this ignominious retreat in the following years.

There was just one sombre note sounded during this year. One night, a former classmate from Benbecula, who was studying radio-telegraphy with a view to entering the mercantile marine as a 'sparks', gave Donald MacRitchie and me, vats of boiling hormones the pair of us, two tickets for the annual Christmas dance at the David Watt College of Engineering in Greenock. The build-up to this epochal event was slow and tremendously exciting. We had decided to conduct an experiment with drug alcohol. Long before the appointed night, the pair of us cased the windows of licensed grocers in Govan, Plantation and Kinning Park researching the prices of half-bottles of spirits. During the weeks preceding the big night, both Donald, who at that time was earning an apprentice carpenter's pittance in the Fairfield shipbuilding yard, and me saved as much money as we could. The way it worked out, my contribution to the pooled resources was considerably smaller than that of my big pal. I had a weekly allowance of only two shillings and sixpence in 1954, although I delivered milk every morning, seven days a week, for a weekly wage of twelve shillings, and I played the bagpipes at a Teuchter territorial association called the Uist and Barra Club every Saturday night for a fee of ten shillings. It goes almost without saying that, resentful little role player that I was, I attempted to display a proper regard for my hard-working mother by turning these earnings, minus half a crown, over to Peigi Bheag. Eventually, with two days to go before the evening of the dance, the pair of us, full of acne and ideals, screwed up our courage and purchased from a licensed grocer in the Govan Road a half-bottle of Jameson's Irish Whiskey. 'Not a drop is sold till it is seven years old.' The longed-for elixir which we considered to be an essential credential in our quest for manhood was stashed in a wardrobe in big Donald's house in Crookston.

I couldn't receive such dangerous contraband in wee Peggy's room and kitchen in Ibrox, of course. If wee Peggy had discovered this poison – she had been exposed to her uncles' alcohol abuse as a child, and as an adult she had witnessed the effects of heavy, Hebridean-style drinking among her own brothers, and was, until the day in January 2005 when she passed away at the age of ninety-eight, totally against the booze – if she had come across a half-bottle of whiskey, Irish whiskey at that, in her home in Brand Street and, moreover, if she had got a whiff of her son's prurient intentions – you know, all that sinful stuff, like, well, *touching* girls at a dance – she would have done her John McEnroe number and punished me in some unspeakable fashion. (God, my heart, fifty-three years on, still goes pitter-patter when I think of that scenario.)

Accordingly, when Benbecula's answer to Tom Cruise hit the dance floor in Greenock that night, I was already besieged by a considerable burden of guilt. After checking out the scenery on the other side of the dance hall, I suddenly went rigid like a gun-dog on point. In the far right-hand corner, standing alone, was a pretty, dark-haired girl, endowed with pert breasts, who was wearing – and I have been able to see this garment and feel its texture beneath my finger-tips to this day – a Black Watch plaid, cotton frock with a fetching white Peter Pan collar and little, white buttons, perhaps five of them, that ran down the front of the dress from cleavage to just above the knee . . . My head swam and I was assaulted by a wave of sexual desire.

It was at this precise moment big Donald indicated by a nod of his head, and a tipping motion of his hand, that it was time. Feeling a little weak in the knees, I took my first drink of alcohol in the gents' toilet two minutes later. The dope kicked in almost immediately. Shame, guilt and sexual frustration were quickly replaced by eupho-ria – a sense of absolute power and control over myself and, more importantly, the cute teenage girl I had spotted earlier. In a flash of sexual desire so overwhelming it made my vision blur, my flesh tingle and my entire being melt, I swiftly intoned a single word: "YES!" I knew with all the certainty of a religious convert at the Presbyterian prayer-meetings of my youth I had discovered my own personal, magic elixir. This stuff would, I was convinced, change my life for ever. Whatever deadly attraction there existed between me and drug alcohol was now solidly locked into place.

The girl in the tartan dress? Sure. It was nothing, really. Ever since that night Norman Maclean, in conjunction with alcohol, became 'I' or 'me'. With the help of alcohol I had found myself. Or, more accurately, I had discovered within me many selves, all of them infinitely more interesting and exciting than the douce little swot with the culturally mixed background who existed before this dramatic introduction to C_2H_5OH.

Five minutes after my first throat-burning swig, I strolled across the dance-floor with all the swagger and insouciance of a Hebridean pimp, fixed my gaze on the dark eyes of Miss Black Watch and casually said: "Can I . . . can I . . . buy you a . . . tractor?" We took a couple of turns round the dance floor. I did a bit of funny shtick for her. She smiled. Then she laughed out loud. Sure, I got her to come outside with me to view the romantic sight of Greenock at night – you know, the cranes, the prison . . . the cops with beer stains on their ties . . . Eventually, I kissed Sandra full on the mouth in mid-sentence, passionately ground my mouth against hers and she let me slip my tongue between her white teeth and on into her mouth . . . Oh, be still, my foolish heart! She detached herself as I began to feel the contours of her Maidenform brassiere under the unbuttoned dress.

"I've got to go," she murmured and fastened the buttons of her dress.

As she vanished inside I employed the never-fail strategy I have used all my life. Because this girl from the Tail o' the Bank had discouraged me from making assaults on her bosom and, as I had hoped, the lower half of her anatomy, I placed the blame on my friend booze. If our courting had gone further I would have claimed credit for myself. Under the influence of alcohol, when something bad happened it was the fault of the drink. If, inebriated, something good happened, this was due to the essential excellence of Norman.

I knew that I hadn't achieved this limited triumph on my own. It was I and my new-found friend, alcohol, who had satisfied my adolescent fantasies. And I was grateful. So grateful have I been for the assistance afforded to what essentially was a timid, insecure, confused boy by drug alcohol that never, during the succeeding fifty years, did I make a serious attempt to terminate for good a relationship which systematically and inexorably destroyed every single facet of human endeavour in which I engaged.

7
Via Veritas Vita

He was trying to spook me. This pugnacious, thick-lipped, dull-eyed face loomed closer, the boxing gloves clenched at his cheeks. "Been at the game long?" he mumbled in the flat accents of Ulster. I nodded with a conviction I didn't know I had, and skipped backwards. My footwork in the gym had always been pretty nifty. Put it down to all those fancy back-steps in Highland dances like Petronella and the Lancers in my teens in Balivanich.

Check me out on my first bout as a light-heavyweight for the University of Glasgow's boxing team. Lean, not particularly heavily muscled, but taut and perhaps over-exercised in the calves and upper arms. My opponent – a fully grown *man* – from Queen's University, Belfast, was a stocky little plug-ugly, very hairy creature. Christ, to me, who shaved maybe once a fortnight, this guy was a freak. He even had hair on his back. I wasn't all that worried, though. At half-an-inch under six feet, I knew I outreached him. In addition I laboured under three separate delusions. Firstly, I imagined I had as good a dig as anyone. On the punch bag in the university gym I consistently punched my weight, greatly encouraged by my instructor who had put the idea in my head of trying out for the boxing team. I didn't run: I leaped at the chance. If I boxed for the University of Glasgow I'd receive what they called a half-blue, a tie, that is, which I knew would be another credential for attracting females.

The fault was that of the youth who sat beside me in Professor Christian Fordyce's Humanities class. His name was Farquhar MacLennan, and he came from the island of Raasay, off the east coast of Skye. We were arranged, some seventy of us, in alphabetical order. The lad sitting to my right was called Lamont. He was all thick-lensed spectacles and acne and held a big fat Parker pen in his fist at all times. He intended to read Honours Classics, and once casually informed me that for his eighth birthday he had received a copy of *Winnie the Pooh* in *Latin! Woo-ee*. I couldn't believe it. Reading a Latin text at the age of eight while I was perusing J.D.Williams and Oxendale catalogues by the light of a Tilley lamp in Benbecula! I was going to have to hustle to keep up with these guys.

Farquhar was the lad who suggested that we go to the gym at ten o'clock at the conclusion of the Latin lecture. "You ought to be getting some exercise," he said, "especially with all that beer, those 'Cobalt Bombs' [a combination of strong cider and Carlsberg Special brews] you're swilling down in the Union bar."

He was right, of course. I was spending too much time drinking. My annual bursary had come through, and without even considering reimbursing my wee mother for the free board and lodging I was getting because I lived, like two-thirds of the intake at the University of Glasgow, at home, I was able every weekend to prop up the beer bar in the Union swilling drink. The strange thing was, I didn't have much of a head for it at the beginning. Returning from the Ossianic Society in the Queen Margaret Union in the early hours of a Saturday morning, I was invariably violently sick on the steps of the all-night ferry that plied its way between Anderston and Plantation. I persevered, however, as I did with my tobacco habit.

I was growing chubby. Accordingly, Farquhar and I enrolled at the university gym for a programme of light exercise. The instructor, a former Scottish javelin champion, who was in his late twenties, was all over me like a cheap suit.

"You're a natural light-heavyweight, Maclean," he said. "Look, we've a tournament in Belfast in three weeks' time, and I'm short of a light-heavy. Fancy it, eh?"

Of course I was up for it.

There followed a hectic spell of skipping, which I was good at, and weight training, at which I wasn't, and long bursts at the suspended punch bag which drew a kind of phoney approval from the instructor. "Good on you, Maclean," he'd shout. "Put your shoulder into that dynamite right cross you've got."

Looking back, he must have realized I'd never make a boxer, unlike those Catholic kids in the lighter divisions, but he needed a full team and superficially I filled the bill for light-heavyweight. I had my own agenda. I needed the credential of that half-blue tie.

Three weeks later, I was in the ring with this squat, hairy man who looked as though he might have to shave twice daily. Then I saw my

chance. I feinted with my left: he dropped his guard on his left, prepared to counter. For a split second I caught a glimpse of his exposed
left jaw and I smacked him with all my might. It was a beauty of a
punch and I caught him sweet on the button. I stepped back, waiting
for him to collapse. (I'd seen this kind of thing before in movies like
The Quiet Man starring John Wayne and Victor McLaglen, and I just
knew he had to go down.)

He didn't. The fucker didn't even blink, and kept pressing forward, bobbing and weaving and snorting and sniffling. Most alarming.

The hell with it. So, I didn't have the punch I thought I had. I'd
get on my toes and with my superior footwork and lightning-fast
reactions I'd pepper him from long range with rapid left jabs, accumulating points.

That didn't work either. He kept attacking my body with vicious
hooks and seemed to be hitting my eyes and bloody nose at will. Bang
went another delusion. It was obvious that my fancy footwork and
rapid reactions was another false belief.

However, I still had a final delusive hope to sustain me. I could
surely take a punch, I thought. Wasn't I the tough guy from Ibrox
who had scrapped with the cream of the 'Slummies' – residents of a
slum clearance scheme in the next block in Brand Street – and who'd
received many a black eye in numerous battles? Yeah, bring it on,
Mick.

That was my last thought. My jaw was ripped with terrific pain.
I burst from within and collapsed soundlessly to the canvas like a
discarded shirt.

I woke up sweating. Green dressing room. Everywhere green. My
trainer smiled down. I was lying on my back on a trolley. The room
was quiet. I reached up to touch my left jaw and felt only a thick
bandage taped to my head. At my touch bolts of pain shot back. The
trainer was moving his lips at me, but I heard his voice as a whisper.
"Broken jaw, lad," he said cheerily. "Saps and milkshakes through a
straw for you for a while." He continued with the false bonhomie:
"Never mind. Cassidy and Mulrine have both won their bouts and
we still have a good chance of winning the match."

A doctor swabbed my arm and injected me. My head dropped
away. There was but one thought that struggled to the surface. Boxing for me was hang-it-up time. That brutal sport was not in my
blood.

My first year at the University of Glasgow, apart from the humiliation of Belfast, was a good one for me. In the Latin class I worked extremely hard to keep up with the true Classicists, the students who intended to take Honours in Greek and Latin, and was rewarded with a first-time pass at the end of the summer term. This was no small achievement, since it was widely known that old Christian Fordyce regularly failed two-thirds of examinees first time round. I was awarded prizes in Ordinary Celtic, and, according to my essay grades in Ordinary English – Beta double plus and sometimes Alpha minus – I was certainly in the top tenth percentile in an intake of about ninety students. Everything was going well. I continued to attend the gym and work out at least twice a week.

I'd cut down on the booze, mainly because I had little money and was kept busy with my singing engagements with Mrs Kidd's choral group. So keen was I to obtain fresh Gaelic songs I almost made a major error upon entering the Celtic Reading Room one morning. An older student from Bragar in Lewis, Angus Campbell, was humming under his breath some ballad of antiquity as he perused his notebook. The arabesques and other vocal embellishments were extremely attractive, and I wanted to steal this little number.

"What's that you're singing, Angus?" I asked.

He looked up, and with the contempt of a senior student for a 'Fresher' he launched into a full-voiced rendering of the song. It was not until he was sixteen bars into the melody that I recognized it.

> 'Some enchanted ee-ee-vening,
> You may see a straeen-jer,
> You may hear him ca-aa-aalling
> Across a crowded roo-oom.'

An additional source of pleasure was my membership of the Officers' Training Corps, who supported an indifferent pipe and drum group. Encouraged by *Ailig Eairdsidh Fhearchair 'ic Iain Ruaidh 'ic Mhicheil*, Alex MacLennan from Lochboisdale, South Uist, I joined the Territorial Army. This corps was meant to be a springboard for a Commission when the time came to do your National Service in the armed forces. For my part, I joined only for the free reeds, pipe bags and the splendid Number One uniform. Membership of the pipe band also gave me the opportunity to dazzle the other pipers with my digital pyrotechnics. These guys, mainly medics and a sprinkling of engineers, had attended semi-independent and fee-paying schools like Glasgow Academy, Kelvinside Academy and the High School of Glasgow. These places all had a strong militaristic tradition: almost every young male was expected to join the Army Cadet Corps and some of them were members of their respective pipe bands. It was with this background that all the rest of the OTC pipes and drums came.

Oh, but their playing was woeful! 'The Old Rustic Bridge by the Mill' and 'The Green Hills of Tyrol', full of chokes and crossing noises, was about their stretch. I like to think that my example – lots of Jigs and Hornpipes – encouraged some of the lads to expand their musical horizons. Without a doubt, I was the big cheese in the Glasgow University OTC pipe band in those days. Predictably, I won the inter-university solo championship which was held in Aberdeen during the summer term of my first year. This was not too difficult. Aberdeen, Edinburgh and St Andrews universities were no higher in piping attainment than our mob.

I was where I wanted to be: the centre of this mini-universe. I adored it.

Socially, I hung about with a clutch of island boys who drank whisky and beer in the Union bar and other pubs like the Blythswood Cottage, the Rubaiyat and the Temple Bar in Overnewton. I was fairly abstemious, but sadly, in time, I discovered that my liver hadn't turned out to be the organ I'd hoped for. (But more about my sordid little flights from reality later.)

I met up with many people who would be lasting influences: Roddy Campbell, *Ruairidh Pheadair*, from Nask in Barra, who became a teacher and who can now frequently be heard on Gaelic radio singing Gaelic songs in traditional style. Another dear friend was John Campbell, *mac Dhòmhnaill Ruaidh*, from South Uist. He was later the best man at my first marriage; he ended up as headmaster of Castlebay Secondary School in Barra. There was the aforementioned Farquhar MacLennan, and my chum from school, the late John Finlayson. I also became quite pally with another lad who to us seemed a touch exotic, Neil Fraser. Neil's father was a Skyeman and his mother came from Lochboisdale in South Uist. (She was the sister of Ailig Eairdsidh whom I've mentioned in connection with the OTC.)

Neil was tall, handsome, poised and natty. He was a natural politician – President of the Union, Chairman of various committees, stuff like that – and undoubtedly had charisma. He was a good guy to have with you if you were out chasing girls. He had the looks; I had the humour. I remember one night we picked up a couple of girls at a dance in Partick and took them on a riotous tram ride into the city centre. Neil's girl was called Tina and I haven't a clue what mine was called. My abiding vision was of Neil and Tina wrestling on the lower deck of the tram as their passion became increasingly heated. Inexplicably, I was laughing uproariously at their antics. When I consider the ill behaviour we displayed I'm deeply ashamed. I suppose we displayed the arrogance of 'students', princes of the universe. This was a deplorable way to behave, just on the verge of being obnoxious.

Neil subsequently had a distinguished career in broadcasting, eventually becoming Head of BBC Radio Scotland. I've been bumping into him, off and on, all my life, sometimes for the good, more often for the bad. Well, he was the guy who gave me the chance to star in my own show on television: on the other hand, I've been obliged to seek help from him on more than one occasion to take me to the Argyll and Bute Hospital in Lochgilphead or to the Priory in Langside to undergo detox. Thoughts of Neil have always been tinged by a compound of gratitude and shame.

During the week I worked hard at my Vergil, Pliny and Ovid and spent some time preparing my English essays every month. I got a real bang from seeing my grades for these attempts. The Ordinary Celtic class, around eight of us, with girls from Lewis in the majority, was pretty easy for me. Prose composition came to me with the fluidity of a dream. I mean, I knew lots of obscure and now even obsolete idioms from my interaction with Seumas Mòr, and all I had to do was carefully express the words in my head on to the page.

But I did get a shock in this first year Celtic class. The senior Lecturer in the department at the time was Derick S. Thomson, later Professor of Celtic at the University of Glasgow. One day he gave us a written assignment. We were to compose two thousand words or so on the subject of *Am Bail' Againn Fhìn*, Our Town. The big reward was that the best effort would be published in the quarterly Gaelic magazine *Gairm*, along with a modest monetary prize. I wanted the glory that would ensue if I won this little competition. I set out to dazzle Thomson with verbal pyrotechnics, and plagiarized gobbets about architecture and history, both subjects about which I knew absolutely nothing. But I was quietly confident that my unorthodox choice of subject-matter would bring the roses to the cheeks of a lecturer who must have been bored rigid, I felt, trotting out the same boring notes year after year. I knew that my fellow students would prattle on about their respective upbringings in rural communities. I was to write about the great city of Glasgow as my town. This ground-breaking strategy would ensure that I gained, if not immortality, some street credibility with the Highland community. Guide books were gutted for facts, and I wove all this stolen material into a kind of epiphany I was supposed to have had as I viewed the buildings surrounding George Square.

I had not reckoned on Kate Macdonald from Balallan in the parish of Lochs in Lewis. Instinctively she had embraced the old adage: write only about that which you know. Her description of her native village of Balallan, the longest established crofting township in the Outer Hebrides, of the abundance of bachelors in the place and of the characters there when she was growing up, was a delight. In unadorned prose, this was a funny and wise story, crowded with anecdotes and observation, which deservedly was published in Derick Thomson's *Gairm*.

When I finished reading this little masterpiece I had to shield my eyes. This was not a gesture of quick satisfaction but rather one of disgust at myself. The Benbecula of my childhood was full of larger-than-life characters: *Iain Ruairidh Fhearchair*, Iain MacLennan, a second cousin of my mother's who was a great source of amusement to Kenny and me when he took us for a spin in his lorry to the Seaweed Factory in Kilphedar. *Dòmhnall Beag mac Mhurchaidh*, Wee Donald son of Murdoch, another granduncle to Peigi Bheag, who was full of tall tales about his adventures and the Red Indian squaw he 'married' in the Rocky Mountains. There was a witch living two houses down from us in Griminish. In short, there was a host of colourful folk I could have written about. But I didn't. I *chose* to write about my new home, Glasgow.

The vertical consciousness of old Lorne Campbell was birling like a U-boat commander's periscope. The descent into madness had begun. There I was, ostensibly drinking from the pure stream of Gaelic culture in my studies, but secretly wanting to be a townie, a boulevardier among the raffish crew who inhabited the West End of the city. Yes, it was definitely time to change courses. But I could not abandon my planned course of action. Perhaps Honours English or Honours Classics would be too difficult for me. What was I doing here? Crazy nights and weird mornings awaited me, I knew.

I learned much later from Dr John Smith, Kate's brother-in-law, who was until his retirement a GP in Carloway, Lewis, that Kate got married, and she and her husband had gone off to teach in Trinidad. Because there were no pensions in that country, they opened their own private English language school and were still grafting away. Kate always professed to enjoy my rendition of *Mi nam shineadh air an t-sliabh*, Reclining on the brae, and in her memory I sang the song and hoped it would nourish her in the Caribbean.

> *Mi 'n seo nam shìneadh air an t-sliabh*
> *'S mi ri iargain na bheil bhuam,*
> *'S tric mo shùil a' sealltainn siar*
> *Far an laigh a' ghrian sa chuan.*
> Reclining on the brae
> Lamenting all that is before me,
> Often my eye is cast to the west
> Where the sun goes down.

Every second Saturday I spent the afternoon at Tinto Park in Govan and supported the local junior football team, Benburg. I was always keen on soccer. In truth, I played a trial for Glasgow Rangers when I was fifteen. Scouts had spotted me when I was playing at inside-right for Glasgow Schools, and I was invited to Ibrox Park along with two other Bellahouston boys, Bobby Norris and George Duncan. Struth, the manager, didn't like my style – "He's too flash and he's not a team player," he was heard to say afterwards. George, a tricky little winger, was signed by Rangers and played for two seasons in the first team until he was replaced by Alex Scott and Willie Henderson. Bobby, a most elegant half-back, who read the game like the *Beano*, was signed by Dundee United. Needless to say, my self-esteem suffered a severe dent after this rejection, but I soon recovered, as I had plenty of other irons in the fire: Highers, girls, music and plenty of disciples eager to hear the colourful spectrum of my views.

On Sunday nights I'd walk through the city to a flat in Carnarvon Street in the Woodside district of Glasgow – easily four miles from my home – where John and Roddy had lodgings. I didn't live in lodgings. My widowed mother and my wee sister, together with my wee uncle Colin, lived together in 191 Brand Street. This seemed a perfectly acceptable arrangement at the time, in contradistinction to the practice of today where youngsters can't wait to get away from the parental home and saddle themselves with crippling debt to rent or even buy their own pads. *Walk*, did I say? Nowadays if I walk to the bank or the Post Office, which ought to take about ten minutes, I have to go for a wee *norrag*, snooze, when I get home. The three of us would discuss term work, Gaelic songs and singers and world affairs. Oh, how we sniggered when we listened to a record of Calum Kennedy singing *An Oidhche Mus do Sheòl Sinn* to *guitar* accompaniment! We considered that the old boy had sold out. What fascist purists we were! When we examined the poetry of Sorley Maclean, a thousand bits of information I hadn't cared about acquired dimension, form and weight. My curiosity about literature and music was stoked.

On the stroke of midnight I'd stub out my last cigarette, take leave of my friends and, that's right, *walk* all the way back home. This time, I'd walk down Woodlands Road, through Kelvingrove Park – you wouldn't get Charles Bronson to do this today – until I reached Overnewton and Partick. Then I'd head for Pointhouse Road, a long, dreary stretch of concrete with weed-infested waste ground on one side and blank walled factories with tiny wooden doors and lock-ups on the other. I'd take the all-night ferry to Water Row in Govan and then wend my way for about a mile and a half through darkest Govan to Brand Street.

On my way through Govan at the corners of Orkney Street, Neptune Street (known as the Irish Channel), Hoey Street and Burndyke Street I'd come across knots of 'Teddy Boys' wearing zoot suits – very long jackets with velvet lapels (some of them had open razors in the breast pocket), tight trousers and suede shoes with crepe soles. Late as it would be, these youths seemed in no hurry to go home. They'd smoke or stretch onto their toes at intervals with their fingers clasped, palms downward over their crotches. They spat a lot, but they would never molest a duffel-coated student type like myself who obviously had no claims on their territory. Sometimes they'd nod companionably as I passed. "Are ye all right, big man?" they'd call as I passed. I'd merely smile and keep walking.

I felt none of the menace I feel today exuding from the young. When I see a group of youths or even girls standing at the entrance of a chip shop, pizza parlour or liquor takeaway nowadays, I cross to the other side of the street. I know that a combination of amphetamines and cheap drink can cause these kids to explode at any time. Many of the boys carry knives – Glasgow has the highest incidence of knife crime in the UK – so I feel it prudent to detach.

My theory, for what it's worth, is that these disadvantaged young people, with their cheeks, eyebrows, lips and God knows what other parts of their anatomies pierced by metal rings, are into pain. They have no sense of respect for themselves, for others or for the environment. This is why they insult passers-by gratuitously and casually litter the pavements with discarded cans, cardboard fast food trays, crisp packets and empty bottles of Buckfast wine. Their loud 'boom-boom' music and rhyming couplets of 'rap' with scatological and explicit sexual references, that blare from ghetto-blasters on the pavement, show contempt for the lousy world we've left them. No work, toxic waste, global warming, the whole nine yards.

(It pains me to finish my account of my first year at university, which was a rewarding one, with this rant about young people today. I find myself in agreement with a friend of mine, Neil Christie. "I think, Norman," he said recently, "we saw the best of Glasgow." I'm convinced he's right.)

Back then in the mid-Fifties, in my first year at the University of Glasgow, all these faces, all these streets and their inhabitants were my future. Now they are my past.

8
Laissez le Bon Temps Rouler

If you've ever walked on a city street, or for that matter in a country park, on a day that the Scottish international football team were playing, and you saw a hirsute character dressed in medieval *fèileadh mòr*, great kilt, with thick hiking socks rolled down over the ankles, and Caterpillar boots on the feet, and a shapeless knitted tea cosy on the head – you know, like Mel Gibson in the film *Braveheart*? – then, blame me. Yeah, I started this fashion for Scotsmen way back in 1957 on the *Côte d'Azur*.

How did I come to dress in this way? It started innocently enough with a visit to St Tropez and my all too brief meeting with . . . (drum roll and trumpets please) . . . Brigitte Bardot! The 'Sex Kitten' has to be mentioned because I've never had good relationships with film stars and the first one I ever met put me off the breed for life.

Professor Angus Matheson, of the Chair of Celtic in the University of Glasgow, looked up from the text of *Léigheas Cas O Céin*, an incredibly boring Scottish Gaelic version of an Irish folk tale published by a scholar called K.C. Craig in 1950, and appeared to notice me for the first time. "Ah, Mr Maclean," he intoned in the sonorous accents of his native North Uist, "I have a proposition for you." Roused from a particularly salacious daydream involving a lot of ropes and blindfolds – this is what priapism did to a healthy twenty-year-old male – I feigned interest. "Mmmm?" I murmured. "Yes," the professor said, "the department has received a request from a . . . a *theatrical agent* in Paris!" He pronounced the last phrase as though his teeth hurt. "He wants to engage a Scottish bagpiper," Professor Matheson continued, "for an engagement in a place called St Tropez in the South of France. Some little French film starlet, Brigitte something or other, has taken a notion to have the Great Highland Bagpipe rouse her from her slumbers every day during the month of August. Are you interested?"

"Would that be Brigitte Bardot?" I trilled. "*The* Brigitte Bardot?"

"I believe that was the name in this . . . ah, *agent's* letter," Professor Matheson said with obvious distaste. "Shall I have him communicate directly with you?"

(Sure thing, get your lucky Scottish bagpiper right here. What's this guy's address? Where do I sign up? Actually, though I'm Pipe Major of the University OTC pipe band, I'm not all that interested in the actual performances. Performances on the bagpipe have been my meat for years. But the South of France has other attractions for a twenty-year-old with terminal acne and a vivid imagination. I can hear opportunity knocking.)

Costume was the problem. My mother, the widow Peigi Bheag, couldn't afford the orthodox Highland dress affected by my fellow amateur pipers – gillie-tying brogues, dun-coloured hose, bespoke kilt, sporran, Harris Tweed short jacket, white shirt, tartan tie to match the kilt and sprigged Balmoral headgear with clan cap badge. To compound things, I was unable to borrow the Officers' Training Corps Number One Dress, since band members would be obliged to turn in this gear after the annual camp in Penrith during the last two weeks of July. When I wore this vision of green melton cloth, gold epaulettes and collar insignia, buckled brogues, blindingly white spats, scarlet sash and flowing plaid, I had to be looked at through dark shades. What was a poor mother to do?

Well, if you were a member of the tartan mafia, you wrote to relatives in the Outer Hebrides. This was exactly what my mother did. She sent an SOS to her cousins Sìne and Màiri in 7 Strumore in North Uist requesting a length of tweed. She knew that her aunties in Carinish possessed a *beairt-fighe* or loom, and that when she herself was a little girl the sale of handwoven Harris Tweed to affluent passengers on board cruise ships anchored in Loch Eport was the sole means of accessing ready cash. Yes, the cousins replied, they had a length of *crotal*, rust-coloured Hessian, that might answer my mother's needs. We received the material together with the obligatory plucked hen a week later.

I donned my designer hat and, like some hand-knitted Giorgio or Gianni, proceeded to grace the world with my beauteous objects. First of all, the footwear: heavy black army boots, the soles bristling with metal studs; thick socks turned down at the ankles to reveal smooth and, unfortunately, hairless calves. The hideous moth-eaten material, a yard and a half wide, was then spread out on the bedroom floor and one half was pleated by hand. I would place my posterior on the pleated half, and, lying face upward on the floor, I would wrap the excess round my waist so that the narrow material hung down to my knees. I'd fasten this with a belt. The plaid part of this dress was wrapped round my left shoulder and fastened with a metal brooch. A collarless over-large shirt of my father's and a shapeless bonnet crocheted by my sister Lorna completed the ensemble.

I figured, correctly as it turned out, that the French didn't have a clue about how a piper ought to dress and I'd get away with it. And I almost did.

I wasn't worried about wearing this alien chic. The image that reeled against my eyelids was of a bronzed stud in off-white linen suit seated beneath a parasol on the terrace of some smart hotel at something that resembled a Cannes Film Festival. Surrounded by desperate wannabes, transvestites, sycophants, pimps and camera-loving female extras squirming out of their flimsy brassieres, I would order a coffee, light a cigar and absorb the aura of other people's glamour and money and pleasure, all to a soundtrack of French, Italian and American voices. What a craven fantasy!

The first indication that not everybody was impressed with my Highland sartorial elegance was received on the bus that took me from Ibrox to the city centre. A Lancashire lorry driver had promised to get me from Dixon Street, just off St Enoch Square, to London Victoria. I had tried to quick-grow a moustache to give me a patina of ruggedness, and my upper lip hadn't co-operated. I proffered my fare to the bus-driver and I distinctly heard a middle-aged couple on the downstairs deck discussing my outlandish appearance. Certainly, I looked like a cross between Shrek on downers and the Michelin Man. "Wid ye look at that, Willie?" the woman whispered *sotto voce*. "That poor bugger's been skipping his medication." "Aye," her male companion bellowed, "he's escaped. That's whit he's done. When we get aff, we'll go to the phone and check the hospital beds." I paid not the slightest attention to this poor couple. Little did these myopic fools know that I was headed for the Big Time.

The journey south was a long one – fourteen hours from Glasgow to my destination – and was remarkable only because I lost my voice yelling "Pardon?" to every utterance of the Warrington lorry driver, who spoke in an impenetrable Lancashire accent.

After stops at roadside 'caffs' for food and a prolonged stay in a bleak industrial estate in south London to unload whatever the driver was transporting, I was deposited on the pavement in front of Victoria Railway Station.

Two hours later I was in the buffet having whiskies bought for me by another kilted gentleman from Edinburgh who, it turned out, was also headed for France. This guy, late forties, looked like an unfrocked scoutmaster, and as the conversation unfolded fitfully, I realized that, hey, he really *was* an unfrocked scoutmaster. He kept urging me to accompany him to the toilet. I kept declining. "Would you like another whisky?" he said. "No, thanks," I said, smiling. I had met guys of that persuasion before and knew that they were always insanely possessive and had a black belt in Karate. I kept on smiling. The douce burgher from Edinburgh continued: "Do you like to experiment?"

(Don't ask. Resist . . . resist . . .) "Are you gay?" I asked, with a catch in my voice.

"Oh, you bet!" he blurted out in a rush. "For sure, for sure, and I want to . . ." His voice was trembling. He stopped in the middle of a sentence.

Despite the fact that he was bankrolling my increasing drunkenness, I decided to try a casual escape act, and with a wave of my hand I marched resolutely to the door.

I have described this scene only to demonstrate that I was willing to toad-lick as long as somebody was purchasing strong drink for me, but that I drew the line at homosexual activity. Pretty sound resolution, I thought.

How I wish that things worked that way when it came to females! Oh, how we adolescent males squirmed on the velour seats of the Capital Cinema at Lorne School, the Lorne and the Imperial in Kinning Park, the Plaza, the Lyceum and the Vogue in Govan, when European actresses burst onto the silver screen in the fifties! First of all there were the Italians: Anna Magnani in *Bitter Rice*. (Wow! Hairy armpits!) Gina Lollobrigida in *Trapeze* brought the roses to our cheeks too. Sophia Loren, I always thought, would provide a handsome ornament for my arm. The thing about these dames was that, unlike their Hollywood contemporaries – Rita Hayworth, Ava Gardner, even the sublime Marilyn Monroe – one could look at these Italian women and say, hand on heart, 'Hey, these girls are real! This could happen!'

Then the French launched Brigitte Bardot in *And God Created Woman*. The girl next door? I didn't think so. This was never going to happen. Little did I imagine I'd get to meet her and be able to ask her personally if she ever attended the 'jiggin', or dancing, at the Locarno or the Plaza.

At midnight on the third of August, I was suffering from travel-jangle – lorries, trains and buses for the previous thirty-six hours – and withdrawal from litres of French wine, as I was conveyed in a taxi up the snaking road that began at St Tropez and ended at *Chez Marie*. This was a villa rented by Roger Vadim on a hillside overlooking the village. On the elegantly paved pathway I lit my last Gauloise cigarette and looked back. A few fishing boats lighted for night fishing were swinging at anchor.

I was filled with considerable nervousness as I clumped my way on diver's boots towards the villa. Then it struck me how happy, how joyful I was, to be meeting the Sex Kitten. (Some kitten! Bardot was all woman, and like a lioness could pounce and disembowel you within seconds if you stumbled.) I was oversupplied with adrenaline as I was ushered into her presence.

Steeled for my Gallic interview, I entered a large, dimly-lit, high-ceilinged room with heavy, intimidating wooden furniture and white flaking walls. Dressed in a diaphanous nightgown, a blonde woman stood with her back to me before doors opening onto a terrace, facing a misty plane of sky and sea. The back of her right hand was cocked against her flexed hip. Her head was thrown back slightly, her face, which I could not see, upturned towards the darkness outside.

"*Comment allez-vous, Monsieur Maclean?* You OK, Monsieur Maclean?" she asked, without turning.

"*Je vais tres bien, je vous assure*, Yes, I assure you, I'm fine," I lied.

"*Bon*. Right," she said, turning languidly and undulating slowly towards me. This woman was a knockout. Nature had blessed her with some spectacular feminine qualities. Her mammaries jiggled as she moved. Say hello to my not-so-little puppies! Her parted bee-stung lips glistened wetly. Her curvaceous flanks, glimpsed through the thin material, roused carnal thoughts. Her eyes troubled me, though. They were bright, unwavering, mischievous.

As my vision became accustomed to the gloom, I saw that there were two men huddled on a couch in the corner of the room. One

81

I recognized as Roger Vadim. The other was a squat, swarthy North African type with a hideous scar running from eye to jaw line. He looked like a sun-tanned razor slasher from the Calton district of Glasgow. Together they rose and trudged towards me.

"*Je suis Roger Vadim, le . . . conseiller des stars*, I am Roger Vadim, the stars' . . . mentor," the taller of the two said. "*Voici . . . Luigi. Il est mon . . . assistant*, This is . . . ah, Luigi. He is my . . . ah, assistant."

"*Je suis très honoré de faire votre connaissance, Monsieur Vadim*, I am certainly privileged to meet you, Monsieur Vadim," I said with fatuous enthusiasm.

"*Bien sûr*? Yeah?" the guy with the Calton eyes said.

"*Je veux faire tout ce que vous désirez, mademoiselle*, I am ready to obey your every command, mademoiselle," I said to Bardot, accompanying my obsequious words with a fluttering hand flourish.

"*Regardez moi lorsque je parle*, Look at me when I'm talking," Vadim said.

I ignored him and again addressed Bardot. "*C'est un honneur . . .* This is an honour . . ." I began.

"*Que désirez-vous boire*? What would you like to drink?" she interjected.

"*Je ne dirais pas non*, I wouldn't say no," I declared affably, "*Un Scotch peut-être*? If I could have a Scotch perhaps?"

I had hardly spoken the words when Luigi left the room.

"*Enfin*, So," Bardot said, "*vous etes arrive, hein*? you finally made it, huh?"

"*En fait . . . ce que c'est passé . . .* Actually . . . what happened was . . . uh," I stammered, "*j'ai retardé à Paris et . . . je suis un peu fatigué*, I was delayed in Paris and . . . uh, I'm pretty tired now." At that time in my life I was a fairly pleasant-looking person in a bony northern European kind of way, and they used to tell me that I had a very engaging smile. As I beamed at this vision of loveliness, however, I became aware that smiles and boyish Hebridean charm were not hacking it.

When Luigi entered the room again, he was carrying a tray heaped with bottles, glasses and jugs filled with ice. To demonstrate an easy manner, I picked up a bottle of malt whisky and poured myself a hefty undiluted measure.

"*Tres bien*, Now, then," Vadim said, "*parlons affaires*, let's talk business."

"*Avec plaisir*, With pleasure," I drawled smoothly, and drained the entire glass of whisky in one gulp. "*Continuez*, Go ahead," I said with some insouciance, as I poured another generous measure.

"*Vous jouez a huit heures précises chaque matin pendant précisement quatre minutes et demi. Compris*? You'll play at eight o'clock precisely each morning for exactly four and a half minutes. You understand?" Vadim said.

"*Parfaitement*, Perfectly," I replied and filled my glass up to the brim once more.

"*Samedi à midi Luigi vous donnera une envelope contenant trois milles francs*, At noon on Saturdays Luigi will hand you an envelope containing three thousand francs," he continued.

The woman spoke: "*Etes vous content du salaire?* Are you happy with your renumeration?"

I sensed a strange vibe in the conversation and I grew suspicious. Time for a dollop of soft soap.

"*C'est un tel honneur de jouer pour vous, mademoiselle, que je ne désire aucune renumeration*, For the honour of playing for you, mademoiselle," I bragged, "I would accept no reward."

"*Bien sûr*, Right," Vadim and Luigi said as one, their voices laden with ill-disguised sarcasm.

I was totally thrown, because by now I knew that I had received a not-so-discreet discouragement of any notion of dalliance. Particularly with a star. Well, I had had my chance to impress and flunked it. The swarthy man with the Calton eyes and I gave each other steely, eyeball-to-eyeball showdown looks.

A strange change had come over me. The booze had kicked in and I was feeling emboldened. What the hell, I'd give Bardot one last shot. Might as well throw in some poetic language. I mean, why stop now?

I pouted like some exotic dancer and, gazing directly at Bardot, spouted words dimly remembered from a Fourth Form reader: "*Ah, que mon coeur est tout remplit de joie et d'amour quand je te vois* . . . Ah, how my heart is completely filled up with joy and love when I see you . . ."

Whereupon, from her luxurious lips issued the words: "*Ta gueule, monsieur!* Watch your mouth, man!"

My eyes were moist as I stared down her rebuke. I'm sure she saw in them human passion, desire and an impulse to control the beloved.

"Gee, you'll regret the day, you scrawny chicken you, that you let Norman Maclean walk out of your life," I whispered, almost silently.

I was tempted to upbraid her in her native language. '*Tu es trop féroce, ma Brigitte, non? Moi, de toute façon, je préfère Simone Signoret*, You're a bit too rich for my blood, Brigitte, aren't you? In any case, I prefer Simone Signoret.' I didn't actually *say* it, but I defiantly *thought* it. Way to go, Norrie, way to go. Nothing for it now but to trap from this place and scourge my flesh.

With as much dignity as I could muster, bearing in mind the French simile '*fier comme un Ecossais*', 'as proud as a Scotsman', I shouldered my pipes and marched to the door playing the second part of a Retreat Air I had written called *My Land*. Why just the second part? That way I was able to take my bottom or right hand off the chanter and wave it in a two-fingered farewell to the film people.

Once outside I kept playing as I wove down the centre of the tree-lined road that seemed to spin before me forever until, to my relief, I reached the village and a bar that was still open. What happened next? I got drunk, that's what.

Sitting in Café Edith on the outskirts of St Tropez, I saw it all clearly. Though zombie-drunk and nervous – three days of booze, sun, no sleep and burned-out adrenaline reserves – when I considered my petulant strop, I was filled with a sense of discovery, of imminent insight. That was the way, I realized, that I had always behaved with females. If they weren't fans I would give them the bullet. I had perhaps been on my own surrounded by girls many times, but I had always considered myself to be in the majority in dialogues with females I had been attracted to.

A wave of regret had massed and was advancing towards me. My need to assume the false persona of a free-wheeling, happy-go-lucky, witty guy had its origins surely in a profound conviction that I was intrinsically worthless and my life was trash.

And movie stars *had* to be rude, I realized. My theory, completely indefensible in a statistical fashion, was that you've got to have a lot of fight in you to make it big in a brutally competitive environment. If you had a hard time in childhood you were being culturally prepared to develop the character traits that would help you become a powerful actor; traits such as vulnerability, courage in the face of slings and arrows, and stamina in the pursuit of goals. You had to go in for colourful pursuits like acting in order to be noticed.

As for Vadim and his low-life minder Luigi, I had nothing but contempt. My face was twitching badly now. The creator of *And*

God Created Woman was nothing but a rude boor who had got lucky. I should have liked to cash Luigi's check. I knew guys in Glasgow who'd have ripped his ears off in a flash. In a wave of loathing it occurred to me that the French and their lack of deference towards a foreign musician were to blame. The incredible truth about my walk-out was that I was not guilty. All I did was act as any self-respecting fellow with a justifiably high conceit of himself would have done.

What if they took me to court for failure to fulfill a contract or something? What if she lied? I would never hear these lies until she took the stand:

'Yes, Your Honour, that's the savage who broke into my house and did unspeakable things to me . . .'

'What did he do, Mademoiselle Bardot?'

'It was so 'orrible . . . he was attired like a cross-dressing barbarian . . . he had insect bite-marks all down his naked legs . . . and . . . he smelled. I don't recall exactly how it happened, but I do know he stole a bottle of my malt whisky and drank most of it before my eyes . . . and then he started making lewd suggestions to me, using words like "coeur", "joie" and "amour" . . .'

No, I was not ready for this. No jury would doubt her lying testimony, especially when she pouted those delectable lips and fluttered her eyelashes. The jury would *know* what unspeakable atrocities I had perpetrated. At least five years playing *petanque* in the mornings in some tropical penal hell-hole did not appeal. Yes, it was definitely time to leave.

The following morning, severely hungover, I hitch-hiked my way to Marseilles, where I boarded a train to Paris and, eventually, I made my faltering way home to Scotland.

9

Via Dolorosa

"You want on the ferry?" I bawled. "Are you kidding me? It's jam-packed already." I gestured towards the little ferry at the Stag Street jetty in Govan where I was attempting to control a crowd of football supporters who were returning to the other side of the Clyde after a football match between Rangers and Celtic.

During the summer vacation of 1956, John Finlayson and I had secured employment as deckhands on the Clyde Trust ferries that plied to and fro across the river, some during the night. It was just my misfortune that I drew the shift on the Saturday of an Old Firm derby. More importantly, I had left my Clyde Navigation peaked cap in the bothy at Meadowside where we reported each morning to have our stations assigned to us. Accordingly, I wore nothing to indicate to the youth who was confronting me at a little wooden gate at the top of the steps leading down to the moored vessel, backed by a queue of very angry men, that in limiting the number of passengers who were allowed to board I was acting in an official capacity. The lad, about my own age, had his tongue sticking out between large teeth, his face was red, and he was making soft oofing noises.

"Look," I blurted. "I *work* here. Whoa. Don't hit me. Whoa, shit." Suddenly, he stepped back. He feinted with his left, but not knowing it was a feint I staggered into his right. My head was turned at an unnatural angle. The young man let fly with a vicious hook that caught me on the chin and sent me toppling down the steps so that I ended up lying face down in the stern of the boat, my feet trailing into the water. Things spun dizzily. My entire body ached. I struggled to my feet in the stern of the overcrowded boat.

Now, things seemed to be happening at a slight remove. Through a screen of gauze I saw and heard a group of men clattering down the steps. Rough hands seized my forearms and I was propelled through the shouting crowd to the bow of the vessel.

"Drown that blue-nose bastard," somebody screamed, and the cry was taken up by everyone on the boat. "Drown the fucker," they shouted. "Drown him, drown him, drown him."

The head of the hooligan who had smacked me at the top of the steps popped into view close by. Something snapped my jaw back, I threw my arms out like Elmer Gantry and balanced on my heels. I looked up. The sky seemed very bright. I felt at least three pairs of hands prying at my chest, waist and legs. Then I was tossed unceremoniously into the polluted waters of the River Clyde.

Now, it was very dark and shockingly cold. First light, now dark. The filthy water poured over my body like the wind sweeping over the machair lands of Uist. Eventually I surfaced, and God be round about me, the strong arms of Dan Shaw, a Harrisman, who had been in the engine room, grabbed me by the scruff of the neck and dragged me aboard. My stomach squeezed acid into my throat. Dan bundled me, shivering, into the engine room, and somehow managed to sail the ferry single-handed across to Partick. The mob outside were screaming like punters at Ayr Races and banging their fists against the tin bulkheads of the engine room. "Get that fucker out of there," they bayed. "Out, out, out."

Of course I didn't emerge from the safety of the locked engine-room. Sopping wet and stuck in a daze, I could hear Dan coming into the opposite dock. He didn't bother to shut down the engine, afraid perhaps that the screaming mob would abduct me and try to drown me again. I could feel each jolt as the little boat kept butting against the steps at Pointhouse Road. Gradually, the ferry rode higher in the water as the passengers disembarked.

I thought my ordeal was over. I was wrong. Stones and clods of grass rattled against the thin tin walls of the engine room. By God, they didn't give up, these Glaswegians.

I hugged myself, waiting, I don't know how long, I don't know what for. I do know that I finished my shift, or part of it anyway, in wet clothes. I was interviewed by a man from Jura called MacKechnie, the Supervisor. He wasn't looking at me when he said, "You've brought this on yourself, Norman. You weren't wearing uniform when you tried to stop these animals. You should at least have had your Clyde Trust cap on. Go home and report to me tomorrow morning at Meadowside." He waddled off, his large frame vibrating freely from side to side.

And I did the same thing in my sopping wet clothes and squelched my way home.

That scary incident was perhaps an omen of things to come. My remaining three years at the University of Glasgow were lived from a core of confusion.

In my studies in second year I took my foot off the pedal. In Higher Ordinary English I was slacking. I skipped literature classes and paid little attention to Norman Davies's *An Anglo Saxon Grammar*. Higher Ordinary Celtic was becoming a little bit tougher. I was expected to learn Welsh and pass the English GSCE examination in that language before I would be allowed to proceed to Junior Honours. I passed the examination, but only just. So things started to go downhill. I spun my wheels for three years. I imagine my name started to come up in discussions among Highland students, because I had lost profile with a lot of them.

"Where is Tormod?"

"That's the piper, isn't it?"

"Yeah. He's stopped coming to the Ossianic Society's ceilidhs on Fridays. Remember, he used to sing at these nights?"

"Yeah, and he was pretty good."

"So, where *is* he?"

"He's not turning up for a lot of lectures and I hear he's never out of the Rubaiyat Bar."

"I heard something about him attending the Royal Scottish Academy of Music and Drama. Part-time."

This was for me a year of stagnation.

There was, however, one glimpse of light. Back in the summer of 1956 I had been allowed two weeks off from my ferry duties in order to attend annual camp with the OTC. This was a condition that had to be fulfilled before you received your 'Bounty', a hefty sum of money and very important to me.

It was in Otterburn in Northumbria that a promising opportunity came my way. We future officers all lived in tents. The members of the Pipes and Drums had their own massive tent with camp beds ranged against the walls. We, the band members, spent a lot of time in our tent playing tunes on our practice chanters and generally loafing around. We would swim naked in a nearby river, but occasionally there was a mandatory route march to be undertaken or a mock assault against our comrades when we had to clamber up hills in full pack, rifles armed with blanks at the ready. These attacks against what we called the Mau Mau were an unpleasant activity, but measured against our idle skiving, enlivened in the evenings by many pints of Naafi beer, the two weeks were tolerable. A highlight of our fortnight was a weekend trip to Edinburgh Castle to play alongside the massed pipes and drums of the Scottish, Canadian and Ghurka regiments at the annual Military Tattoo during the Edinburgh Festival.

On the last night of our stay in Otterburn we assembled in a vast marquee with the top table occupied by all our commissioned and non-commissioned superiors. We were treated to a delicious four-course meal, a remarkable feat in field conditions, and encouraged by the officers to drink as much free whisky as we liked. (I think they were trying to teach us how to drink like officers and gentlemen. This didn't work with greedy Norman. I drank to excess as I found myself doing more and more every time I was exposed to drug alcohol.) The meal over, the real heavy drinking started. In my elevated state the voices of my comrades became a murmur and the sense of the words dropped away. The smell of cigars and cigarettes floated in on a louder noise – laughter.

The members of the corps were performing party-pieces – mainly ribald poems and the odd badly sung rugby song. And they were all entertaining. Maybe it had something to do with their attendance at fee-paying schools and the self-confidence these institutions generated in their charges.

I couldn't contain myself. Out I went to the top table and regaled the company with an Irish song about Brian Boru's contraceptive.

"I was up to my oxters in sh--, sir,
Just doin' me bit in the bog,
When me spade struck something quite hard, sir –
A stone or a stick or a log . . ."

At the end of the night I was approached by the Chaplain, a Captain in the Territorial Army. "Maclean," he said, "you have a very good voice. I'm going to arrange for you to have an audition with Professor Frederick Rimmer, the Head of the Music Department at the university. If he thinks you're good enough, he can arrange for you to receive a bursary to allow you to do an LRAM at the Royal Scottish Academy of Music and Drama."

It was the word 'bursary' that floated my boat. I could always use extra money, as my expenditure on booze was increasing on a weekly basis. The additional letters after my name were an attractive prospect for someone shallow like me who liked to grandstand. The clincher was that I'd get to wear another multi-coloured scarf, setting me yet again apart from the hoi polloi.

"That's fine by me," I slurred. "You'll be in touch at the beginning of the firsht term, won' you?"

"Don't worry, lad," the Captain said, "Frederick Rimmer and I will surely get you your bursary."

I saluted smartly as he departed.

Well, I auditioned for Rimmer some time near the end of October. He played three-note chords on the piano and I was asked to sing the middle note. I'd love to be able to report that the man was overwhelmed by my ability and said something along the lines of 'Under what bushel have you been hiding your light, young man?' but he merely grunted and I was dismissed.

Okay, I got the bursary – a huge sum for a youngster who was fast developing a ferocious whisky habit. All I had to do in return, I thought, was attend Machell's Studio at St George's Cross once a week, and practice breathing exercises with an attractive young blonde voice coach who'd place her hands on my abdomen and have me inhale and exhale repeatedly. It was no hardship to be pawed like this before she took me through my latest aria. She'd lend me big, fat 78 records of Peter Pears, Beniamino Gigli and Jussi Björling, and at home I'd sing along with these great tenors as the records spun on the turntable of my sister Lorna's portable record player.

This pleasant life, at the expense of my academic studies at the University of Glasgow, ended one afternoon before Christmas when I had to appear at the college itself, situated in what is now called Nelson Mandela Square, just off Buchanan Street.

The old lady who headed the voice-training team sat behind her desk, her hands clasped in front of her on a desk.

"Your voice tutor," she said, "tells me that your singing is coming along splendidly. I feel I must ask you about your theory."

"My *what*?" I mumbled. What was this crone trying to say?

"You know," said the lady, "chords and harmony. It's all in the primer we gave you when you started here."

She took off her glasses, breathed on them, and started to wipe them with a handkerchief. "Well," she said. "How's it going?"

Via Dolorosa

If truth be told, it wasn't going at all. I hadn't cast an eye on the primer and, having no wish to embark on a new course of study, I immediately decided to abandon the LRAM course.

"I'm leaving," I blurted out. "I've decided to terminate my relationship with the Royal Scottish Academy of Music and Drama. Goodbye." I turned on my heel and strode out the door. This kind of precipitate action was becoming a habit of mine. If I encountered a difficulty in my life, rather than face it, I would detach. And I'm afraid this pattern continued throughout my life.

"Your choice, Mr Maclean," she called out, and I thought I heard a sob in her voice as I exited.

From that day until this tears often come unbidden to my own eyes when I consider how rash I had been not to have persevered with the LRAM. I may not ever have made the chorus of a professional opera company, but I would have learned how to preserve my voice, which would have stood me in good stead when I entered showbusiness – a career which started some eighteen years later.

Horace once wrote: 'The passing years steal from us one thing after another.' Life for me in the final months of my second year, a succession of pounding hangovers and frequent bouts of morning sickness, caused me frequently to weep with shame. My hands would often be tingling and affected by a gross tremor. I felt myself dizzy and weak as I rode the Underground from Copland Road station (now called Ibrox) to Hillhead. All too often, as I forced myself to walk up University Avenue to attend Higher Ordinary English lecture on the metaphysical poets, I'd change my mind at the last minute, turn around and slip into a public house in Dumbarton Road to order a double whisky to pour balm on my troubled soul. The trouble was that my self-medication worked. After a couple of drinks I'd vow to knuckle down and get into the same groove I occupied in my first year.

Though I'd vow to change, I just couldn't climb back on that horse. I wanted to be a free-spirited youth. Yet I was emotionally muddled. Sleep was a turmoil. A lot of times as I started to drift off, I felt myself drifting back to the time I slept in the bedroom with my father in his coffin not eight feet away from where I lay.

Dreams floated in. Bad dreams. A recurring nightmare involved me and the Zulu warriors. *Click, click* . . . faintly at first I heard the clashing of spears against shields. I stood at the corner of Midlock Street and Brand Street looking eastwards down Brand Street towards Lorne

School. Round the corner from Govan Road and swinging into the far end of Brand Street came a troop of Zulu warriors, half-naked, brandishing spears and oval shields. Their bare feet raised clouds of dust as they pounded their way towards me.

I had to make my way to Elizabeth Street at the end of the block, race up that street and seek refuge in a 'dunny' which lay at the base of a common close just round the corner in Paisley Road West. Why I didn't scurry up Midlock Street and, passing the intersections of Middleton and Ibrox Streets, make my way to Paisley Road West that way I don't know. I suspected that, knowing myself to be slower than my attackers, I stood a good chance of being overtaken on the long stretch of Midlock Street.

This decision meant that for a hundred yards or so I was running *towards* the advancing fleet-footed Zulus. Two warring motivations fought inside my head. I had to move as quickly as possible to the far corner of the block in the *wrong* direction, even if it meant heading towards danger. On the other hand, my drugged, leaden feet were rebelling and I seemed to be losing ground to the approaching horde.

I'd wake up, my heart pounding. My face would be hot and my entire body would be bathed in sweat. I'd open my eyes and give silent thanks that I had emerged from a nightmare. I'd press my hands against my head to stop its twisting. Eyes clamped tight shut, I'd step into my trousers, my head swimming with tiny sparks of light. Somehow I'd perform perfunctory ablutions, and with a surly snarl inform my poor mother, who was already hunched over her sewing machine, that I was off to 'yooni'.

This happened again and again.

Where was I to sign up for happiness? Small waves of depression would ripple over my body like water over a smooth stone in a Highland stream as I plodded down Woodville Street towards the Underground Station at Copland Road.

It was a source of wonder to me how quickly I abandoned former moral precepts. I saw no shame attached to leeching from my drinking companions. Never once did I fail to register my preference when asked in the Temple Bar, "What are you having, Norman?"

One night in the Blythswood Cottage in Park Road I was feeling pretty flush – the LRAM money must have come through – and I, for a change, was buying. The barman approached with the order of assorted shorts and beers and I handed him a fiver. He turned to make change and seconds later I heard his query as he looked over his shoulder in my direction.

"Was that a tenner you gave me, Jimmy?" he said.

"Mmmmm," I stammered. "I'm sure . . . umh, I think I gave you . . . ten pounds."

The barman handed me a five pound note and some silver.

"Listen, boys," I whispered urgently, "I feel we have to get out of this pub immediately." I was nervously shuffling from one foot to the other. "Move, lads," I screamed. What followed was a stream of dialogue from an American gangster movie.

"No, listen," I ranted, "We've got to escape right now. They'll probably discover their mistake any minute . . . O MY GOD! HE'S COMING THIS WAY!"

As I sank to the floor, I uttered in a long, quavering groan the immortal words: "You guys go on without me."

The barman only wanted to know if we wanted anything else. My performance had given my friends a severe jolt. They were speechless with shock. There they were enjoying a rare burst of munificence from the notorious sponger and suddenly they got side-swiped by this deranged fool, me.

It came as no surprise to me or anybody else that, given my dissolute lifestyle, I failed Higher Ordinary English in the degree examinations in June. I got no kick out of seeing my face in the mirror dripping egg. Arrogantly, I decided not to take the re-sits in September. (I didn't *need* the English pass for my proposed Honours degree in Celtic Language and Literature.) My summer schedule was full between my job with the Clyde Trust and the second annual OTC camp, this time in Milton Bridge Barracks outside Edinburgh. Oh, I assured myself hollowly, during my Junior Honours and Final years I'd be a changed man.

All addictions are mindless. You have to block your mind to things that are too painful. It's about filling the emptiness of childhood wounds by somehow reinventing them, and making the stakes higher. The nature of addictions is to be closer to ourselves, yet also torn away from ourselves.

Therapists have always told me that I could only change myself. I could not change alcohol or, for that matter, people, places or things. To control-freaks this was distasteful advice. I was a control-freak about everything in my life – my words, my musical instruments, my clothes, my files – but in my relationship with alcohol I was out of control. It controlled me. Was this a nice little holiday for me? I used to think so. The core of this relationship was the struggle for control.

I used to think that anything that didn't involve a struggle was just too easy and therefore not worth having. Also, I wanted to be a bad boy. The alcohol abuse was about expressing some wild part of me, the part that didn't want to be nice, nurturing, worthy. I too want the right for wildness of soul.

Why did people get attracted to risky, dangerous behaviour? Attraction was about fear. I tried to separate fear from excitement. I was competitive: that was how I stretched myself.

How could I change? I took me some time to realize this: nobody, myself included, ever changed. 'Change' was a misleading word. People could put on different outfits – look, I'm not wearing black any more. 'Change' was about facing yourself: yes, I was like this. An acceptance of what I was. Could I live with it? If I couldn't, I needed to do something. I came to the conclusion that I had to change my behaviour, or shut up and get on with it.

I had to set about reorganizing the software of my mind by taking away the symptoms. What did I want? Why wasn't I getting what I wanted, and what was causing this? For instance, if people were not living up to my expectations, I would have to trace it back to the fact that I had tried to put them under my control – that I had communicated something to them that allowed them to treat me in a particular way.

I was to visualize myself as my optimum self. How was I feeling better? What was the difference? I had to see and hear and look through the world from my optimum self. Know the centre of it. Visualise being inside this self handling a difficult situation, and know the difference, know how much easier it was. I was convinced that my behaviour would change, and that I would feel different, and this would manifest itself somehow.

What I hoped would manifest itself was a belief that I did not have to change, but could handle who I was. I didn't have to believe that real passion should stay untangled from ordinary life. Although I could still believe that bad boys and girls are where pleasure meets pain, I could choose whether to relive that or not. The choice was mine to enjoy it or despair of it. Or at least I thought I had that choice.

10
Heavy Sigh, Sad Heart

I sit here staring at total whiteness on the screen, and know that never again will I completely get over my last two years at the University of Glasgow. The banshee wind and the drilling of the workmen have subsided and I have a suspicion that this is but the calm before the storm.

I think for a moment, unsure. I come to realize that I did not have feelings about my undergraduate life that were not thoroughly contradictory. I was weary of writing essays, but irresistibly thirled to scribbling; I found the endless wrestling with Welsh grammar exhausting but in a strange way invigorating; I grew tired of poring over impenetrable Irish texts, but was constantly filled with awe at the industry of these medieval scribes; enjoyed the escape — for a short time — from the squirrel-cage of daily drinking and ached to get back to it. My sour recollection of the time I came to realise I was not a scholar is fast assuming form. The air grows chillier in the unheated flat and in the next ten minutes or so the sleet patterns the windows. It began as thinly scattered needles, not even noticeable; but the wind rose until it was blowing with fury and with it came great masses of snow. Shivering constantly, I resolve to confront what I call àm mo dhunaidh, the time of my mischief, head-on. I show a kind of fixated resolve, as if the sole method of dealing with this black memory is to steam into it and get it over with. I take a deep breathe, inhaling in my imagination large snowflakes as I do so, and slowly exhale.

We have a proverb in Gaelic: *Cha tig osnadh trom bhon chridhe a tha sunndach*, The heavy sigh comes not from the cheerful heart. And many a heavy sigh issued from my banging heart during my last two years at the University of Glasgow.

Before I started my Junior Honours year I took part in the annual OTC camp, and, as in the previous year, the pipe band played at the Military Tattoo in Edinburgh Castle. One Friday, after playing with the massed bands, I experienced an odd encounter. Most of the guys were tired and wanted to make their way back to our base at Milton Bridge, near Penicuik, Midlothian.

I was restless, however, and wanted to explore the bars on Leith Walk on my own. I *had* to. This walkabout had been *necessary* in order to maintain my vitality and to avoid having my charisma in the pipes and drums dented. This adventure was breathtaking! I had lost my senses.

Round about nine o'clock I was standing outside a bar near the top of Leith Walk counting my money. I was in full Number One dress – bottle green Melton tunic with gold-embroidered epaulettes, MacKenzie tartan plaid, kilt and hose over buckled brogues. I knew that I cut quite a dash.

Out of the corner of my eye – *something* moving. I looked up with a start. A man stepped out from the shadow of a theatre awning. "What would you say to a cool glass of lager – *laagagh*?" the figure drawled. His accent was educated middle-class Scottish embellished by the foreign-sounding voice he employed to identify the proposed refreshment. Well, I thought, if he's got the money, I've got the time. I was intensely interested in money.

We entered a dimly-lit lounge bar and my tall companion ordered two glasses of lager – *laagah* – chilled. He extended his hand. "Hamish Henderson," he said in a rich baritone. I told him my name and explained that I was a student at the University of Glasgow and that I was reading Celtic Language and Literature.

"How very interesting!" he said in a measured, carefully modulated, almost crooning voice. "I myself have more than a passing interest in Scottish Gaelic. *Cia às a tha thu?* Where are you from?"

I told him Benbecula, but it struck me that this obvious boulevardier wasn't all that comfortable in my native language, and the rest of our conversations were conducted in English.

"You see, Norman," this smooth man said, "I lecture in the School of Scottish Studies at Edinburgh University – Lallans and Scottish folk tales."

This information pricked my curiosity, and I determined to get close to this sophisticate – obviously highly educated and, most importantly, comfortably affluent – and discover if there was a career opportunity for me somewhere in the department he had mentioned.

More drink, Hamish paying for every round. He was, he told me, a graduate of Cambridge, where he had studied Modern Languages.

During the war he had served as an officer in the Intelligence Corps, interrogating and debriefing Italian and German prisoners of war. I was impressed, and soon I was enveloped in an alcohol-induced cocoon. I relaxed with my thighs spread ajar in an athletic sprawl.

It was after my fourth or fifth malt whisky – we had eschewed the *laagah* in favour of shorts because of the approach of closing time – when my new friend made an odd proposition.

"I say, Norman," he said, his eyes glinting and a wry smile on his lips, "how do you fancy coming back to my flat – it's just round the corner in Prince's Gardens. We'll take some bottles back and you'll get to meet the two German girls I've got staying with me just now."

The combination of more drink and perhaps the opportunity for dalliance with girls from Coburg, Bavaria, proved irresistible to me. I agreed to accompany him. The subsequent events, though recollected through a screen of drunkenness, will remain in my head forever.

As we trudged up the brae with clinking bags towards a handsome white terraced house, I cast sidelong glances at my labouring companion. He was tall and gangly with a decidedly flat-footed gait. He had dark wavy hair, and a bushy moustache bristled over unnaturally red, well-defined lips.

When we reached the front door we entered a spacious hall paved in gleaming white marble. We mounted more marble stairs with a rich, red runner of thick carpet in the middle until we reached a sturdy oak door which opened to a spacious living room with a long trestle table in the middle littered with papers, envelopes and stacks of opened books.

Hamish invited me to sit in an over-stuffed armchair backed by a massive bay window. He reached for a book on the table.

"Would you like me," he said in hearty, jolly, manly tones, "to read you some of my poetry?"

"Yes," I said with a weak smile. I spoke with great politeness and utter lack of conviction. I felt I had to have the light of this intellectual giant fall upon me. He might, just might, be able to give me *entrée* to a new academic arena.

The next hour or so was an ordeal. Hamish began reciting, chanting really, verse after verse of obscure poetry, none of which I could get a handle on. I could hear a sawing sound coming from my chest. I was hyperventilating. My social radar was picking up an unusual vector to the drama being enacted in front of me and I grew wary.

Hamish was sitting cross-legged in front of me, and in his enthusiasm he was salivating, drenching his moustache and over-red lips with spittle. Though I saw him as the fabled main chance, I had no intention of allowing him to get any closer to me. Surely he wasn't . . .

To the March 'Farewell to the Creeks', composed during World War I by Pipe Major James Robertson of Banff, Hamish recited passionately the words he had composed in Sicily in the summer of 1943.

> The pipie is dozie, the pipie is fey,
> He winna come roon for his vino the day.
> The sky ow'r Messina is unco an' grey,
> An' a' the bricht chaulmers are eerie.
>
> Then fare weel, ye banks o' Sicily,
> Fare ye weel, ye valley and shaw.
> There's nae Jock will mourn the kyles o' ye,
> Puir bliddy swaddies are weary.
>
> Fare weel, ye banks o' Sicily,
> Fare ye weel, ye valley and shaw,
> There's nae hame can smoor the wiles o' ye,
> Puir bliddy swaddies are weary.
>
> Then doon the stair and line the waterside,
> Wait yer turn, the ferry's awa.
> Then doon the stair and line the waterside,
> A' the bricht chaulmers are eerie.
>
> The drummie is polisht, the drummie is braw,
> He canna be seen for his webbin' ava,
> He's beezed himsel' up for the photy an' a'
> Tae leave wi' his Lola, his dearie.
>
> Sae fare weel, ye dives o' Sicily
> (Fare ye weel, ye shieling and ha'),
> We'll a' mind shebeens and bothies
> Whaur kind signorinas were cheerie.
>
> Fare weel, ye banks o' Sicily
> (Fare ye weel, ye shieling an ha'),
> We'll a' mind shebeens an' bothies
> Whaur Jock made a date wi' his dearie.

Then tune the pipes and drub the tenor drum
(Leave your kit this side o' the wa').
Then tune the pipes and drub the tenor drum
(Leave your kit this side o' the wa').
Then tune the pipes and drub the tenor drum
A' the bricht chaulmers are eerie.

I asked Hamish why he had formed what was in essence a small 'private' partisan army, working in liaison with the British Army in Italy in 1944. He replied in the words of Dante: "*Libertà va cercando, ch'è cara,/ Come sa chi per lei vita rifiuta.* Freedom he is seeking, which is so precious – as they know who gave up their lives for it."

"Where . . . what happened to the German girls?" I stammered.

"Oh," he said nonchalantly, "they'll be down on the green in front of the terrace. Come on, we'll go and fetch them."

A wave of relief swept over me as we at last left the room and descended the broad staircase to the front door. I didn't really believe in the existence of these girls, but once outside free I'd make my excuses and get an all-night bus back to the Barracks. There was something sinister about this guy, but maybe I was wrong . . .

I was truly astonished when Hamish cupped his hands to his mouth, rattled off gouts of guttural German, and was answered by two female voices issuing from the green slopes of the communal gardens down below the roadside.

Two strapping girls stepped through a wrought iron gate and Hamish made the introductions. To speed things up and get to the checkered flag, we all went back to the flat, where the girls made a massive fry-up which I devoured greedily, washed down by copious drafts of laagah. Nothing untoward happened, and Hamish and the girls escorted me to St Andrew's bus station, where I caught a bus to Penicuik. On the way to the bus stance we linked arms, and though I didn't understand more than half of the song I sang lustily, I felt greatly elated as we all stepped together to the words of the *Bandiera Rossa*.

Avanti. Popolo, alla riscossa, bandiera rossa, bandiera rossa! Bandiera rossa la trionferà, evviva il comunismo e la libertà! The girls offered their cheeks for farewell kisses, but Hamish, to my surprise, embraced me and assured me he'd be in touch.

He was true to his word. Shortly afterwards I received a letter inviting me to join him and a certain Dr Bobby Botsford, an American folklorist and anthropologist, on a tour of the north Highlands in the footsteps of a famous clan of Travellers, the Stewarts, through Ross-shire and Sutherland. I was to be the transcriber of any Gaelic songs and poems that *Ailidh Dall*, Blind Alexander, Stewart might have. (And he had a lot.) The three of us drove in a Landrover from Edinburgh, to Perth, then Newtonmore, where we found a huge Traveller encampment, on to Kingussie, Inverness, Bunchrew, and into the barren moorlands of Sutherland. From Altnahara we traveled north, accompanied by Ailidh Dall's tribe of Stewarts: Essie, a handsome girl of sixteen, and Gordon Stewart and various *cailleachan*, old women, to Brae Tongue by way of Naver Bridge, Armadale, Bettyhill, Strathay and Melvich. We pitched our tent on a brae above the white sands of the Kyle of Tongue.

Ailidh Dall, a piper and a singer, was the man Calum MacLean, of the School of Scottish Studies, described as 'the best Gaelic storyteller ever recorded on the mainland of Scotland'. From the ancient song '*Am Bròn Binn*, The Sweet Sorrow' to the story of '*Am Maraiche Màirnealach*, The Weather-Wise Mariner', the old man gave me a treasury of gems to transcribe.

I never again experienced the joy of that trip. What I learned from Hamish Henderson and Bobby Botsford was that I was not at all well read. In comparison to their vast reservoir of knowledge of the arts I was just a barefoot boy. That pair never talked down to people. They assumed that all three of us had a mutual frame of reference. To me, the actor, it was mind-blowing stuff, and I'd nod sagely when references were made to Giovanni Boccaccio, Vincenzo Monti, Proust, Voltaire, Molière, Goethe, Thomas Mann, or to musical giants like Mahler, Stravinsky, Mozart and Verdi. Wow! I treasured their perspectives which were wiser and more wide-ranging than my own.

I pledged to myself that I would concentrate on my Old Irish and Middle Welsh texts. My latest spark of hope was that I'd get a good degree and join Hamish Henderson and John MacInnes at the School of Scottish Studies. It had been hinted that I might fill the post of Archivist there.

Mine was a hollow vow. Instead of cracking the books I preferred to run around with an older raffish crew of islanders who were into dissipation. Neil MacKinnon and 'Griff' Macdonald, both from Skye, and Neil Macleod from Harris had completed National Service and seemed to have plenty of money for whisky and beer. They viewed me, I think, as a comical Glasgow Highlander. I loved to drink –

loved the taste, loved the buzz I got from downing a couple of large ones, loved the smell of stale drink in the spit and sawdust pubs I frequented, and loved the sight of a glowing array of inverted spirit bottles on the gantry of a bar at night.

I took great pleasure when, after the pubs closed, we four would trudge up Wilton Street to the lodgings of three trainee nurses, Peggy MacAskill and Chrissie from Harris and Dolina Something-or-other from Lochs in Lewis. Griff would bark out on an epic tale of low humour in a loud voice. The subject of his monologue could be as mundane as a visit to the cinema, but with extravagant arm-gestures and twitching grimaces, Griff would infuse his narrative with dramatic detail. The key to his humour was that he started laughing even before the first words came out of his mouth, and his gasping laughter swept you along like a wave, no matter what he was actually saying.

After these outings I'd usually be feeling too fragile to contemplate opening books. Also, since I didn't have the spur of degree examinations at the end of my Junior Honours year, I interpreted this as freedom to be idle. I'd make it all up in my Final year, I promised myself.

To be honest, I can remember only one lecture I attended more or less regularly during my third year. That was the one given every afternoon by a lecturer in the Celtic department, a Welshman called Rowlands. I found myself getting slightly stimulated by the *Mabinogion* and I was slowly but surely becoming literate in Modern Welsh.

At the occasional lecture given by Professor Matheson (I was the only student) I'd have an overpowering urge to yawn. I had to fight my jaws to keep them from flexing. My lips would expand laterally and my nostrils would flare. I used to hope that Matheson, droning on about *Dà Chluas Chapauill air Labhraidh Loingseach*, didn't notice.

I can remember trying to study at home. Slumped in the 'big' chair – the one I'd inherited from my late father – in the kitchen, a drawing board on my knees, I would try once more to get to grips with an obscure Welsh text. I would sigh as I drifted from the text to the verbiage of a boring and ill-written Welsh grammar book, taking very little in. I'd often close my eyes, because if I opened them I would see my scruffy surroundings and start thinking again: and if I started thinking I'd have to face the horrible possibility that my presence at the university was a ghastly mistake.

I hated what I'd turned into: an alcoholic. And I hated the course

I had undertaken. I'd hold my trembling hands up before my face and intone: "It's just . . ." I couldn't complete the sentence. "I'm stuck in this nightmare and I just have to get on with it."

My weak token of industry wasn't really enough, though. During the summer vacation between my third and fourth years I spent two months working as a barman – a barman! – in a hotel in Criccieth, on the Lleyn Peninsula, ostensibly to practice demotic Welsh. I chatted with the few locals who frequented the public bar of the George Hotel. They were not big drinkers and there was little conversational buzz in the place. I made up for the customers' frugality by stealing miniature bottles from the gantry, and sipped them in my room during work breaks.

The question asserted itself unbidden. Why didn't my family recognize that I was drifting far from the bourgeois values of my childhood – order, moral rectitude, courtesy, co-operation and, above all, respectability?

Something had happened in the summer term of my third year. It was a Saturday morning drinking session in the Curlers Tavern on Byres Road after band practice. James Ross, a distinguished part-time broadcaster for the Gaelic Department of the BBC, was in the company. So was Colin MacAulay, a Clydebank Gael of Lewis descent. There was another man of whom I had only a vague recollection drinking along with us.

When he expressed an interest in acquiring a practice chanter with a view to learning the Highland bagpipe, I had no hesitation in delving into my pipe case and dragging out the chanter I was using at the time.

"Here, Jack," I said. "Give me thirty shillings, and this nearly new instrument is yours." I was desperate for a couple of quid to allow me to continue drinking

The deal was concluded with a celebratory round of drinks and I thought no more about it. Word, however, soon got out that I had sold MOD property for filthy lucre and I was summoned into the august presence of Lieutenant-Colonel Treloar, the CO of our outfit.

"I'll need all your kit, Maclean," the Commanding Officer said, in the distorted accent of his native New Zealand. It was a dreadful, shameful, humiliating defeat.

My shame, my shame. . . . Not only would I miss the Saturday morning practices and the attendant bevvy sessions, but also I knew I'd miss the company of the middle-class students who were my charges. These fellows were expanding my horizons – on the horizontal plane, of course – at a rapid rate.

The answer to my question above is that my mother was too busy earning cash from her marathon sewing sessions; my sister, who was seven years younger than I, didn't count. My uncles and their spouses were just thrilled that I was attending 'yooni' at all, and assumed, when I regaled them with war stories, that all was well. The gravamen of the indictment against me was that after my father's death I had become the man of the house and was allowed to behave as I liked.

Back in Wales I hooked up with a female English holiday-maker, a broad-beamed country lass whose lower abdomen swelled out against her skirt and whose prominent breasts I was allowed to fondle in a field behind the village and on the rocky foreshore. She was extremely strong and liked to show off. Her favourite trick was to invite me to attack her with an imaginary knife in my right hand. She'd grip my wrists in her powerful hands, abruptly spin round so that her broad back was in front of me, and then she'd hoist me off the ground so that my feet would bang against the back of her calves, and I was helpless. I'd feel strangely disturbed and incredibly aroused. Heavy petting every afternoon when the bar closed for a couple of hours was the routine. When she had to return home to start her training as a nurse in Nottingham, we promised to correspond. As I assured her, I knew that I had no intention of writing to her. What the hell did I think I was doing? Why should I, a young man with a glorious future ahead of me, make a long-distance play for a plain young woman whose greatest aspiration was to become a nurse?

At the end of September I took the ferry from Holyhead to Dublin. I wanted to get the atmosphere because I had received hints from Professor Matheson that there might be funding for me to attend University College Dublin after graduation. There then followed a halcyon period, which was good, because my Final year was an unmitigated disaster.

11

Avalanche

On my arrival in Dublin, on a grey and damp Sunday morning, after an all-night drinking session on board the ferry with various groups of Irishmen – my kind of people – I was terribly weary.

Though I was low on funds, my ability to reason hadn't entirely vanished. I was determined not to stay in one of the scruffy lodging houses that dotted my route from the Quays to the city centre. (Some of them were offering Bed and Breakfast for twelve shillings!)

I entered a restaurant in Grafton Street and ordered a sirloin steak with onion rings and a beer. I was starving. The cost was a little over five pounds, a massive sum for someone who had about eighty pounds in his pocket that had to last me God knew how long. I had to eat.

A group of four lads who looked like students were seated at an adjoining table. They appeared to be three or four years older than me. I started chatting to them and, despite my fatigue, must have been in scintillating form as I recounted my latest adventures, because they made appreciative noises and snorted with suppressed laughter as my narrative unfolded. Casually, I let drop that I was a singer too and would be glad to perform for them. They were intrigued, and invited me back to their flat in St Stephen's Green. A couple were engineering graduates, one was completing his studies at Vet School and the other was about to defend his Ph.D. thesis in Biology. They liked a drink and I was delighted when they told me I could move in with them . . . for nothing.

I 'skippered' – lodged without payment – for around two weeks, eking out my money by breakfasting on 'Tayto' Cheese and Onion crisps and pints of Guinness. I was seriously thinking of returning home to Glasgow in the near future. I had lived off the goodwill of these kind Irish boys for too long.

Then, at an impromptu party in somebody's flat in St Stephen's Green, I met Maeve Ryan, a widow in her late thirties.

I literally bumped into her, hip to thigh, at the drinks table. Wavy red hair flowed down to her assertive breasts. The low-cut dress told me that she wanted people to know that she had a body. She beamed at me and her face, with small regular teeth, was about six inches away from mine. Undeniably, she had a libidinous presence. She looked into my eyes and smiled – very warmly.

"Congratulations, Scotty," she said in a low voice.

"What for?" I said.

"Your singing," she said. "You have a beautiful voice, and that Gaelic song was truly lovely."

(I had moaned my way through a fairly modern song made by *Dòmhnall Ailen Dhòmhnaill na Banaich*, Donald Macdonald, who was from South Uist.

'*Ghruagach òg an fhuilt bhàin, èist ri bàrdachd mo bhilean* . . . Young maid of the golden tresses, listen to the poetry of my lips . . .')

I felt confused and woolly-headed, which was a better way of putting it to myself than *drunk*. The compunction about falling for an older woman, however willing she might be, on one hand, and rising lust, on the other, were locked in combat in my woozy head.

"Will you see me home, young man?" she said with a salacious leer, giving off whiffs of frisky trouble.

"I'd be delighted to escort you," I said with mannered dignity.

"Are you sure?" she said. "You're not just saying that?"

It was true. I was just saying that, and I meant it. There was an overwhelming itch in my groin, and this older woman seemed only too happy to relieve it. Hand in hand we walked slowly to a taxi rank at the top of Grafton Street. She did something with her forefinger in my palm, a grip that I knew was the prelude to love-making.

When the taxi deposited us at her home in Ballsbridge I was gobsmacked. The mansion she lived in was most impressive. An expanse of stone-clad wall with a double wrought-iron gate ran the length of this large property. Behind the thick vegetation close to the wall a swelling green lawn adjoined the paved path that led up to the porch of the house.

The interior was no less imposing. I made out a broad staircase as we swept through a vast reception hall with a marble floor, into which were scattered random circles of maroon tiles, and entered the living room. There was a large floor-to-ceiling window at the far end of the room that looked out onto a well-tended lawn, about which were scattered round iron chairs with awnings and cushions. The floor was covered by a thick green carpet. A massive couch and three easy chairs were upholstered in tan tweed. On the mahogany-panelled walls there hung half a dozen paintings, oils and watercolours, that I was sure cost a lot of money. One wall was entirely filled with shelving supporting scores of books I was anxious to get my hands on. A huge stone fireplace holding a nest of logs was the focal point of this extremely comfortable room.

"Real cosy place you've got here, Maeve," I said.

"Thank you, Norman," she said.

I repeated the phrase in a low whisper, talking to myself, "Yes, this place is really cosy . . . really cosy . . ."

"You can be cosy here as long as you like," Maeve said.

A young man could get to like these surroundings. I didn't hesitate. I rose to my feet out of the chair in front of the window where I had been slumped and quickly darted between a solid ebony glass-topped coffee table and the fireplace to where she was standing, hands on hips. I held her face in my hands and kissed her. She responded passionately and, inevitably, we undertook a romp on the couch. She displayed a lasciviousness I had never encountered before. She was eight stones of pure joy, and she made love with all the fervour of someone who had been deprived of intimacy for too long. I loved her shameless mouth, her girlish breasts – nipples like little buds – and her uninhibited response to my thrustings.

I spent six weeks in Ballsbridge, bundling with Maeve of the well-turned calves every day. I read a lot during the day, everything from lurid true-crime stories, based on real events, to lavishly illustrated books on the castles of Ireland.

Maeve had been married to a prominent Dublin architect who had succumbed to a massive cardiac infarction at the young age of forty. He had obviously left her pretty well off. She defrayed the costs of domestic and horticultural help by working. She taught every night, of all subjects, technical drawing at a college of further education in the city.

She had an animal vitality about her . . . something marvellous and robust. I can still see her smiling face with the dainty little teeth and startling green eyes turning from side to side, wisps of damp red hair plastered to her forehead, her mouth agape as she reached climax.

For six weeks I lived like a mediaeval prince, eating well and drinking in moderation – maybe a glass or two of red wine with a delicious meal of breaded lamb chops with vegetables and tiny roast potatoes when she returned from her evening classes – and indulging in riotous rutting.

Unfortunately, the looming final year at university demanded my attention. I had written to my mother informing her that I'd be home at the end of October, refreshed and ready for my last session. At the final parting on the North Wall as I prepared to embark on an overnight crossing on the passenger ferry that sailed directly to the Broomielaw in Glasgow, Maeve was crying openly. Her face was shockingly contorted. I felt guilty myself, and the thought of the coming term was making me feel miserable. However, I'd deal with that, I thought.

I really did make a determined effort to recapture the easy flow of things I enjoyed during my first year at the institution. I blew the annual grant money on a second-hand Lambretta scooter. I suspect that unconsciously I wanted to establish the credentials of a final year student. And the machine would keep me off the drink, wouldn't it? It didn't really. When I fell off the wagon, I used to mount my steed with impunity and didn't give a fig for my own safety or that of others.

I attended the Ossianic Society for the first time in years and renewed acquaintance with a host of Highland and island students. I attempted desperately to assume the persona I had lost two years previously. In company, I had a smile and ready quip for everybody. In the privacy of the bathroom in Brand Street, however, it was a different mask that revealed itself. My face was blurry because of my obdurate insomnia. God, I was tired getting out of bed. All I could make out in that face was pain. I couldn't begin to relax enough at night to sleep.

"Working hard, Norman?" one girl at the Ossianic, Kenna Campbell, said.

"You bet," I said loudly, a congealed smile on my face. I beamed at her for a long penetrating moment.

"That's good," she said. "It's good that you're back on the rails again."

Well, I was attending Old and Middle Irish fairly regularly. I had also cut back on the drinking. I could not deny that there was a hole in my life where drinking used to be. I found it hard to con myself into thinking that I was living a glittering and thrilling existence. The tapering off from my lover was necessary, as I was awash with debt. One minute I would be pawning my piping medals, some of them 14 carat gold, beseeching the counter clerk to give me a break on the prices – and the very next I would have to grind through the gears, tune up my central nervous system, put on a false mask and become a cool, happy, relaxed personification of trust, in order to persuade *anybody* to lend me some money.

One source of funding was Harry Garvie, the unlicensed money-lender who flew small amounts of cash out of the Kensington Bar in Ibrox. He charged four shillings in the pound per week as interest. He was a short, heavy-set, dozy-looking man of about forty, not very prepossessing, yet everybody who frequented the pub knew that he was ruthless when he was forced to confront a slow payer. I knew that he didn't dislike me. He thought, I'm sure, that the presence of a university student raised the tone of what was essentially a working-class establishment.

The first time I approached him for the loan of a pound was embarrassing. Harry, on hearing my request, arched his eyebrows in what I took to be an expression of astonishment. "All right, Nor-man – *Awright –*" he said with more than a trace of scorn in his husky voice. "I'll give you one note – *Ah'll gie ye wan note –* but remember, I want either one pound four shillings or the four shillings this time next week."

I paid him off the first time, but I returned several times after that and borrowed larger and larger sums of cash that I had no business looking for in the first place. The strain of avoiding Harry and the young louts who provided muscle for him when he had to deal with recalcitrant clients left me paranoid. Oh, the entire business was stress-ful, stressful.

Delegations of young toughs sent by Mr Garvie were visiting my mother's house quite regularly. They'd announce that their boss wanted his money. "You have no choice but to pay, Mr Maclean," – meaning, "We can come round and break your hands if you don't fork out . . . soon."

I was facing Panic.

My solution was to steal and sell my late father's gold watch and chain. I went to a precious metal dealer in Oswald Street, climbed a

Avalanche

steep, narrow staircase and entered a cubicle with a counter, not two
steps away from the door, topped by a wire grille.

A middle-aged man with a swollen belly, grubby shirt sleeves resting on a shallow counter, gave me a pinched stare through thick
spectacles.

"Help you?" he said with indifference.

"I've got a gold watch and chain I want to sell," I said. "How
much will you give me for them both?"

Without a word he examined the jewellery I had pushed through
a slot in the base of the grill.

Suddenly, he looked up at me and said: "Okay, I'll give you fifteen
pounds for them." His look was one of tried patience.

"Fifteen pounds!" I exclaimed. "That watch is eighteen carat gold
and must be worth at least fifty pounds." I was stunned.

"Fifteen pounds is my limit," he said in a matter-of-fact voice.

"This is . . . not fair," I said. "Can't you put it up to twenty at least?"

The man studied the watch and chain for a moment, as if he were
willing to reconsider his offer. Then he looked up.

"If you can get twenty pounds for this stuff, go and get it," he said
tonelessly. "Fifteen's my only and final offer."

I started to stammer out some lie about tradesmen having to be
paid that day. He cut me off in mid-flow and said contemptuously,
"Take it or leave it, Jimmy."

By now he had his left hand inside a drawer. His fist emerged
clutching a clump of crumpled pound notes. He slowly spread his
fingers and pushed the greasy money under the grill.

I snatched the money up in trembling fingers and, aflame with
anger and humiliation, I wheeled about and hurried out of the cubicle.

Harry just took the money with a dour look. His indifferent attitude was as humiliating as that of the swollen belly in the cubicle. He
was used to dealing in a cool, contemptuous fashion with losers. I was
aware that a door had closed in my face.

Despite this and my insomnia, I was making some progress with
the prescribed texts. I'd hit upon a scheme to enable me to catch up
on my neglected Irish books. I went to the home of a young woman,
Chrissie Dick, who had North Uist connections and who had gradu-
ated with Honours the previous year. From her I borrowed copious
notes she had made in her Junior Honours and Final years. These fat
notebooks, chock-full of detailed commentary on set texts which I

109

hadn't bothered to read, I consulted all too infrequently, particularly in the run-up to my Finals.

The rot set in over the Christmas vacation. I had taken a temporary job with the Royal Mail, delivering letters, cards and parcels during the busiest time of the year. It was during this twenty-day period that I became friendly with an older tough from Whiteinch called Matheson. He was about forty, with prodigious upper arms, chest and shoulders. His nose was thick at the bridge and obviously had been broken a few times. He took a shine to me mainly because I sang Country and Western ballads – 'loser music' – while we were sorting the mail at the start of the shift.

One day he loomed over me as I tossed letters into pigeon-holes with destinations stenciled above them.

"Hiyah, Norrie," he said, "What are you doing for the New Year? – *Whit urr ye daein' furr the New Year?*"

A red alert burst forth in my skull, but I found myself saying, "Nothing really."

"Come over to mine after the bells and we'll have a wee swally," he said.

Nervously I took down his address. I don't know why I made the decision to accept his invitation. From his scatological monologues, full of references to fornication with fruity housewives, perhaps I imagined I would meet one of those women, and – who knew? – I might get lucky.

In the early hours of the first day in January I knocked on the door of his flat in a tenement in Whiteinch. He was alone. I hid my disappointment at the absence of women and accepted a full glass of cheap fortified British wine bearing the legend *El Dorado*. I took a sip. I loved it. There was no dawdling over the tumbler. I had an overwhelming urge to knock back another glass of this cloyingly sweet concoction. I downed a second glass in three gulps and indicated to Matheson that I wanted another one. Soon I felt as liberated as a prisoner released after a long period of incarceration. Over the following two hours I drifted on a torrent of words issuing from the scarred face of my host. He spoke of fights he had been engaged in, robberies he had taken part in and jail sentences he had served.

Like a neural wave, though most of the time I was tuned out, satisfaction flowed through me. This hooligan was confiding in me because he somehow regarded me as an equal – a *man*.

I parted with him, both of us pretty much in the bag, a little after four in the morning. I didn't know it then as I walked a trifle unsteadily down to the all-night ferry, but, by indulging in this little bout of dissipation, I was inviting the avalanche to begin.

The next two terms were disastrous. I resumed my habits of the previous two years – drinking to oblivion in the evenings, having sleepless nights, and suffering excruciating hangovers. Classes were regularly missed. (I must say that Professor Angus Matheson, Chair of Celtic Language and Literature, did not enjoy good health and often cancelled his lectures. I can't pretend I felt like curling up and dying whenever I'd see his apologetic note pinned to the lecture room door informing me that he was indisposed. My heels would be striking my bum all the way down to the Union, where I ran a tab.)

In short, with a head that felt like a husk most of the time, I dithered about. I got into the habit of taking a *norrag*, forty winks, in the afternoon. I'd start to sink, and then the sentry in my skull would yank me into consciousness. In the middle of the day, lying in the bed with my eyes closed, I would sigh. Christ . . . Who was I? How the hell did I get here? I realized these questions had been crystallizing in my mind for the past two years at least. The answers, I knew, were alcohol and vanity, maybe alcohol more than vanity. An avalanche of guilt descended upon me. The Final Honours degree examinations were fast approaching. The pile of debt I'd accumulated was a nagging worry. The time of reckoning was fast approaching, I thought.

There was an opening of sorts, though. My Adviser of Studies summoned me to his office one day in the Easter term to make me a remarkable offer.

"Mr Maclean," he read from prepared notes. "We are aware that Professor Matheson has been in poor health recently."

"Yes?" I said.

"You have missed a critical number of lectures," he said.

"Mmmmmm," I agreed.

"Accordingly," he went on, "the Senate have agreed to allow you an additional year in order for you to be fully prepared for your Finals. What do you think?"

I was in *trouble*. No. Another year in this place would unhinge me completely. No. Another year of catatonic despair? There was no way to cope with it. I sagged like someone taking a bullet.

"Postponing the Finals for a year won't help, sir," I said calmly. "I want to graduate this year." What I needed was the ticket, and for these nightmare days to end. I picked up my worn briefcase, which contained only a battered copy of *The Lost Weekend*, and made it clear that I was anxious to be away.

"Have a think about it, Mr Maclean," the Adviser said.

"I will, I will!" I bellowed.

The degree examinations had to be dealt with. Whisky would be absolutely essential to get through this obstacle course. Frequently I'd run out and be forced to ride my scooter to out-of-the-way pubs to get a half bottle of whisky. One night, late on, I found myself sitting on the bench seat of the upstairs lounge of Ibrox House, a rough pub about a mile away from where I lived. I paid over the odds for my take-away and suddenly felt guilty. The Finals! I patted my pocket and raced downstairs to the car park where my Lambretta stood in splendid isolation. Losing control, I glanced through the windscreen and to my horror saw that the keys were still in the ignition. I didn't hesitate. I picked up a building brick and started to pound it against the perspex windshield. It didn't break. An old man approached me warily.

"Whit are ye daein'?" he asked.

"I'm trying to get my keys," I gasped, continuing to rain blows on the unyielding windscreen.

The old man brushed past me and, reaching easily into the machine, extracted the keys from the ignition barrel.

"Here's yer keys, son," he said and handed them to me. "Whit wurr ye battering the windscreen furr?"

I mounted the scooter, impatient to be free. Suddenly it occurred to me in a lunatic flash that I could talk my way out of this mess.

"No harm done," I said. "I always test windscreens that way. For stress factors. I've got a heavy date with the *Mabinogion*. Got to go, pops." I twisted the hand-grip on the left-hand side of the handlebars and revved the throttle on the right. Releasing the clutch rather too quickly, I lurched into Broomloan Road and sped home.

Madness, madness . . .

When I opened the first paper I felt a spurt of alarm. I heaved a heavy sigh and suddenly my heart started banging away in my rib cage. I set to scribbling, battering out nonsense, X-ing out hopeless mistakes and making many false starts. My memory of the twelve papers I sat in the Baird Hall – sometimes two papers a day over about nine days – is that these were the worst days of my life. What kept me going was the prospect of a mammoth drinking session I intended to enjoy in the Rubaiyat with Griff and the two Neils after my final paper. And what a session that was! At one point in the afternoon I found myself on the roof of the terraced house in Belgrave Terrace where Griff was renting a room. I was whooping and screaming at the passing traffic on Great Western Road. God alone knew why.

I left the University of Glasgow with a Third. *Humiliation* . . . well, I had to face facts. I'd let Jake MacDonald and myself down. There would be no postgraduate degree at a Cambridge college. The parchment I'd receive from Glasgow would have no value. I gave in . . . I began to feel hugely sorry for myself. I was wiped out . . . *utterly*.

Then, an escape route opened which I took without a second thought. It was a chance to emerge from the bitterly cold loch of shame that enveloped me. Jake was being elevated to the post of Lecturer at Jordanhill College of Education. Donald Alex Macdonald, Jake's assistant at my old school, was about to become Head of the Gaelic Department. In a breathless telephone call he told me he was willing to have me as his assistant. All I'd have to do was attend teacher-training college for only two terms – such was the paucity of trainee teachers – and I'd be earning honest, good money after the Easter break next year. I accepted his offer in a compressed millisecond and experienced the first surge of spirit of the preceding three years.

Oh, I knew that what I was about to do would not provide a good fit with my imagined future – but I did it anyway.

12
Farewell, Ella

Ella MacDonald, daughter of Alex MacDonald of Moidart and sister of the finest piper of his generation, Pipe-Major Angus MacDonald, sat on the pillion seat of my Lambretta scooter with her arms around my waist. We came careening up the dirt and gravel track towards *Cuinnich*, the wind scratching our eyes. I was going to show off my beautiful new girlfriend to *Seumas Mòr* and *Màiri* and to my cousins, Bella, Nan, Murdo and Christopher. Delirious with egotism, I had succeeded in anaesthetising my wounded feelings concerning my recent academic failure by drinking regularly and making new amorous conquests.

The latest of these was the fair Ella. I met her in her father's home in 102 Berryknowes Road, Cardonald. Alex, the old man, had invited me up for Sunday dinner after an epic drinking session in the Viceroy Bar at Paisley Road Toll. The following night I was pleased to discover that a seventeen-year-old, extremely pretty girl looked after her policeman father in the two-bed roomed flat. The evening was spent sipping whisky and frequent cups of tea and nibbling sandwiches prepared by the ever-attentive daughter.

Alex was an engaging raconteur with a full range of facial expressions and a good ear for mimicry. His tales of the exploits of the Glasgow Police Pipe Band had me rolling on the carpet like somebody who didn't have the sense our Creator gave a turnip. One riotous tale of his was about the trip the band made to Paris just after the war to play at an amateur football match involving Queens Park and a team of French gendarmes.

"Like I said, Norman, the band had a little problem over in Paris," Alex said, a rueful grin on his chiseled lips. "Not a problem for the band. An embarrassment for me, sure, but Johnnie Johnston, the gold medalist from Islay, took the whole thing like a traffic accident. Of course, we younger bandsmen allowed Johnnie a certain degree of derangement because of his talent. So for a long time he got away with murder. He had a serious handicap with his speech. On top of the sing-song accent of his native island he had a pronounced lisp and a seriously guttural uvular 'r'. 'I want the respect – *rrrethpect* – and trust *–trrrutht –* of all pipers – *piperrrth* – everywhere – *everrrywherrre'* he used to say to us."

"And was he a good player, Alex?" I said.

"Bet your life," Alex said. "Only thing was, he loved playtime. Give him a dram, and it guaranteed trouble down the line. The sand really hit the gears in Paris, though."

Alex cleared his throat. "When the plane touched down in Paris the French were lining the tarmac to welcome the footballers. First to come out was big Charlie Scott, all six feet three and eighteen stone of him. With the addition of his feather bonnet to his already impressive height he must have looked like a giant to the nervous French football team. He was followed by more monsters in full Highland dress. We were all grim-faced and giddy from the flight in a chartered aircraft and from, as I remember, a great many drams. As we swaggered towards the reception committee, singing and whooping, the French reeled backwards in confusion.

Alex waggled the fingers of his right hand to indicate rapid flight. "High-pitched, excited gabbling in their native tongue," Alex said, "accompanied their retreat. It was like the evacuation of Dunkirk. No boats, just the *casan*, feet."

In an attempt to impress Ella, I improvised a panicky outburst that might have approximated the shouts of the scared hosts. "*Zut! Ça sera impossible! Ces montagnards, ils sont trop forts pour nous!*"

Alex grinned. "Right," he said. "Sounded a lot like that."

I was delighted. I laughed and slapped my right arm on the arm of my chair. "Damn," I said, "this is a hoot." A sidelong glance in Ella's direction confirmed that she had appreciated my interjection. "What happened next, Alex? Did the Pipe-Major have an, um, itinerary?"

"Naw," Alex said scornfully. "The one fragment of a plan Pipe-Major John Macdonald and the members of the band had was to find premises that sold alcohol, and drink as much booze as their bellies could hold, and they fulfilled that with ease, more or less . . ."

Our narrator failed to tell Ella and me whether the band actually played in the afternoon and what the result of the football match, if it ever took place, was. Instead, he performed a linguistic jump-cut to late evening and the interior of a bistro adjacent to the barracks where they had been put up.

He spread his hands, palms up and open. "Look," he said, "I was used to the Scottish licensing laws where public houses had to close – oh, I think, at nine o'clock. We went crazy with the freedom afforded by the laid-back attitude of the owner of the little bistro, who was kept busy refilling glasses of Cognac and half litres of draught lager."

"I bet the owner had never seen as much money in the till in all his life," I said.

"Well, geez, I don't really know about that," Alex said, widening his eyes and arching his eyebrows in simulation of the delighted bar owner. "All I know is that he was really happy."

"How long did he keep the drouthy bandsmen re-ordering?" I said.

"Oh, eventually, around two in the morning," Alex said, "he decided that he had made enough and he declared that he was closing up."

I saw a further opportunity to show off my linguistic and thespian skills. In an adenoidal whine I intoned: "*Je regrettes, messieurs, mais c'est nécessaire de fermer. C'est finit. Buvez et allez-vous en!*"

"Christ!" Alex said. "You must be a psychopath, Norman. That's exactly how the man sounded." Seeing my gratified smirk, he pressed on at some speed. "The boys got the message. Right away. To a man they besieged the bewildered owner with requests for 'carry-outs'. Old habits die hard, and back home you never leave the pub without ensuring that you have drink to go."

"Which you do," I said.

"Which we do," Alex said. "But it was the choice of drink that was odd. We were all given bottles of Chianti in raffia baskets. This was because the Pipe-Major had pointed out the prettily packaged wine first. The rest of us just mumbled, 'Same' and handed over clumps of greasy francs. Soon the men would have been a sight to see if anybody had been on the Rue d'Orce to see them, but the douce burghers of Belleville were all fast asleep, and were spared the sights and sounds of drunken Scotsmen, each with woven baskets dangling daintily from hairy wrists, arguing about the pointing of 'Inveraray Castle' and 'diddling' reels in ex tempore *canntaireachd*, mouth music."

"Did you call it a wrap, then?" I said.

Farewell, Ella

"No, we didn't," Alex said. "At least Johnnie and I didn't. He lurched up to me on the pavement and said: '*An gabh thu dram, a bhalaich*? Do you fancy a dram, young fellow?'"

At this point, Alex got up and stood beside the chair, and looked at the floor as though he were reliving the dilemma. He exhaled heavily. "What you've got to understand," he said, "is that I wasn't long out of the Camerons and lusted after danger and adventure. I said okay. Foolish perhaps."

"You must have been a little nervous, I mean going off with a, um, *volatile* character like Johnnie," I said.

"I was scared *shitless*," Alex said, glancing briefly at the serene face of his daughter, "See, if it'd ever got to the ears of the Pipe-Major that we had continued to drink after the session in the local bistro he would have dumped us like hot phosphorous. 'Where can we get a drink at this hour,' I asked him. 'Follow me,' Johnnie said, marching purposefully to the edge of the pavement. As we swayed there, I was asking him things like 'Well, where are we going?' And he said, 'We're – *We'rrre* – going to a night club.' Then I pointed out that neither of us spoke the language. 'Watch and listen, Alex,' he said. 'I speak fluent French – *Frrrench*.' He then marched into the middle of the road, towards an approaching Citroen car with orange lights on the roof, and with his arms outstretched over his head, he bellowed, 'Taxi – *Tacthi*!' The car halted, and before making for the rear door Johnnie gave me a triumphant look. 'You see, Alex,' he said smugly, 'that's the French – *Frrrench* – for taxi – *tacthi*.'

"We sprawled in the back seat of the cab," Alex continued, "and once more I had doubts about Johnnie's command of the language. The driver, a skinny, pale-faced man, with long hair caught up in a pony-tail at the back, said something that I took to mean 'Where to, gentlemen?'"

"Probably something like, '*Alors, messieurs, où allons-nous?*'" I said.

"Yes, Norman," Alex said, trying not to sound irritated, but failing. "I asked Johnnie how he intended to give the driver a destination. 'No problem,' he said confidently. He pressed his mouth to the grilled partition, and, in a sibilant whisper, said, 'Driver – *Drriverrr* – take us – *uth* – to the bad places – *plathes*.' The driver understood immediately, and with a lewd wink at us drove off at some speed. I overheard him say something in a conspiratorial murmur about Montmartre, and I assume that's where he let us off, in a dimly-lit side street."

Alex took two paces to his right and then two paces back. "So there we were," he said, "in a shabby night-club somewhere on the South Bank, seated at a table littered with empty glasses. As usual we were talking shop. 'You know, Johnnie,' I said, 'I think our Pipe-Major, Seonaidh Roidein, is the best piper I've ever heard. When he puts his pipe up at the practices in Orkney Street Police Station,' I said, 'the rest of us pack up our instruments and listen with our mouths hanging open.' Johnnie Johnston seemed stunned. He just sat there and looked at me for about a minute. 'What about me?' he said after the long silence. 'Did you know that Willie Gray – *Grrray* – before he retired – *rrretirrred* – recommended – *rrrecommended* – ah, he wanted *me* to be the Pipe-Major?' 'No, I didn't,' I said. Inwardly I thanked God that the brass had favoured the South Uist man over this manic, competitive person in front of me.

"At this point, a tough-looking waiter in a tight tuxedo arrived at our table," Alex continued. "With a flourish he laid a silver tray that held a grubby piece of paper in front of us. 'Kind gentlemen,' he growled. This was the bill. All I could see were zeros, and I remember my palms becoming sweaty and a heart-pounding feeling, like: what was going to happen? What would Johnnie do?"

There seemed to be a new edge of anxiety in Alex's voice. "Johnnie picked up the bill between forefinger and thumb, glanced at it briefly, and crumpled it in his fist before dropping it on the stained carpet. He ignored the waiter and focused on my white face. 'Listen – *Lithen*,' he whispered fiercely. 'You get the carry-outs – *carrry*-outs – and make for the door – *doorrr*. I'll hold this big clown back.'" Alex broke off and clenched his fists. "Well, I did as I was told. I grabbed the wine – I mean, I don't – I don't know what came over me. When I paused in the doorway and looked back an astonishing sight met my eyes."

Alex gaped and inhaled through his mouth. "Jesus Christ," he said, "there was Johnnie on his feet, waving the ornamental claymore which all pipers carry on their waist-belts in the face of the retreating waiter. It wouldn't have cut butter, but the large dirk had a fourteen-inch blade and looked dangerous." Alex straightened up, and throwing his shoulders back, mimed the imaginary sword-play. "Mad Johnnie was on his toes like a ballerina," Alex said, "waggling his sword in circles and thrusts. He was screaming in his high-pitched voice: 'Stand back, stand back. My father was the finest swordsman in Islay! *Thtand back, thtand back. My fatherrr wath the finetht sworrrdth-man in Islay!*'"

Seated, Alex concluded his narrative. "We got away with it," he said thoughtfully, keeping his voice low. "Look," he said massaging the back of his neck with his hand, "I'm on early shift tomorrow. Do you mind if I make for the nest now?"

Ella and I shook our heads. "Okay," he said, moving towards the door. "Ella, you make Norman a cup of tea, or you can pour yourself another dram, if you like. I'm off."

And so it was that I found myself, a good hooker of whisky clenched in my fist, alone with Ella in the living room. It seemed the most natural thing in the world. There was this gorgeous seventeen-year-old female, black wavy hair framing a heart-shaped face with a prominent, upturned upper lip, smiling at me from a three-seater couch on which she was curled up, her ripe, womanly haunches swelling the blanket that covered her lower body.

Ella punctured the dead air that lay between us. "Your singing was lovely, Norman," she said.

I accepted the compliment with an actor's bashful panache, and I found myself abandoning my manners and vocabulary by blurting out: "You're an absolute doll, Ella." She had about her an air of vulnerability. I desperately wanted someone to love me. Someone modest and kind. Someone under my power.

I scooted from my easy chair and stood above her for about fifteen seconds. Slowly, I leaned forward and, taking her trusting face in my hands, I tenderly kissed her cushiony lips. She surrendered her will, and, although sensing she was afraid, I lowered my body onto hers, sucking at her mouth, her tongue, and cupping her head in my hands. I felt myself floating in warm water, never so happy as then, if only then were forever.

In my imagination the outer winner had masked the inner loser. Ella would be, I decided, from this time, my true love. In the subsequent tension, however, between disguise and display that characterised my attitude towards that sweet girl, I did not behave well. I loved her fraternally, but not passionately.

I didn't take her out. Our intimate moments were crammed into the last half hour of my visits to her home. The principal part of the evening would be taken up with alternating tunes on the practice chanter, war stories and the sipping of tiny little shot glasses of whisky. My courting of Ella never got beyond languorous kissing and the cradling of each other in lazy arms.

Two warring motivations burned inside my head. On one hand, I felt protective and manly in her company. But, as I frequently reminded myself, she was only a shop girl working for a Dutchman called Van Zanten in Ingram Street in Glasgow's Fruit Market, while I was a graduate, with Honours, of the University of Glasgow. What an asshole! Norman Maclean, lucky to have the M.A. ticket, was thinking himself so sophisticated and superior, just because he immersed himself in the passionate streams of the piano *intermezzi* and the clarinet solos of Brahms.

Nevertheless, I chose to ignore her wise voice, her perception and quiet dependency on me. Once, suffering from a teeth-grinding hangover, I sat with my elbows on my knees, quivering like the tip of a fishing rod. I confessed to feeling afraid.

"What are you scared of, Norman," she said.

"I'm afraid to go home," I said.

"Why?" she said calmly.

"I'm afraid I won't waken up tomorrow morning," I said.

"Listen," she said calmly, "you're either going to waken up or not. If you are alive in the morning, you'll have to deal with your problems – without the aid of alcohol – or if you aren't, you won't have to worry any more."

She was completely relaxed when she took my hand and looked into my eyes. To attempt to describe her without mentioning her beautiful face would be crazy. She dazzled me with those soft brown eyes, and with that slightly curved delicate nose, joined to the forehead without a bump, ascending above the altar of lips so rich and sweet . . .

At times I've thought that the attraction of 102 Berryknowes Road was just a pretty face in thrall to my dynamic personality. Oh, and the free whisky. That and the slow burgeoning of an almost father-son relationship between Alex and me. Ever the since the death of my own father, Niall Mòr, I suspected that unconsciously I had been seeking some father-figure replacement. It was strange, when I reflected on my own life, how often my father kept wandering in and out of focus. Maybe it was not so strange after all. Maybe Proust had it right when he wrote that autobiography was the search for one's father.

When we reach Cuinnich, Ella and I, on my new Lambretta scooter, we're greeted with courtesy and kindness by everyone in the household. After a perfunctory wash, Crisdean and I depart for a spin on the scooter to Spean Bridge. We were ostensibly giving the new machine a work-out, but secretly we planned to purchase whisky at the hotel and have an old fashioned ceilidh with Seumas Mòr and Murdo on our return.

The public bar of the Spean Bridge Hotel was crowded. Dressed in the plus-four trousers and tweed jacket of my grand-uncle, I drifted from one little knot of drinkers to another, accepting glasses of whisky topped up with lemonade from each hospitable group. I wonder now what my passion for uniforms meant. In the deathless legend imprinted on a T-shirt I saw once in California, I was a true believer: 'Forget meaning. Means are OK.' Without a taste for philosophy or self-examination, I concentrated on means, not meaning. For me, the meaning was written on the tablets of Moses: to impress people and be popular. I've always had tremendous dependence on what other people thought of me. Did I have basic inner feelings of inadequacy and a driving need to compensate? Today I believe I did, though I believe too, that as far as neuroses are concerned, I could be classified as within the normal range.

I was not behaving normally at closing time. I hooked up with Cristean, each of us with a half bottle of whisky protruding ostentatiously from the hip pockets of our trousers.

"*Bheil thu deiseil gu falbh*, Are you ready for the off," I said.

"Yeah," he said, his broad face flushed with drink. "But we're not going to Cuinnich."

"We're not?" I said.

"No," he said, "there's a dance on in Onich and that's where we're going. Are you fit?"

Challenged over my extraordinary tolerance for alcohol, I informed him with some hauteur that I would easily drive the scooter. After a lot of mounting and dismounting to transfer the whisky bottles to the inside pockets of our jackets, and a great deal of revving of the engine, we wobbled to Onich in a cloud of Scotch.

From the moment we entered the pub in Spean, I never gave one thought to the poor girl I had abandoned among strangers on the shores of Loch Arkaig. I knew that Bella and Nan would be kind to her, but they were so much older than this young girl. They

121

didn't have a mutual frame of reference, nor was Ella fluent in the language.

At the rodeo in Onich I was oblivious to her plight. Under a suspended Tilley lamp, we swivelled and stomped to the strains of the 'Cumberland Reel' in the Strip the Willow. I had no hesitation in accepting the invitation of four female hotel workers from Lewis to a party in a hotel in Corpach, where they were working the season.

Dòmhnall Ailig Moy, Donald Alex Macdonald from Moy farm, ran the girls to their cottage on the grounds of the Achterloo Hotel, and Crìsdean and I followed on the scooter. Seumas Mòr always described Dòmhnall Ailig as *'fear dhe na daoine again fhìn*, one of our own people,' when, in the uniforms of the Royal Navy, he and his brother Angus would visit Cuinnich on a Sunday afternoon, the percussion of the bottles they carried in an old leather shopping bag accompanying them as they strode across the pasture towards the house.

In the annexe of the Achterloo Hotel, the four girls were standing against one wall and clapping their hands to the music of Bobby MacLeod's 78 record 'After the Games'. We males had our buttocks pressed up against an enormous table that ran the breadth of the room. Donald Alex raised his arm and snapped it down in some kind of a signal. He and Crìsdean broke from their positions and ran towards the women. I trotted after them and, following their example, seized hold around the waist of a tall blonde with heavy breasts. I spun her round and promptly fell backwards onto the carpet. We were suddenly thrashing about, twisting, her breath panting whisky fumes right up into my face . . . Her hot crotch pressing down on me and I inhaled the terrible smell of her sweat. Suddenly her fingers were squirming and squeezing around my upper thigh. A wave of pleasure swept through me . . .

As the Spanish proverb has it, *Noche alegre, mañanita triste*, A night of revelry, a morning of sorrow. This certainly described me and my cousin as we trudged into the kitchen at *Cuinnich* house late the following afternoon. Ella was seated at the table, tears streaking her smooth cheeks. She had taken on an injured silence as though in heavy mourning.

"Where have you been?" she said.

"We met some people in Spean and went to a party in Aonachan Gardens afterwards," I lied. "I'm tired and I want to go to bed for a *norrag*, nap."

Her voice lifted in anger. "No, don't go," she said. "Don't you dare. For the love of God, I worry for twenty-four hours because you're off gadding about on that damn scooter, blind-drunk, probably."

"Ella," I said, "I'm truly sorry that I left you on your own for so long. You know I love you."

"You've never loved me, Norman," she said. "You just loved the fact that I loved you."

As I clumped up the stairs to the bedroom where Christopher was already snoring, I reflected on her words. What she had said was true. She offered me the flattering mirror of her attention, and invariably I felt protective of her when she was around. Unfortunately, she wasn't to be around for much longer. I heard her sad valediction from the doorway.

"Norman," she shouted, "your cousin Murdo is giving me a lift on his Panther into Fort William. Don't bother to keep in touch when you get back to Glasgow."

I made my way over to the bed and sat on it with my head in my hands. It wasn't until I heard the front door slam shut that mean, scattered thoughts filled my skull in slow transfusion. *I need a drink, and I need it right now.* Dry-mouthed, I recalled the flask with three inches or so of whisky in the inside pocket of Crisdean's jacket, roughly six feet away where he had discarded it. I retrieved the bottle and drank with the air of a man long deprived, and grateful. I remember thinking that I should get off this bed and follow Ella and Murdo. I *should not* have another swig of whisky. Surely *should not* – but one more can't hurt.

I descended into that familiar black hole, comforted by a lurid compensatory fantasy playing in my head. Shit, I'm out from under that mousy bitch. I've a good mind to tell her to go to fuck. I don't need her. I'm free and clear now, nobody's fiancé needing to feel guilt because I'm being regarded by Ella's big tearful eyes when I haven't paid sufficient attention to her . . .

I come to sitting bolt upright on my swivel chair in Bellahouston, dizzy, trying to swallow. The sharp odour of self-hatred issues from my pores. Bitter regret floods my being and I stumble into the kitchen. With claws of shame I cling to the fridge, squeezing the metal to the point of pain. Aaagh! I feel like – it is weird to think about that weekend nearly fifty years previously. Gradually, though, my grip slackens and I begin to feel both exhilarated and a shit. I gaze at the moon and pray that its cold light is falling on Ella, far distant and lonely in a faraway bed.

13
Stag in the Mist

The yarn went like this: *Dòmhnall Beag mac Mhurchaidh*, Wee Donald son of Murdo, he of Rocky Mountain fame, had been carousing with far-flung neighbours for a week. When he decided to come home he found himself hopelessly lost. He knew he had a bottle of whisky and a comforting squaw 'wife' waiting patiently at home, but he couldn't reach them because he didn't know where he had been. The moral of this story, among the many recounted by my mother, was that you might know where you wanted to go, but you'd find it difficult to reach your destination if you didn't know where you had come from.

One foggy night in February 1960, with only a couple of months to go at Jordanhill College of Education before I'd be earning real money in a respectable job, I was in exactly the same condition. I didn't know where I'd been.

I was trundling along the gutters somewhere along Great Western Road astride my trusty Lambretta, doing around fifteen miles an hour. It was a real pea-souper. In the early Sixties, so many coal-burning fires compounded by naturally occurring mist made travelling on some occasions nightmarish. I was in a nerved-up state, meaning sex was imminent, delicious in anticipation, and suddenly I had no idea where the hell I was.

I knew where I wanted to be: Clydebank High School, where I taught Gaelic to a little group of mature students. They weren't all mature. A young seventeen-year-old, Sandra, to whom I used to give a lift at the end of the class, used to masturbate me in her back garden. It didn't look as though that might happen tonight.

I puttered to a halt and rested one foot on the pavement, the other in the well of the scooter. Silence. There was no traffic in either direction. Fog hung in shrouds about me. My eyes could not penetrate anything.

The story, in a minor way of course, had resonance for me. The magnified version, to do with my past and my future, was nebulous. The problem was that I did not know where my future lay. What was I looking for? Happiness? I knew that rarely lasted. Diversion, maybe – diversion from the ineluctable depressing facts: there is death, disease, impotence and dementia ahead.

Of course, I know my own back-story. My mother, Peigi Bheag, gave me all the information about my ancestors. I decided, as I waited for the fog to clear, to start with my maternal side. *Anna Bheag, nighean Aonghais 'ic Iain Mhòir*, Annie MacDonald was my maternal grandmother. It seems she was a bit of a tyrant. She was the only girl, with five brothers, and was undisputed head of the family. My sole memory of this formidable lady is of standing as stiff as a poker in her kitchen, aged about ten, and asking her if she wanted a good Gaelic song. "*Siuthad thusa, ghràidhein, gabh thusa òran math Gàidhlig dha do sheanmhair*, Go on, dear, and sing a good Gaelic song for your grandmother," she said. Ramrod-straight, arms rigid at my sides, I launched into '*Mo Chruinneag Ìleach*, My Islay Lover'.

> *Och, och mar tha mi, 's mi 'n seo nam aonar,*
> *Gur cianail dh'fhàg thu mi an dèidh do chòmhraidh –*
> *Mo chreach 's mo dhìobhail nach robh mi 'n Ìle*
> *'S mo chruinneag Ìleach 's mi dol ga pòsadh.*

> Alas for my condition, all alone am I,
> Bereft you have left me after your words –
> My destruction and my ruin it is that I am not in Islay
> With my Islay lover and me about to marry her.

With a great beam of pleasure on her almost Sicilian swarthy face, she'd reach into the pocket of her apron and reward me with a couple of mint sweets. Oh, I was the gold-plated kid, without a doubt.

Fortune kissed me too during my short stay at Jordanhill. The course was not onerous, and attendance at lectures was not strictly monitored. I had wheels; I had my grant and the Wednesday night class with its lubricious overtones. Above all, I had a job guaranteed for Easter. Accordingly, over two terms I think I attended perhaps three lectures. A tweedy psychologist gave us an intelligence test, and it turned out I was in the top three percentile for my age group. I really didn't give a fig. This information didn't scrape any tartar off my teeth. I attended a lecture on statistics and became convinced that we indeed live in a binary world. Oh, yeah, there was a cockamamie final exam on which I relied heavily on the work of an American educationist called Dewey. My one ambition in college was to go to the cinema more than anyone else in history.

It was time for me to go back to tracing my personal genealogy, and pick up on some anecdotes concerning Anna Bheag. Her sons, Allan, Angus, Norman, Jimmy, he of the fine arched brows, Roman nose and jaw, and Wee Colin, were dead scared of her, and she was pretty tough on her only daughter, my mother, too. I have a photograph of this squat pillar of a woman, printed over a century ago, that is more distant from today's sensibility than a postcard from Monet. She is decorated with black chiffon and laced black boots. She had prominent thyroid eyes, black eyes with heavy, dark lids. Her tales to my mother were a catalogue of torment – *Murchadh Iain Bhig*, Murdoch Johnson, her grandfather, being hunted by dogs on the north shore of Lochboisdale as the landowners' lackeys rounded up the displaced crofters for shipment to the New World.

For some reason – I suspect it was to be near the man she had decided to marry – she had left Old Mill, Benbecula, and rented a two-room-and-kitchen flat in Mair Street in the heart of the Plantation district of Glasgow. She duly married *Tormod Ailein*, Norman MacKinnon, who was a mariner all his life. He came from Cladach Baleshare in North Uist. This man had taken some adventurous life-paths: he'd jumped ship in South Africa and in Australia. My mother told me that her father had the *dà shealladh*, second sight. Indeed, he foretold his own death at sea.

"*Annag*," he said to his wife one afternoon while he was on shore leave during the last year of the Great War, "*cha till mi tuilleadh an turas seo*, I'll not return this time."

"*Dè phrablais tha thu cantail a-nis*, What rubbish are you talking now?" replied my grandmother, with some asperity.

"No," he continued in Gaelic, "I'm going down with the ship this time. I saw it clearly in my sleep. I want you to see that the children are taken good care of. The Navy will see you comfortably off."

"*Feuch an dùin thu do bheul, amadain*, Won't you shut your mouth, fool," my grandmother said.

But it came to pass. The irony was that he really shouldn't have been on active service at all. He was forty-four at the outbreak of hostilities, and was deemed too old by the Royal Navy recruiting panel. Such was his loathing of life ashore, despite obtaining a good job as a shore bosun when he retired from the sailing ships, that he was desperate to get back to sea. The inescapable fact was that he was unable to sleep on dry land. After liberal application of Cherry Blossom Black Boot Polish to his silver hair, he presented himself at the Royal Navy recruiting office once more and coolly lied about his age. He was accepted.

My mother had much anecdotal information about this man. It seems that he was of medium height, narrow in the shoulders, and had the reputation of being a snappy dresser. He had an abhorrence of dripping taps in the kitchen. He maintained that it reminded him of the cruel drought he and his shipmates on board a Dutch clipper suffered when they were becalmed in the Straits of Magellan. When native Indians launched their war canoes from Tierra del Fuego, the crew repelled those fierce invaders, who had a reputation for cannibalism, with fire hoses.

The reputed second sight seemed to have let him down somewhat. Just days before the sinking of the *Holderness* he had requested a transfer from his cabin close to the engine-room to another berth in the bow of the ship. Everyone there perished, but the seamen berthed amidships and in the stern were all rescued. I was glad that I avoided travelling by ship if I could. There was no sense in taking chances. I mostly took the airplane.

I frequently asked my mother if 'Papa' MacKinnon took a drink, and the answers were always equivocal. I think I was slowly realising I was becoming psychologically dependent on drug alcohol myself.

"Oh, sometimes he'd visit the home of an old shipmate in Kinning Park, *taigh a' Bharraich*, the house of the Barraman," she'd say. "He'd maybe crack a bottle with his old friend. But, Norman, I never saw him the worse for drink. I wish I could say that about his sons, my brothers." Another refuge for him when he was home on leave was *taigh Chiorstaidh Eachainn*, the house of Kirsty, daughter of Hector. She was a North Uist lady who presided over a brood of children in Cornwall Street.

The sepia-coloured photograph in my mind's eye I had of this hazy figure was of a man, terribly restless, with a lust for new places and new encounters. Maybe his Christian name wasn't the only thing he'd bequeathed to me.

His widow, Annag, who had always been bossy, even back in Old Mill over her brothers, Murdo, George, Alasdair and James, was, predictably, the role model for my own mother, *Peigi Bheag*, Wee Peggy. Wee Annie worried about the welfare of her siblings and, in particular, that of her youngest brother James, *Seumas Mòr*. When her mother died in the twenties, James, who was the only unmarried member of the Macdonald family, went to hell . . . on wheels. Excessive drinking, neglect of the beasts on the croft, falling into drunken comas in the houses of neighbours where he'd been regaling an entire household with his *ròlaistean*, or tall tales, were just some of the symptoms of his decline. When word reached her that her youngest brother was engaged in a life of dissolution, she commanded my mother to write a letter. (She herself was illiterate, never having attended school.) In it she recommended that James should get married without delay, and she even had a prospective bride in mind. The girl's name was Mary Patterson, and she belonged to one of the few Protestant families in Daliburgh in South Uist. Unfortunately, but, as it turned out, fortunately, there was an illegitimate boy, Kenny, in the frame. It was reputed that the infant's father was a member of the Royal Family, a party from which had been on a fishing trip to Uist when Mary was working as a sixteen-year-old chambermaid in Grogarry Lodge. Repeat, reputed. Who knows?

This was the best move Seumas Mòr ever made. She proved to be an excellent wife and helpmate. To me personally she was extremely kind. When I was a competing piper she used to make me kilt hose. She didn't buy the wool in a haberdashery. No, she collected the wool from the fleeces of the sheep. Carding, spinning on the *cuibhle-shnìomh*, spinning wheel, she manufactured her own yarn before starting to knit.

Big James deserved praise too. He gave the baby the Macdonald surname, and treated the child as his own. When *Coinneach Sheumais*, Kenny son of James, was killed at El Alamein, the old man was dealt a devastating hammer-blow that he never really got over for the rest of his life.

How could I ignore my paternal side? I cherished my family archives: scraps of romance and physical action, family tales I've tried to press from my distant and fractured memories of my mother's monologues.

My paternal grandfather, John Maclean, was from 'The Green' on the island of Tiree. His *sloinneadh* or patronymic was *Iain Eòghain*

Ruaidh, John son of red-headed Ewan. For an islander, he was almost unique. He never took alcoholic drink during his entire life. He didn't go to sea. He was a horsy man, a drover, a bouncer, and a farm labourer. He possessed a sweet lyric tenor voice. My recollection of his singing when he lodged in our house in Brand Street for a time after his wife died was of a kind of home-knitted Andrea Bocelli. I have a silver medal, won at Falkirk Tryst, bearing the inscription 'Awarded to J. MacLean for the singing of a Gaelic song'. He drifted into Glasgow's Gallowgate, where, in the tough essentially Irish pubs of the area, he was employed as a 'chucker-out' because of his fast fists and because he, unlike his drunken opponents, was always sober. At the turn of the century, he was an 'orraman' or general farm labourer in a farm on the outskirts of Newton Mearns, south of Glasgow. The owners of the farm were of Islay descent and were called MacLellan. There were three lads and one girl, Flora, in the family. What did John Maclean do? He fell in love with the farmer's daughter. My father was actually conceived and born in Newton Mearns. This was a disgrace and a scandal to the well-doing MacLellans. Whether under pressure, or just to prove that he could do it, John did the romantic thing. In the dead of night he placed the ladder against Flora's bedroom window, snatched the daughter and his infant son, Neil, and promptly took off for Tiree.

The brothers didn't take this abduction lying down. They hired a fishing boat in Ayr and sailed to Tiree to liberate their sister and retrieve her infant son. Good intentions, major mistake. In an epic battle on 'The Green', John Maclean laid all three of them out, and the sturdy farmer's sons, battered and bruised, were obliged to return to Renfrewshire, their mission unaccomplished.

He spent some time in Argentina breaking horses. My father spoke Spanish fluently, having being immersed in the language from an early age. John Maclean's next move was to North Uist, where he drove a 'gig', a one-horsed carriage, for the owners of the Lochmaddy Hotel, taking tourists to places of interest on the island. He adored Uist and the people there. My father was enrolled in Lochmaddy Primary.

He then went to *Ruairidh Ruadh MacAmhlaigh*, Red-headed Roderick MacAulay, over on the west side, as groom to the horses. But again there was a falling-out resulting in fisticuffs. It seems that MacAulay's pride and joy was a fine stallion. One day, the beast bit my grandfather on the forearm. Maclean decided to teach the horse a lesson and demonstrate who was boss. He buried the animal, belly deep, in a dungheap, and proceeded to leather it about the head with his fists. When MacAulay emerged from the house and saw the treatment being meted out to his stallion, he was incensed. Words turned to blows. The result was predictable. MacAulay, who had the reputation of being a fair scrapper himself, ended up on the deck and John Maclean, wife and son, returned to Tiree in disgrace. Two more sons, Hughie and John Neil, were born there. It was Uncle Hughie who blamed my father for breaking his mother's heart by running away to sea at the age of fourteen. "Yes," he'd intone in a sepulchral voice, "when Neil left the island, she just turned her face to the wall and passed away."

I knew very little about Flora MacLellan. She had no Gaelic and never integrated either in Uist or Tiree. The film was faded, barely intelligible. There were many blank frames there. My own theory was that she did not die of a broken heart. Rather, she succumbed to some form of renal failure, a genetic weakness that claimed the life of my sister Lorna at the age of twenty-five.

Back on my scooter, there was no let-up in the filthy mirk. I decided to make for the chequered flag and relate to myself a couple of stories about *Anna Bheag*, Wee Annie, my maternal grandmother. After the drowning of her husband, she somehow managed to get word to Cladach Baleshare that my mother and my uncle Norman, who had been exiled to the home of *Peigi Thormoid*, Peggy daughter of Norman, their paternal grandmother, should come home to Glasgow immediately. (Weird, the way the same Christian names keep cropping up every second generation among the Gaels. It resembles Chinese ancestor-worship.)

My mother, who'd be about eleven at the time, and her brother dutifully returned to Mair Street and joined their siblings, who were complete strangers to them. From the off, she got into trouble. One Saturday, my granny asked her to take her youngest brother, Colin, outside *gu 'm faigheadh e osag gaoithe*, for a breath of fresh air. Reluctantly, I'm sure, she took the four-year-old out into the street. There, she was accosted by a girl her own age, Carrie McGee. (If they weren't 'Hielan' in Plantation at that time, they were Irish.)

"Come on, Peggy, and we'll go to the 'Imps'" – the Imperial Picture Palace – "and we'll watch the *Perils of Pauline*," Carrie said.

This was a silent film, with tinkly piano backing, featuring an attractive blonde who got into one bad scrape after another. Without even a backward glance at her young brother, my mother and Carrie went off to the cinema. While they gazed from the stalls, mouths agape, as Pauline was tied with chains to railway tracks with an express train thundering towards her, Wee Colin wandered off into Paisley Road West and promptly got lost. A policeman picked him up and, fortunately, a female neighbour recognized him as he started crying for his 'mammy', and exclaimed: "That's the wee boy MacKinnon, Constable. I know where he stays." Accordingly, the three of them, the woman, the policeman and a sobbing Colin, made for my granny's house in Mair Street.

Two hours later my mother swung into the close and was accosted by an irate Annag Bheag who was armed with a furled umbrella.

"Norman," my mother used to say, "that woman thrashed me across my . . . my buttocks and the backs of my legs with the umbrella up and down the close for a full twenty minutes. The bruising was so bad that I couldn't go to Rutland Crescent School for three days."

I took a perverse pleasure in this story. It proved to me that Peigi Bheag, that workaholic – frequently, in our house in Brand Street, a young woman would be standing on a chair in a slip: my mother, with a mouthful of pins, would be circling her, pinning paper patterns and swatches of material on her – hadn't always been endowed with the deep repressive Puritanism of the respectable working-class. She had been at one time a carefree and careless young girl.

Finally, there was my granny's first sighting of her future son-in-law. One Sunday evening, *Anna Bheag* had been spying from the bedroom window when she saw her daughter and a tall young man chatting at the corner of Mair Street and Paisley Road West.

"*Cò am fear mòr a bha bruidhinn riut shìos an sin?* Who was that big fellow who was talking to you down there?" she demanded.

"Oh, he's just a seaman we met up at the *Drochaid*" – the 'Hielanman's Umbrella' as they called it, where young Gaels performed a kind of tartan *paseo* every Sunday night – "and he's from Tiree," she replied in Gaelic. "But, mother, he went to school in Lochmaddy." This would be an attempt by my mother to persuade Granny that *Niall Mòr*, Big Neil, was almost one of our own, irrespective of the fact that Uist is a good five hours' sailing from Tiree.

Quick as a flash, granny said sneeringly, "*Nach e chaidh air an astar dìreach los gun ionnsaicheadh e mar a dhèanadh e cunntas*! Didn't he go some distance just so he'd learn how to do arithmetic!"

How about that from an uneducated *cailleach*, old woman?

The filth of these suburban roads was dense. My contractual arrangements with my Creator had gone awry on that evening. It was the way Sandra treated me that swept up my hair. But that was not going to happen, I realised. There was nothing for it but to do an about-turn and hope that the dirty haze that had settled on the city was dispelled slightly the nearer I got to the city centre. I was lucky. The traffic lights at Anniesland Cross abruptly poked through the soiled lumps of fog. From here I could make it home, but it would be a close thing. A nervy animal, urgent with only one purpose, I eventually, an hour later, parked the Lambretta at my mother's close at 191 Brand Street.

14

Gus

After the dissolution of my relationship with Ella I enjoyed a period devoid of romantic encumbrances. I also enjoyed my introduction to teaching. I was good at it. More to the point, I enjoyed having a good wad of money in my wallet.

One night, when I was toddling home from the flesh-pots of Govan, a car, a handsome old Sunbeam Talbot, drew up beside me and the driver, blurred by the film of dirt on the passenger window, hissed: "Pssst! Wanna buy some feelthy peectures?"

This was Gus Matheson, to whom I referred briefly in the chapter on my growing-up in Brand Street. His offer of a lift was accepted graciously by a tired and slightly emotional Norman. I sighed as we moved off, not in the direction of Ibrox, but towards the Anderston area of the city on the other side of the Clyde.

"Where are we going?" I said.

"For a drink," he said.

"Don't be daft, Gus," I said. "The pubs are all shut now."

"Pubs aren't the only places where drink is sold late on," Gus said.

"They're not?" I said.

"No," he said in what I thought was a slightly patronizing manner. "Listen – have you ever been to a shebeen?"

"No, no, never," I said with a nervous giggle.

"Well," he said firmly, "we're going to the house of an Italian lady, Mrs Gerrardi, over in Argyle Street. They know me there, and, once we're in, here's the deal: all drinks cost half a crown – whisky, rum vodka, brandy, wine, beer, it doesn't matter."

"I haven't much dough, Gus," I said hesitantly.

"That's okay, Norrie," he said magnanimously. "I'll stake you this time. I'm working as a Linesman with British Telecom and I'm pretty well off."

"Thanks, pal," I said. Then a sudden thought struck me. "What kind of people go to this . . . ah, shebeen?"

"Oh, the usual flotsam and jetsam," he said airily. "You know, housebreakers, off-duty taxi drivers, working girls who've scored earlier on with rich punters." He looked slyly across at me as he recited this last category. "You'll love it, Norrie."

This *was* getting exciting. My admiration for Gus's street smarts, however, was tinged with a hint of envy that he, as the Italians say, 'was coming out of the shop when I was barely going in'. Also, I resented the implication that the presence of prostitutes would be a turn-on for me. (Actually, it was.)

We were admitted to a room and kitchen two floors up in a tenement in Argyle Street. The décor was cosy, working-class: in what used to be a bed recess stood an over-stuffed sofa occupied by a blowsy middle-aged bottle-blonde. She beckoned me over and proceeded to cover my face in wet kisses. Her name was Lena, she told me, and she had had a good night on the game. Soon, Gus approached with a glass of clear spirit, and the next two hours passed in a haze of cigarette smoke and fumes of strong drink. I was in my element, and Gus seemed to be quite happy, talking animatedly with a leather-jacketed hoodlum with sideburns that proclaimed he was not a tax-paying citizen. Lena was very chatty, and I admit I enjoyed her company. The most risqué thing that happened that night was that she told me a joke which I found very funny. At the time.

"This young guy goes into a pub in the city centre," she said. "He sits on a stool at the bar next to a fat lady of about fifty-seven. That's mah age, Norrie. Ah'm fifty-seven as well. Anyway, they get talking and he buys her a couple of brandies and she gets really pally, you know, stroking his thigh, and leaning closer to the young guy."

At this point, Lena herself had a firm grip on the inside of my thigh.

"Hey, be gentle, lover," I said.

"Ye're aw right, son," Lena said. She had a lascivious smile on her painted lips: "Right," she said. "The old bird is making no secret that she fancies the young fella, and the young fella is getting really *hot*. 'Do you want to see me hame?' she whispers in his ear. 'Aye,' says the young guy, thinking – okay she's fifty-seven, but what the fuck! 'Aye, Ah'll see ye hame.' 'Do you fancy a Sportsman's Double?' she says. 'What the fuck's a Sportsman's Double?' he says. 'You know,' she says. 'A mother and daughter kinda thing.'

"The young guy is really horny now. 'Aye, Ah fancy that, hen,' he says. 'C'mon, we'll get a taxi to your gaff.'"

Lena had me in stitches as she mimed the young guy's ardour, all rapid movements of her tongue and excited panting. She continued, her voice rising in excitement: "Well, they get tae her hoose in Riddrie or some place. As soon as they're inside the door she takes her coat aff and stands at the bottom of the stairs. 'MUM?' she shouts. 'Can ye come doun the stairs and meet a young friend of mine?'"

Both of us dissolved in laughter. Aah, come on, you had to be there.

I was embraced by Lena and Mrs Gerrardi, who kissed me twice on the cheek at the door. "*Una bella festa, ragazzi,*" she said, and with many a merry ringing laugh we clattered down the stairs to the Sunbeam. We got home without incident.

He didn't have the looks of a matinee idol. What Gus had in abundance was confidence. I was sure he had never experienced a moment of self-doubt in his life.

Some of his exploits, a few witnessed by myself, and others related by reliable witnesses, were hair-raising in their recklessness. On one occasion, a Tuesday night, bored and without money, we drove in his works van to the Locarno Ballroom in Sauchiehall Street. We took various cables and electronic gadgets from the back of the van in full view of patrons who were patiently waiting to gain admittance. The scam was that we were pretending to be reporters from BBC Radio. Uncoiling a massive cable with some mensuration device at the end of it passing as a microphone, the bold Gus marched boldly up to the line of waiting patrons, and exclaimed in a fruity Kelvinside accent: "Make way for the BBC. Make way, please. We're conducting interviews with people on the street. Want to find out what you think of Glasgow's Licensing Laws."

Now, some of the people in the queue were very unsavoury-looking characters indeed. The lads were dressed in long, drape jackets with velvet collars, narrow pegged trousers, and to a man they wore suede shoes in various hues distinguished by thick crepe soles. Most of the guys had scars or 'Mars Bars' on their faces, and the thought asserted itself unbidden in my brain, that were our cover to be blown, we would undoubtedly face dire consequences from these toughs. Undeterred, Gus approached a couple – a pseudo-gangster and his lightly clad gum-chewing moll – at the head of the line.

"Excuse me, sir . . . and madam," he intoned in a voice like a baritone saxophone. "What do you think of the present Licensing Laws in the city?"

"Whit dae ye mean, ya bampot?" the shifty-eyed youth said.

"Well, you know," Gus said. "The pubs close at nine-thirty at present. Do you think that responsible drinkers really have enough time to enjoy and savour a . . um, wee refreshment before coming to places like this?"

"Too true, mate," the Teddy Boy said. "It's a diabolical liberty, so it is . . . um, sir. You've goat tae get yer kerryoot at all costs, and your bird his tae plank it in her handbag before ye come here."

His partner patted her shoulder bag with lurid red fingernails. "Goat it right here, mister," she said.

The voice of the first interviewee, who was still protesting at what he obviously considered a social injustice, was being drowned out by an increasingly loud chorus of affirmations from others in the queue. *Right ye urr, mate! . . . You tell him, mucker! . . .*

"The way I myself see it," Gus said, inclining his head towards the 'microphone', "it's high time the city fathers, and the police, revised their policy on extended hours. Why should they dictate that respectable, law-abiding citizens of the second city of the Empire should be forbidden to seek for themselves . . . RECREATION?"

The entire group, with not one respectable, law-abiding citizen in their midst, exploded with cackles, whoops and guffaws . . . *Oh, aye! . . . Fuck the polis! . . .Whoee . . . heh, heghggh . . .* From out of the confused uproar came the chant: RE-CRE-AY-SHUN FUR RA PEE-PULL! RE-CRE-AY-SHUN FUR RA PEE-PULL! RE-CRE-AYSHUN FUR RA PEE-PULL!

To my horror I realized that Gus wasn't satisfied with causing a near riot.

"You'll all get fifteen pounds each," he said. "That is, if we use the piece in our programme. Just give your names and addresses to my assistant, the sound-mixer, over by the van. Yeah, the guy with the white face standing with the clipboard over there. That's N . . . er, Nigel."

Damn! I thought. We couldn't make a getaway until I wrote down the particulars of some thirty people – maybe more than that, as additional spectators, drawn by the uproar and the promise of fifteen pounds, were joining the host of extras. Soon, to the accompaniment of snorts and snuffles from Gus in the driver's seat, I was busily taking down dictation from the conscientious hedonists, all the time fearing that one of those greedy bastards would ask me for ID.

Eventually it was all over. Could we leave now – at last? Gus took one hand from the steering wheel and waved it from the open window of the van, and before taking off, in a gesture of benediction said: "Thank you, thank you, brothers and sisters. Remember – Jesus loves you."

I couldn't believe it. *Jesus loves you!* Quivering with relief, I huddled in the passenger seat, casting from time to time reproachful glances at the Caucasian Sammy Davis Junior beside me.

"Thanks, Gus," I said, my voice dripping with insincerity. "We could have ended up getting plunged back there. Do you know that?"

"I know," he said simply.

And that was the key to his fearless behaviour. Everything he undertook had to be charged with a powerful undercurrent of danger. This adrenaline rush was highly contagious. I myself quite quickly became addicted – in a vicarious way – to the thrills provided by Gus.

Gus was a storyteller such as might have beguiled Odysseus. The exploit that earned Gus the most admiration was his scam with the 'Bedtime Bazooka'. During his National Service in the Corps of Signals he was posted to Egypt. Because of his natural athleticism and outstanding eye to foot co-ordination, he was chosen as a striker in a British Army football eleven who were scheduled to play a team from the Royal Navy in Alexandria. He was the only non-professional footballer in his team. I daresay he could have played professionally if he had been so inclined, but as a dedicated party-boy he had no aspirations to follow in the footsteps of his father, who, before the war, had played professionally for Queen of the South.

Unfortunately, or fortunately for Gus, he was seriously injured in the second half of the game after a particularly brutal tackle from an enraged sailor. He was stretchered off the park with the front of his right thigh pressed against his upper body. In short, he couldn't straighten the leg.

"It wisnae sore," he told me, "but it was weird, Norrie. I was immediately wheeched away to a field hospital wearing nothing but shorts, football boots and the team strip. I stayed there for a couple of days, and then they gave me a galabiya to wear and transferred me by airplane to a military hospital in Malta.

"Once there, I was fitted out with a pair of crutches, and I spent most days hirpling about the ward on them, still dressed in the Egyptian robe. I looked like the Mad Mullah, but this was a good thing. You see, I had no Army kit, and since I was kidding on that I'd lost my memory, they couldn't identify me. 'Ah, yes,' this great poofter of a psychologist said to his students who followed him everywhere, 'here we have a classic case of retroactive inhibition. The psychic shock induced by his accident – by the way, we don't know with certainty how he sustained his injury: he remembers nothing of his past life – has wiped his memory clean.' What a load of bull!

"But, you've got to believe me, the best thing the medics in Malta did for me was to introduce me to this mad electronic device that was meant to prevent wastage of the muscles in my right leg. It was just a wee black box, about the size of a twenty packet of fags, with two leads with suction pads on their ends coming out of it. The idea was, you attached the pads to your thigh. There was a round dial and a rocker switch on top of the box – the dial to control the charge and the rocker switch to turn the gadget on. When you pushed the thing on – *Whooeee, baby, right to the moon!* – you got a jolt of electricity that made your leg straighten with a kind of painful jerk. These half-wits left me with the machine with strict instructions to use it at least four times a day. Well, I did, and maybe it did me some good. But never mind, I had other plans for my new toy.

"It wasn't long before I put them into action. Galabiya flowing in the wind, I swung myself on the crutches down to the dockside bars of Valetta. They were all crowded with sailors on shore leave. In the first one I went into I captured a group of tipsy matelots. Oh, I came on soft in my spiel. Coughing and spluttering in cod Arabic – you know how those rag-heads always talk as though they've been eating cats – *staanuchwyaahuchwyaahhh* – I socked it to them.

"'Gentlemen,' I said, 'you know how sometimes when you're in bed with a woman you have a spot of difficulty in . . . er, rising to the occasion – especially if you've had a little too much to drink. Worry not. Help is at hand. I, Doctor Hasaan Entebbe, one-time former personal physician to the late King Farouk, have the solution to any problems of . . . ah, a sexual nature you may experience. I have pleasure in presenting to you my own personal invention, THE BEDTIME BAZOOKA!'

"The sailors stood there, suddenly interested, in a tight little clump, most of them thinking – Aahhh, this might be the answer. 'How much for a go at your 'Bedtime Bazooka', Doc?' one guy with a London accent said. 'Two shillings for ten seconds' worth,' I said. 'It won't hurt, but it'll do wonders for your love life.'

"The guy who asked the price stepped forward and handed me a two-shilling piece. 'What do I have to do?' he asked, eyeing the black box and the leads suspiciously. 'Relax, my very good friend,' I said. 'Just grip these pads in your hands and we'll start you off with a mild buzz.'

"The grinning sailor took the pads in his fists and nodded for me to start the treatment. I footered around with the dial, turning it back and forth until I thought that I'd got a safe voltage. Didn't have a clue what I was doing, but all this faffing around added to the suspense. 'Ready?' I said. 'Ready,' he said in a squeaky voice. Poor guy was sweating bullets. I flipped the switch and immediately the sailor began to convulse like someone in a detox ward . . . *bizzumbiz-zumbizzum* . . . went the machine and . . . *chittachittachittachitta* . . . went the sailor for fully ten seconds.

"The guy had obviously been given a mild electric shock. He was pink with pleasure as his mates congratulated him for having been the first to subject himself to the 'Bedtime Bazooka'.

"I cleaned up, Norrie. Bigtime," Gus continued. "See, the combination of drink, masculine pride and the plausible promise of an enhanced sex life had the Pommies queuing up to be blasted by the 'Bedtime Bazooka'. Of course, what you've got to remember as well is that anybody who chooses to enlist in the Royal Navy is by definition a thicko. Did it work? I've no idea. What's for sure is that nobody was going to complain. 'Excuse me, Doctor, I tried your "Bazooka" and I couldn't perform.' That was never going to happen with those macho men.

"Well, I set up a circuit of around a dozen bars in and round about the red-light district, and I'll tell you, it was a poor night when I didn't clear at least fifteen pounds. That's no' bad going for a one-legged Egyptian with no memory."

Actually, the leg, though straight now, gave him intermittent problems all the time we hung out together. He had shoulder pains and bouts of Tennis Elbow too. Like all aspirants to physical perfection, he suffered from numerous injuries incurred in weight-training and endurance running.

I myself didn't go in for that kind of nonsense. Exercise for me was confined to weekly swimming sessions in the municipal baths in Clynder Street, Govan. Oh, and I considered my playing the Great Highland Bagpipe to be a form of exercise. It *is* a very demanding, physical instrument. My focus was mainly on breathing and relaxation. I didn't go in for the punishing regime that Gus and others like him endured on a daily basis. You know, where you hang for hours from wall-bars and beams, climb ropes and lift weights until your entire body becomes a mass of knotted muscles that have to be unravelled in Casualty.

I regarded Gus and his fellow addicts with detached amusement on the few occasions I accompanied them to the Health and Fitness Centre. I used to sneer as they struggled with barbells, grunting like wild animals with the effort required to hoist them over their heads. *Aaaghrrr! Aaaghrrr!* – they would roar. If I was ever tempted to emulate them, I used to lecture myself with my own words of wisdom. "Norrie, my lad," I used to whisper softly, "if you have to lift something – anything – that makes you go, *Aaaghrrr! Aaaghrrr!* there's only one thing to do. Put the fucking thing down!"

At this point in the chronology of our friendship I appear to have broken down. My diaries of this period, particularly when describing a grand tour of Europe in the summer of 1962, have been encrusted with some kind of liquid. We took a ferry from, I think, Folkestone to Ostend. Details are a little hazy because of the vast amount of beer we drank on the voyage.

Anyway, it was dark when we reached Ostend. We found ourselves in a big pub where a stand-up comedian was socking it to an appreciative audience of *Flamands*. The guy was obviously to the taste of those well-fed Belgian folk, and my competitive instincts were aroused. Before you could say *Mannequin Pis* I was on the stage belting out 'The Smith of Chilliechassie', a driving reel played at speed. I got a good hand from the crowd and effusive congratulations from the comic. I remember thinking as he shook my hand that some day I might have a go at this comedy racket. Oh, it was coming round the mountain all right, though I didn't know it at the time. One of my unvoiced gripes about piping was a nagging suspicion that the instrument itself formed a barrier between me and my audience. How much better it would be, I mused, if I dispensed with the bagpipe altogether and connected with a potential audience using nothing more than gestures, facial expressions and voice! My chance was coming, though not for another few years yet.

We took an overnight train from Ostend to Cologne, where we stayed with a middle-aged married couple, Hans and Ursula Schmidt, for about a week before taking off on a drunken pilgrimage to the south.

The only firm recollection I retain of Cologne is of a guy being thrown out of a café one night. It appeared that he had been sooking away at a glass of coca-cola laced with aspirin. I had thought this was another urban myth – you know, a cheap concoction that'd give you a buzz – but I have to admit the guy was completely rubbered when he was eventually persuaded to leave by a brawny waitress. Of course, perhaps the German was staving drunk when he entered the café, and his boxed treat would have had little effect on him. Nevertheless, I found myself mentally filing this little trick with a view perhaps to employing it myself in the future. Oddly enough, I have never been desperate enough to medicate myself in this fashion. Yet. I've just been lucky, I guess.

Eventually, we reached Koblenz, and almost immediately got a lift from a US Army Captain who took us to the charming city of Trier. My recollections of the following stages of our journey are pretty nebulous, mainly through over-indulgence in the Moselle wine of the area. Somehow, we made it to Luxembourg, where, in a bar, we got chatting to a Corporal in the Royal Canadian Air Force. On discovering that we were Scottish and that I carried a set of bagpipes with me, he became ecstatic.

"Gee, guys, this is a blast," he said. "My wife's folk are from Scotland – MacDonalds. MacDonalds of Glencoe."

"Is that right?" Gus said. "I bet your wife would just love to hear Norrie here playing 'Women of the Glen' for her."

"Oh, boy," our new Canadian friend said. "She'd adore that. Can you do it? Look – why don't you spend the night at our place? We've loads of room."

"Could we get a shower?" I said. "We both stink to high heaven."

"Of course," our new friend said. "*Mi casa es su casa*. That's what the PRs in Toronto say: Your house is your . . . um, my house . . . ah, fuck it! Let's go."

It turned out that the Royal Canadian Air Force base was actually on the Belgian-French border in a tiny place called Longwyon.

Deposited by taxi on the uniform streets of the base, we marched, all three of us, to the strains of 'Scotland the Brave' or some other piece of piping kitsch, until we reached a brick semi-detached house, no different from neighbouring dwellings, which was the home of Corporal Bill Jackson.

With drunken pride, he loudly confided that his wee, red-haired, almost-Scottish wife would welcome us with open arms.

Well, she didn't. The outside door opened suddenly, and framed in the doorway was this huge middle-aged lady with grey hair and soft and shapeless figure, whose looks, red hair and all, had deserted her. She seemed to have surrendered to the ageing process without a fight.

But she was not without fight. With a perfectly delivered right hook that Tyson would have been proud of to the left jaw of Bill, she decked him, leaving him sitting up, dazed, on the flagstones of the garden path.

"Get in the breeze, you drunken sot!" she bawled. "And take these two bums with you!"

Alors, que faire? Bill picked himself up, grinned apologetically and strode off up the street.

"Told you," he said almost proudly, "she was a feisty little Scotch dame, didn't I?"

"Where are we going now?" I said.

"To my best friend's place," he said. "Frank Durant's his name, and he's a corporal too. It's just about – *aabaaoot* – two minutes' walk away."

When we arrived at Corporal Durant's quarters, the door was opened by a very well put-together Mme Durant.

"Come in, Bill," she said graciously. "And you guys can come in too. He's in the lounge."

When we entered the living room, Durant was sprawled in a leather lounger with an array of Labatt beer bottles, mostly empty, on a low table in front of him. It soon became clear that he and his wife, long-legged and slim Sylvie, were experiencing some marital difficulties. Whenever she came in from the kitchen with more beers she served me first, contriving to brush her fingers against mine in teasing foreplay. After a while it was decided that we'd visit the Servicemen's Club on the base. I was flattered when Sylvie linked arms with me and announced that she was coming with us. Yeah, I know, in situations like that, at that particular stage of my life, the body always reacted first.

In the crowded little bar in the club, Jim Reeves was groaning in supplication from six speakers.

Put your sweet lips a little closer to the phone.
Let's pretend that we're together, all alone.
I'll tell the man to turn the jukebox way down lo-o-o-ww,
And you can tell your friend there with you he'll have to go-o-o.

Half a dozen couples were swaying in time to the music on the postage-stamp-sized dance floor. I escorted the delectable Sylvie to a spot as far away from my three companions as I could manage, and there, enveloped in a bubble of privacy, we swayed on stiff legs to the slow pulse. Sylvie, who was technically an 'older woman' – she'd be in her early thirties, I figured – put her hand on the back of my neck, pulling my lips towards her smooth bare shoulders. As I sang along with the country singer I felt myself being drawn to the warm comfort she offered. She was, of course, married, but never mind, she was ready to go, and I found this illicit activity incredibly exciting.

Next, back to the table, hand in hand, to find no sign of Gus or Bill. Instead a couple of Military Policemen, tall, crew-cut, blond, with piercing blue eyes, like they had just stepped out from an episode of *Baywatch*, were speaking softly to drunk Frank. "Come on, Corporal," one of the cops said, "you know, and we know, you're well over the limit." "Yeah," his buddy said. "Let's all go down to the guardhouse and you can sleep it off. You're in no condition to drive a car." The tone hardened. "Move!" the first cop barked.

Frank's despairing cry of "The car, Sylvie. Take the car home, darlin'," rang in our ears as he was hustled from the club by the two cops. We were alone at last.

"Can you drive, Norman?" Sylvie said, that lover's glow in her eyes.

"Of course," I said confidently, though in truth I had a superstitious dread of the Durants' automatic-drive Opel.

Sylvie grabbed me just outside the door and kissed me. Hot and breathless, I clasped her shoulders to keep my balance.

"God, you're beautiful," I said. "Let's go."

After a lot of kangaroo hopping – I had left the shift in Drive, and when the engine petered out, as it did lots of times because I wasn't giving it enough throttle, I resorted to a series of jump-starts – in a familiar nerved-up state meaning sex was on the horizon, I finally carried Sylvie over the threshold of her kitchen door.

Soon we drank from various assorted glasses of beer, rum, wine, a giddy mix of tastes in my mouth and the surprise of fumes rising like hot wires through the nasal passages and up into the skull, and the yet more profound sensation of heat, burning, going down, coating my throat with fire. I took the glass from my lips and placed it carefully on the work-top and kissed her, hard. I gripped her shoulders, hard. As she gripped me – my arms, my back. Suddenly and passionately. Sylvie as eager as I. As hungry.

I had never confronted a female as direct in her appetites as Sylvie. We entered the bedroom, me first, Sylvie holding the door open, and started kissing beside the bed.

"Hurry up, Norman," she whispered as she lay down, kicking off her sandals and drawing off her jeans and panties, while she shrugged her way out of her peasant blouse and unsnapped her bra. Naked myself, I lowered my body and placed mouth, chest, belly, thighs and feet against mouth, breasts, belly, thighs and feet. Then I moved into her, swiftly and easily. Soon she started to moan, low and steady, as I grabbed onto her thrashing hips and rode, rode, rode. I began to lose it as, in my pumping frenzy, my consciousness lurched towards extinction.

She told me, cradling me in her arms, "Norman, honey, thank you. You're pretty damn good, you know."

"You're pretty good yourself, Sylvie," I said.

Her face suddenly split into a grin. "I hope," she said, "you have a brilliant time down in the South of France. I'm sure you'll make love to loads of young girls on the beaches there."

With wifely solicitude she kissed me awake much later. I was a man on the move. After a quick shower, I dressed quickly in clothes borrowed from Frank's wardrobe. I had to find Gus and get out of Longwyon before her husband was released from the guardhouse.

After a quick farewell kiss on the doorstep, I made my way to the outskirts of the village, where, under a sign pointing in the direction of Metz, Gus lay fast asleep. He and Bill had spent the night in another of Bill's friends' houses and I made no mention of Sylvie and our passionate love-making session.

By way of Metz, Nancy, Dijon, and Chalon-sur-Saone we progressed in short rides as far as Lyon. There we pushed the boat out and dined on steak, French fries and wine. The extracts relating to Marseilles and Cassis are impossible to decipher.

All I remember is Gus performing a death-defying dive from the corniche to a crescent-shaped beach about three hundred feet below. I had had enough. "Gus," I said, "it's over. Let's go back home."

We turned round, and as we walked all the way back to Marseilles, I reflected that Gus would never change and would always act first and think later. This suppression of inner objections, feelings of cowardice or confusion, was beyond me, and I vowed that I would never again try to play with the big boys. Big girls and big drams, yes; boys, no.

It should be clear from the above paragraphs that, while I still retained some morsels of common sense, I was attracted to the reckless behaviour of my pal. This diversion into fond recollection reveals a facet of my personality that disturbs me. I sought intensity of experience and I knew instinctively I wouldn't find it on my own. There was always a hope that I would find it with others. I found it with Gus. What I have learned in this affectionate account is that I *thought* I was a tough guy, but I was clinically deluded.

15

Playing with Fire

"Mr Maclean," this gorgeous young Prefect said as she loomed over me, "may I have this dance, please?" The occasion was the Senior School Christmas dance on the last day of term. This was what was called 'Ladies' Choice'. I was sitting alone on a stool near the bandstand with my hands in my pockets, surveying the rotating herd of adolescents with a superior smirk on my face. In truth, I was half-smugged because I had hidden a half bottle of whisky in the pocket of my duffel coat in the staffroom, and had been nipping away at it all night.

I stood up and there followed an embarrassing foot-shuffling silence from me. I fixed the girl with a disbelieving smile. Okay, I'm a young probationary teacher and she's a pupil. But, after all, there were only four years between us with regard to respective ages. I believed in each of my lives. This time I'd be the good-natured sport who enjoyed playing with fire. Her invitation made my heart bang away madly. Now, I've always been a womanizer, drawn compulsively to female flesh. And there was an abundance of that stuff before me. All of these thoughts, compressed into a millisecond, flipped through my mind.

Margo McGougain – everybody, pupils and staff, had noticed this lass – was a sexy big number . . . luminous skin, a great mane of chestnut brown hair, lovely sensual lips and the finest pair of big – and I mean really big – breasts I've ever had the pleasure of viewing. She was wearing a white cotton blouse with a drawstring that tightened round her proud bosom.

I knew better, but I couldn't help myself, and we took to the dance floor to perform a modern waltz. During these sweeping gyrations she rubbed my back. She awakened desires in me as she held me in her consuming warmth.

"Are you going to walk me home?" she whispered in my ear. Everything about this girl exuded mischief.

147

"Okay," I replied casually. Jesus, this was a no-no. Suppose any-body noticed us slipping out together – a teacher and a pupil – but I had already lost my mind to this forward young girl. I wanted to know what she was up to, just so I could figure out what kind of dance step she'd oblige me to do later on.

Once we reached the entrance to her parents' flat at Paisley Road West she grinned broadly and said, "Do you fancy going into the back close for a bit?"

"Not half," I responded with alacrity.

We stood face to face against the wall of the tenement that over-looked a drying green. She gripped my waist without warning. I heard myself ask, "Do you mind, Margo, if I warm my hands inside your coat?"

"Of course not, Mr Maclean," she said, kissing my mouth, draw-ing her tongue along the edge of my lips.

There were a lot of unruly and unsavoury things rattling around in my mind. I said, stroking her breasts, "You know, Margo, I'm going to regret this, but I've got to see you again."

We made arrangements to go shopping in Paisley the following day, Saturday. I bought her a chunky sweater in Marks and Spencer, and in the evening, after a steak meal, I took her with me to a ceilidh run by the Paisley Highlanders. (I had started to sing, semi-professionally, at various little Highland gatherings throughout the Central Belt.)

On the Sunday night I had dinner with the family and I twinkled like . . . well, if not a star, certainly a night-light. The courtship would certainly have become more intense but for the fact that I was off to Barra on the Monday in pursuit of a girl from Brevig, Katie Ann Haggerty. I'd like to stress in mitigation that, apart from attending a police-sponsored dance in a hotel in Gordon Street in the city centre where we had a photograph taken, I didn't take the affair with Margo further until she had left school and was taking a kind of gap year working as an assistant librarian in Elder Park, Govan.

I got on well with her father, Bill McGougain, and his wife. Bill was an ex-cop from the Govan Division, based in Orkney Street, and because his people hailed from the Lochgilphead area he never tired of listening to my rendition of the English language Argyllshire song, 'The Green Hills of Islay'.

Very soon, after her parents had retired to their bedroom, we got into a routine where Margo would spread herself on the couch and summon me over to join her. I'll never forget the night she unhooked her brassiere to reveal billowing breasts with honey-coloured aureoles and nipples like little buttons. I kissed, sucked and bit. She cradled my head in the crook of her arm, and with her other hand she reached down to the zip on my pants. Oh, God be round about me, I was happy, never as happy as I was then, lips, tongue and teeth all working overtime. Her parents could not hear my soft moans as she swung into the final strokes of my coming. No one could hear my final plaintive cry.

At the beginning of my courtship I thought I had found the girl who one day would be my wife. Until, that is . . . Christ, here we go again . . . that cursed afternoon session. A slightly rosy soft focus comes into my mind of the two of us together in the flat at Paisley Road West one Saturday afternoon. Mum and Dad were off visiting friends somewhere and we had the house to ourselves. I was scribbling in a notepad and she was smiling benevolently at me as she looked up from her knitting. Suddenly, she clutched at me. Hot, breathless, so hard that I was pushed into the back of the couch. She said, "God, Norman, you're so beautiful! I love you."

"I . . . I'm very fond of you. I love you, too," I lied. "Fuck it," my internal voice whispered – I hated being trapped like this. I had to confront difficult issues, and I much preferred the mindless ecstasy of ejaculation under her skilled fingers. I knew what was coming and I was convinced it would be a kind of Rubicon for me. I didn't figure just yet on having a co-skipper in the voyage of life.

"Norman," she said, "why do you think I'm dressed in my house-coat at three o'clock in the afternoon?"

"To relax and be comfortable?" I ventured tentatively, playing Mickey the Dunce.

"To make love," she announced. "Come on, then." The intensity of her gaze frightened me, because it reminded me of a slow glide towards death.

"Wait, Margo," I said. "Let's think about this."

She stood abruptly, extending her hand. "Come through to the bedroom, darling," she said. "Mummy and Daddy won't be home for hours yet."

I rose stiffly from the couch and plodded along by her side. Mine seemed to be a kind of slow march. This was what it was like to be throttled by fear.

"I think at times, Norman," she said, "you don't seem to want me. Is that right?"

"No, no, no . . ." I stammered. "Margo, you're just a kid."

"I am, huh?" she snorted indignantly. "I'm a woman. Look." She shucked off the top of the housecoat and held her glorious breasts in the palms of her hands, proffering their ripeness to me.

"Are they the breasts of a kid?" she simpered.

"Well, no," I admitted. "They're magnificent, Margo."

Next, she dropped the entire garment to the carpet. There she stood, entirely naked, in front of me. What a body! Her curvaceous hips and well toned thighs framed a truly vast and dense bush.

"Is this the body of a kid, Mr Maclean?" she asked with the assurance of somebody who knows she is all woman. She spread her fingers wide and buried them in her hairy crotch.

"My God," I exclaimed, "you've got more hair down there than me."

"Let's see, shall we?" she suggested, and proceeded slowly to take my clothes off until we both stood naked gazing at ourselves in the dressing table mirror. After a fairly long time she laid her lovely hand on my penis and led me to the bed.

Under the sheets, not surprisingly, I had an erection. The subsequent coupling was a disaster. I entered her in triumph and as I did she exclaimed. My excitement mounted and I felt her inward tightening. I was in a pumping frenzy as my consciousness staggered towards oblivion. Suddenly, I heard her gasp: "Norman Maclean, don't you dare come inside me." That's women for you. You never know on which side they're going to start doing their *pas-de-bas*. I didn't know what was going on in her mind and wouldn't hazard a guess even today. I hastily rolled off her, put my clothes back on and said, "Goodbye, then, Margo," plunging my hands into the pockets of my trousers. I turned on my heel and made for the front door. Naked, she followed me, screeching and wailing.

"Norman," she sobbed, "you just can't walk out like this. Darling, it's early yet. I was going to make *penne* with that Irish stew sauce. I'd like to be doing that, caring for you, for the rest of my life. Pet, why don't we get married and I'll be the mother of your children."

"Dream on, dunderhead," I shouted as I walked down the stairs.

"Norman," I heard her cry, ever more faintly, as I descended, "I love you, don't leave me."

"Ah," I said bitterly, "get more fibre in your diet, you fantasist."

There is a fine line between drama and melodrama. The final soap-operatic quality of this scene was a direct consequence of the pair of us having watched hours of television while waiting for her parents to retire. As I toddled home I asked myself why I didn't put up more of a fight right at the start. There was more than a touch of greed in my decision to go along with her, as I see it now. Self esteem leaked out of me like air from a porous pipe bag. I was guiltily aware that I had incurred an erotic debt which could be called in at any moment.

Of course I went back to her, and for a year and a half I suffered a kind of premature middle-aged angst. I seemed to be locked into a treadmill of repetition. When it suited me, or when I ran out of money in the pub, I'd stagger into Margo's parents' house, half drunk most of the time, and babble for most of the night. After watching television for a while, her parents would go to bed, and Margo and I would start the heavy petting again.

I recall one exchange we had after one of our steamy sessions. "You know, Norman," she said wistfully, "I think you want to have your cake and eat it."

"That's right, child," I replied. "Who wouldn't want to have his cake and eat it? Am I going to waltz into the baker's, order an expensive sponge cake, pay handsomely for it and announce to the counter hands, 'I have my cake, but I don't want to eat it. I want *other people* to eat it,' eh?" I had never been able to make sense of this stupid proverb.

Some nights, if I had money, I wouldn't go out at all except to buy Scotch and drink it alone in my room. I was constantly anaesthetizing myself with alcohol, buying a few hours of oblivion at the cost of feeling the next morning as if my head had been stuffed with cotton wool during the night.

My ability to teach properly was being eroded, too. When I started off, I enjoyed the work. I indulged my thespian talents: I had a captive and mostly appreciative audience who enjoyed my shtick, and I genuinely believed that the body of knowledge which elders are obliged to impart to succeeding generations was truly important. Though I say it myself, I used to be pretty good at this game. I'd write little playlets for the pupils to enact. And I didn't neglect grammar and spelling either. I've always believed that the foundation of stable bilingualism is literacy. Today, most Gaelic speakers are non-literate, and this is apparent in the continuity scripts I had to correct when I worked in Grampian Television and Scottish Television. The presenters and continuity announcers at the BBC are severely limited in vocabulary and authentic idiom, too. I suppose that's why I've had four Gaelic language novels published to date and am working on a fifth at present. Unless bilingual Gaelic speakers become literate, the language will remain the prattle of the hearth.

After the failed attempt at penetrative sex with Margo, my attitude towards the pupils changed. One disturbing feature of my behaviour in school was the ease with which I lost my temper, particularly with high-spirited boys. At Bellahouston Academy, staff wore gowns and I'd be bustling round this Victorian pile with my rather thick Lochgelly draped over my left shoulder. And I wasn't shy about administering corporal punishment with the strap either. I used to make jokes on the slightest pretext at the expense of some miserable spotty youth. "Do you work in a circus, boy, or do you always dress like a clown?" I'd bellow. Yes, yes, I knew jokes were a disguised form of aggression. What was especially disturbing was the disgust I felt towards myself when I indulged in this brutal behaviour. Behind the thin rationale that discipline had to be maintained at all costs, there were stabs of pleasure to be obtained from beating these boys who, I knew, would never fight back. There was a narrow margin between the gratuitous cruelty of corporal punishment and righteous indignation. I supposed that this was how my father felt when he chastised me.

After about a year of this less than happy time, I decided to emigrate to Florida. I had resigned from an unrewarding teaching job and accepted a post as manager of a citrus plantation in Tampa. A citrus plantation! Though I knew a bit about growing potatoes and turnips, I had no experience of citrus fruits. MacMillan, my sponsor, however, was oddly reassuring when I had expressed misgivings over the transatlantic telephone.

It had started during the school summer holidays the previous year. A minister of the Church of Scotland, the Rev. Somerled MacMillan, who had a high profile in Gaelic circles – he had compiled a well-regarded collection of the poems of a South Uist bard, Donald MacIntyre, under the title of *Sporan Dhòmhnaill*, Donald's Purse – invited me on a jaunt with American and Canadian visitors from the Clan MacMillan Society of North America. My duties, for a period of two weeks, were not arduous – play reveille on the bagpipe in the morning before breakfast, and pipe the guests into dinner in the evenings in the various well-appointed hotels we visited throughout our tour of the Highlands. Sometimes I relieved the Rev. Somerled at the microphone at the front of the bus, and I'd regale the rapt tourists with largely fictitious glosses on the landmarks and ruins en route. Singing, lying and piping, I enjoyed a pleasant tour, travelling first class all the way and with generous pay at the end of it. I knew it was all an act, though I had always found my acts enjoyable – pedantic teacher, hard man, funny guy, singer, Scottish historian. I was able to be a good anything, if it was only part-time.

One American, a Mr MacMillan from Florida, seemed to be taken with me. One night this well-padded old Cracker invited me for a nightcap in the comfortable cocktail lounge of an upmarket hotel in Grantown-on-Spey. He placed his malt whisky on a low table, cocked his head and gave me a long, fixed stare, the way a person does when he is about to say something of far-reaching importance.

"I *jes* was wondering, Norman," he drawled, "if you ever – *evuh* – considered emigrating to the US."

"No," I admitted, though I was now considering the new idea with considerable interest.

"You'd do well in my country," he said. "You have good appearance, you're educated and extremely articulate for your age. Above all, boy, you're the right colour – *culah*."

I was briefly flushed with a warm sense of approbation. Over the succeeding days I convinced myself that another main chance was on the horizon.

In late night conversations, employing tones of assertive command, MacMillan of the piercing blue eyes cajoled and flattered me. I learned that this ageing country boy was immensely wealthy and influential in Florida. He wasn't kidding when he offered to obtain for me the coveted 'Green Card' all foreigners needed for employment in the US.

"*Unnh-unmh-unnnnhhhhhh*," he'd sigh. "It's cool, Norman. Senor Gonzales, my foreman who runs the place, will keep you right – *ryutt*. He's Cuban and he keeps the negroes – *niggras* – on their toes."

So, in the autumn of 1963, I took off for Windsor, Ontario, on my way to conquering the New World.

16
Florida Interlude

The line at Immigration in Buffalo Greyhound was a long one. Mine was a slow march as I shuffled forward towards the stout black officer whose fat backside spread like butter over an aluminium stool, visible through the glass sides of the kiosk-like booth over which he presided. He was conversing with a middle-aged woman, whom I pegged as being Greek. She shivered in her cheap threadbare coat as the fat man questioned her, and confessed loudly: "Don't know *Eenglish* too good."

This was going to take a while.

I studied the queue, looking for the most likely foreigner who would speak up and get things moving. But nobody made a movement or said a word.

Well, should I? Did I dare? I was the smartest-dressed and youngest person waiting for the counter to be free. I looked positively mediaeval in my Maclean tartan kilt, green tweed jacket and fawn-coloured 'Balmoral' headgear. I was also getting a little buzz from the cans of beer I had been steadily sucking from since I left Toronto in the early afternoon. It was 21.25 and the connecting bus to Miami didn't leave until 23.00 hours. I had plenty of time. Nevertheless, I found myself pushing up to the front and saying in a deep baritone voice:

"Excuse me, Sir," I crooned, in a carefully modulated voice designed to impress upon the officer that I had complete mastery over his own language. "I was wondering if – the thing is – we could – you know, hurry things up here . . ."

The black guy turned and stared at me through narrowed eyes. "You're gonna get your turn," he barked. "Now get back in line."

Nevertheless, he completed my own inspection rather quickly, and I soon found myself seated on plastic in a low-slung Departure Lounge with my pipe case at my feet. The hermetic silence of my long journey south from Canada was driving me crazy. I needed to talk to somebody . . . anybody.

Then, in the middle of the raggedy loungers who dozed in their chairs, surrounded by damaged luggage and plastic bags, I saw him. He was a skinny, fortyish man with a prominent Adam's apple, shiny-faced, and he wore a grubby seersucker suit. He would do. Without thinking or rehearsing what I was going to say, I rose, grabbed my pipe-case and sauntered across the concourse to where he stood gazing at the ever-changing lettering and figures on the Departures and Arrivals board.

"Hi, sport," I said jauntily. "I crave a favour . . ." Where this quaint locution came from I do not know. *Crave a favour*! Give yourself a break, Norman.

"Will you keep an eye on my bagpipes, please, while I make a phone call?" I said politely. The man ignored me as if I were a beggar. But why? I was dressed in full fig and I imagined my rig-out and my Sir Harry Lauder accent would stimulate his curiosity. Then, I'd get a chance to dazzle him with the wide spectrum of my views on North America. But no: he shuffled sideways, all the time gazing fixedly over my head.

"Unh-hunh," he grunted.

Leaving the pipe-case at his feet, I strode purposefully towards a bank of telephones on a wall about sixty feet away. I had no intention of phoning anyone. I picked up a receiver and pretended to be in conversation, all the time keeping watch on the skinny man. Apart from prodding the case with the tip of his broadly welted shoe a couple of times, he hardly moved from the spot where I'd left him.

After a decent interval I marched smartly over, and with hollow volubility started to babble:

"This is really civil of you, Sir," I gushed. "I'm truly grateful to you for standing guard over the precious bagpipe of a poor lost soul from Scotland." I burst into song:

"Bonnie Scotland, I adore thee,

Though I'm far across the sea . . ."

I was merely observing the common decencies, no? I continued to amp up what I hoped was my country charm, unnecessarily as it turned out, for he cut me off.

"You're from Scotland, are you?" he said.

"Spot on, Sherlock," I snapped back, indicating with sweeping arm gestures my Highland outfit and the bagpipes. I wasn't going to have a conversation with this retard. Despite being provided with numerous hints and opportunities to start a dialogue, all he could say was 'You're from Scotland, are you?' I bent down to pick up the pipe-case, when I felt a limp hand on my shoulder. I wished this grumpy old prick in hell. So shoot me.

"What part of Scotland are you from?" he said, in a strange accent I couldn't identify.

"You won't have heard of it," I said curtly. "I come from the Outer Hebrides."

"Which island?" he said, surprising me with his awareness of that remote archipelago.

"Uist," I replied dismissively.

"North or South?" he said.

I looked more closely at the rubbery face with the dark rings under his eyes.

"Benbecula," I said, wondering how he knew the area.

"*Bithidh Gàidhlig agad, mar sin*, You'll have the Gaelic, then," he said.

"*Tha gu leòr . . . làn mo chinn*, Plenty . . . my head's full of it," I stammered, stunned by the direction the conversation had taken.

His thin prominent nose twitched in excitement as he filled me in on his back-story. He had come from South Uist to the United States twenty-five years previously in response to an advertisement in the *Oban Times* seeking to recruit pipers for the Worcester Kilties Pipes and Drums. He drifted westwards, taking low-echelon jobs in factories, warehouses and sawmills and eventually settled in Cleveland, Ohio.

"You play the pipes?" I snorted.

"Yes," he answered sheepishly. "Everybody of my generation in South Uist played the pipes."

I glowered at him for a couple of beats, then gestured at my own pipes which were lying between us. "This is ridiculous," I exclaimed. "Why didn't you tell me all this when I first approached you?"

"You talked too much," he said with the trace of a smile.

"What?" I said, angry all over again.

"In my experience in the United States – *Yew-United States* – ," he said in English, looking at me right in the eyes, a little half-smile, half-sneer on his thin lips, "I've found that if someone talks to you at length, he's fixing – *fixin'* – to make some money out of you."

My breath had been knocked out. I accepted his extended hand but I could not avoid hesitating to take it, as if fearing contamination. Hot, loose-jointed bones: I gave them a squeeze and said, "Well, thanks for the tip, my friend. You've made my entry to the USA truly memorable."

And he had. I shook my head disdainfully and turned away towards a little kiosk selling newspapers, cigarettes and magazines. To my delight, they sold liquor too, and I bought a pint of Jim Beam.

As I approached the bay from which the bus to Miami was departing, I tried to buck myself up by considering the glories that awaited me in Florida.

After the depressing monologue from the stranger from South Uist, I considered briefly that my emigration to America might be the equivalent of purchasing a one-way ticket on the *Titanic*. The Yanks, according to him, didn't like talkers, and boy, could this boy talk! Not wanting to go down that gloomy line of thought, I gave up on it.

I took a swig from my bottle in a crouched position at the back of the coach and experienced an infusion of courage. In a couple of days, after an overnight in a lodge outside Philadelphia, I'd arrive in Miami, where I'd kit myself out with clothing more suitable for the tropics before proceeding to the MacMillan plantation in Tampa.

As I settled back in my reclining seat I spoke to myself in a calm whisper: "You're going to be all right, Norman. You've made the right move."

Thirty-six hours later, stiff and half in the bag, with my sinuses encrusted with soot, I arrived in hot and humid Miami. After a taxi ride across the Biscayne Waterway to Miami Beach, I booked into one of the dozens of fly-blown daily rate hotels that were a prominent feature of the decaying area. It was called Plaza Cubana.

After taking a short nap in a shabby room, I purchased sandals and shorts from a seedy men's clothing store nearby. But I was restless and went on patrol down Collins Avenue. The pavements were dotted with groups of Hispanic females, with clusters of black girls here and there. There wafted an odour of failure throughout the strip, a smell compounded of pending criminal charges, lack of money, spousal or pimp abuse and joylessly consumed drugs and alcohol.

Miami obeyed jungle laws: eat under the cover of darkness, and find a patch of shade in the hotel garden to sleep through the long, humid day. As I strolled along Collins Avenue that night, I heard my rather heavy Scottish brogue shoes scraping on the sand-covered sidewalk, squelch-squelch, squelch-squelch. I began to recite Gaelic poetry in my head. That was a little game I played often when drifting in pursuit of excitement down streets in strange, alien cities, something to pass the time.

> O gur sunndach mi air m' astar,
> Falbh gu siùbhlach air bheag airtneul,
> Dol a chòmhrag ri Bonaparte . . .
> How happy am I,
> Departing swiftly without tiring,
> Going to fight Bonaparte . . .

The neon light of a Bud advert in the window of a cinder-block bar showed like a fire across the freeway.

> 'Illean cridheil, bitheamaid sunndach,
> Seasaibh onair bhur dùthcha . . .
> Hearty lads, let's be merry,
> Uphold the honour of your country . . .

I sauntered across the wide street, my right arm and index finger extended stiffly to slow down speeding cars, and headed towards the door of the Flamingo Bar and Grill. All I could hear was the faster skliffing of my footsteps as I approached the push-pull double doors: squelch-squelch, squelch-squelch.

What I really lusted after was the more affluent stretch of South Beach, however. This was Miami Beach in all its kitschy glory. I had observed from afar the patrons of these sumptuous places, and only the conviction that the people and the prices were too rich for my blood kept me from entering these watering holes which were drenched in Salsa music. I craved the sight of other young people who exuded an aura of glamour, money and pleasure. All these well-toned young studs in white jackets, women with augmented breasts squirming out of their bikini evening wear, reeled against my eyelids. I wanted to belong to that tribe.

My night-time circuit ended in an edgy burnout saloon near the Plaza Cubana where I drank myself nuts, courtesy of two shirtless, almost certainly gay, gym bunnies. Dark thoughts that the mind phrases to itself in my native language assailed me. '*Nach tu th' air a dhol bhuaithe, Thormoid!* How low have you sunk, Norman!'

I awoke the following morning to an orchestral arrangement of "For All We Know", relayed to the room by way of two clapped-out old speakers attached to the wall above my single bed.

I quickly showered and shaved and descended three floors in a creaky old escalator to Reception, where I paid the middle-aged Hispanic woman at the desk. I left with my canvas grip and pipe-case in one hand and with a languid wave of the other I bade farewell to Plaza Cubana. I was off to confront my destiny in Tampa.

From a payphone in Miami Greyhound I placed a call to MacMillan in Tampa, informing him that I'd be arriving in four hours' time.

As the coach trundled through the Everglades, past swamps on the nearside punctuated by wooden shacks with poorly dressed black families standing listlessly outside, and on the other side huge groves of live oak garlanded by shaggy Spanish moss in long gray strands, I reflected on the genesis of this adventure.

Everything went with the fluency of a dream, and here I was with a black servant at the wheel of a Lincoln pulling up in front of a big-breasted structure of brick with two immense columns before the front entrance. In the boiling sun, as hot waves roiled from the sand-covered driveway and mirage slicks flared up in front of my eyes, I caught a glimpse of a big white clapboard building cantilevered on stilts over a swamp.

"Foreman's place," the black man said.

MacMillan was right there in the open doorway. "How you doin', Norman," he said. "Welcome to Tampa." He was wearing a long-sleeved blue work shirt and jeans topped by a bright red visored cap that emphasized the gray of his temples. He ushered me inside – sumptuous furnishings, all white-on-white with a Lucite staircase and what I took to be a real Monet painting on one wall.

"Make yourself at home, boy," he said heartily. "Please allow me to introduce my daughters."

I had noticed a pair of dumpy girls, late teens or early twenties, in skintight madras shorts, over beside an elaborate hi-fi system at the far wall. With their floppy asymmetrical breasts encased in tight t-shirts bearing the legend 'Just hand over the chocolate and nobody will get hurt', and their posture of jaded yearning, I felt a stab of revulsion. It hurt to look at them. I'm talking real *ugly* here.

One of the girls waddled over, her lips glistening and her pointy Cadillac-fin glasses glinting in the sunlight, and started to speak in an adenoidal accent:

"Hi, Norman," she whined. "I'm Holly and that's my backward sister Jeannie over there." She then kissed me wetly and I was pressed into the vast pillows that were her breasts while she thrust her fat pelvis into mine.

I wanted to be excused from this class immediately. When her equally ugly sister joined us she was bearing a silver tray crowded with assorted drinks. I downed three vodkas, bang, bang, bang. I detected a sinister bass note in MacMillan's airy dismissals of my concerns over my employment and the duties they might entail.

"Stay chilled, Norman," he said. "You're going to be living with the Gonzalez family down in the Swamp House. Can't have a good-looking young fellow like yourself hovering over my fine examples of Southern womanhood." He paused, smiled and spoke with satisfaction: "Maybe later . . . when you become acquainted with my girls . . ."

"Whatever you say, Mr MacMillan," I said, more out of politeness than conviction.

Ben, the black servant who had met me at the bus station, picked up my cases and indicated that I should follow him. As I trotted down the hard-packed meandering dirt path towards the cantilevered wooden house, I felt fear. What was the sly old fox planning? He was looking for a suitable husband for one of his daughters. I could sense it: I could feel it: somehow I *knew* it. As we entered the surprisingly cool interior – the door was unlocked – I was thinking *This is my life ticking away*. F. Scott Fitzgerald himself said there were no second acts in America.

Suddenly, the warm voice of Celia Cruz burst forth from what I took to be a kitchen. When I stepped forward to discover the origins of that heavenly sound, I saw that a boom-box by the window had been turned to full volume by the most gorgeous girl I had ever seen. I was stunned. With her little bottom in faded blue jeans, her bare midriff, her tube top and long, black glossy hair, she swung her hips to the pulse of the song. Her jeans were low slung, and her top was so high on her chest, I could see her light-caramel-coloured flesh. Her lissome young body writhed and spun. Her mouth displayed a playful smile. Abruptly, she turned off the music and advanced, her hand extended in greeting.

"*Ola*, Norman," she said in a low-pitched voice. "*Me llamo Adelita*, My name is Adelita."

I acknowledged her introduction, averting my eyes from those big sensual lips, for fear of wanting to stare at her, which I did. With my heart banging in my rib cage and an undeniable stirring in my groin, I started a dialogue in ungrammatical but effective Spanish. (Nobody has acquired a foreign language as quickly as I did in the company of Adelita. Sexual attraction is indeed a powerful stimulus and motivator.)

It turned out that she was not much younger than myself and attended a Community College, studying Accountancy, up in Connecticut. During vacations she returned home to Tampa to look after her widower father and three younger siblings.

Ben was dismissed with a wave of her hand that set the gold bangles on her wrist jangling. I haltingly asked her to play the music again, and I was exposed to the most erotic display of my life. Millions of volts of energy and excitement charged her body as she teased me, grinding her hips and projecting her breasts, and touching the top of the fly of her jeans with both hands as if at any moment she was about to unzip them, all with a salacious leer on her lips and a lubricious look in her eyes.

I couldn't help myself, and walked over to stand beside her. She spread her arms. Slowly, incredulously, I sank into her embrace. All at once she was kissing me wildly, probing my mouth with a furious tongue.

It didn't take long for Adelita and me to get our rumba going. This was the start of a summer of swallowing greed. I visited the citrus plantation on only three occasions, receiving no rebuke from Senor Gonzalez or Mr MacMillan. Adelita and I made the most of our freedom. In a big-assed Cadillac convertible loaned to me by my boss, we tooled around the back roads of the county, listening to an easy-listening radio station where we heard 'Surfin' U.S.A' by the Beach Boys, 'Sugar Shack' by Jimmy Gilmer and The Fireballs, 'Blue Velvet' by Bobby Vinton, 'If I Had A Hammer' by Trini Lopez and 'I Love You Because' by Al Martino. We bathed naked in creeks and made frantic love in the searing sun. Adelita liked it good and reckless. I recall one occasion as we sauntered alongside Tampa Bay when we were drenched in a sudden, warm shower of rain. I proposed going for the afternoon to a hotel where we could make love in a double bed. Adelita promptly agreed. The cracker in Reception didn't want us.

"This hotel don't speak Spanish," was how he put it as he looked disgustedly at the Latinate cast of my Cuban lover. He slumped into resignation, however, when I offered him two twenty dollar bills. Welcome to downtown Tampa.

At night we would listen to Salsa music, drink Bacardi rum, and often my lovely teacher would, with a dictionary and a daily Spanish newspaper, encourage me to extend my tenuous grasp of the language. After a supper of fried *pollo* – chicken and brown beans – we'd say goodnight to her father and the children clustered around the television and make for Adelita's narrow bed. There we would dissolve into one another, utterly, and my pride and happiness flowed into her – ah, the joy of sin.

It couldn't last.

Margo McGougain paid a surprise visit from Scotland.

I was seated on a wooden kitchen chair, a glass of Cuba Libre on the table before me, and Adelita was cradling my head, slowly lowering her cheek against mine. Something caught my eye: Margo was standing in the doorway.

"I think that's enough," she commanded, her face an impassive mask. "It's time for you to come home with me, Norman."

How was I to deal with the choice that was eating away at my gut? To stay, or go. I didn't answer. It was easier that way. I looked down into my drink and drained the last of the rum in one swallow. "*Adios,* Adelita," I croaked, my throat constricted. I crept out of the room in Margo's wake. A wave swept through my central nervous system and told me I was about to wash away a summer of pure delight. I have starred in this movie a couple of times since then, and I'm now familiar with the scalding feeling that sweeps over my brain in these circumstances. I followed big Margo without as much as a glance at the love of my life. What could I say? I'd always hated confrontation.

An additional factor in my resigned decision to return to the UK was Vietnam. The war over there was heating up, and since, as a recent immigrant, I had a very low number, I knew it was only a matter of time before I was called up to serve in the forces of my adopted country. Two rounds in the head and a final resting place in a rice paddy didn't appeal to me.

I remember the looming visage of Secretary for Defense Robert S. J. McNamara on the television reciting the following doom-laden announcement:

"I and General Maxwell D. J. Taylor reported to the President and the National Security Council that the security of South Vietnam is a major interest of the United States as other free nations. Our basic presentation has been endorsed by all members of the Security Council and the President and by Ambassador Henry Cabot Lodge.

"Major U.S. assistance in support of the people of South Viet-Nam to deny this country to communism and to suppress the externally stimulated and supported insurgency of the Viet Cong as promptly as possible is an important interest of the United States.

"I and General Taylor have reported that our judgement is that the major part of the U.S. military task can be completed by the end of 1965. The political situation in South Viet-Nam remains deeply serious. It remains the policy of the United States, in South Viet-Nam as in other parts of the world, to support the efforts of the people of that country to defeat aggression and to build a peaceful and free society.'

Put it down to remnants of the *fiosachd*, second sight, but I knew this meant trouble for me. I resolved to register as a conscientious objector if I ever got called up. A few years down the line the world heavyweight boxing champion, Muhammad Ali, arguably the most widely recognized man on the planet, used the same appeal before the Supreme Court. "I ain't got nothin' against them Viet Congs," he said. "No Viet Cong ever called me nigger." He was sentenced to five years in prison for refusing to kill 'slopes'. *Five years*!

This frisson of worry, I'm sure, drove Adelita and me to ever more frenzied paroxysms of sexual dissolution. *Fanny Hill* by John Cleland, banned in the U.K. but freely available in Tampa, gave us inspiration for new and exciting erotic experiences.

All that was over.

As we jetted back to Glasgow from Miami, Margo fell asleep almost immediately, her head lying on my shoulder, her breath on my face. I thought I would sleep too, but I didn't. My mind was too full of Adelita and what it meant to be going home. We hardly exchanged three words. I looked at the mask beside me from time to time and couldn't shake a plummeting feeling of anxiety for the future.

17
Heartbreaker

Back home again, my behaviour towards Margo was as boorish as before. When the beautiful girl, now started her primary teacher training, freely offered the delights of her sumptuous body, more often than not I'd knock her back in a childish and spiteful attempt to exact vengeance. With her non-stop frothing about getting married, buying a house and raising children, I was becoming increasingly irritated. It seemed as though she was ripping apart the seams of my life.

'Jesus, I haven't lived my life yet,' I thought to myself one night, as I gazed at my doleful reflection in the gantry mirror in the public bar of the Kensington pub. For once, I eschewed the racy chatter of Harry and the other toe-rags.

I was conducting a kind of stream of consciousness monodrama. Did I desire Margo, and did she desire me? The answer to the first question was "No", and the answer to the second was an enthusiastic "Yes". Marriage? That was a possibility as remote as my popping over to a beach bar on the Copacabana in Rio and ordering a half and a half pint. The thought of Brazil gave me an idea. How about if we got engaged first of all in some exotic place? This would give me time – a year at least – before I fast forwarded out of her life. Neat, huh?

Margo and her parents thoroughly approved of my cunning plan. Becoming engaged before marrying was, in their opinion, the correct and proper thing to do. With a rather flashy engagement ring in my pocket – rubies and diamonds were predominant in the setting – we spent a delightful week in Paris at the plush home of a friend of mine, George Hertz. He was a charismatic man, an Austrian Jew whose father was from Czechoslovakia and whose mother was Russian. The family escaped to Chicago after Hitler annexed Sudetenland. This background left him fluent in at least six languages. I've heard him on the phone speaking in Russian, Swedish, French, Italian, Spanish and, of course, German. When he spoke in English he sounded like a particularly erudite American gangster. By profession he was some kind of metallurgical engineer. He had doctorates in both Chemistry and Physics and had attended 'school' until he was almost thirty. When Margo and I visited him in Paris he was head honcho with a French plastic manufacturing company. He occupied an extremely well-appointed town house near Place de la Nation. We had become friendly during the course of a two-week piping school in Staffin, Skye, run under the aegis of the College of Piping. Thanks to the influence of John MacFadyen, the oldest member of a renowned piping family, I was a kind of Junior Instructor, and George was one of my pupils. (In passing, I must pay tribute to the kindness and generosity shown to me by the MacFadyen family who lived in Carham Drive, Cardonald. I had long ago pawned my own instrument, bought for me by my poor late father, to obtain cash for drink, and if I had an engagement to pipe at, a wedding for example, Big Duncan, the father, would lend me a set belonging to one of the boys, Duncan, Hector or Iain.)

As a piper George was no great shakes – he couldn't hear the pulse of any tune – but cerebrally he made me look like a barefoot boy. I learned a great deal about public speaking from George. He never talked down to others. If he explained something to you in nasal polysyllables, he never worried about whether or not you understood. He, Hamish Henderson and Seumas MacNeill were the influences I've carried in my own verbal palette to this very day. These guys spoke in sentences and were very fluent. My own efforts to emulate them backfired on me. Back in 1991 the Head of Documentaries and Drama at Grampian Television, Ted Brocklebank, made a documentary about my life and sordid times called *A Talent to Abuse*. The structure consisted of my comedy act filmed in Stornoway, Harris, North Uist and Skye, interspersed with monologues from me in various island locations. This hour-long programme had great resonance with the viewers – I still get feedback from Lowlanders who have never been north of Drumchapel. *A Talent to Abuse* was nominated for a BAFTA award in 1992. We, the Grampian team, didn't win. The prize went to the BBC for a documentary that everybody has forgotten by now. I remember being gobsmacked by the comment from one hack who was reporting on the event for a provincial newspaper. "Norman's pieces to camera were over-written," he said to Ted at the conclusion of the viewing. Good God, what a numptie! Nothing I said was ever scripted. That's the way I talk, you moron.

In Paris, George was a splendid *vademecum*. He was phenomenally clued up about the City of Light. He took us to the Arc de Triomphe, Opera, la Cité, Notre Dame, the Louvre and the Eiffel Tower. In addition, he treated us at all the "in" Parisian restaurants, and also took us to more plebeian bistros. In our base at the town house there were lochs of liquor and a huge store of cigarettes, domestic and foreign. I don't know if Margo enjoyed the break, but I was in my element. Exposure to George, however, had a downside. It made me realize how circumscribed and myopic my own world had become. I wanted to *be* Monsieur Hertz.

It was no surprise that, back home, life asserted once again its jog-trot, boring rhythms. The stations of my personal cross were home, school, pub and Paisley Road West. I had to come up with another delaying tactic, or, better still, break free altogether. Why didn't I just talk to Margo and discuss the future realistically? I wasn't the kind of man to explain, or even to apologize. What it boiled down to was that I just didn't have the *cojones*.

A holiday of four weeks' duration in Caldetas on the Costa Brava did little to improve relations. Margo, who had by this time completed her first year of training as a primary school teacher at Jordanhill, arranged everything. There was some kind of a deal available to students to have a four-week vacation in north-eastern Spain at a very low price. Somehow she succeeded in qualifying me for this cheap holiday in the sun. I went along with everything she suggested. We took a bus from Glasgow Sheriff Court to Edinburgh Airport, boarded a charter flight to Paris and proceeded to Caldetas by train.

Despite having scrutinized intensely every map of Spain I could lay my hands on, I have been unable to locate this village. It existed and lay somewhere north of Badalona and Mataró. This place for me was a wonderful choice. The hostel, on the main street running at right angles to the railway track which you were obliged to cross on the way to and from the beach, was clean and, most importantly, observed a strict segregation of the sexes policy. This meant that Margo had to sleep in the female dormitory while I was two flights up in a single room. Sure, I allowed her to come up late at night and accepted her loving ministrations to me. But as soon as I had shooed her off to the women's dormitory, I'd put my clothes back on and make for the

'Barrels', a bodega deep in the heart of the only hotel in the village. There I'd carouse with the Catalans until the early hours.

"You like to travel, Norman, don't you?" Margo said one evening in our bed. "I want to keep you around, darling."

"I'm not going anywhere," I responded.

"I'm worried you'll take off for someplace like Uist, where your heart is," she said.

"My heart is here with you, Margo," I said.

She took one of my hands and kissed the fingertips. "Thank you for saying that, pet," she said.

I wasn't sure she believed me. I wasn't sure I believed myself.

Breakfast around noon consisted of juice, croissants and black coffee. After a smoke of the local cigarettes called 'Celta' I would toddle down to the beach and join the girls already sunbathing in their favoured spot, near the upturned hull of a fishing boat. There was a kiosk just in front of the railway line that sold ice-cold bottles of San Miguel beer, and for the next six hours, every day, I'd indulge in an alcohol-fuelled drift into reverie and nothingness. I was lucky. Margo took good care of me. I have the type of fair skin that turns bright red in the sun, but she made sure by slathering creams all over my body that I didn't burn. Within a fortnight I sported a tan, though I say it myself, that was the envy of the visiting Scottish students who arrived with only two weeks' vacation to enjoy. The days flowed by in a drunken haze.

What Margo did not know was that I had a cunning plan for my finale: a few days before we were due to leave, I had received a money order from the Australian Mutual Insurance Company in the amount of twenty pounds. I had cashed in my life policy two weeks before our departure. I was going to Barcelona to have a little fun. Without Margo.

Christ! As I gazed at her bronzed curves, I felt guilty. If she had known what I was about to do, she would have cut my head off. The notion of decapitation stimulated a mad reverie. Despite feeling nauseous, my fevered brain started to expatiate surreally on what it would be like to have no head.

Must be tough having no head. Finding suitable clothes would be a problem. I mean, you'd have to find t-shirts with no hole at the top. Friends would find it difficult getting you Christmas presents. 'What do you want for Christmas, Norman?' 'I don't know.' 'I suppose a tie would be out of the question?'

I actually used this routine, or something like it, twenty years later during my stand-up period. I'd conclude by complimenting the audience on their sophistication. '*You know, folks, when I tried this shtick in wherever a few weeks ago the people didn't laugh. They thought I was making fun of the handicapped or something. Come on – there's no such thing as a headless person! Did they think that a headless family – dad, mum and three kids – were going to come into the show and start heckling me? 'Boo-hoo, boo-hoo, I suppose you think you're funny, you sicko. Look how upset my kids are.' You know, ladies and gentlemen, I hate headless people. And I'll tell them that straight to their face!*'

In Barcelona I was struck by the visible symptoms of an oppressive Church and State: knots of smug priests ensconced at café terraces; a loaded machine gun at every street corner. Franco's dictatorship was quickly forgotten when I stepped out of the taxi at a bank at the top of the Ramblas. After an extremely long wait, I was served graciously by a handsome middle-aged matron who placed a pile of pesetas and some centimes in a large envelope. This would be the equivalent of over three hundred pounds today.

Deliverance! I stepped onto the pavement and immediately lost control. Many drinks in many bars in the Barrio Gótico left me with a head full of gin and coca-cola and hazy memories of the two days and nights I spent in that menacing city. Barcelona loved drunks. I was fresh meat for the pimps, taxi drivers and prostitutes who infested the place.

Suddenly it was dark . . . I was losing my grip on the bar, sinking slowly to my knees. A heavily made-up woman clutched at my belt. "You speak excellent Castilian," she said. "Just stand up, please. Your command of Spanish is most impressive."

"Listen, madam," I croaked, "I'm a great Spanish speaker down here where I am. You'd go bonkers if I stood up and started to speak Gaelic."

Later on that evening, much later on, my hands were clawing uncontrollably at a bedspread I was sitting on in a room I had no recollection of hiring or even paying for. I could hear myself breathing heavily. In the bathroom next door I used someone's razor to have a quick shave. In the middle of a down stroke I noticed something glinting in a soap dish: a gent's gold signet ring. I picked it up, admiring its weight and the embossed coat of arms. Could I steal it and make my escape? What would I say to the arresting policeman?

What? This gold ring you found in my pocket? Well, you see, sir, I was strolling along Via Layetana when this gentleman from my native island, Benbecula, stopped me and in the vernacular asked me to do him a favour. Yes, he was a merchant seaman, you see. He thrust this ring into my hand with the command that I should deliver it to his brother in Liniclate. Then he ran away into the darkness. So that is why I had that ring in my pocket. Can you believe that?

No. He'd consult his notebook that contained details of the complaint made by the rightful owner of the ring and closely inspect me against the description the complainant had given. Although my command of Catalan would undoubtedly improve by exposure to five years in a Barcelona prison, I decided that the risk was too great. I nervously replaced the ring in the soap dish and hurried out of the tenement flat I had spent the night in.

The following day and night was spent in a frenzy of bar-hopping and hysterical drinking. Short and long taxi rides were punctuated by long periods of solitary drinking in honky-tonks in the Barrio Chino and round about the Estación de Francia. I believed I was in the grip of a potentially fatal alcoholic episode. Just sitting there on a stool in a dimly-lit bar in a side street to the left of the Ramblas, an empty glass of rum in front of me, I couldn't move. Death, I was sure of it, was not far off. At least there was no pain. I reasoned that I'd probably black out in the next few minutes, and after that it wouldn't matter.

Of course I endured this self-induced paralysis, and around midnight I was able to talk and move . . . but I was still not free of alcohol. Somehow I scraped together some peseta coins and bought a single train ticket as far as Mataró. I have strange memories of meeting a young man there, originally from Andalusia, who splashed water from a communal fountain in a cobbled square on my face in an attempt to clean me up. He also gave me some paper money which enabled me to travel on to Caldetas.

Margo greeted me with open arms. She took me up to my room and put me to bed. For the next four days, until it was time for our departure from Spain, I remained there, alternately shivering and sweating, and she administered lukewarm bed-baths and cool sponges to my quivering body. She brought soup and crusty bread up from the refectory. She never once asked where I had been for forty-eight hours.

On the Friday we checked out and took the train to Paris. It was then I started to hallucinate. At the beginning the visions were not too alarming. Heat waves on the brown earth of the fields outside the carriage were solidifying in the air like the waves of a Paisley-patterned shawl. Grazing cattle turned into packs of leopards. One of these great cats was running parallel to our train, and his savage jaws were but a foot from my window. I lurched backwards into the soft body of Margo and buried my head in her ample breasts.

> Pillowed upon my fair love's ripening breast,
> To feel for ever its soft fall and swell,
> Awake for ever in a sweet unrest,
> Still, still to hear her tender-taken breath,
> And so live ever – or else swoon to death.

But Keats was almost a goner when he wrote that, and so was I. Who would rescue me from this insane, self-lacerating ordeal?

Yes, it was Margo. That night, we shared a bed in the dormitory of a lycée somewhere on the outskirts of Paris, and we didn't care what anybody thought. I had been pegged as an eccentric character by then anyway. As we queued for our evening meal I noticed that two teams of mechanical footballers, about three inches high, were playing enthusiastically on the stainless steel surface of the serving plate. "Come away the Blues," I bellowed. As an Ibrox man, I favoured them over their opponents, who wore red strips.

"Shhhh," Margo whispered in my ear. "What are you talking about?"

"Look at them," I shouted. "The wee footballers. They're clever, those Japanese." I grinned at the serving man. "*Ils sont formidables, les Japonnais, en effet!* The Japanese are terrific, right enough!"

The guy shrugged. "Norman," Margo said plaintively. "There *are* no footballers." She led me away.

"Okay," I said. "I think there's something wrong with me."

There certainly was. All through the month of September in that horrible year of 1964, I oscillated wildly between feeling that I ought to be grateful to Margo for all her kindnesses and wanting to flee as far away as possible from someone who was slowly poisoning me with her cloying solicitude. I had no empathy, no sympathy. I could not step back and view a situation from another person's point of view. When the guilt over betraying Margo, which was being generated by one rebellious negative cell in my body, started to well up, I fought it down before it could erupt in my mind. I could not admit that I was the one who had become engaged to the girl. I could only moan inwardly that I had been wounded.

What I did to break the malevolent cycle that was destroying the quality of my life, my mind and my soul was typically cowardly. Without telling anybody about my plans, I applied to Aberdeen Teachers' Training College to study for a Primary Teacher's Certificate of Competence, a session of only two terms. I had as much interest in teaching under-twelves as I had in nuclear physics. The move north was just a means to enable me to detach. One night I was passionately necking with my fiancée; the next morning I boarded the Aberdeen train at Queen Street Station. New exciting experiences awaited me, I felt sure. One experience I was not prepared for was my first admission to a psychiatric hospital, the Ross Clinic in Queen's Cross, Aberdeen . . .

I began my studies in the Teachers Training College in October. I dismissed the DTs I had suffered two months before and started drinking again. The money must have come from my grant. It didn't last long. By mid-November I was skint again and drinking a subsidized cup of tea in the students' canteen in St Andrew's Square. Suddenly, I keeled over. When I came round, a young woman I recognized as being in one of my classes was kneeling beside me. "Are you all right?" she asked.

"Yes," I said "I'm fine – just a touch of the 'flu."

"My fiancé is a doctor and he's collecting me in ten minutes," she said. "I'd like him to take a look at you."

The doctor fiancé duly arrived in a smart car a few minutes later, took one look at me and said: "How long have you been drinking for, Mr Maclean?" I told him six weeks, too tired to resist. "Look," he said urgently, "I have a psychiatrist friend in the Ross Clinic who'll help you. Come on."

Dr Jim certainly did help me. After a seven day period of detox, ingesting prescription drugs, he struck a deal with me. He'd keep me in the four-bed ward for as long as I wanted to stay, provided that I did not touch alcohol. When I told him about my Teachers Training course he said that I was free to attend classes until I obtained my diploma, again stressing that there was to be no booze. I readily accepted his conditions, and there followed a halcyon period of around four months when I enjoyed free food, clean bedding and

Sickness Benefit money on a weekly basis. I even got myself invited to spend Christmas with one of the pretty nurses, Dorothy MacKay, at her parents' home in Tomintoul.

Over the next forty-three years, my life would be peppered with these stays in hospitals. Sometimes I'd be inside for a month, at other times perhaps for a couple of days or a week. One of the reasons I presented so frequently was that I lived an itinerant lifestyle. Landladies, hotel managers, even girlfriends and wives, simply did not know what to do with the hulk who would, within a two or three hour period, drink a bottle of whisky.

The intervals between hospital admissions could vary between weeks and years. I would get cognitive behaviour therapy where I'd be given a programme conditioning me to avoid drink and reward myself with little treats in order to avoid being anxious or depressed. Every time I left one of those places – Craig Dunain Hospital, Inverness, Stobhill Hospital, Glasgow, Dykebar Hospital, Paisley, the Argyll and Bute Hospital, Lochgilphead, the Crichton Royal, Dumfries, Kingseat in Aberdeen, the Priory, Glasgow, the Roosevelt Hospital in New York – I was determined to remain abstinent. Sometimes I succeeded; more often, I failed. I supposed I had never really subscribed to the theory that it was better to get high on life . . .

I think I'm inclining towards the psychiatric model in the treatment of alcoholism, where the doctor tries to uncover the hidden cause of a neurosis so that, when a traumatic event in the past is remembered, one doesn't suffer the neurosis any more. The trouble is, it can take a long time to discover suppressed traumatic experiences, assuming they existed in the first place. Maybe this little literary exercise will disclose some event, long obliterated in memory, that will help me to accept who I am.

A sudden gust of wind from the south-west whines against the living room window to my right. This breaks my reverie and I am relieved to abandon the subjects of hospitals and Margo McGougain. I acquiesced in my own seduction by a sweet, essentially innocent girl, and then callously discarded her. Going back over the history of this relationship in detail makes me realise that the top and hem of this appalling chapter is that I broke a young girl's heart. For me she might as well not have existed.

18

First Marriage

My decision to become a husband was, to put it delicately, erratic. It was driven by panic. When you've been conditioned to believe that marriage is written on the tablets of Moses, you think that unless you aspire to this condition and move towards it at reasonable speed, you must be doing something wrong. Or you must be condemned to a lonely old age. I fell victim to this delusion. I allowed alarm bells about the future to blot out every rational thought in my head. Panic has a crazy momentum. In its grasp you refuse to view your position calmly. Instead, you give in to hysteria. Your situation is hopeless. You Cannot Get Out. A solution has to be found *now*. You end up making decisions. Wrong decisions. Very wrong decisions. Decisions that change everything. Decisions that you come to loathe. How do I know this? Because I married Greta Macdonald of Aberlour, Banffshire.

She had been a colleague of mine in the Primary Department of Lossiemouth High School, where I had taken a post after leaving Aberdeen. While she worked down in Aldershot for a school term, I wrote poems and soppy, sometimes steamy, love letters.

Of course I didn't love her. I didn't know her. I had, however, enough confidence in my thespian ability to think that I could fake being a model husband and, hopefully, father. The festering cancer in my soul told me I *needed* to marry somebody.

After the wedding ceremony in a Roman Catholic church in Duffton, we rented a two-bedroomed 'executive' flat in the New Town of Cumbernauld and she began work in a local primary school while I took up a post as Depute Head Teacher in a sin-bin in the east end of Glasgow, Garthamlock Secondary. My working life didn't lack drama. I had imagined that I knew Glasgow, but exposed to the crime, poor living conditions and all-round wretchedness of the inhabitants of this sink estate, my head churned like a spin-dryer.

Most of the children I supervised belonged to single-parent families. Either the husband was doing 'one to three' in Barlinnie Prison or he had just gone up the touchline and simply disappeared. Many of the boys were sleeping rough in abandoned houses. These kids should have been sent to school in handcuffs and locked up afterwards.

I relied on corporal punishment to subdue them – girls as well as boys.

If you pulled that kind of rough discipline today, you'd be ringing your lawyer before sundown. The pupils at the Annexe were a different species. They would steal fire extinguishers – Christ, *fire extinguishers*! – and anything that wasn't chained, locked, screwed or nailed down.

They were a cool bunch all right. Most of them had never been west of Glasgow Cross in their lives. They accepted their dysfunctional families and squalid lifestyles with equanimity. The way they lived was *normal* in their eyes. Every Monday new faces would stare at me in the office and explain they had just been released from Polmont Borstal. On one occasion I was attacked by two new arrivals. Their advocate, one William McClymont, was going into a long rigmarole about how the two brothers had been 'done' for 'screwing hooses'. The new boys were as bored as I was. They grew restless. They hadn't heard of my fearsome reputation as a brutal disciplinarian, and acted accordingly.

"Right," one of them shouted, "Gie tartan-heid the message." With that, his brother leaped onto my back and began pummelling the back of my head with his fists. The brother who had made the initial war cry grabbed my tie and pulled me towards him across the desk. I heard a distinct crack as my upper body hit the edge of the angular piece of furniture. After subduing them, with extreme difficulty, I discovered I had sustained three cracked ribs. Just another day in the zoo that was the Annexe.

On another occasion my jaw dropped to the floor when I was interviewing a little thief whom I'd caught red-handed hiding a purse he'd stolen from one of my female assistants when she left the classroom to take a toilet break. He was hiding the purse in a trash bin in the playground when, on a regular tour of inspection of the premises, I discovered him and quickly manhandled him into the office. On my desk stood the old Underwood typewriter I used to compose my weekly 'Glasgow Letter' for *The Oban Times*. I decided to type up a confession, purporting to come from the thief, which was full of pseudo-legalese. This, when signed, would save me trouble when the CID officers visited, as they did frequently. This young hoodlum stared at me impassively as I said in a deep brown voice meant to impart sincerity, and even sympathy, "Now look here, Billy, sign this piece of paper and things will go more easily for you. Of course, you'll go away, but a confession will mean a shorter stay in Polmont."

The self-possessed thirteen-year-old smirked, and in the undifferentiated tones of a trade union spokesman reading a prepared statement, he intoned: "I-am-not-prepared-to-sign-this-document-without-my-solicitor-being-present. I-have-a-criminal-lawyer-on-retainer-and-at-this-moment-in-time-I-have-nothing-further-to-say."

I stared at him incredulously. This kid was light years ahead of me in street smarts. I capitulated, reached for the telephone and summoned the CID.

The female pupils provided problems too. To show that they liked me, they would shower me with stolen gifts. Each lunchtime they would descend on the big stores in the city centre and shop-lift an embarrassing load of gear – shirts, jumpers, ties, socks, slacks, records, electrical goods like tape recorders and cassette players. This was third-degree-burn stuff and I was forced to hide it in the spare bedroom.

The main bone of contention between Greta and me was the amount of time I was spending away from home as newly appointed Pipe-Major of Cumbernauld Caledonia Pipes and Drums. After a stressful day spent trying to impose order on wayward pupils in the Annexe and escaping occasionally to the sanctuary of my office to type up my weekly feature for *The Oban Times* – this, along with singing engagements, paid quite well and formed part of the welcome additional income I was generating – I'd spend two evenings a week scouring the mean streets of the city, picking up drummers, taking them to gruelling practices in the village hall, and delivering them back to their various homes in Glasgow late at night. My new bride wasn't best pleased.

"Norman," she complained bitterly, "Gie up that fuckin' pipe band." She had a mouth on her. "You're supposed to be a singer. Fit wey div ye nae ging back tae the singin'?"

I had made myself radioactive. "I don't know if it's hang it up time yet," I mumbled.

"I'm not asking you," my new bride said, "I'm telling you."

So that's what I did. Tendering my resignation to the band I resumed my diaphragmatic breathing exercises and sang along with Björling, Gigli and Peter Pears every night and at lunch break in school.

I soon took my first faltering footsteps on the Stairway to Fame at this time. First of all I was invited by John Alick Macpherson, a recent recruit to the Gaelic Department at the BBC, to write and read on radio a short story. Instinctively, in front of the microphone, I didn't think about the thousands of people who might have been listening. I imagined that I was talking to one person I was fond of. I must have made a fair fist at the assignment, because, shortly afterwards, he brought me into the studio and recorded about a dozen unaccompanied Gaelic songs. Some of these have been digitized and played by Morag Macdonald on her radio programme, *Mire ri Mòir.* They stand up very well and there was hope a while back there that Macmeanmna, a Gaelic record company based in Skye, might release a kind of 'legacy' CD. The project fell into some kind of black hole, however, and I did nothing to pursue the matter.

My singing was really taking off. Not only did I cut my first album, entitled *The Bard Sings*, I also won the Gold Medal for solo singing at the National Mod held in Glasgow. For good measure, I was crowned Bard for the composition of an epic poem entitled *Maol Donn*, or 'MacCrimmon's Sweetheart'. This twentieth century piobaireachd poem is divided into three movements: *Ùrlar* or Ground, *Taorluath* and *Crunluath*. I set the poem in a piping competition where I am watching and listening to Pipe Major Donald Macleod, and I reflect on the likeness of a piper struggling to finish his performance without error and my own struggle to get through life.

> *Bu tu a' chraobh leatha fhèin an lios nan sùil,*
> *Bha glòir dhut dlùth 's bha 'phròis ag at do chlèibh,*
> *'S nochd thu tiamhaidheachd nad anam rùisgt'*
> *Nuair sheòl bàt' do chiùil gu cala rèidh.*
> You were the only tree in the garden of eyes . . .

The entire poem appears in both languages in an anthology of twentieth century Gaelic poetry, *An Tuil*, edited by Ronald Black, formerly of Edinburgh University. Actually, I feel a pang of shame when I think of this work. It was motivated solely by pride. I knew that the Bardic Crown hadn't been awarded the previous year and the thought of winning it in Glasgow appealed to my larcenous, pot-hunting soul.

After my triumph, I *did* get a lot of print and television coverage. This was due to two main factors: firstly, I was young – generally Gaelic poets were retired ministers, priests or head teachers: they were so old that they farted dust – and secondly the venue, Glasgow, was the media centre for print and broadcasting. Interviewers didn't have to travel far to have a word with this newly discovered polymath. (This was the description of me by columnist and author Cliff Hanley.)

It was shortly after this I made a breakthrough into television. Fred Macaulay, the head of Gaelic broadcasting, asked me to take part in a light entertainment programme called *'Se Ur Beatha*, You're Welcome'. Groups were all the rage in the sixties, and Fred had manufactured a male trio called the 'Innis Gaels'. Calum Cameron, a baritone from Soay, was the acknowledged leader, while Louis Stewart from Lochaber was the bass, and the singing dentist, Alasdair Gillies, was the tenor. Gillies wanted out to pursue a solo career and I was chosen as his replacement.

Controversy erupted at the first rehearsal. I had received a contract that stipulated I was to receive the sum of eighteen guineas for each programme. I considered this a fair reward. However, when chatting to Louis, I discovered that he was receiving twenty guineas. I marched over to Fred and told him that I was a better singer than Louis and deserved at least a similar fee. The Head of the Gaelic Department suggested we discuss this later, in private. A battle of wills began between Fred and myself.

I was having none of it and stormed out of Broadcasting House and spent the afternoon fending off increasingly anxious calls from Queen Margaret Drive. The trouble with this severely edited account of the fiasco of my first television appearance is that a lot of the detail is ebbing away. I remember in the Contracts Department telling me they observed a strict league table approach towards the remuneration of on-screen talent. Premier League luminaries included Stanley Baxter, Moira Anderson and Kenneth McKellar, while Gaelic tyros like me languished at the bottom of the Third Division.

I must have accepted this analogy, because I found myself within the week in the company of Calum and Louis, marching like Russian soldiers up and down the length and breadth of the studio floor. In truth, the fatal flaw with the Innis Gaels was a clash of conventions. The musical arrangements of the Musical Director, Ian Gourlay, were clever and modern, but they didn't suit the content or the traditional, old-fashioned singing style we had been brought up with.

Further television spots in *'Se Ur Beatha* followed. I guested in shows hosted by the likes of the Macdonald Sisters and Mary Sandeman. Soon I was presenting a series of this programme myself. I always had a two-year supply of confidence when it came to performing. I felt an up-tick of adrenaline as I entered the studio. For an instant I was frightened by the glare of the television lights. I was aware of small red lights turned my way. They were the red lights that indicate the television cameras are on and filming.

I thought I had acquitted myself well when Fred summoned me up to the gallery. He was sitting in a swivel chair in front of a bank of monitors. "*Suidh sìos, a Thormoid*, Sit down, Norman," he lisped in the soft consonants of his native North Uist. "*Tha mi airson beagan comhairle a thoirt dhut*, I want to give you some advice." In his gentrified island accent he came on like a member of the War Crimes Tribunal. "Norman," he said in Gaelic, "a presenter has to be seductive. You can do this easily. We know that you're a scallywag at heart. However, you have to feign affability." He was dead right. All my life there existed an obdurate tension between disguise and display, and I foresaw no problems. If television presenting is all about pretence, then Fred was preaching to somebody whose entire life, to some degree or other, had been founded on deceit. He wasn't finished. "Comedy, Norman," he continued, "works best when the audience likes you. Don't be grinning like a pools winner. A wry smile, the raising of an eyebrow and even the pretence that you don't know you're being amusing works very well, too.

"You're not trying to get your audience admitted to the splitsides' ward. And, finally, make your hand and arm gestures small. *Tha sgàilean an telebhisein cumhang*, the television screen is narrow," he said. "*Cha ruig thu leas a bhith a' crathadh do ghàirdeanan mar am fear a bhios a' stiùireadh nam plèanaichean aig a' phort-adhair*, You don't need to be waving your arms like the guy who guides the planes to their parking places at airports."

I took his words to heart. On telly I abbreviated the epic gestures and minimized the facial expressions. In speech I adopted an intimate tone. Before the green light came on in the recording studio the words '*Calma*, Norrie' seeped into my head like a mantra. A key had been found.

Money was pouring in, and we moved from the 'executive' flat to a three-bedroomed house in the charming village of Eaglesham in Renfrewshire. The birth of our daughter Temora coincided with the move. I knew that this adorable child represented a new domestic manacle. I was piling up obligations. I knew that never again would I be in charge of my own destiny. At the same time, my appearances on telly meant that my semi-professional weekend engagements doubled and became more lucrative.

For months the relationship with Greta Macdonald had been deteriorating, and the added pressures of feeding Temora in the middle of the night, along with the stresses of running the sin-bin, were contributing to the inevitable dissolution of the marriage. I was constantly hovering over the boundaries of depletion. The whole time I was working in Garthamlock and doing wee Mickey Mouse gigs in places like Aviemore, Pitlochry and Mallaig, I was still binge drinking. I didn't see it myself, but the wheels of my marriage were falling off. Every day, after school, I'd stop at a café in Giffnock for a cappuccino and a fag, just to postpone the inevitable arguments that would ensue when I got home. What sparked off these vitriolic exchanges was generally fairly trivial. Though she liked the additional money my weekend performances brought in, the gravamen of her indictment was that I should do more around the house and spend more quality time with our daughter, Temmy. I considered these accusations grossly unfair.

"You haven't done anything about cutting the grass, Mr Showbiz," she'd screech as soon as I came in the door. After driving for about an hour to get to school and spending my days wrestling – yes, physically *wrestling* – with future murderers and rapists, I'd be so exhausted that I'd fall asleep for a half hour or so before taking Temora up to the woods in front of our home and regaling her with fantastic, fanciful tales about 'Galoomchiks' – a kind of benevolent gremlin – and other fantastic creatures. After the evening meal I'd slump in the chair and try to get some shut-eye, for I knew I'd be up during the night when Temmy would wake up with colic or the painful after-effects of serious burns. These she had sustained from getting into a bath full of boiling water. I had always blamed my wife's carelessness for this, though it has to be said she never took this view of the incident.

Temmy had suffered third-degree burns to her feet, shins and lower body. As I lay on the carpet in her room listening to her sobbing, I'd wonder why Greta, at home all day, didn't cut the fucking grass herself. The weekends and the gigs brought some relief. The post-ceilidh drinking sessions were great fun at first, but by the time the consequences manifested themselves, a pattern of conditioning and reinforcement had been set up. You never get something for nothing when alcohol is involved.

On my way down from a gig in Carrbridge I was almost capsized by an unwelcome upheaval to my emotional barometer. I kept hearing a small angry voice in my head. In my head rant I planned to avoid confrontation by lapsing into silence. I thought that this strategy would be ironic – a public blether who chose not to speak privately.

I had packed up the gear, with difficulty. I had run out of cigarettes. The whole situation was verging on the desperate. My entire system was in irritability overdrive, motoring nothing short of mania. Greta had inserted herself into my consciousness like a spike, badgering me, bothering me and persecuting me. There were times, perhaps too many times, when I considered murdering her.

I trudged up the stairs to bed, nursing a corroding indignation. I slid next to Greta. (Oh, we still made love fairly regularly. Not with passion, but civilly.) I snuggled up against her back, but she was fast asleep. Very soon I myself was dead to the world, too.

Temmy started bawling it seemed like three minutes later, though I think I was sleeping like a stone for at least three hours. Greta nudged me with her elbow.

"Go and see to your daughter," she grunted sleepily. She rolled over and covered her head with the duvet.

I rose shakily from the matrimonial bed, quickly pulled on a pair of trousers over my pyjamas. When I'd heated up her bottle in the kitchen I climbed the stairs to the squalling infant's room and she scoffed the lot quickly. When she had fallen asleep, with a weary sigh I inserted myself into the sleeping bag that was permanently folded at the foot of the cot.

After about three hours I was wakened by the cawing of the rooks in the woods. Quietly I got up and toddled down to the living room. Greta was sitting on the couch reading a magazine.

"You never listen, do you?" she said accusingly.

"What are you talking about?" I said.

"You told me that you'd not be hanging about with the wet-heads after the concert, and I said I needed you home for what's left of the weekend. You think three o'clock in the morning's a reasonable time?" she snorted.

"Sorry," I said.

"And so you should be," she shouted.

'*But I am,*' I felt like shouting back at her. '*I am so sorry for just about everything in my life.*' I tried to touch her hand. But as soon as I extended my arm she flinched. "What's up, Greta?" I whined. She ignored me, spreading her arms wide, like Elmer Gantry, and yawning.

"I don't know what's happened to us," I said.

"Don't you?" she said, not looking at me.

"No, I don't," I said.

"Tough luck," she said.

"What the hell is that supposed to mean?" I snapped.

"Work it out," she said.

"Why are you acting like this?" I asked plaintively.

"I'm not acting," she hissed.

"You're always sniping at me," I said, "bringing me down, when I'm doing my damnedest to provide for you and Temmy."

"I don't want to talk about this just now," she said, rising and leaving the living room and heading in the direction of either the kitchen or the dining room.

Silence. I heard the sound of a screwtop bottle being opened. I sat in the armchair staring listlessly at the books on the shelves lining the wall opposite me. Eventually, I got up, and on tired legs moved into the dining room.

Greta was slumped at the table, a whisky bottle and half-full glass of amber liquid before her. She looked up lazily as I entered and drawled, "You're a teacher and a father, Norman. But you think you're a singer. Some hope."

I could have garroted her. "I'm a serious family man, Greta," I said, "and you know it."

She looked up at me, her face flushed with acrimony. "You don't like your life, do you, Norman," she said. Her tone was glacial.

"I hate my life," I replied. It was at that point I saw out the corner of my eye a baby's bath half full of grey scummy water lying beneath the window. "What the fuck's that?" I said angrily.

"What's it look like?" she replied with a triumphant smirk.

"Bath water that hasn't been emptied," I said, raising the volume.

"Oh, I gave Temora a bath yesterday, I think. Can't remember . . ." she said coolly.

"Why didn't you clean up afterwards?" I demanded.

"Thought I'd leave it for you," she said with a flash of teeth.

That's when I lost it completely. "Sure, I'll take care of it," I said, through gritted teeth. An adrenaline charge of rage swept over me. Swiftly I seized the bath and in swinging motion I hurled it through the dining room window. The tinkle of broken glass was strangely pleasing to me. I heard Greta's screams of alarm as I rushed out, slamming the front door behind me. I experienced an explosion of rage. In my anger I felt a wild moment of surcease, as after intercourse.

I jogged, my pyjama top drenched in sweat, across the Fenwick Moor to the village of Newton Mearns, where I knew I could catch a bus into the city. Fortunately, I had the previous night's fee in my hip pocket. I was at least solvent.

While waiting for a city-bound bus in Newton Mearns I studied my reflection in a shop window. This image was not pretty. My complexion was as pale as milk, and two blackened smudges underlined deeply haunted eyes. I was a guy who had done more wandering than any minstrel. Though conscious of my pyjama top and slippers, I didn't allow my dishevelled appearance to bother me. The curiosity of other people about how I looked was a matter of indifference to me. In the event, nobody seemed to pay any attention to me for the duration of that day. My gut had turned into a furnace and what I needed was a stiff drink.

Thus, much later in the evening, I found myself in the West End Hotel in Edinburgh. There I sat between Dr John MacInnes and a writer from Uist, Uisdean Laing, at that time resident in Australia, who dedicated to me a copy of his book of translations and his own compositions called *Gu Tìr mo Luaidh*. I was completely gacked. I was deep in my own forest. Robertson, the proprietor of the West End, kindly offered me a free room in which I slept for around four nights.

19

Myself the Actor

During the years of my courtship of and marriage to Greta, 1965 until 1971, I did the rounds of various hospitals and psychiatric units. In the autumn of 1965 I spent time in the Royal, Aberdeen, and in Craig Dunain in Inverness. These sojourns were by no means totally unpleasant: after a five-day detox, I would begin to eat and thrive. My two admissions to Stobhill Hospital in Glasgow when we were living in Cumbernauld followed the same undeviating pattern. I did not diminish the seriousness of my bouts of prodigious drinking and their aftermath. At the time. And it has been ever thus. Once discharged, sooner or later I would attempt another experiment with drug alcohol. On the morning after the break-out I would be feeling not too bad, and I would want to go out and celebrate the fact that, in my warped thinking, 'I had cracked it'. From my posh residence in Eaglesham I was dispatched to Dykebar Hospital in Paisley a couple of times. Alas, I was becoming used to these boundary stones in my life.

The indices of differentiation I sketched in my dealings with Brigitte Bardot in a previous chapter were exactly the ones that drove me to become a stand-up comedian. Since I was my own producer, director and star in stand-up, I had all the credentials to be an actor. I have been an actor all my life. In my ongoing quest for validity I have inhabited the characters of many types: Hebridean peasant, city slicker, intellectual manqué, acerbic polymath, pleasant and easy-going companion among many other personae.

My insatiable appetite for approval led me, a few days after my light from the family home in Eaglesham, to my most ambitious and least successful role of all. That was a short, a midget-sized, part as a hotel owner. This is a long yarn about a little stroke I pulled about thirty-five years ago when I thought that I was going into withdrawal on the shores of Loch Fyne in Argyll, and that death would find me there. Long imprisoned memories have made it difficult for me to narrate the circumstances that led to what I considered a good little trick. I was now living in my mother's house in Brand Street, but spending a lot of time in Strachur with a statuesque divorced lady, Lindsey Martin, who was about my own age and whom I had met at a ceilidh in the George Hotel, Inveraray.

She was a blonde Scandinavian type, brought up in Manitoba, and stood hunched over a chopping board in the kitchen. I could see from the hang and sway of her breasts that she wasn't wearing a bra.

I went up behind her, encircled these breasts with my arms and kissed her neck. "Leave it out, leave it," she said. "Horny Norman."

"What's wrong?" I said. She turned round to face me, the kitchen knife pointing at my belly. "I've got a lot on my mind," she answered curtly.

When I quizzed her further, it emerged that the owner of the hotel where she worked as a cook – let's call him Sir Ludovic Maclean – was about to sell up. "He'll be in Edinburgh all week talking to accountants and lawyers," she said. "I might be out of a job soon, Norman, and I'd have to give this place up. Maybe move back to Canada, you know?" The 'place' was a rented cottage on the outskirts of Strachur owned by a trio of American submariners based in the Holy Loch at Dunoon. The cocktail cabinet and Lindsey's magnificent breasts were what attracted me to visit Mid-Argyll at least twice a month during 1971.

The price old Ludo sought for his eight-bedroomed hotel sits lightly on my recollection, but the figure of fifty-seven thousand pounds asserts itself unbidden.

I paid little attention to Lindsey's worries, and the weekend passed in usual fashion: sexual high jinks fuelled by lots of hazelnut vodka, peach schnapps, corn liquor, cherry brandy and other exotic brands of alcohol left behind by the American owners.

On Monday morning, after a light coma full of theatrical nightmares, I stood in front of my lover, and asked her if she had any money in her purse. Wordlessly, Lindsey handed me a five-pound note. As I stir the memory soup, in my head the only gobbet that surfaces is the rapid emotional transition from apprehension to relief. Funny thing that: every time I have begged someone for money, always to buy drink, my fear has rapidly turned to euphoria and mounting triumph. I know that shortly, with enough drams of the 'water of life', my quivering body will cope with the toxins I've poured into it.

Lindsey adjusted my tie, ran a comb through my hair and dusted the shoulders of my new suit with spread fingers. I was the picture of the handsome, distinguished man whose profession might be, vaguely, an entrepreneurially cultural academic, print journalist, television or radio director or producer, actor, solicitor, publisher or accountant even. Thick, luxuriant hair just slightly on the long side, curling over the collar of a light grey Austin Reed single-breasted suit. Japonica Swiss cotton shirt under a blue and orange power tie, and the whole ensemble completed by two-toned burgundy and cream Moreschi slip-ons. These gestures towards *dandyisme* had been purchased five days previously in Edinburgh on a maxed-out credit card, when my precipitate flight from the matrimonial home after the row with my then wife meant that I was forced to stagger across the capital, from Robertson's West End Hotel in Palmerston Place to a formica-tabled Indo-Pak restaurant in the University district, dressed only in a pyjama jacket, trousers and slippers. Today, however, as my grandmother might have said, '*Cha mhilleadh a' ghràndachd idir mi*, It wouldn't be ugliness that'd spoil me'. My inward reality, of course, was that of an unco-ordinated wretch. My fine clothing hid a heart like a stone.

Before I parted with Lindsey I took a quick slug of Scotch from a half-full bottle on a coffee-table. The stuff went down like molten pumice. Instantly I felt sick. I padded into the kitchen and, at the tap, I drank long and breathlessly. I splashed some water on my face and was rubbing it with a kitchen towel when I looked up and saw her standing before me. Now go, I told myself. "When will I see you again, Norman?" she said. "Uh, I'll try . . ." I said haltingly, "to . . . er, get up . . . next Friday." "You gonna be drinking?" she asked. "You better not stand me up." I left quickly and marched briskly to my Volvo 122S. I took off like a rocket, heading for Glasgow.

As I drove northwards along the eastern shore of Loch Fyne, heading for Glen Kinglas, the angle of the sun made the water a sheet of burnished silver. Petrol and blood alcohol levels were perilously low. Four miles out, I felt the first symptoms of withdrawal. My entire body oozed sweat as I halted at the petrol pumps in St Catherines, and, though bone weary, my hands clawed with some vigour at the steering wheel. My head seemed to be adrift from its moorings. My heels were dug into the floor mat, with both knees locked. It was hard to swallow: my tongue felt like a giant foot. I was in the bosom of death. I was sure of it. I was going to *die*. Just sitting there on the leather car seat.

I was not in any pain, except for the rasping in my lungs as I coughed endlessly without inhaling. Probably I would black out shortly, I thought, victim of the dreaded heart attack, and after that nothing much would matter any more.

A full half-hour passed before I was able to move. Get petrol? Big spit in a bucket. I intended to proceed forthwith to the public bar in the hotel across the road. Abandoning my car in front of the pumps, I scurried across the road and into the welcoming gloom of the pub. A youth with a large hooked nose and bad teeth framed by particularly virulent acne leaned across the counter. The whiff from his heavily-oiled hair smacked of baleful rituals in front of mirrors.

"Double-double, Mr Maclean?" he asked knowingly.

I nodded, not trusting myself to speak.

"Grouse, Norman?" he said.

I nodded. These Argyllshire people are familiar with my habits, I thought. This boily boy even knew my name. I assumed he'd attended one of my gigs in Cairndow or somewhere; he was obviously a fan. As I drank – no, inhaled – the quadruple whisky, neat, I decided he was all right. I mean, you couldn't help it if you'd been born ugly, right?

"Same again, Norman?" he asked, and, without waiting for my response, called over his shoulder: "This one's on the house." The guy was probably gay and had memorized my name just in case his dream lover should enter his premises.

The real reason, which didn't occur to me at the time, was that I had placed my pipe-case, which bore the legend in crude lettering 'Norman Maclean, World Champion Piper, Glasgow', on the counter. The young barman could see it clearly from his perch beneath the gantry. Maybe he assumed that I was a famous piper . . . or maybe not; maybe he was just humouring me because he reckoned that any well-dressed professional laddie crazy enough to carry such an identity card around with him almost *had* to be a Heavy Dude, and perhaps even loaded.

None of this made any difference to me with a snout full of double-double whiskies. Savouring the Scotch, diluted this time around with water, and the relaxed feeling it induced, I considered my next move. Though feeling no pain, I was concerned, as I always am once I've started, about where my next drink was coming from. I started to mumble distractedly about 'low prices at the Oban lamb sales . . .'

187

Just another hill farmer in elegant Italian shoes passing the time of day. Indeed, I thought it might be prudent to engage in routine small talk.

"How're you doin', young man?" I brayed. "I suppose you're wondering why I've got a face as red as a lobster and why my hands are trembling? Yes! Well, damn it, man! Ever spent a weekend in Ludo's hotel? . . . You'd never believe the skinful we had last night."

"That'll be the last of the wild weekends, then," said the lad, who was now becoming more like an earth person with every drink I downed. "I hear that Sir Ludovic is looking for a buyer."

Bingo! That's what I'd do. I'd buy the hotel. Well, why not? I could pass myself off as a relative and casually drop the figure of sixty thousand pounds into the conversation I might have with the person in charge of the place. Equally casually, I could request a large snifter of brandy: on the house, of course. They wouldn't refuse the new owner, would they? No point in hanging around here any longer.

I paid my new-found friend who had given me the brainwave – what a splendid fellow he turned out to be! – and limped outside, taking care to obscure the tell-tale identity lettering against my right thigh. Right there, Norman. Show whoever is looking after the place that I bear the same surname as Sir Ludovic.

Eventually, after driving at a fast clip back to Strachur, I make it to the Reception area of Ludo's hotel. Bearing the pipe-case at the port with my name showing outwards, I took deep deliberate breaths and rapped smartly on the Manager's door. I was devoid of fear. I was a budding actor dedicated to my craft.

The door opened and a short, fat, middle-aged man wearing a light blue suit stood before me. He had a silver identification bracelet on his left wrist and a bulky metal Breitling watch on his right wrist. He was absently eating crisps from a cellophane packet. He stared at me for a long time. I would have to be very careful with this guy. Finally, he spoke: "Help you?" he asked in an adenoidal whine.

I didn't trust this butterball. He was making me nervous. I was getting a wave of ugly vibrations from his sparse grey hair that he had plastered to his scalp. My opening line was supposed to be something like, 'Good evening, my man! All I want is some tea and tab-nabs in your residents' lounge!' The long silences had over-primed my pump. I was trying to make too much of my affected upper-class Oxbridge accent. I was grimacing in what I thought was a supercilious way, twitching my nose and rolling my eyes around. Perhaps the drink had something to do with my overheated performance, too.

"G-G-G-Good evening, my m-man! [shlobber-gnash-foam]," I gushed. "Allsh I want [spit-foam] is s-s-s-some tea and t-tab-nabs in your R-R-R-Residents Lounge! [sneer-salivate-twitch]."

"Uh-huh," he grunted as he crammed a handful of crisps into his crabbed mouth.

"Ya," I barked. "Got some accounts to do before I take off for Edinburgh."

"Don't want a room, then?" he enquired, spraying crisps before him.

"No, thank you," I responded with a civility that bordered on the obsequious. "Actually," I honked, "I'm hoping to hook up with Sir Ludovic at his lawyers' office tomorrow. Lots of boring business to discuss."

"Every man's got his own twitch," the man said uninterestedly as he brushed past me. His name tag encased in plastic and reading 'Duncan MacDougall' bounced on his lapel as, with extended arm, he pointed to the sliding doors that led to the lounge. He was about to return to his office when I stopped him dead in his tracks.

"Ya," I drawled casually, "I've just bought this place from my . . . er . . .ah, fellow clansman."

Wham! His bored expression changed abruptly. His mouth opened in a startled O like in the *Scream* painting by that Norwegian fellow.

"Tea and biscuits . . .er, Sir, you wanted?" he whined plaintively.

"No, I've changed my mind," I snapped in tones pitched about C sharp. "Do me the favour of bringing me a large brandy and soda and . . . oh, ya, *and* a packet of Bensons." I waved my hand languidly in a gesture of dismissal.

Once seated in a leather chair before a smoky-glass-topped table, I hugged my chest in triumph. I was stardust, I was eighteen-carat gold-plated.

The Duncan chap entered the lounge carrying a silver tray bearing a large brandy glass, a soda siphon and a bottle of Courvoisier.

"Where are my cigarettes?" I demanded in hectoring tones worthy of a subaltern in the Green Howards, which I could have been if I had been bothered to sit my Cert. B test when I was in the OTC.

"Uh, I forgot," he said, in some embarrassment. "I'll go and get them right away . . . er, Sir."

"Mister MacDougall," I said sternly, "I can see where you and I have got to get some things straight. We don't seem to understand each other, and that makes me even more nervous than I was before." A captain in the Scots Guards couldn't have done it any better. "You've got to get it into your head that I will do what I like as the new owner of this establishment," I said in the clipped accents of a Major in the Queen's Own Cameron Highlanders. "Fetch me my cigarettes. Come on, now, chop-chop."

When he returned with the cigarettes he made a big production of peeling the cellophane off the packet, removing the silver paper and producing a light from a gold-plated Dunhill lighter.

I inhaled and blew the smoke in his face. "You, my friend," I say, "are going to get on fine with a former Lieutenant Colonel in the brigade of Gurkhas. Now be a good fellow and bring me some ice. Dismiss, Sergeant!"

I relaxed. Everything was going right: I was finally getting the breaks.

Duncan MacDougall returned with the ice. I resumed work on my 'accounts' on the inside of a cigarette packet. Without looking I poured myself another bumper of brandy, spilling part of the contents on the table.

"You need anything else . . . er, Sir?" he said.

I stared fixedly into his watery eyes. "You'll take me on a tour of the Cocktail and Public bars," I shouted like a Colonel in the Royal Scots Dragoon Guards.

The cocktail bar was deserted when we entered. I clucked my tongue and started muttering about 'wet t-shirt competitions on weekends . . .'

Duncan was radiating disapproval. I heard human voices next door in the Dining Room. "MacDougall, Quick march!" I commanded. Some teenage girls were desultorily setting the tables for breakfast. I marched past them swinging my right arm, thumb over clenched knuckle, like the old soldier I surely was, and kicked open the door to the Public bar.

This was a heavy night in downtown Strachur. The clientele, all male, were dressed in blue boiler-suits and dung-stained calf-high industrial boots. They stared at us in silence. The barmaid, a middle-aged harridan who must have been a remarkably ugly child, was impassively hostile. Finally she spoke. "What do you want?" she snapped.

I was on a roll now. "I'll make it easy for you," I said, just like General Montgomery. "You're sacked! And so are all the ugly bitches in the Dining Room!" I barked. In ten seconds I went from soft-spoken Ulsterman general to frenzied cleric in the mould of Ian Paisley to bellicose Jihadic terrorist. It pains me now to recall that Old Mary, who had worked in the kitchen since Lazarus took a nap, fainted clean away upon hearing this news. "Go! Go! Go!" I bellowed. "I'm bringing in Filipino girls! They're cheaper and better-looking than you lot!"

MacDougall shrugged apologetically to the gob-smacked punters and led me away. This guy is just another wet-head hotelier, his expression seemed to say.

Back in the Lounge with my bottle of brandy, I hunkered down in the padded leather chair. It was all over now. There was no doubt in my mind that something ugly was about to happen. It was important, I thought, to get out of this hotel immediately. I would need to organize some booze for the road, however.

When MacDougall entered again I launched myself into my appeal. "Here's the problem, my man," I said. "I have to leave here right away. Must see Sir Ludovic at nine o'clock tomorrow morning." Plummy accent was slipping.

He shrugged.

"Look," I said in a tremulous voice, so different from the commanding tones I had employed earlier. "I was wondering . . . I wondered . . .yeah, I thought maybe I could get something from you to help me get down the road . . ."

"What?" he said.

I hesitated then blurted out in a broad Glaswegian accent: "Any chance uv a karry-out, Jimmy?" This was a nifty little line from a graduate of Jesus College, Oxford, what?

The policeman from Skye, summoned no doubt from Inveraray by my erstwhile batman, Duncan MacDougall, put the arm on me. "*Chan eil buintealas agad ris an àite seo, a Thormoid*, You don't belong here, Norman," he said quietly. '*Thugainn a-mach*, Come on outside."

I went quietly with him to the front entrance. "Where's your car?" he said.

"What car?" I parried.

"The one you've been driving while blind drunk."

191

"Look," I said. "I don't care about the car. I'm seriously knack-ered. Just take me to jail."

He laughed. "No, you're not going to jail," he said. "If your sur-name hadn't been Maclean and if you'd pretended that it was, you'd be facing a custodial sentence for sure. As it is, I'm taking you to the Rest and Be Thankful. You'll spend a shitty night in the open but we'll just put it down to a drunken prank."

Sir Ludovic didn't get his price and kept his hotel. Lindsey got married to a hotelier in Dunoon and opened a gourmet restaurant called 'Lindsey's Kitchen' in the place. Duncan agreed to attend a psychotherapist for about three years afterwards. Old Mary took to drink and eventually went into rehab.

20
Tinker Woman

In the summer and autumn of 1972 I was conducting a steamy affair with a married lady in Lochaber. On my discharge from the Crichton Royal Hospital in Dumfries, paid for at great expense by my widowed mother, in the spring, I had tried to observe my vow to abstain from close relationships with the opposite sex 'to the best of my ability'. The 'best of my ability' was none too impressive when it came to sex. But it was now time to end this shameful liaison. I was headed for our place of assignation, arranged by telephone the previous evening. Yes, I was headed for the old schoolhouse at the head of Loch Arkaig where I intended, in dignified fashion, to break the news to the lady.

The afternoon was growing dark and sashes of sleet fell randomly out of a lowering sky. Occasionally, I glanced at the loch on my left as its colour became steadily blacker, and I sensed some connection between the lengthening shadows on it and my ability to call to mind my youth. Perhaps when night would envelop the glen, and that would not be long now, my childhood would disappear in the darkness. But still, away up at the far end of the loch, the dying winter light left a wash the colour of ash on its surface.

Where the little narrow road curled around bays of shingle and rocky promontories its career was smooth and level, but in places, hills and gullies set it to rearing and plunging steeply. It was still no wider than single-track, but a tarmacadam surface had replaced the cart furrows that were here before. Nowadays, travellers no longer had to throw two stout trees across the many burns in order to traverse them.

I parked at the schoolhouse alongside a mud-stained Landrover and a tapping sound of metal on metal came to my ears. There was something intrinsically sinister about this tap-tapping noise. *Thunk, thunk, thunk . . . poinng.* It was the dangling hasp on the door, padlock long gone, banging against the corrugated walls of the schoolhouse in the wind.

That afternoon I was extremely nervous. There came the low sound of singing from inside. I hesitated. Another sound was heard. I grabbed the dangling hasp and rapidly released it. "Unghhg . . ." I grunted. "*O, Dhia, seall!*" – I was bent double clutching a cut in the palm of my hand. There were one or two seconds of silence. A drop of blood glistened on a paving stone. I fastened a handkerchief roughly around the wound, pulling the knot with my teeth. The schoolhouse door creaked as I entered the single room, my heart in my mouth.

My mistress Liz was sitting on the teacher's high chair gazing at the flames that were already rising from the round opening on the top of the wood-burning stove. A black duffel coat lay on one of the tiny desks. She was wearing black ski-pants and a white sweat-shirt that clung to her large, round breasts. The long, black hair had been arranged in thick coils high on her head, and her broad face, as she smiled at me, glowed bronze in the firelight. If I had sought evidence that she had prepared carefully for our encounter, I needed to look no further than the tiny blood-red earrings, the same colour as the lipstick that covered the tender mouth with its white teeth. Liz was of tinker stock – her grandfather was Robbie Stewart, a famous Sutherland traveller – but when I met her she was a housewife in Fort William where she was married to a comfortably-off builder who had been left with a young son when his first wife died. From the outside she appeared content with her lot, but behind the great, black eyes an unnatural hunger gnawed at her.

When we used to meet, mostly in woods around Fort William, we succumbed to a kind of fit and gave ourselves over to ceaseless kissing and caressing of one another.

Without speaking almost, with reaching hands we used to tweak, cup, tickle and suck, and while she never denied me ejaculation, I had never been allowed to slide into her moist depths. Where Liz's pleasure lay I did not know, and neither could I say why we kept on meeting.

That afternoon in the schoolhouse my gaze was fixed on her plump red tongue as she deliberately moistened her lips.

"You don't really know what I like, do you, Norman?" she said in a low-pitched, husky voice as she moved towards me. "I know what you like, though. Ever since that first time – the night you were singing at the Royal?" I blushed as I recalled what had happened after

I met her and her party at a table full of drinks. I had written my good wishes on a slip of paper proffered by Ally her husband, a thickset little man of about forty or so with the smell of whisky on him, when Liz led me to the dance floor. Elegant in high heels and a short black chiffon dress, she enfolded me in shapely, bare arms, and the repeated thrust of her thigh between my legs as we twirled and swooped, along with her warm breath spluttering in my ear, caused my will to melt. Ally had to leave early to meet a friend. Minutes afterwards, on the bed in Room 34, we lay down together fully clothed. She kissed me, starting at my ears and eyelashes, then sliding down to my neck and chest, undoing buttons, buckle and zip as she moved her mouth. Her hands reached down and measured the length and breadth of my bulge. The more uninhibited her ministrations and the rougher her fondling of me became, the more I was convinced that some uncanny passion beyond my knowing was behind her urgency. Quickly I drew her up, turned her onto her back and moved onto her. "Wait, go easy," she whispered. "Let me bring you relief by hand. Please, Norman." She arched her spine and effortlessly rolled me over. Within seconds I felt her hands on me once more, less frenzied this time. I had no choice. In a short while, as my fingers were tangling in her hair, my head turning from side to side on the pillow, I tried to prevent Liz from seeing the weakness in my eyes if she should raise her head from her labours. Swiftly and smoothly her fingers moved up and down and as the familiar tightening in the groin and belly built up, so I despised myself. The weaker I became, the more her strength was affirmed. Suddenly came the thrusting upwards as the time of my spending overtook me. It was only a brief glimpse I caught of her dark eyes as she raised her head, and I was about to turn away to the wall, but I saw they were half-closed, her expression beatific . . .

In the little schoolhouse of Srathan that afternoon a powerful magnetism forced me closer to her. I took a couple of steps in her direction. I stood stock still, my face turned away from her. "Liz," I said, "I can't take it any more."

"Can't I help you?" Liz said, fear in her eyes as she slowly got to her feet.

"You know, Liz," I said, taking a step backwards, "we've got to talk."

"Plenty time for talk later, Norman," she said, standing upright now. "We've got the rest of our lives."

I walked across the room towards the teacher's stool. I was amazed at how lust and mental agitation combined to push me towards her again. I sat on the stool. I wished I had headed for the door.

Liz approached and in one swift, fluent movement sat on her heels before me, gazing boldly upwards. She was like some robber, I thought, who was about to steal from me. My face was turned away from her.

"Hey, Norman, I'll be good to you," she said. "I've always been good to you, haven't I?" She placed the palms of her hands on my thighs. "Norman? What's wrong?"

I attempted to moisten my lips, but found it impossible, as my entire body had become parched.

"We've got to pull the pin on this . . . this *charade*, Liz," I said, and I had never heard my voice so muffled.

She stared at me, as though she was trying to figure out whether or not I was joking.

"But, Norman . . . what about . . . I thought that this is what you wanted?" she stammered, as her hot hands roughly massaged my legs from calves to thighs.

My entire body stiffened and I said, "Listen, Liz . . . No . . . Listen . . . I don't love you – and this is killing me . . . because . . . because I know that you think I belong to you . . . but like I said, I don't love you."

Liz ignored this, and proceeded to wrap her arms round my back. Her fingers gently pulled my shirt from the back of my trousers.

"You think maybe you could kiss me?" Liz said. A high tide of fear was in her eyes as she leaned more heavily against my lap and began to stroke my arms. "I want you, Norman," she said.

"You don't understand," I said. "I'm exhausted doing things I know are wrong. Like . . . you know, us being together like this? You're married, for God's sake! Maybe nobody else will show me as much love as you have done, but I've got to hope that out there . . . somewhere . . . Look, what I'm trying to say is . . . this has to be our last meeting."

She remained silent, shrugged off her sweat shirt, which had streaks of blood on it where my injured hand had touched her breasts, and unhooked her bra.

With my eyes fixed on the door I kissed her softly.

Liz carried the kiss on, her lips moving from my mouth to my neck and down to my chest.

I remained slumped on the stool as Liz undressed me. I neither hindered nor assisted her. Why, I asked myself, do I have to pretend to be like other men, by attempting to make conversation, when I recognize that what I should prefer is that I no longer have the ability to breathe?

Placing her hands beneath my armpits, Liz dragged me upright so that, completely naked now, I was up against her and our tongues were flowing together and I wriggled to get even closer to her, wanting, wanting something, wanting a sheltered, safe place that would wrap me in warm softness. I turned my head away from her for an instant. "Liz," I said breathlessly, "I need . . . need to get away . . . From me."

I entered Liz in triumph and my excitement quickened as her thighs gripped me with surprising strength. There was a tension in her body that communicated itself to me, and caused me to cup her thrashing head in my hands. I was in complete control. I felt her lifting herself to me, as if hungry to swallow me up. I grabbed on to her writhing hips and rode, rode, rode, until I could hold back no longer and the rock shattered beneath me and vertigo overcame me. An electric current passed through my body and the command of the blood, to reproduce itself, to live for ever, was finally obeyed.

I saw in the dim light her pendulous hugeness, and my head swam. Liz placed her hand on the back of my neck.

"Don't do that," I said.

"Why, pet?" she said.

"I'm afraid," I said, "if you peel off my old skin – Christ! I sound so melodramatic."

"You've been doing tap dances for others all your life," she said, shaking her head.

"But they're so real, those people," I said. "Especially the ones from the past."

"But many of them are dead," Liz said. "You can't change that."

We lay in silence. I decided that I would go. I sat up. With my right hand I rummaged among my discarded clothing searching for my stockings.

"You hate letting other people see the real Norman Maclean," Liz said. "Don't you?"

An unbearable itch covered my arms. The door was about ten feet away from the spot where we were lying. I wished I was fully dressed.

"I've been searching," I said.

"Searching?" Liz said.

"Searching," I said. "You know – searching? I kept thinking how many women were out there . . . and how one of them . . . might, I don't know, absolve me."

Liz laughed. "And by moving on, you think you'll change?" she said.

"That was the idea," I said.

"So," Liz said, "were they as helpful as you thought? Those other women?"

"Of course they were helpful," I said. "They were very helpful. You're helpful." I raised my arms, palms upward, fingers bent rigid. "I've tried intimacy time and time again," I said. "Trouble is – it doesn't hold, right?"

"Wrong, Norman," she said. "Believe me – intimacy will last, if you want it to. But you've really got to want it."

I pulled on my trousers, then my shoes. It was time for me to get out, I thought. Her words had challenged me, and I had no thoughts but to escape. "My problem," I said, "is that I cannot give myself completely to others. I don't know how to tell anyone about me. All I do is improvise."

That made her smile. "It's like you're in a never-ending film where everybody knows the script, except you," she said.

I quickly twisted my head around to look at her more closely. There was sweetness and comfort in that tender mouth, I thought. "That's it," I said. "That's exactly it."

Right in the middle of putting on my jersey, the thought came to me that I should remain a little while longer. I shall stay with Liz another ten minutes, I decided.

I lay down beside her, and supporting myself on one elbow looked down at her naked body. When I lightly placed my fingers on a nipple she covered them with both her own hands.

"Of all the folk you've met in your life," she asked, "which ones did you get really close to?"

Reluctantly, a sigh rose from deep within me. I was wearying to get away from these questions. What I found most strange, however, was that I lacked the strength to extricate myself from the situation. I tried again to tweak her nipples with my fingers. Liz stopped me with her own hands.

"Since Seumas Mòr I haven't needed any other people," I said.

"That's a lie," she said.

Suddenly a tide of regret overwhelmed me. Why was I still here? What kept me a prisoner in the little schoolhouse of Srathan attempting to participate in a discussion with a woman whose every word pained me? I moved my hand from her breasts to her neck. A little vein throbbed there. I could feel it beating strongly, and the certainty grew in the core of my being that it was from this power source that my own emotional good health would be restored.

"There must be someone in your past you miss," she said.

I hesitated. Then a powerful message straight from the heart made itself known.

"My father," I said. "I never really got to know him."

I could not think of anyone else. Suddenly I felt as if there was a lump in my throat, and I was very close to the point where I might begin to weep.

"Look, Liz," I said, and my eyes suddenly filled with tears. "I don't want to talk any more about intimacy or relationships."

"But Norman," Liz replied, "you've got lots of friends. You've worked hard at forming relationships."

"But I know who my worst enemy is," I said.

Liz seemed confused.

"My worst enemy is lying here on sheep shit in this fucking schoolhouse. It's me."

Now crying openly, I said, "I'm the one who can't accept success. Right on the brink of success a voice inside me says I don't deserve it, and I snatch it away from myself by hitting the sauce."

Without conscious thought I leaped to my feet and found myself standing in the doorway. I stood, facing Liz, with my hands tucked into my armpits, feet separated, like a mannequin in a shop window.

A heavy sigh came from Liz as she put her clothes on. "Norman," she said, "I feel sorry for you. You're hollow, man. Okay, you're attractive, but you're a taker. Your tongue's worn thin saying 'Gimme, gimme, gimme.'"

I turned my head so that I was looking away from her, and I said: "Yes, I know what you mean." And I did know, because at that very moment I was struck by a particular thought. However often I might find myself alone with a woman in the future, I should never be completely certain about what I was seeking. It was not friendship, or love, or even sex that motivated me. I grasped her wrists and dragged her hands down to her sides.

"You're cursed," she said. "No woman who has enough regard for herself to be able to give love to another person . . . she'll never hate herself enough to get involved with you." She paused and gave a short laugh. "And the ones," she said, "whose self-esteem is so low that they'd want to take you on . . . well, they don't know what love is, and they won't be able to show it to you."

I stood resolutely at the doorway as she made to brush past me.

"No," she said, "we won't ever meet again. There's nothing to talk over. You hate talking, Norman. Poor you." She took a heavy breath and turned slowly away. "Fuckin' rat," she hissed, her eyes narrow and her lips curled in disgust. "You never knew, Norman," she said, "what kind of woman I was, did you?"

"Well . . ." I said.

"And I don't suppose," she said, "I'll ever know what kind of man you are either."

Liz turned abruptly and walked out of the room.

I was devastated. My noble speech of renunciation had been aced by a tinker woman. After twenty minutes or so dragging at cigarette after cigarette, I jumped into my car and angrily drove at speed to Glasgow and my mother's new address in Mosspark.

I had been staying in 90 Ascaig Drive with my mother and wee Uncle Colin for about three months, reading, watching television and performing the odd semi-professional gig, when I started drinking again. The inevitable happened. An ambulance took me to the Southern General Hospital in Govan, where I remained for three weeks. There was something different about this visit. First of all, I was shaking so violently that morning that my mother, despite her life-long abhorrence of drink, sent my uncle out to the licensed grocer's for a quarter bottle of whisky. I remember drinking it in the ambulance taking me to the hospital. Propped up by my only friend, I was able to walk into the ward to which I had been allocated. The recovery proceeded at glacial speed. However, recover I did. I put this down to having chosen my parents very carefully. Despite never treating my body like a temple, I enjoyed robust health until very recently.

When I was discharged, I was filled with new resolve. I promised myself that I wouldn't touch alcohol ever again. This period of abstinence lasted a full year. On the advice of Iain Christie, the law-yer who was handling divorce proceedings on my behalf, I applied for and was accepted into a course in Strathclyde University leading to a postgraduate diploma in Personnel Management. I had really wanted to study for a degree in the Law, but there were no vacan-cies in the faculty. This Personnel Management qualification would have to do.

This one-year course proved to be a healing experience for me. I enjoyed the lectures on Sociology, Behavioural Psychology and Sta-tistics. My fellow students, about sixteen of them, were by definition mature. I myself was thirty-seven years of age, was less in awe of the lecturers and threw myself into my studies with enthusiasm. I felt I had something to prove academically, and was greatly encouraged by the very approachable teaching staff.

I didn't lack for female companionship. I had taken to visiting the home of a younger girl from Barra, Mary Catherine Macneil, in a flat in Iona Court. In her company I regressed into the Gaelic reservoir of culture that lapped within me. She was the best Gaelic speaker I had ever encountered and our nights were filled with dalliance and shared memories of our respective childhoods.

In the summer of 1975 we took a fortnight's holiday in a coastal resort near Genoa. Sunbathing and window-shopping occupied our days.

"*Tha e air a bhith mìorbhaileach, a nighean*, It's been marvellous, girl," I said on the eve of our departure for Glasgow.

"It has been good, Norman," she said. "But it's just an interlude in time. When you go home you have to do that month in the British Aluminium Factory in Fort William for the practical experience you need to get your diploma. I'll go back to the telephone exchange in Anderston and we'll both move on."

Beautifully tanned, I made my way to Kilmonivaig, where my cousin Nan was married to Archie MacColl. I intended to stay with them for the month's practical factory experience. But for some strange reason I stopped at the Kings House Hotel at the foot of the Black Corries on Rannoch Moor for a celebratory pint. Perhaps I was rewarding myself for my abstemiousness during the preceding year; maybe I was secretly worried about my ability to work in a factory environment; perhaps I was regretting having broken up with Mary Catherine. The whole potpourri was of course multi-factorial. All I remember of the ensuing two or three hours was admiring my brown forearms on the counters of various bars in the town of Fort William and quaffing a great many pints of beer.

On the east side of the River Lochy on the neat little road that ran north to Kilmonivaig I gracefully glided off the tar onto a flat pasture where Charolais cattle dozed. I had not even attempted to apply the brakes. I was very drunk. On foot I reached my cousin's home and told them my car had been abandoned about a mile back. Archie promised to tow me out in the morning. And he did just that, but I insisted on going on to Spean Bridge Hotel for a 'curer'. This was the start of an epic debauch that took me from Spean to Glenuig in Moidart and back again.

I remembered my last night of freedom. I had been drinking in the public bar of the Spean Hotel until closing time. Sadie Cameron, married to Iain Beag, was a former girlfriend of mine. She was in the Cocktail Bar and offered me a lift back to Nan's, but in my perverse way I refused her offer and decided to walk the two or three miles to the farmhouse. It was the cattle that unhinged me. As I loped past the MacPhees' house, the only dwelling between the main road and my destination, I saw these monsters lying in heaps on the pasture. They were not Charolais cattle. They were giant elephants. I knew it wouldn't be long before they roused themselves and trampled me to death. "Holy shit, they've spotted me," I whispered to myself. "Run, Norman, run!"

In the morning I awoke to find Archie MacPhee, our neighbour, leaning over me.

"Norman," he said, "Nan's phoned for an ambulance. You're going to Craig Dunain."

The room looked like the site of some drug dealer's pad after a raid by armed police. The chest of drawers was lying on its side against one wall. The wardrobe was leaning at a precarious angle against my bed. A grim memory and vivid flashbacks of my battle with the elephants in my room loomed up.

"Here," Archie said, extending a half bottle of whisky. "Take this for the journey up to Inverness. Get dressed." He shook his head sadly.

"Thanks," I said, distractedly.

21
Heady Times

I did not know it then, but my stay in the psychiatric hospital in Inverness in the summer of 1975 was to signal the start of the best thirty months of my life. As usual, arriving in reception around noon, I was more dead than alive. Liberal doses of Valium and multi-vitamins soon worked their by now familiar magic. Soon I was out and about, mixing with a sizeable group of Hebrideans from Lewis, Harris and the Uists.

I was also seeing *another* girl in Craig Dunain. In fact, I was seeing rather a *lot* of her – only she didn't know it at first. I was *stalking* her. Audrey was a married patient from the Hilton district of Inverness, and had suffered some kind of stress-induced breakdown. She was a tall, striking blonde in her late twenties, with bright blue eyes and high cheekbones. Under the influence perhaps of our respective prescription drugs, we'd play a little game. Every day I'd wait for her to emerge from the dining room. Then I'd follow her to her ward. She would start to run . . . and *I* would run after her. She would make cute little sounds: *Oh! Oh! Oh!* Then I would make cute sounds back at her: *Urrgh! Urrgh! Urrgh!* I just knew she *loved* our little game.

One day I caught up with her. We began to chat. In no time she was smiling; then laughing. That was the start of a brief but intense relationship. I had long since retrieved my car from Kilmonivaig, and every second afternoon or so Audrey and I would take a spin to Scorguie woods. After the first love-making session on a carpet of pine needles, we both knew we would be taking our relationship further. This woman launched my world in exciting new directions. She was totally uninhibited. We took to wrestling naked, and I was initially pleased to allow her to subdue me. Straddling my aroused groin, she would insert four fingers into her vagina and masturbate herself with rapid strokes before roughly inserting my penis into her well-lubricated crotch. After a while, though, I became slightly afraid of this unquenchable sexual appetite of hers. Though I was living in the past, with the Gaelic speakers, and in the present with my voracious lover, I was planning for the future I was convinced I was going to have with . . . someone else.

Another source of comfort to me was the injection of three hundred pounds into my meagre savings account by Martin Macdonald, Head of Gaelic Radio in BBC Inverness. He visited me while I was in hospital, and offered me the money if I would assign to the Beeb the rights to half a dozen songs I had recorded for John Alick Macpherson nearly a decade previously. I agreed with alacrity. I was solvent. I was sober and healthy. I decided to accompany a couple of the Lewis men, who were being discharged with me on the same day, to Stornoway.

These were heady times indeed! Bleached of self-esteem after summarily dismissing Audrey, I was ready to pursue romance again. I installed myself in a comfortable hotel called the County, in Church Street. It was there I first cast an eye on *Peigi an Nullaig*, Peggy Martin, daughter of Donald (who was born around Christmas.)

Peigi was working as a chambermaid and waitress, and served my table in the dining room. She looked like someone who could have made a career in television.

I was struck by her radiant beauty, prominent cheekbones, gleaming golden hair and graceful carriage. She was wearing a black dress with a spotless white apron which did not disguise plump décolletage. I immediately fell for her, and contrived to be in her company as much as possible. I reasoned that the love I craved deserved a second chance. I wanted the best for the most beautiful girl on the planet.

She told me that she was divorced from her husband, a merchant seaman, and had three children: Kareen, thirteen; Donald, eleven; and Martin, eight, her favourite, and, soon after I got to know him, mine too. She lived with her widowed mother and the kids in the Poligan. (The place-name was taken from a concentration camp in South Africa built by the British during the Boer War: it must have been a grim place in the days when the returning heroes from the Great War 'raided' the grazings of Gress Farm and hacked out crofts for themselves.) The postal address was 10 New Street, Back, Isle of Lewis.

But it was not just her physical beauty and calm, soothing demeanour that attracted me. We had a mutual frame of reference in our shared Gaelic heritage. Her uncles, seamen all, had their counterparts in my own family. We had grown up listening to the same thick 78s of Neil Maclean, Archie Grant and a new hero and pioneer, Calum Kennedy. We effortlessly swapped stories about ghosts, second-sight and 'characters' we had heard about in our childhood. I experienced a feeling of coming home. I had no doubts about this woman. She was definitely the one.

One afternoon I was visiting the Poligan and I was overwhelmed by a feeling that was greater than happiness. I felt renewed. There was so much ahead of us, so much to be looking forward to.

Peigi had one arm draped over the back of the sofa, throwing her ample breasts into prominence. Her face, with the narrow brow and prominent cheekbones, displayed anticipation.

"*Tha thu àlainn, a nighean*, You're beautiful, girl," I said.

The thin-lipped mouth widened in a smile. I moved a little towards her, and she immediately came into my arms, yielding and eager. I kissed her mouth, her throat, her lidded eyes.

It was then she invited me to move in with her. This could work. I knew it. Peigi was the one I had always wanted. I AM LOVED I AM LOVED I AM LOVED. . . caused my innards to levitate. What I wanted was unconditional love, and I got that from Peigi.

I took a job in Lionel Secondary in the parish of Ness as a teacher of Gaelic. This was most rewarding. In the staffroom I had two established Gaelic writers, Norman and Alasdair Campbell, with whom I had long, Socratic dialogues about art and literature. The children were the brightest it was ever my privilege to teach. A fact I remarked upon was that the high flyers in my third-year class had no inhibitions about expressing themselves in Gaelic, indeed seemed quite proud to do so, while the less intelligent pupils in my other third-year class were more reluctant to communicate in their maternal language. It seemed to me that they imagined that every Gaelic word they uttered diminished the store of English they possessed. They understood every word of Gaelic, but most of the time opted to use English. This attitude is prevalent to this day among a significant proportion of bilingual Gaelic speakers. I leave people to make their own inferences as to the self-esteem of these folk.

A diversion that gave me much pleasure was the formation of the Ness Pipers Society. A dozen or so pipers, the majority of whom were ex-Seaforth Highlanders, met on a Wednesday night in the Cross Inn, where Tom Patterson, the proprietor, served free tea and sandwiches.

We'd practice sets on the chanters for about an hour, then we'd get the big pipes out and blast away for another hour or so. Peigi approved of my involvement in this little club. This was a first for me, and endeared her even more to me. In addition, Norman Mackenzie, the proprietor of the swankiest hotel in the Western Isles, the Caberfeidh, offered me a monthly singing engagement in the function room, for which I was paid a lot of money.

I might have remained in Lewis forever, if it hadn't been for the disapproval of Peigi's mother, *Annag Eachainn*, Ann, daughter of Hector. She was a deeply religious woman, much given to attending weeks of Communion in every parish in Lewis and in Harris too. These black-clad elderly women followed particular preachers in the same way that the secular youth of today follow pop stars. I'd had to have been particularly insensitive not to realise that she found it offensive that her daughter shared a bed with a papist from the southern isles. She was convinced all her life that, because I came from Uist, I was Roman Catholic. My solution was predictable. I'd move away. I talked Peigi into going with me to South Africa, where I hoped to get a teaching job. When settled there, we'd send for the kids. I went so far as to teach myself Afrikaans, to fulfil a condition in the Republic that all employees in the public sector had to be bilingual.

On a cold February morning, Peigi and I left 10 New Street, Back, in my little Datsun Cherry car, for a new life in the Orange Free State. We didn't make it. Instead we ended up in Oban, Argyll. On a leisurely drive south from Ullapool to my mother's house in Askaig Crescent, Mosspark, I took a notion to make a diversion to Oban. Descending *Bealach an Ruigh'*, the Pass of the Ridge, we viewed bonny Oban Bay which lay before us, a mirror of silver framed by the snow-topped peaks of Mull. Peigi was enchanted. She must have had some sort of epiphany.

"*Am faod sinn fantail an seo airson greis*? Can we stay here for a wee while?" she said.

"*Is cinnteach gum faod*, Surely we can," I replied.

And so it came to pass that Peigi immediately got a job as chambermaid and waitress in the Corran House Hotel, while I booked into the Park Hotel and proceeded to run up a daily tab for dinner, bed and breakfast. Mr Kirk, the manager, didn't press me for immediate settlement of the growing bill, but I was aware that I'd have to get some kind of employment soon.

One night I was in the cocktail bar of the Park sipping coke – I was still abstinent at this point – when Billy Ford, Neil Sinclair and Colin (the Giant) Campbell, remnants of Alasdair Gillies' backing band, were entertaining the mainly English visitors with popular Scottish melodies. Since they had provided instrumental support for me many times at the ceilidhs run by Gillies in the Milton Hotel, Fort William, I wasn't shy about giving them a pull during their break.

"Listen, lads," I said, "I'm looking for work as a singer, and I know you guys are well connected in this town. If you hear that some hotelier is looking for an entertainer, I'd be grateful if you'd let me know."

The trio from Colin Campbell's Highland Dance Band examined their shoes and cast sidelong glances at one another. It was like being in a Swedish film where there was no speech, just the sound of swallowing. Not one of them had the *cojones* to tell me that holidaymakers in Oban during the summer season weren't looking for a traditional Gaelic singer to entertain them. They wanted a 'Son of Andy Stewart', or a folk duo like the Corries, or an old-time variety act like the Alexander Brothers.

The following night, Neil Sinclair, accordionist and pianist from Connel Ferry, called me. "Listen, Norman," he whispered over the phone, "how do you fancy being a folk singer for David Hutcheson up in Soroba House Hotel? The hippy guy who did the gig and who had a heavy blow habit freaked out last night, and took off for his home in Edinburgh."

"I'm pawing the carpet as you speak," I said. "Sure, I'm up for it. Pick me up at seven tomorrow night and we'll nail this sucker down."

Well, we auditioned for 'Touchy Hutchie' and we reached an agreement. I would entertain for a minimum of two hours, six nights a week. In return, he'd allow me free accommodation in a caravan behind the hotel and pay me sixty pounds, cash in hand, per week.

My first night was filled with ignominy. Neil Sinclair gave a voice-over introduction. It was full of references to my being a double gold medallist at the annual national Gaelic arts festival . . . blah, blah. And it didn't mean a thing to the middle-aged tourists from the north of England and the scattering of local adulterers. What I hadn't thought about was that I knew the lyrics of only three English songs: 'The Bonnie Lass o' Fyvie', 'The Bonnie Lass o' Ballochmyle' and 'The Green Hills of Islay'.

Dressed in a tailored blazer, open-necked silk shirt, with multi-coloured cravat and grey flannels with black and white two-toned shoes – some folk singer! – I swished up to the mike stand like a ballerina *en pointe* and exhausted my entire English repertoire in ten minutes flat. That's when I knew I was in trouble. It was crazy, but that was when I made up my mind to talk to the members of the audience individually. I posed inane questions like, 'Where do you live, madam?' and 'What do you do for a living, sir?', and depending on the responses I'd consult my mental rolodex of stolen jokes and trot out some old chestnuts.

It worked, and I left my first gig as a full-time professional comedian-cum-vocalist greatly enthused. There followed a steep learning curve I embraced enthusiastically. Every Scots song in the canon I gleaned from cassettes, and quickly memorized them. I brought the pipes into my act. Likewise I employed the clarinet, though not very well. But the smartest things I included in my act were monologues delivered in costume by Highland 'characters'. There was the drag act of the nymphomaniacal waitress from Lewis, the Free Church Elder, the policeman from Uist working in the city, the merchant navy deep sea skipper from Barra and the effete steward on the Cal-Mac ferry. The great thing about these characters from my point of view was that once I had the verbal routines on my tongue, I didn't have to think any more. In addition, the audiences seemed to appreciate these interludes. Indeed, the place became busier as the summer wore on. Over the twenty weeks I worked there, a significant infestation of island people took to visiting at least three times a week – lounging young fishermen from Tiree, Barra and Uist, clutches of female hotel workers from all over the Highland region, and Gaelic-speaking couples who had settled in the town, starved of authentic Celtic entertainment, all flocked to Soroba House Hotel to hear this 'Teuchter' entertainer who had burst upon the entertainment scene. 'Touchy Hutchie' was making plenty of money, and he generously shared it with me. It was a great time for Peigi and me. She had become my best friend as well as my lover.

I soon left the caravan, and with my share of the proceeds from the sale of the matrimonial home in Eaglesham, I bought a one-bedroomed flat in 12 High Street, an old tenement. There we nourished the culture of our respective homelands. This was the happiest I had ever been. The boys joined us, and despite having to sleep in a recessed cupboard in the hall, seemed content. I personally enrolled them in the appropriate schools, Martin in Rockfield Primary and Donald in Oban High School. Kareen, my step-daughter, chose to remain with her grandmother, Annag Eachainn, on Lewis until she had at least finished her fourth year in secondary school in Stornoway. When I came home from a gig, I used to gaze upon the two handsome boys, Donald twelve and Martin nine, and my heart would swell with pride. Peigi would make a big bowl of fritters and after liberal lashings of salt and vinegar the men in her life would gobble them voraciously. I vowed to be a good father to the boys, and a good husband to Peigi.

It was small wonder, then, that I determined to go on the road with my act. I recruited John Carmichael, who himself had given up a comfortable career in teaching to accompany Alasdair Gillies, the singing dentist, to Halifax, Nova Scotia, to record for television a massive series of Scottish entertainment programmes. Gillies had gone back to pulling teeth in Drumchapel, and John was looking for work. The deal was this: John would travel up to Oban by train and spend an overnight with us on the eve of our departure for the north. I drove and paid for the fuel. Our fee was sixty pounds per night, and the disposition of the net profits was two-thirds to me and one-third to my accompanist. The term 'accompanist' sounds patronizing. John was far more than an accordionist in my back line. On the long drives to hotels and village halls in places like Durness, Corpach and Ardrishaig, he subjected me to a crash course in the business of touring. The mysteries of PA speakers, combo amplifiers, leads, microphones, instrumental introductions and musical bridges were all patiently explained. I was fairly mature when I made the leap into performing for cash, and I knew nothing. I greedily assimilated the information he gave me. I don't think I've ever applied myself as intensely to any other activity in my entire life. I had not used my mind in such a constructive way for some time. Of course, this all-or-nothing approach to life and its activities can be a bane as well as a boon. I didn't realize it then, but I did afterwards.

During a period of about six months, every week, John and I traversed the roads of the Highlands for at least four days at a time. A roll call of venues would be boring, but suffice it to say we visited all the entertainment hotspots west of an axis drawn between Wick and Campbeltown. In the spring of the following year we attracted an old stalker. In Roy Bridge, Gairloch and in Nairn, a wee old man would hang back and engage John and me in conversation. He'd buy a bottle of beer for John and a coke for me. When I asked John afterwards who this gnome was, he informed me that this was the legendary John Worth of Inverness, one-time manager of the Playhouse Theatre and the guy responsible for hiring luminaries like Andy Stewart, the Corries, Moira Anderson, Calum Kennedy and a host of other well-known names in Scottish light entertainment.

"What's he want with us?" I asked.

"Well," John replied, with some reluctance, "he wants me to take part in a wee show he's established in the Cummings Hotel in the town. It's seventeen weeks of well-paid work, Norrie."

"Oh," I said, with some chagrin. "Any chance of me getting a turn?"

"Actually," John said, "I think there is. His first choice of headliner was Alasdair Gillies, but the dentist is dragging his feet. His wife and in-laws are churchgoing folk and would disapprove of Alasdair working on the blessed Sabbath. I think you're 'het', man."

Eleven am the following Tuesday, it was a telephone call from Inverness. "Hello, John Worth here. Meet me for coffee in the Spean Bridge Hotel tomorrow at ten."

Floundering in over-stuffed armchairs, we got down to business. Well, Mr Worth got down to business. Everything he said in the elongated vowels of his native Manchester had my head bobbing up and down like a fishing float. But I listened intently to him. He came from a family of impresarios and theatrical producers who worked in Lancashire, and he knew everything about running a light entertainment show. "You're a very funny [*foony*] man, Norman," he said. "I think we could have a profitable arrangement if you were willing to join the cast of 'Cabaret at the Cummings' in June."

A charge of apprehension assailed me, however, when John described payment.

"Budget is tight, Norman," he sighed. "Five might not be all that acceptable, I know."

Christ, five nights at a fiver a night, irrespective of board and lodging, which he was willing to pay for, was a lot less than I'd been making in Soroba House. Playing for time, I lit a cigarette. John noticed my less than enthusiastic response to his offer, and rapidly expanded on his proposed remuneration. "Of course," he spoke rapidly, "that's not counting what you'd make on the 'Bank Raids'."

"'Bank Raids'?" I enquired. "What are they?"

"That's when I sell the show on Fridays to outlying towns and villages," he announced proudly. "I promise you, you'll receive £120 additional wages on a Friday night. That's on top of your basic five hundred pounds for working in Inverness."

Five hundred pounds plus per week! Some kind of braying sound must have issued from my mouth, because I saw Worth's face register 'startle'. This moment was the pinnacle of my existence, and I floated down the road to Oban to give Peigi and the boys the good news.

At Rehearsal Day One I was intimidated by the obvious talent displayed by the supporting cast. Bob and Maggie Donaldson, known professionally as 'The Marlettes', sang Country and Western songs, Scottish ballads and cover versions of current pop songs with enviable composure. Our drummer, Billy Nelson, had a lot of experience playing in pipe bands. Bill Clements, keyboards and clarinet, possessed a singing voice of extraordinary power and range. The Maggie Firth Dancers were comely and athletic and tackled Highland, tap and Rock and Roll with equal aplomb. John always wanted to finish the show with a big production number involving the entire cast. I had the bright idea of having the cast do something different at this finale. The dancers sang '*Plaisir d'Amour*' in four-part harmony. Bill left his seat behind the keyboards and electrified the audience with his rendition of 'Jerusalem'. John Carmichael did a visual gag involving an exploding accordion and an emerging chicken. Wee Billy Nelson delivered a seven-minute stand-up spot. The Marlettes did a slick version of the Highland Fling, and I modestly confined myself to introducing the acts with suitable hyperbole. John Worth, the audiences, and, most importantly, the cast, loved this turn of events. I got brownie points from the back line for my magnanimity. My bringing them forward to display hitherto hidden facets of their personalities did much to dissipate the whiff of resentment I detected early. Who was this raw loudmouth with little prior experience of showbiz who was now headlining the show? I'm sure my fellow entertainers asked this question a lot at the beginning. My strategy paid off, and I ended up very much *persona grata* with the cast.

I was learning a lot of things. The greater part of them came from John Worth. After each show he and I would retire to the Residents' Lounge for his double malt whisky and my coffee. In his slow drawling accent he'd recount vignettes of comedic greats, gossip about fees and generally wonderful show business chat. To this day I owe him a debt of gratitude for his generous help, his enlightenment, and great kindness.

Some sort of sleety rain is falling diagonally across the double-glazed window to my right. I have long since turned off the electric fire and it is turning quite cold in my living room . . . but I don't feel it. I have my face turned up to welcome the chill. Internally, I am aglow as memories of my times with my second wife, Peigi, slowly unspool.

22
Poster Boy

There was a little movie-star magnitude in my life now.

John Worth paid me the compliment of changing the name of his summer show to 'The Norman Maclean Show'. Some of the cast were puzzled by the name change. John explained in his resolutely solid northern drawl that his decision was entirely based upon the harsh reality of commercial drawing power.

The second season in Inverness was even more rewarding than the first. I was given the freedom to perform my own vocal compositions and to experiment with new comedy routines. I actually polished up a routine involving the questions 'Where do you live' and 'What do you do for a living?'

"I'm trying to get agency representation," I'd begin, "and I visit the home of a noted booker. 'Okay, let's hear your act,' he says. I start off with my well-tried opening gambit. 'Where do you live?' I ask. 'Right here, you idiot,' he snaps irritably. 'Okay,' I gabble. 'What do you do for a living?' 'I audition cretins like you,' he retorts. The sense of humiliation is complete, folks." The reception to this goofy routine was usually friendly.

The accordionist this year was a youth from Bucksburn, Aberdeenshire, called Stuart Anderson. The squeeze box was the perfect instrument for this restless soul. His fingers fairly flew over the keyboard and, after bonding, we worked together for a number of years thereafter. In fact we still keep in touch, which is a rare thing in the ephemeral liaisons of show business.

Visits to Fort William were taking up a great deal of my time. Fergie Macdonald, Allan MacCall from Ardnamurchan and I had formed a little recording company called 'Shona Recordings'. Administration of this fledgling company involved spending a lot of time in our office in Cameron Square, Fort William, attending meetings and having my ear bashed by telephone callers. We released three albums that I know about: 'It's Scotland's Oil' featuring Fergie, 'Teuchters Laugh Too', my own first comedy album, and 'John Carmichael Tears the Tartan' an experimental selection of piano accordion music by the eponymous soloist.

In our wee office in Cameron Square I used to cringe when I heard Allan MacCall negotiating fees for me on the telephone. "Yes, friend," he'd drawl, as he sprawled back on the revolving typist's chair, "if you want the best, you have to pay the top fee. We're talking ceilings here, my good friend, ceilings." Nine times out of ten he'd get the inflated fee he was asking for.

Fast forward a year, and in my new much larger flat in Argyll Mansions I got a call from Neil Fraser of the BBC. He had secured funding to make an eight-programme light entertainment series for television. The way things worked back then in Gaelic television was that you committed all your resources to Current Affairs one year, and the next year you lavished your budget on Light Entertainment. Roddy John Macleod from Port nan Long in Skye was the anchorman for Current Affairs, and a cracking job he made of it too. The Light Entertainment shows relied heavily on vocal and instrumental music. Indeed, I had taken part as a guest, under the guidance of Fred Macaulay, in many of them myself.

In the Italian restaurant in the west end of Glasgow where we had *penne*, Neil, dressed in a light-grey worsted suit, projected confidence. "There is a project," he said in his mother's Gaelic, "you might be interested in doing, Norman."

"What is it?" I said, failing to keep the quiver of excitement out of my voice.

"It's a comedy series, Norman," Neil said. "Eight programmes, half an hour each. We'll record them on Sundays over a period of two months, starting in December. I've got Finlay J. Macdonald on board, and we're going to make the best light entertainment series ever attempted by the Gaelic Department. Do you fancy it?"

"That's not even a question, Neil," I replied. "I would work for nothing on a project like this."

"By the way, I'll see you get your *per diem* right now," he added. The *per diem* consists of the marvellous cash-in-hand expenses which you get when actually shooting.

The prospect of doing something like this flooded my veins with glee. All too soon Neil, Finlay J., who had a detectable sense of humour and an enviable fluency in written demotic, and I were beavering away in a rather untidy office, trying to come up with fresh comedy scripts. 'Cutting' and 'shooting', I found, had nothing to do with the Glasgow street gangs of my adolescence. They had to do with film, and I quickly picked up the jargon. The fact that we communicated in Gaelic made for a cohesive atmosphere. The overall ambience was relaxed and productive.

Unlike meetings I attend today, the rank odour of budget hysteria was never present. The formula was not epochal. Studio-based with lavish sets, each programme would open with me delivering schtick, a mixture of anecdote, perceptive observation and straightforward gags stolen from various sources with the serial numbers erased. I'd be seated on a stool dressed in a trendy Cecil Gee lounge suit. I went for a kind of Ken Dodd, joke every twelve seconds, approach. There followed a number of comic sketches – right-down-the-middle gags with strong punchlines. Guest singers and instrumentalists performed a couple of spots, and we closed with a 'stramash' involving everyone. Nothing was improvised. I barnacled myself to this duo and the two months of filming made me euphoric. Our script meetings were peppered with phrases like *"Fuirich diog,* Wait a second . . . How about we try doing this?" . . . "Or maybe doing that?" . . . "Or maybe if you do it like this you can . . ."

My straight man in the sketches was Donnie Macleod, later known as 'Donnie Dòtaman' in a long-running children's television series called *Dòtaman*. I had my doubts about Donnie at first. I knew he had been brought up in Peterhead where his father had been a prison officer. While I was aware that his older sister Margaret spoke in the fluent tones of her parents' native Point, I had assumed that Donnie might have been overly affected by the Lallans of his boyhood, as my own young sister had been by the slurred consonants and glottal vowels of Govan. I needn't have worried. Donnie, as rhythm guitarist of the folk group 'Na h-Òganaich', consisting of sister Margaret and Noel Eadie, had his knees well tanned in the hot and steaming village halls of the Highlands and Islands. He had an amazingly good ear, and as well as being the possessor of a light tenor voice, he had a talent for mimicry that rivalled my own. Rehearsals, conducted in cod Cockney or Mancunian, were a delight. We hit it off right away, and our pleasure and mutual admiration was apparent in every sketch.

The post mortem analyses on Mondays were also a source of great pleasure. Neil created an incredibly casual atmosphere. The fact that we communicated in Gaelic made for a feeling of cohesion in that small office.

All three of us were relaxed and productive as we sketched out the scripts for the following Sunday's shoot. I felt about as alive as I'd ever be. We were like family, and proceedings were so easygoing that you couldn't help wondering why every Gaelic programme didn't involve a team of writers. (I already know the answer to that. The BBC can't afford it. At present, they're skint. The so called 'independent' programme-makers are in worse financial straits. A programme I watched recently being filmed in Kelvinhall was so strapped for cash that they couldn't afford make-up!)

Comparatively speaking, *Tormod air Telly* was made in big budget land. Neil didn't bat an eyelid at requests for a couple of 'overnights' for guests appearing on the series. He wasn't profligate, but he was sensitive. I particularly appreciated the trust he showed in me. Often I'd say to the lads, "Look, I know, this sketch seems a tad light on paper, but I can assure you I used the same gag in Tarbert last week and it got the laughs. Trust me, it *is* effective." And Neil, perhaps with some internal misgivings, allowed the sketch to go through.

There was, however, one sticking point: the signature tune. An accomplished line-up of session players – keyboards, drums, guitar, saxophone, flute and clarinet – opted for a kind of Annie Ross jazz medley. I took the liberty of suggesting a little pipe jig I had composed for a set of lyrics called *Cion a' Bhuntàta*, Scarce of Tatties, sent to me by Donald John MacMillan from South Uist, who was employed as Prime Minister Harold Wilson's armed bodyguard at the time.

Neil listened to me playing the wee tune on the practice chanter, but I could tell he wasn't sold on it. He stared at me with frightening intensity for a long time, then seemed to reach a decision. "Right," he said in a firm tone, "let's go down to the College of Piping in Otago Street. We'll let Duncan Johnstone hear it and he'll make the final decision."

We trooped down to the College. I played the little two-part jig for Duncan and was immensely gratified when the great composer himself approved of it. "Neil," he said, "I myself would be proud to put my name to that little number."

We hurried back to Broadcasting House and, with the session guys really cooking in the background, I recorded the tune on the Highland pipe in two takes. My faith, and Neil's, was justified when the series was broadcast and a host of young pipers, less hidebound than their elders perhaps, picked up on 'Tatties' and submitted it in competitions and included it in recitals. The fact that I had written this simple little melody stood me in good stead when I was over in Oman assisting Gordon MacKenzie, Director of Military Music for all the Sultan's squadrons of pipes and drum corps, in setting up and training a mounted pipe band for a massive military tattoo to be held in the capital, Muscat. Gordon, whose fingers I set on the chanter first of all in 10 New Street, Back when he was a boy of about eleven, introduced me to the young Arab recruits who were about to become the camel-mounted pipes and drums of the Royal Omani Guard. When he casually mentioned *en passant* that I was the composer of 'Scarce o' Tatties', the bandsmen went ballistic. They crowded round me, eyes and mouths forming Os, and gushed compliments my way over cheering and clapping. I was engulfed by brown faces, all barking gutturally in Arabic and broken English, telling me that I was some kind of cross between Mozart and Neil Diamond. Eva Peron must have experienced this screaming adulation in her heyday. "It's insane, man," opined Gordon. "Just because I gave them what after all is not a very demanding tune to learn, they all think you're a male Madonna."

"Och, Gordon," I protested shyly, "it's not as good as 'My Land'." 'My Land' was my first composition for the bagpipe and had a wild trajectory. It started off as an opening song with English lyrics for Andy Stewart. The wee man knocked it back, and I sent it with Gaelic lyrics to the singing dentist, Alasdair Gillies. He displayed impeccable taste by employing it as his opener, in both languages, for many years. The next thing I knew, the late John Weatherston, Pipe-Major of the Red Hackle pipe band, was asking my permission to include the tune, with fiddle and organ accompaniment, in an album the band were about to record. What was I going to say? 'No, John, I don't let anyone record my music.' The Red Hackle duly recorded 'My Land' to good reviews, and the upshot of this publicity was that His Excellency the Governor General of Canada adopted my wee Retreat Air as his own personal tune, to be played at all his public appearances. Unless you've been living in a tree, you will have heard 'My Land' played on the bagpipes. Practically every bandsman, from the exalted gods of Grade One to the minnows of wee marching bands from the Great Uncut is familiar with and plays 'My Land'. Here's what Brian McGeachan, a young journalist friend of mine, has to say about the tune.

"The first time I heard the tune it immediately stuck to my ribs. I instinctively wanted to rush over to Hampden and don the Scotland football kit, convinced that the thundering anthemic nature of 'My Land' would ensure my scoring a hat-trick!

"For years I pressed Norman to write lyrics for what I consider to be an exceptional alternative to 'Flower of Scotland' and 'Scotland the Brave'. I'm certain that modesty has prevented Norman from both writing those lyrics and promoting the piece as fully as he should.

"We have this ongoing national debate about a new anthem for a young generation of Scots. We want a tune that will both reflect the new Scottish Government in Edinburgh and appeal to our beloved Tartan Army. I think 'My Land' is it."

Surprise, surprise, Brian! Here's a set of lyrics I prepared earlier:

> 'Side by side we stand together
> 'Neath the flag of blue and white:
> We salute you now and ever,
> And our souls are filled with pride . . .'

Och, I've quoted this rather overblown piece already earlier in the book, in relation to Beijing.

Life had never been that magnanimous to me ever before. Then, as Joseph Heller has it, something happened. One Monday evening, when driving home from my last script session for *Tormod air Telly*, I was forced to abandon my car a mile or so west of Tyndrum in a blizzard. This was a complete white-out. Unable to distinguish the highway from the surrounding moorland, and having difficulty in breathing due to driving snow, I stumbled in and out of ditches until I made my laborious way to the Invervey Hotel in Tyndrum. Power lines were down and illumination was provided for the sizeable group of refugees by flickering candles. Emerging from the white storm outdoors, we all felt cosy and safe in this warm haven.

The proprietor had provided sandwiches and hot soup, and there was camaraderie among the hill walkers, stranded motorists and locals that was most engaging. A couple of hill walkers to my left at the counter had ordered drams of whisky, and the aroma of the spirits wafted to me and filled my lungs with a longing more intense than I had felt for two and a half years. The craving was a need, as if my soul was bone dry and nothing on earth could satisfy it except a glass of spirits. The unexpected glimpse of a bottle on the gantry behind the bar caught me unawares. An inverted litre bottle of Martell brandy winked at me in the candlelight, and I could taste the sweet, powerful spirit, could feel the bite of it at my throat, the hot rush flowing down my gullet, the warmth spreading across my entire body. The first swallow of brandy was paradise. I heard celestial music. I could not believe I had gone thirty months without this.

Alcohol addiction, if you subscribe to this diagnosis, is a progressive malaise. In relapse, once an addict puts that first drink in his mouth, he doesn't have to worry about the wife or the job or bills. All these mundane concerns are blocked. Now the one task before him is to keep pouring the stuff down his throat. More peats have to be thrown on the fire. The price, however, is always larger than the pay-off.

Why did I keep relapsing? Once in a while I couldn't stand the self-imposed control I had placed myself under and the resultant stress. I had the need to break out, drink too much, become a zombie. That night in Tyndrum, I felt very strongly I needed to break out. One minute I was happy working, perhaps over-working, on the scripts for the television series with Neil and Finlay J. I was travelling all over the north of Scotland to perform a very physically draining act involving playing the bagpipe while lying on my back and dancing. I was spending too much time on Shona Recordings business. Then, out of a clear blue sky, I blew all these achievements away by rendering myself a vegetable through alcohol abuse. I considered this behavioural paradox a reflection of my all-or-nothing approach to life. Whatever I'd be tackling – music composition, teaching mathematics or Gaelic, gigging or writing – I used to throw myself into the activity with abandon. After a spell of intense effort, I would come to resent the pressure I was exerting on myself. 'Give me a break,' my internal voice would squeak piteously. From then on it was only a matter of time before I decided to self-medicate with drug alcohol.

Well, my break-out on that occasion didn't last too long, but I was left with a profound sense of loss. It is undeniable that what was laughingly referred to as my career in showbiz suffered because of my sporadic abuse of alcohol. Other people recognized the danger even if I myself was in denial. Billy Connolly, in 1980, sussed me out. Sponsored by the motorcycle manufacturers Kawasaki, the 'Big Yin' was cycling from Glasgow to Inverness, stopping en route in Perth, where Jimmy Shand provided the entertainment, and in Aviemore, to which he'd invited me. In the cocktail bar of our hotel all drinks were free, and I greedily took advantage of this bonanza as we chatted into the wee small hours. He told me three things that have stuck with me. Firstly, he put a stop to the endless recital of gigs I had lined up by saying, in the slightly effeminate Glasgow voice he affected, "Why are you doing this to yourself? You know, taking on stacks of these small engagements? They can't pay much. You'd be better off concentrating on half a dozen big, big gigs every year for a lot more money." It was then that I had an inkling that I was an adrenaline-junkie who got a buzz out of fatigue.

I put this heretical thought to the back of my mind, and listened intently to his second pearl of wisdom. "You know, Norrie, you've got a talent," he said. "Nice things are going to happen to you. But not if you carry on drinking the way you've been doing all night."

On the eve of his departure for England, where Michael Parkinson, the Duchess of York, Pamela Stevenson and the worshipping aristocracy awaited, Connolly was right on both counts.

It was his third observation that struck a responsive chord with me. Talking about his own experiences onstage, he said, reflectively, "You know, Norrie, sometimes when I'm doing stand-up, I find myself performing actions that I haven't rehearsed, haven't even thought about. I'll be describing a Glasgow Bobby when, suddenly, I find myself actually assuming the gait of a middle-aged cop. It's uncanny, man. I don't know where this comes from. It's like I'm being manipulated by some master puppeteer who's turned me into a marionette, and he's pulling my strings."

An interesting aside: Allan Henderson, the talented young fiddler, piper and raconteur, told me recently that Connolly had been asking after me. He and fellow members of the successful string ensemble Blazin' Fiddles had been invited to provide the musical entertainment at a soirée held in Billy's mansion in rural Banffshire. "Connolly remembers you, Norman," Allan said. He came up to us after the break and said, 'Which one of you guys is from Oban?'

"Aidan O'Rourke admitted that he came from the town," Allan said.

"Know a guy called Norman Maclean?" was the next question posed by the comedian and film actor.

"We all admitted that we knew you, Norman," said Allan.

"That was one funny guy," Connolly said. "You know how you Teuchters aren't noted for your humour – but that Maclean was a genuinely funny man."

I asked Allan if Sir Sean Connery had been present. It seems that he had graced the occasion. "Was he asking for me?" I enquired.

"No," Allan replied. "He was just swanning about being James Bond, and he didn't even speak to the hired help."

I believed the lad.

Anyway, back to *Tormod air Telly*. When the time came for the transmission of the programmes, I was slightly apprehensive. I needn't have worried. We had a smash. The various elements were slick and fast. Audience reaction was phenomenal. There were two main reasons for this: one, each episode in the series was intrinsically good; two, bilingual Gaels were intrigued by any television programme that featured their native language. In contradistinction to audiences today who are being exposed to cheap programming from all sides, viewers a quarter of a century ago were *faithful* in a way that producers and directors now can only enviously dream about. Such was the popularity of *Tormod air Telly* that wedding receptions in the Highlands were interrupted when screening time neared.

It is a source of pain that archivists in the BBC have lost or destroyed most of the footage from this seminal series. I am confident that the film would stand up today. But I would say that, anyway, wouldn't I? At the very least, the advent of video and DVD would have ensured its longevity. I don't know if the Gaelic Department in Pacific Quay will ever dare to replicate these halcyon days. I have my doubts. In the present climate of budgetary constraints, the temptation to spread available resources exceedingly thin is almost irresistible. The programme makers must know that they are in danger of losing a fast diminishing audience. Gaelic on television is at the beginning of a vicious cycle.

23
Hijacked in Quebec

Back in 1980 I had a psychotic interlude in New York after a record-breaking season in the Park Hotel in Oban. During the last few days of this triumph I started doing without sleep and writing little notes to myself. I can never be sure, but I'm convinced that my subsequent manic outburst in the Big Apple was a consequence of getting my cerebral wires crossed in some pernicious way that made me convince myself that I was omnipotent.

My erratic behaviour evinced itself at first in my increasingly hostile attitudes towards my pals, Billy Ford and Neil Sinclair. These were the guys I was going to divvy up the season's takings with at the end of September. Nevertheless I could not refrain from taking potshots at them on stage. "Billy Ford," I used to confide to the audience, "had a dream last night when he saw God . . . Then he remembered he had a mirrored ceiling above his bed." A lot of local people resented Billy, because he had recovered from alcoholism. Maybe I did too, subconsciously. It didn't matter. The snide line got some laughs. Neil too was the butt of some of my sickest routines. "Not many people know this, folks," I used to say in a conspiratorial whisper, "but Neil Sinclair has a glass eye. True. He lost his eye in a childhood accident. When I'm talking to him I can't help staring at his glass eye . . . waiting for it to *move*. I've known him for about twenty-five years and it's still fascinating. Then I got to thinking: 'What good does the glass eye do for him?' It does him no good whatsoever, folks. It might as well do me some good. So . . . if you're going to lose an eye . . . put maybe a digital clock in your eye socket . . . Then when I'm talking to you I can go: 'Dearie me, is that the time it is? Listen, I've got to run.'"

Peigi was understandably worried over my increasingly erratic behaviour when we eventually arrived in New York. Everybody had advised me not to make the journey: Peigi herself, the Rev. John Macleod and my own mother, with whom we spent an overnight. But I was determined to go, and with a fistful of currency and cheques, I arrived in JF Kennedy convinced that I was about to be awarded the freedom of the city, because I had made a scene on the aircraft in the mistaken belief that we were about to plunge into the Atlantic. I diverted the doomed passengers by running through the highlights of my act, including songs, as I pranced about in the aisles. I paid taxi drivers with excessive amounts of travellers' cheques. I made knowing hand gestures towards cops in police cars in mid-town. I spouted from the Book of Leviticus. An alarmed wife delivered me to the Roosevelt Hospital in Manhattan where, after giving the staff an exhibition of Olympic class floor exercises, I was promptly assigned to a straitjacket and a padded cell. I received a short course of cortical depressants which enabled me to sleep soundly for the first time in weeks. Once restored to the general population, I made a rapid recovery and began to lobby vigorously for an immediate discharge. This I secured with much difficulty. I didn't realise it at the time, but it was in the hospital's financial interest to keep me in dock for as long as possible. As it turned out, the bill, eventually paid for by an insurance company, was a stomach-cruncher. With the aid of written testimony from our local GP, Dr Ronald Firth, a lovely gentleman, I got out of that fix unharmed. I have never had a reoccurrence of this malaise, but I always ensure that I get *some* sleep every night.

Together, in the autumn of 1981, Peigi and I flew to Montreal, where we were to hook up with Stuart Anderson, the virtuoso accordion-player. Things did not augur well for our tour of Quebec and Upper Ontario. Stuart's precious accordion had ended up in Montreal's second airport, and he was on the verge of apoplexy. In his thick Buchan accent he was remonstrating with the baggage handlers. "Fit wey kin yese nae ging o'er to this ither airport and fetch my valuable machine?" he ranted. The handlers made Gallic shrugs of non-comprehension – and no wonder: I could scarcely make out his excited delivery myself – and turned their backs on him. That's an odd thing I noticed about the Quebecois. Though they are fluently bilingual, they are better disposed, marginally, to Anglophones who at least make an attempt to speak their *langue maternelle*.

Stuart eventually resorted to taking a taxi to the other airport and retrieved – God knows how – the errant instrument. Later on, at a gig in the Renfrew valley, north of Ottawa, I almost wished he hadn't. We were playing in a swish community centre and we had a fair house. My opening piping set was greeted with polite applause. Once I started on my warm-up spiel, however, I sensed that something wasn't quite right. Eighteen-carat gags, tried and tested, were greeted with universal apathy. I attempted to jolly the audience up by asking them, "What's wrong? Am I talking in French or something?" This got an immediate response. "*Mais bien sûr, Monsieur Ecosse,*" they shouted. "*Parlez en français. Français, Français, Français.*"

I realised with mounting horror that we had been booked into a predominately French-speaking region. In the light of this little landmine, I suppose I coped reasonably well. If I had been given enough time I could have cobbled together a reasonable comic script – in fact, I did so many years later at a gig with the Clan Wallace and the Lomond and Clyde Pipe Band in a place called Niort in north western France – but to attempt to translate my prepared routine on the hoof to a surly bunch of Canucks, who must have been remarkably ugly children, was a task I could certainly do without. When I found myself talking in Japanese – *Na-ho weeki weeki hah keiro* – I barked out commands to Stuartie, 'Northern Lights', D, 'Dark Island', D, or 'Flower of Scotland', C.

Relieved that we had survived this cosmic jolt without curling up and dying onstage, we collected a very generous fee for our troubles and motored back to the Macdonalds' home in Ottawa. This was the ex-pat who had invited us over in the first place. Stuart and his new bride, Joyce, promptly took off for a delayed honeymoon in Niagara Falls, and Peigi and I, loaded with Canadian and American dollars, jumped a Greyhound bus, destination New York City.

Around five o'clock on a late November afternoon, in the Montreal Greyhound Restaurant, at a horseshoe-shaped bar, four thugs in leather jackets sat on stools opposite us sipping coffee and casting anxious glances towards the automatic door every time someone entered or departed. In my airline bag I had a half-pint of Bourbon. I wondered if I should make the trip to the rest-room for a quick swig. I decided to take a chance. Ducking down beneath the level of the counter, I quickly unscrewed the cap and gulped from the bottle. Peigi had seen my sly move, but didn't say anything. She sipped her coffee, and from time to time glanced at the customers sitting on stools opposite. I sat upright on my stool, lit a cigarette and waited for the first waves of alcohol to rill through my system.

The French-Canadian hard men were staring at me curiously. I remember having the fleeting thought that I had never seen uglier people than these Canucks in my travels. *Tant pis*, as they say in Quebec, I'd soon be boarding my through bus from Winnipeg to New York. I had been working, doing stand-up, singing and playing clarinet and bagpipe in gymnasia and little clubs in the Renfrew Valley and had accumulated about three thousand Canadian dollars. I intended to spend some of the loot on my wife in the Big Apple, and then we'd make our way to my cousin's home in Windsor, where we'd chill for a week or so and cut loose from North America thereafter.

After the bilingual announcement that the New York bus would leave in five minutes' time, I swung off my stool and tried to be graceful as I picked up my travel bag and bagpipe case. Then I blundered towards the bus's door without a backward glance at poor Peigi hirpling in my wake.

I sat by the window in the very last seat at the back of the bus. People still massed at the door – struggling with shabby kitbags and disposable plastic sacks. They were mostly black or Hispanic with a light scattering of Canucks and white Americans. Without crouching down to conceal my actions, I applied the liquor to my lips, lit another cigarette and donned the headphones to listen to some Vivaldi on my Walkman. In a little while I fell asleep and dreamed about a man slowly drowning in a *poll-mònadh*, peat bog. Was it a dream about the past, or a dream about the future?

Around eight-thirty in the evening, my eyes came open. Headlights from approaching vehicles cut across our flight and swept through the sleeping darkness of the travellers. I looked out the window to my left and saw a hefty, yellow-coloured van overtaking us. Suddenly, there was a loud crash as the van veered towards the left-hand side of our bus. In a second, the same thing happened again. This dangerous manoeuvre got the attention of D. Sanchez, our driver, a very tidy number who wore a close-fitting two-tone blue uniform. "Listen up, please," she rattled in clipped Spanish-accented English. "Has any passenger left behind an article of luggage at the supper rest-stop in Montreal?" she asked. "We appear to have the driver of a yellow van trying to attract our attention." Crash! As I looked out I realised that I was a drunk man sailing towards the international border between Canada and the United States and marvelling at an impressive piece of driving on the part of the madman who controlled the yellow van.

Abruptly, the van swerved in front of our bus, obliging the comely D. Sanchez to brake violently. Then, gradually, the pace slowed as the intermittent glows from the van's brake lights showed its rear a constant yard away from the front of the bus. Eventually, both vehicles came to a halt on the hard shoulder of a six-lane turnpike that sliced through the dead cornfields of Quebec.

The engines of the van and the bus were left running for a few seconds too long. My elbows on the backrest of the seat in front were numb as I peered ahead. I couldn't feel my mouth in my face. All my fellow passengers were now awake, and all of us, instinctively, wanted something to happen.

It did. The rear doors of the van burst open. A man with a nylon stocking covering his face, and a shotgun carried at the port, jumped out and scampered to face our front door. My attention was diverted from him as the yellow van suddenly lurched into motion and sped away from us. The sensible and courteous D. Sanchez must have pressed a button. The bus door opened with an asthmatic whoosh, and the gunman was inside in an instant. He smashed the butt of the shotgun into the side of our driver's pretty head and she slumped sideways to the floor. Her attacker swivelled the vacant driving seat round and sat facing us. He raised his shotgun and addressed the passengers in English: "Hey, bitches," he said softly, "money, billfolds, passports, jewellery on the floor." He raised his voice dramatically. "Now!" The poor blacks and Hispanics who were unfortunate enough to be seated near him started reluctantly to throw paper money, rings and watches onto the floor.

The armed robber started to bellow: "You can't do better than that, you can take a couple of shells in the head. I'm serious. Now lemme see that green stuff." He rose, and his lips and squashed nose beneath the stocking looked terrifying from thirty feet away. Moving swiftly towards us, he smashed the barrels of his weapon against the temple of a Puerto Rican matron who had been crying over and over again, "*Perdona nos, Senor*, Spare us, Sir." He pounded the woman's skull methodically, each blow audible and followed by howls of pain. This was truly revolting, but in comparison with what happened to me ten seconds later, these were the good old days. The lunging barrels and their now supine target prompted a shower of wallets and passports. I extracted my hoard of dollars, passport and airplane flimsies from my travel bag and slipped them down the front of my pants. Fortunately, I had broken a twenty dollar bill in the rest stop in Montreal for my coffee, and had been given change in singles. These I fanned out ostentatiously and let them flutter, one by one, to the floor of the coach. The masked man sat down again, gun trained steadily on us. "Now," he said, almost patiently, "I want you people to leave the bus in an orderly fashion. Don't take anything with you. Just move your sorry asses. Now!"

I got to my feet groggily and reached up to the luggage rack to retrieve my bagpipe, a silver and ivory set of 1907 Henderson drones with a silver-soled Sinclair chanter dating from the mid-seventies. Very stupid stroke to pull. In an instant the robber was behind me in the aisle. I was alone, my terrified wife pressing in panic against my back, with a psychotic armed hoodlum. "Leave it, Scotty," he rasped.

All the things you might think I'd do in that kind of situation, I didn't do them. The fear froze me. "Look," I gasped as I slowly turned to face him, "this instrument is a family heirloom. I was left it by my mother's first cousin, *Uilleam Alasdair 'ic Aonghais 'ic Iain Mhòir*, Willie Macdonald of the Muirhead and Sons pipe band."

"Leave it!" the gunman hissed. He might as well have said: 'The tumour's malignant.' As I watched the muscular grip of his right hand on the shotgun butt, I vowed I'd never take strong drink again.

I said okay, and made to sidle past him in the direction of the door. I saw the bandit's left arm slicing backhand towards my head. I tried to avoid the blow but it connected hard with my mouth and sent me reeling, stumbling to my knees. He hit me with a right uppercut, butt first, to the mouth. He asked: "You gonna leave, hero?" I nodded my head, and he hit me again, this time above my right ear. I stumbled towards the door, blood pouring from mouth and head. I leaped out the bus and, obeying some primitive instinct, proceeded to run at right angles to the bus towards the rows of broken stalks glazed with ice, away from the thirty or so passengers who stood shivering in the lee of the bus. Of course, you've guessed it, in my headlong flight to escape from being turned into hamburger meat, I tripped on a fence wire and landed face-down on the edge of a field. I lay there rattling for what seemed an eternity, until I heard the diesel clatter of the bus engine being revved up and looked behind me in astonishment as the pirate drove off at speed in the direction taken by his accomplice in the van.

We stood miserably by the side of the road (the pretty D. Sanchez sat, her knees against her chest, and the unfortunate Puerto Rican woman lay on the grass verge covered by various coats) as the descending cold coated us like an aerosol spray, waiting for rescue. Numerous lorries passed by, hooting their horns, but nobody stopped. A young half-wit – Canadian or American – braced me and said: "Excuse me, sir: you look like a military person. Didn't you think you could have disarmed that guy? After all, he was on his own." To cut him off, because I have an aversion to dealing with the handicapped, I replied in Gaelic: "*An ann às do chiall a tha thu*? Are you clinically insane? The guy had a shotgun trained on me. Maybe Sean Connery could have dealt with him, but James Bond I'm not." My wife spoke up: "*Tha mi mionnaichte, a Thormoid*, I'm convinced, Norman, that guy winked at me beneath the stocking mask as we came out the front door of the bus."

I turned away and lit a cigarette. I had been forced to recognise, in front of the woman who was going to make the second half of my life a wonderful time of love and companionship, that I belong to a tribe of people who sing under the threat of violence. That's a pretty large tribe, I think.

Eventually, a passing truck stopped, picked up the wounded and made for the nearest provincial police post. After an hour or so, representatives of various police agencies – Provincial Police, Montreal civic detectives and even a quartet from the Royal Canadian Mounted Police – arrived on the scene and took depositions from us. The bus was found about five miles down the road, cleaned out, and was driven back to the scene of the hijacking. Individually, we were escorted across the turnpike and invited to make an inventory of what was missing. Peigi and I boarded the bus in the company of a Montreal detective. I was considerably more sober than when the crime was committed. We saw a trio of Puerto Rican boys scooping up coins that the robbers in their haste had left behind. I ignored their guilty stares as I slowly made my way to the rear. My airline bag was gone. But, *taing dhan Àigh*, thanks be to God, my wooden pipe box was still resting in the overhead rack. Having checked that the bagpipe was still there, I gave a silent prayer to the Creator for my deliverance. I had only a chipped tooth and a sore ear for my night's work.

Then, in the words of the old man from Barra when describing any dilemma he might face, I was in a 'quadrangle'. The Provincial troopers said we had options: we could be driven back to Montreal, be put up for the night in a hotel and make a list of stolen property for which we might or might not be reimbursed in the future; or we could press on, with a police escort, to the border and enter the States. Perhaps I made the wrong decision. We went on to the border. There, after a superficial interrogation by a surly black Immigration Officer, we were admitted to New York State. Some of our fellow travellers were not so lucky. One poor soul, a bona fide US citizen, was refused admission at the turnstiles because he had given up his passport on the bus. God knows, he could be hanging about on the Canadian side of the border to this very day.

On a new Greyhound bus we journeyed southward to the Big Apple, where a squad of mouthpieces from the bus company debriefed us and purchased all twenty of us Danish pastries and coffees. That was all, Jack. There was no compensation, and there was no enquiry into what had been stolen. I was in such a hurry to get out of New York that I didn't initiate a legal action against Greyhound. *Och, cha robh e gu deifir*, it didn't matter. Not then, anyway. We had money, passport and flight tickets. We were alive and headed for Scotland with a stopover in Windsor en route. Nowadays I might have done the backstroke and considered my choices more carefully. Naw, I'm kidding myself. I wouldn't have had the moxy to inflate my losses to the authorities.

I have a certain level of self-awareness, and I am now candid about my chances of ever growing up and behaving in an assertive manner. If there's an easy way of dealing with a problem, that's the one I'll take.

24
Bad Hands

I realized that things were creeping downhill for me after I resumed drinking following what was for me a long period of abstinence. When I was in my cups my actions were problematic. I'm not saying that every time I went on a bender I got into trouble. But it is true to say that every time I betrayed my rather strict moral code and behaved in a way that was the antithesis of my regular way of life, for sure, drug alcohol was involved.

During my third season at the Cummings Hotel in Inverness, an interested spectator at many of the shows was a famous television producer at the BBC called Iain MacFadyen. He wasn't just there for the laughs. No, he was working, and I was the focus of his interest. He was to loom large in my professional life in the future.

At this point I mentally backtrack to a season I spent in the Corran Halls, Oban, opening for 'the Voice of Scotland', Kenneth McKellar. Such was my willingness to be deluded that I imagined that this would be a rewarding experience. It was anything but. McKellar had an inflated opinion of himself, and constantly classed himself as one of the top ten tenors in the world. With a top note of A above middle he was okay, but not exceptional. His interpersonal technique left something to be desired, too. One night, after the show, a young girl from Northern Ireland came to the dressing room. I discovered afterwards that she had been sent to Scotland by some aid agency or other to escape the violence and terror that reigned in her homeland during the Troubles.

"Mr McKellar, sir," she piped in her marked Ulster accent, "may I have your autograph, please?"

McKellar, dressed in leather jacket and trousers and wearing calf-length boots, bustled past her, ignoring the proffered book, and made for his Harley Davidson motorcycle, which, for the duration of the sixteen-week run, he used to commute between the cottage

230

he and Heidi had rented in Kilmore and the theatre. What a boorish display!

I myself didn't see out the full season. 'The Voice of Scotland' and I had a major fall-out in late August over, of all things, the volume of applause I was getting at the 'calls', when impresario David Webster would mince onto the stage, microphone in hand, and re-introduce the entire cast. Invariably I got the biggest hand at this point.

McKellar took the cream puff, assumed a *bus*, a pout, and methodically set out to sabotage my act. I used to finish my warm-up spot with a song, and was informed by the star of the show that this was unacceptable.

"There is only one tenor in this show," he said pompously.

"That's okay," I chirped. "I'll drop the song."

What I did was conclude the warm-up with a wild selection of jigs and reels on the Highland bagpipe that fairly stimulated the audience. McKellar objected to this development as well. "How the fuck do you expect one of the top ten tenors in the world to follow that . . . cacophony?" I ended up doing a tap dance taught to me by Maggie Firth in Inverness the previous year. Neil Sinclair would play a slow 6/8 march to which I'd do a sub-Bruce Forsyth shuffle round the stage. It didn't affect the 'calls'. I consistently received more applause than the headliner.

Eventually, I got so fed up with his carping criticism that, after a liberal infusion of whisky to give me Dutch courage, I left the show and notified the MU that I felt I was the victim of constructive dismissal. I doubt that they read the letter. David Webster, predictably, adhered to the showbiz adage 'Keep your eye on the money', and supported McKellar right up to the death throes of the show.

Marooned and bereft of self-esteem, I did what Connolly specifically told me not to do. I accepted a slew of gigs that had humiliation sown in their fabric. What would frequently happen was that I'd look at my diary, and if I came across a virgin page, I'd be gripped by unreasoning panic. I must find work at any cost, I'd tell myself. Consequently, I found myself on many occasions in settings where if Groucho Marx himself descended to entertain, he would have found it extremely difficult to be funny. One such blighted engagement was at the Port Glasgow Celtic Supporters Club held in the Hibernian Halls. First off, the club members resented being pulled away from their games of bingo. Then, before my spot, the catering staff served up soup and dishes of revolting stew. My introductory rap was drowned out by the sounds of clanking crockery. CLANKCLANKCLANK CLINK and CLANKCLANKCLANK. The sobbing, big-dipper vocal swoops of Glen Daley singing the 'Celtic Song' continued to blare out from a giant ghetto-blaster perched on the bar counter throughout my spot. It was impossible to get the punters to shut up. They were all screaming like . . . well, Celtic supporters at Parkhead.

The secretary of the club was a white-haired man who wore glasses with milk-bottle thick lenses and heavy black frames.

"Whit dae ye want?" he said.

"I've come for my wages," I said.

He stared at me, giving no sign that he had heard.

"Sir, could I have my fee for the night, please?" I said after a long pause.

"Fuck off," he grunted. "You're no' worth a fee, ya bam."

My mood, reasonably bright at having survived this ordeal – actually my singing of 'Danny Boy' and 'The Rising of the Moon' went down fairly well – immediately turned sour.

I was threatened with physical violence only once in my career and that was in the inappropriately named 'Stardust Lounge' in Thurso. Stuartie Anderson, the accordionist of the flying fingers, and I were engaged by John Worth to play this tip of a pub, a magnet for the lowlife of the town. The place was full of MacDendrums the night we turned up. Singlets and tattoos were much in evidence among the clientele. And as the old music hall aside has it, that was just the women! We had to change into our kilts in full view of the curious audience who were obviously up for a party. I knew there was going to be a hot time in the old town that night when, just as I was inflating the pipe bag for the start of the show, a full beer bottle of Newcastle Brown Ale came crashing through one of the narrow rectangular windows that lined one wall and exploded with a loud bang on the concrete floor. Which disgruntled former customer was responsible for this outrage was a matter of indifference to the revellers. What was remarkable to us was the aplomb with which the audience received this sinister warning. The ladies calmly picked shards of broken glass from their long hair and clambered on top of the tables to jig in time to the fast reels I was playing. Indeed, it was the blasts on the pipes that saved the evening from complete disaster. The audience loved the sonorous sound of the noble instrument.

They had little time for the jokes and songs, and showed almost no appreciation of the digital pyrotechnics of Stuart on the accordion. The young man displayed wisdom beyond his tender years by cutting his normal twelve-minute spot to a record-breaking forty seconds. He it was who alerted me to the approach of an ill-dressed, unshaven monster who was marching purposefully towards the tiny stage. I have no idea to this day what element of the show riled him, but there was no doubt from the threatening expression on his face and the bunched knuckles of his hands that he was not seeking to buy my latest comedy album or obtain my autograph. "Play the shaggin' pipes, shit-face," he mumbled through wet, blubbery lips. I held the mike stand with its heavy base across my upper body and pretended to be about to use it. "You want to hear the pipes, do you?" I snarled. "Okay, just for you, Clint, I'll do it." No sooner had the High A of the chanter cut through the stuffy little room like a laser beam than the monster retreated backwards, flashing two thumbs up in approval, Once more, as I launched into a rake of jigs at breakneck speed, I expressed silent thanks to Pipe-Major John Macdonald for getting me out this jam.

When I complained to John Worth about our treatment in Caithness, he sympathized and promised to blackball any requests for talent from that quarter in the future. "Speaking of which, Norman," he said, "I've got to keep you working, so when were you thinking of getting on that bicycle and back on the road?" I stared at him in disbelief. His smile in return was extremely attentive. Needless to say, I immediately resumed working on the circuit from Hell.

My later trip to Las Vegas was not without incident either. The circumstances leading up to this jaunt were peculiar. An exiled Scot, John D. MacLennan, 'the Singing Swinging Gael', who was resident in Irvine, Orange County, California, had organized a series of gigs meant to celebrate Saint Patrick's Day in the Sahara Hotel and Casino in the Mafia-dominated town. A thumbnail sketch of this larger-than-life character would have to include his chequered career as a singer and hotelier in the Old Country. The premises he owned in Moray and Ross-shire were both mysteriously destroyed by fire or flood, and John D. and his feisty bride, Joan MacKenzie from the Lochs district of Lewis, began a new life, first of all in New Jersey, then in California. "There's more money on the west coast, Torry," he used to say, with many a nudge and knowing wink. ('Torry' was his abbreviation of the

Gaelic version of my Christian name, Tormod.) Suffice it to say that John D. was a survivor, endowed with charm by the carat-load and handsome in his impeccably-cut Highland dress. In less formal situations, without his well-made hairpiece which disguised a head like a giant thumb, and with his prominent gut hanging over the waistband of his shorts, he resembled a cross between Shrek and a jolly Buddha. In my mind he was typecast for envelopes of cash. I jumped at the chance to perform in this Mecca of show business.

I remembered the words of Lena Martell, who spoke to me briefly at a gig when she was performing in the Rangers Club in Ibrox. I was knocked out by her act and remain to this day an avid fan. "When, Norman," she drawled in a mid-Atlantic accent, "did you last play Las Vegas?" Las Vegas? I had recently returned from Lochmaddy, and thought I was pretty hot stuff. Now I would be upsides with our own Glaswegian diva, I thought.

John Carmichael, the accordionist who was invited, was less enthusiastic. Of course, he had worked with John D. before, and suspected squalls of emotional turbulence on the horizon. "You know, guys," he confessed to Charlie Cowie, the fiddler, and me at Heathrow International airport as we waited to board a non-stop flight to Los Angeles, "I'd prefer to be doing a gig in Govan Town Hall." I couldn't understand his attitude. He obviously needed more fibre in his diet. But after what transpired in Nevada, I found myself in agreement with him.

I received the first blow to the good conceit I had of myself at the muster for the noonday Saint Patrick's Day parade. The giant car park in downtown Las Vegas was overflowing with green ribbons attached to blindingly white linen suits – no women took part in this event: they'd be milking the cows in their ranch-style villas or planting 'praties' in the desert, I suppose – and the *green* beer was quaffed from polystyrene cups in copious quantities. The marshal of the parade, a lanky Ichabod Crane character, heard me tuning up and stalked over to me.

"Who're you?" he demanded.

"I'm Norman," I slurred back at him, licking foam from my lips, "and I'm a comedian."

He thought I had said 'Canadian'. "No kidding! A Canadian? *Man* – ain't that a kick. I don't care where you come from with your poncy English name," he snarled.

I thought he was insinuating that people from my country couldn't be funny. "I'll have you know, Paddy," I declaimed haughtily, "that Sir Harry Lauder was considered one of the best comic turns of his generation, even here in America."

"I don't give a fuck [*fook*] who you're related to," he gabbled back, fast losing it. "What do you think you are – a comedian?"

"Look," I said, articulating slowly and clearly. "This morning I'm your piper."

"Where's the rest of the band?" he enquired anxiously.

"What band?" I enquired, genuinely puzzled.

"Glasgow fuckin' [*fookin'*] Police Pipe Band," he blurted out. "Thirty-six champion pipers and drummers who are the fuckin' [*fookin'*] World Champions."

I immediately sobered up and entered a state of extreme agitation. Not that I was worried, I reassured myself, I could stand some competition but – well – you know. A solitary piper leading a horde of white-suited Irishmen who had been expecting to follow nine-times winners of the World Championships! I wished I was dead. I shouldered the pipes and over what seemed like a five-mile route march I played 'Garry Owen' and 'Kelly the Boy from Killane' about fifty times each. I was knackered at the end of it, and understood clearly that I'd been well and truly John D.'ed. The budgetary parameters had obviously been interfered with, but certainly not to my advantage. When the parade reached our destination, the Horseshoe Club on Fremont Street in the heart of downtown Las Vegas, the legendary patriarch of the Binion family who owned the club, Benny Binion, handed me an envelope stuffed with dollar bills. He obviously wasn't aware of the switch, and a good job too, because this old guy had a reputation for dishing out his own brand of frontier justice to anyone who offended him. While in Dallas, Texas, this avuncular old man was a suspect in several slayings, but because of his friendship with the District Attorney he got off with a suspended sentence for the shooting of one Frank Bolding, and later, in 1936, he was charged with the murder of a racketeer. Three years later the charge was dismissed. His son, Ted Binion, was murdered in 1998 by his live-in lover, Sandy Murphy, and her secret lover, Rick Tabish. I may be a wee bit stupid at times, but I knew immediately that these folk were just too rich for my blood. I took the money and, as the song has it, ran. I was extremely lucky, I guess.

My luck didn't hold that evening, though. My nemesis arrived in the Sahara Hotel and Casino. In front of an all-white audience of about two hundred, I opened the show in my usual fashion. Dressed in a white cutaway jacket dripping with gold braid, dress Menzies tartan kilt, matching tartan hose with silver buckled patent leather shoes, I swung into a selection of 6/8 marches. My crowning glory was a white Balmoral bonnet with red and white dicing that I wore in approved military style, the headband absolutely horizontal two inches above my eyebrows and the front of the bonnet pulled down to the level of my eyes. This was what caused all the trouble. As I counter-marched across the spacious stage, executing flashy turns with raised knees, I became aware of the audience convulsing like patients in a de-tox ward. Bulging eyes and angry mouths were all I could make out. I couldn't hear what they were actually shouting because of the din from bagpipe, accordion, fiddle and drums onstage, but when I stopped playing, the braying of the incensed patrons immediately became clear. " BRITS GO HOME, BRITS GO HOME, BRITS GO HOME," they roared in chorus.

I was unable to move my lips and my throat had dried up. What had this animosity, nay, this naked hatred, to do with me? Then it struck me like a hammer blow. It was the way I was dressed, and my militaristic marching that had offended the audience. All these third and fourth generation beefy Irishmen had been exposed to propaganda issued by the republican fund-raisers Noraid, and the cool bonnet I wore reminded those generous donators to the cause of filmed images they had seen of infantrymen from Scottish regiments like the Black Watch and the Highland Fusiliers kicking down the doors of Catholic households in the Falls Road. Somehow we staggered to the end of our hour-long spot, when we were afforded an hour's respite before we had to go on for another hour.

The second spot was different. We slung the Highland dress and donned trousers tucked into long hose to resemble knickerbockers. Shirt sleeves were rolled up and regular skipped caps were worn. Fortunately, the Canadian dancers who were on with us had suit-able props for the Irish Washerwoman dance, and they disported themselves vigorously with clacking tap-dance shoes and brandished shillelaghs. We also assumed new identities. I was Brendan Mulcahey, John became Ciaran McMahon, all-Ireland accordion champion, and Charlie, who had drunk too much and hadn't bothered to get out of the kilt, was Brendan O'Malley, all-Ireland fiddle champion. My introduction in a cod Guinness twang was greeted with roars of approval. "Aaaaaaaand, Ladies and Gentlemen, a soft eeeeevenin' to yez all. I, Brendan Mulcahey from the laaaaand of kings, proudly preeeeeeZENT THE LEPRECHAUNS." We got away with it. And while it was a schmaltzy, naff show, I couldn't help feeling pleased with myself at having turned the thing around.

I've always believed that between performer and audience there exist only four permutations. You can put up a good show and the audience loves it: you can perform well, but the audience is indifferent: you can be lousy and the audience, deservedly, barracks you: but you can do a rotten show and, inexplicably, the audience approves of you. My debut in Vegas fell into this last category.

My first feature film role, in 1983, I remember with a bodylong shudder of sorrow. Earlier that summer, I succumbed once more to John D. MacLennan's blandishments, and returned to the West Coast. It would be about three o'clock in the afternoon, Californian time. I was emerging from the main doors of LAX when I sensed movement alongside of me. I was just starting to turn when a black hand fastened on my shoulder and propelled me into a massive concrete pillar by the entrance.

The mugger came right after me. He was about the same height as me, in his early twenties, though his bushy Afro gave him a couple of inches more. He was dressed in white sweat shirt and baggy denim trousers as favoured by the inmates of San Quentin. The most notable and alarming thing about him was that he was swinging a tire-iron in his right hand.

He said, "Motherfucker, fuckin' motherfucker. Gimme your money, you motherfucker. Gimme it, gimme all of it, gimme it, or I break your arm."

I thought, Where the hell is John D. MacLennan? Slowly, ever so slowly, I took my wallet out of my hip pocket and extended it to this desperado who had the effrontery to brace me in front of a milling crowd of travellers who were going in and out of the main airport building.

I said, "You can have it, you're welcome to it." The wallet fell from my trembling fingers. "Sorry," I said, "very sorry, wait and I'll get it," and crouched down to retrieve it. I bent my knees and planted my feet firmly under me and I thought Right! I quickly straightened up, sustaining a glancing blow on my upper left arm as I drove my head full force into his nose.

He stumbled back against the wall behind him. The next thing I observed was a huge pair of hands squeezing off my assailant's carotid artery in a debilitating choke hold. This was John D. MacLennan to the rescue. I allowed him to take me to the hospital, where I had pins inserted in my left humerus. The operation was a success, though the arm isn't as mobile as it was before.

It did prevent me from playing the Great Highland Bagpipe for a couple of months, though, and to pay off the medical bills I was obliged to join John's team of solar heating salesmen based in Santa Monica. I studied MacLennan's technique by going with him on numerous home visits, and when I eventually went out on my own I found to my delight I was good at this sales lark. For a brief while, John and I led the sales league table – there were about a dozen different teams from all over southern California involved in this project with names like the 'San Diego Hotshots' and the 'Longbeach Energy Team'. I proved to be extremely good at selling what was, admittedly, a good product with liberal tax benefits. I used John's pseudo-psychological patter with remarkable success. "Yes, sir," I'd say to the off-duty cop to whom I was pitching, "what you've got to do is set your goals for the future, project ten years or so down the line, and describe accurately in writing how you're going to triangulate between your professional life, your duty to your family and your own core being." After all, selling is all about pretence. I'd had bags of practice at blethering, and did so well that I was in line to enjoy a vacation in Tahiti as a reward for my success.

All thoughts of Tahiti and the Polynesian women so celebrated by Gauguin were banished by a long-distance phone call I received from the UK one morning.

"Suzy Figgis on the line for Norman Maclean. Can you get him for me, please?" a Kelvinside female voice asked.

"What do you want?" I said, in a shaky voice.

"I'm casting director for Bill Forsyth's new film, *Comfort and Joy*. He's seen Norman in some telly stuff and he thinks he'd be good as a Highland psychiatrist in this project."

A Highland psychiatrist! Well, they couldn't have found a head so full of suppurating neuroses if they'd tried for another ten years. But I wasn't prepared to agree to anything without playing hard to get.

"Listen, Ms Figgis," I said sternly, "Norman Maclean is sick and tired of accommodating producers and directors cheaply and agreeing to comply with their every whim. He's off to Tahiti shortly on vacation and it'd have to be for a generous fee that he'd give that up."

"Oh, I can assure you, sir," the posh voice whispered silkily, "Bill Forsyth is no cheapskate. How does five hundred pounds a day, plus per diem, for a twenty-day shoot sound?"

I was frozen. This was riches beyond the dreams of Croesus. A feeling of total shock and paralysis lasted about a week. In fact it lasted only about a couple of seconds.

"Hold on," I blurted, "I'll get Mr Maclean."

When I picked up the receiver again after a suitable delay, my voice had deepened and was markedly more Highland in its lilting cadences.

"Ms Figgis?" I crooned, "This is Norman Maclean."

"Mr Maclean," she said, "did your secretary tell you about the film . . . and the financial arrangements?"

"Yes," I replied in a seemingly bored voice. "We're inclining to view your offer favourably."

"That's good," she said. "Bill will be so pleased that you'll come and read for us. When can we expect you?"

"I don't know," I said and immediately regretted it. "I mean . . . um . . . er, I'm stuck here in L.A. and I don't know if I can afford to buy a plane ticket home. You see, I'm still owed money from my present employers and . . ."

"Don't worry about a thing, Norman," she interjected sweetly "Give me your fax number and address and I'll have a copy of the script and a Business Class air ticket sent over to you. I'll give you a ring at the end of the week and we'll firm up an audition for a fortnight's time. Okay, darling?"

It wasn't really. I felt sick and guilty. I had a return Economy Class ticket in my wallet. I bet they knew. I bet they didn't think much of a guy who couldn't afford the fare home. They'd cancel the best offer I'd ever received in my life and think I was a loser.

And so, fourteen days later, I turned up at Bill Forsyth's production office in Park Circus. I was pleased to be home, but had no great confidence that I'd actually get the part in the film. Forsyth, auteur of *Gregory's Girl* and *Local Hero* was, I had to admit it, not only a brilliant director but something of an icon. We got on like Ryan O'Neil and Ali McGraw in *Love Story*.

He chortled appreciatively at my descriptions of America and the Americans. The interview and the reading that never took place were concluded by the great man saying, "See you at the end of the month. I've enjoyed your yarns. And I know you'll gobble the part of the Highland psychiatrist. It's nice having you on board. Goodbye, Norman."

It was my first day, a Friday, in the employ of something-or-other Productions Limited. I parked the Audi in the car park of a swish hotel in Bothwell Street, and a gloved hand opened the door, got my case and me into the lobby of the hotel. At Reception, I was booked in with commendable speed and informed that anything I needed, absolutely anything, should be charged to the film company. A little voice was coming up inside my head saying, 'Brrrilliant, Norrie!'

It did not turn out that way, of course. I swooped down in the lift to Reception and raced excitedly up to St Vincent Street and onto Argyle Street, headed for the comfort and familiarity of a Teuchter pub called the Park Bar. There I met dozens of acquaintances I hadn't seen for some time, and very speedily I was completely rubbered and had to be taxied back to my hotel.

In the morning a large whisky provided by room service steadied my derailed nerves. I was chauffeured down to Inchinnan to have still photographs taken of me aboard a fifty-foot yacht. (It seems the shrink was a sailing buff.) These would be used to decorate the walls of my office in St Vincent Street. 'CUT,' was called, and I couldn't help noticing there was a gross tremor in my hands as I hurried to get into my street clothes. Forsyth gave me the address of the lawyers' offices that were to double as my consulting rooms and asked me to meet him there at three o'clock in the afternoon. I made it, only just, after imbibing large drafts of spirits, and it was immediately apparent to the director that I was unfit.

"Listen, Norman," he said in a kindly fashion, "why don't you go home and rest for a bit. I don't need you until Monday morning. Come down on Sunday evening, fully rested, get a good night's sleep in the hotel and we'll film some great footage on Monday. What do you say?"

"That's very . . . er, civil of you, Mr Forsyth," I stammered. "The thing is . . . I'm a bit short of cash and . . . um . . . I'd be grateful if you could help me out with an advance to enable me to buy some petrol."

"No problem, Norman," he said with a broad grin on his face. "Clive, Clive, come in for a minute," he shouted in a loud voice. Clive was the accountant, and he bustled in clutching a bulging briefcase.

"Clive," Forsyth said in a commanding voice, "I want you to give Mr Maclean three – in cash – immediately."

As the bespectacled middle-aged accountant rummaged in his case I reflected that three pounds was a kind of niggardly advance. *Jesus Christ*, I thought, *you'll not get much fuel with that, Norrie. You'll maybe stretch it to a pint and a couple of nips.* Clive peeled off a fan of twenty-pound notes from an enormous roll of banknotes and extended them gracefully to me. *God save me, they were offering me, not three, but three hundred pounds!*

Hands were shaken, grins were exchanged, thanks were muttered and I left the room in a state of high elation. The following thirty-six hours were a fandango of dissipation. It took me about twelve hours to get home to Oban, the delay occasioned by frequent stops at pubs and hotels en route, and I just had time to shower and change before departing on the never-ending return journey. On the Sunday night I had the bright idea of telephoning, on the courtesy phone, every bust-out Teuchter freak in the Glasgow area whose numbers I had in my address book and inviting them to my room for free drinks. The response was enormous. By midnight in the trashed hotel room there must have been around thirty boozed-up Highlanders strewn on beds and carpets, all talking to God privately. Everything slow-motioned for a while. Brandy bottles, empty glasses and prone bodies were all over the place. My heart and head were dislocated. This explained why my entire body was vibrating. I pondered the idea that I had been stupid – worse, greedy. I knew that I'd blootered, big time, and mercifully passed out.

My exit from *Comfort and Joy* was accomplished smoothly and rapidly. Loud banging at the bedroom door was followed by the entrance of a shocked chambermaid with a pass-key. She was accompanied by Saturday's chauffeur, and together they politely ushered the stragglers from my Bacchanalian circus outside. I was hustled down to my car and the chauffeur ran me home to Dunbeg without a word. Well Martelled by the time we got to Camus Road, I was able to summon a taxi for the driver to take him to town, where he would catch the Glasgow train. I have to say that Bill Forsyth behaved throughout with commendable restraint. He didn't berate me, and immediately summoned up a well-known Glasgow comedian, Arnold Brown, to take my place. Scalding shame prevented me from viewing the completed film, but from what I know of Brown, I'm sure he would have made a good job of whatever part he was offered.

A final very bad hand that I dealt myself was to hook up with the most famous Gaelic singer of all time. The fact that I should in all likelihood have refused Calum Kennedy's invitation to accompany him and various other artistes on a tour of the Highlands and Islands at Easter 1990 is not why I choose this hiccup – correction: bout of whooping cough – for retelling. Rather, this odyssey was remarkable in the way a Scottish entertainer, who would certainly have featured in a poll of the top three Scottish singers of the twentieth century, bore witness to the showbiz adage: never try to come back.

I was lodging with my mother and Colin in Mosspark, Peigi having told me that she could no longer live with me, when the telephone call came.

"Yes, Norman," the high-pitched voice proclaimed. "I *need* you to be second top of the bill on this tour. I've got a roadie and a drummer recruited already, and I'm hoping to engage George Smith from Fort William, Johnny Bogan from Muir of Ord as second comic and various female dancers and singers. Do you think you could get Billy McGuire, the button-key box player, to come along?"

"Probably," I said doubtfully. McGuire was the *enfant terrible* of accordion players, a man with debilitating physical problems – psoriasis and asthma among them – and a serious drink habit. As a composer and player, however, he was light years ahead of anybody else in the field. I got to know Billy during a particularly toxic debauch in Normandy, where we were expelled from the nunnery we stayed in for playing the bagpipes and accordion in the showers after lights out.

"The money?" Calum squealed. "The sky's the limit, *a bhalaich*. You and I will split the net profits fifty-fifty. We're going to clean up."

"How long will the tour last, Calum?" I asked.

"About four weeks," he answered with only a second's hesitation.

"When do we start?" I said, having given Calum a buyer's signal by my use of the first person plural.

"On the third of April," he said. "We'll all meet at the beginning of the month in the Station Hotel in Inverness . . . yes, we're kicking off in the town . . . I'll give you a list of the engagements if you come down to the Eglinton Arms Hotel in Ardrossan soon. I want you to meet my new wife, Christine, and my new wee daughter Eilidh." (The Voice of the Highlands had been married to Anne Gillies, older sister of Alasdair the singing dentist, and had daughters by her who were now off his hands. Anne died at a tragically young age – of what, I knew not.)

In a stupid attempt to be 'cool' and 'hip', I had taken to having the flyers I sent to potential bookers bear the punk-sounding legend 'Stormin' Norman and the Scabby Knee' – this was the back-line of pick-up accordionists, drummers and guitarists I might have at any time. I had been having trouble finding work.

My only source of income was the providential, but random, repeat fees I received for doing Gaelic voice-overs for John Smith of the BBC for the children's cartoon *Postman Pat*. These voice-overs, for *Fireman Sam*, *Danger Mouse*, and *Dragan Sgeul* provided honourable work, though I didn't fancy having testimony to this effect on my headstone: *He was a terrific Postman Pat*.

I enjoyed this kind of tightrope walking, courting catastrophe. I embarked on a terrible month-long journey into the hot and steaming village halls of the Highlands and Islands. My diary for that month is as meaningless as if written in Urdu. Venues, from the north coast of Sutherland, Caithness, down through Easter Ross, Inverness-shire, Argyll, the Isle of Arran and the Outer Hebrides, merged into a blur. All I can remember was that we had packed audiences everywhere. Of course, Calum didn't perform at all the concerts. If he had sold the show for an inflated fee as he'd done in Alness, Wick and Fort William – and I actually got a glimpse of Kennedy's double book-keeping when Iain Munro, the proprietor of Tingle Creek in Erbusaig, just outside Kyle of Lochalsh, showed me a notebook left behind on the last engagement of the tour – then the 'Voice of the Highlands' would deign to sing two or three medleys comprising his most popular songs. More often than not, at the 'suck-it-and-see' gigs, he would apologise for the throat problem that had assailed him during the night. 'Ladies and gentlemen,' he'd announce: 'I'm sincerely sorry that I won't be able to sing for you tonight. However, we are extremely fortunate in that we have a man here who will delight you all. He's a piper . . . He's a singer . . . He's a poet . . . He's a comedian . . . He's . . . the one and only . . . Norman Maclean!'

And I would be left to carry a skeleton cast of performers on my own. (Various members of our troupe had departed, either voluntarily or against their wills, at regular intervals from the off. First to go

243

were the dancers; then George Smith was sacked in his home town of Fort William after ruining his van by transporting gear and bodies all over the north; and Johnny Bogan, after he had outlived his usefulness as the taxi-driver of his smart new car, was dispatched in Mallaig.)

I was enveloped in a cloud of foreboding when Calum decided unilaterally to purchase a clapped-out old Peugeot 306 in Inverness early in the tour. The roadie, who had a bad back, had no driving licence. Consequently Norman Maclean, banned three times already for drunk driving, was obliged to keep the show on the road. My efforts towards the end were persistent but tiring. What kept me going was the knowledge that I would be in for a massive pay-day on completion of the tour.

The decision Calum made to do without the services of Billy McGuire was a bad one. At Uig pier in Skye, about to embark on a Cal-Mac ferry to Tarbert, Harris, I was jammed behind a queue of vehicles waiting to board the *Hebridean Isles*. Billy emerged from the Bakar Bar, comsiderably the worse of drink, and demanded money from Calum. With cruel impersonality, our leader threw a twenty-pound note through the window on the passenger side. Predictably, McGuire was incensed.

"Come on, you bastard," Billy shrieked. "I've worked an eight-day week for almost a month for you, and this is what you offer me! Ah'm going to sort you out!" He wrenched a metal stanchion from a fence and began to rain heavy blows on the roof and windscreen of the Peugeot.

"Drive, Norman, drive," Calum shouted, and pretended he was trying to get out of the car to sort things out on a one-to-one basis. There was nowhere to drive to. I was completely hemmed in.

"That's all you're getting from me, you psychotic Irish bastard," Calum shouted, as McGuire redoubled his efforts with the metal bar. Paint-chips were flying in sprays from the bonnet when eventually the queue moved forward and we entered the hold of the ship. Once aboard, the 'Voice of the Highlands' took charge of the on-board telephone and tried to cajole and bribe various island accordionists to accompany him in Tarbert and Stornoway. To a man they all turned him down.

McGuire, to his credit, made it aboard and spent the entire voyage strapped to a bed in the skipper's cabin, imagining that he was somewhere on the wine-red seas of the Caribbean along with former island shipmates. After suffering a beating from a nephew of Calum's outside John Macleod's Tarbert Motel, and spending the night locked in the motel toilet with the hand-dryer the only source of heat, Billy McGuire, the bravest man I've ever known, performed in Stornoway Town Hall the following night to rapturous applause.

After our last gig in Erbusaig, McGuire was grudgingly paid out and I ran him to Kyle of Lochalsh, where he would get a bus to Glasgow. My driving days were not yet over. Calum, in a voice I had learned to distrust over forty years before, said: "You did very well, Norman. Me and Christine and the wee one are going to take a two-week break in my condominium in Torremolinas in Spain next Sunday. We'd like you to come with us. Fancy it?"

"Ye – yes, Calum," I said, sensing that another hustle was on the way. "But what about my money?"

"Later, Norman, later." He gave a gravelly snort. "Now I want you to drive me, Jimmy and the roadie" – this latter hadn't lifted a finger to help us all through the tour, and every night he used to drink himself sodden – "down to Ardrossan, and you and I will go to a box-ing tournament I've got tickets for in Kilmarnock tonight. Christine has already got your tickets for the flight tomorrow."

Oozing plausibility, I explained that I needed money to repay his wife and have something to jangle in my pocket if I was going on holiday.

The man shrugged. "Plenty of time," he said.

This was the first of several rude disappointments. I remember very little of that intimidating drive to Ardrossan, except its close. The boxing tournament provided me with an additional hundred pounds. There were so many knock-outs in the first half of the programme that one of the organizers approached Calum and asked him if he would do a twenty-minute spot. He bottled it and offered me the gig. I accepted. Doing stand-up in a boxing ring to a couple of hundred drunk toughs with only a bingo-caller's microphone was horrendous. Performing ninety-degree turns every few minutes in a futile attempt to engage at least a quarter of my audience at a time, my efforts were dogged but dispiriting.

Later that evening, in the shabby living room of the Eglinton Arms Hotel, a decaying shell which Calum had purchased as a home for his family, he offered me a packet of Smarties.

"What's this for?" I said.

"The dogs," he replied.

"What dogs?" I asked.

"You see, we keep the Alsatians in the dining room," he said, "and since you're going to be sleeping in Room Thirty-two over in the west wing, you'll have to go through the dining room to get to the stairway that leads to the bedrooms. Here's the keys."

I bade my host, his wife and wee Eilidh goodnight, and nervously descended the stairs to the dining room.

"Remember, Norman," Calum shouted in parting. "Give the sweeties to the dogs and they'll not interfere with you."

I pushed open the heavy oak door and entered a scene from Dante's Inferno. Ten or more massive hounds with lolling tongues and glistening teeth surrounded me in anticipation. The truly huge dining room – the Eglinton Arms had once been described as the 'jewel of the Ayrshire coast' – was covered in dog excrement. In a panic, I scattered the Smarties over my shoulder as I picked my way delicately through the muck to the far door.

Eventually I made it to my room, and what a hovel it was! Peeling ceiling tiles, various bowls to catch rain drips, damp nylon sheets and no pillow was my lot for that night of horror. In the morning my head was covered with white dust from the crumbling overhead tiles. I looked like a Yeti.

We departed in the old Puggy shortly afterwards for Glasgow Airport. On the way there, I tried to broach the subject of an accounting. Calum produced a sheaf of papers, and for the forty-five minutes it took to reach our destination I had to endure a detailed summary of the expenses he had allegedly incurred in putting together the tour. His litany was incredibly detailed. I noted with astonishment that he had recorded the purchase of a toastie for Billy McGuire in Allan Hamilton's bistro in Lairg at the beginning of our commando course.

"All I'm asking, Norman," Calum said, dropping into gentle con-man tones, "is that on top of all the expenditure I've described already, fares, food and lodging, et cetera, I should take fifteen per cent of the gross for being the agent in this enterprise. That's what Peter de Vries would charge."

It was too late. I was locked into this.

"This is a *business*, Norman," he explained piously, oozing show-biz sincerity and so forth. "All you have to do is accept this eleven hundred pounds. Here, take the envelope."

I took it, changed some of it into pesetas at the Bureau de Change and flew off to Malaga. Calum didn't actually have a condominium there. He had a timeshare in a Dutch-owned apartment block in Benelmadena. Because business was slack in April, I was easily able to hire a very comfortable self-catering apartment in the complex for about two hundred pounds for the fourteen nights.

The punchline was that I had a thoroughly pleasant time over there. Calum didn't emerge from his apartment in daylight. He was not a sun-lover. I spent most mornings and afternoons at the pool with Christine and Eilidh and enjoyed myself hugely. Taking things gradually, tanning and swimming, by the end of the first week I had revived my aquatic skills until I ended the up the Mark Spitz of Benelmadena.

I met Calum only twice in the years between that invigorating spring holiday and his death a couple of years ago. The first time was in Islay, where Ted Brocklebank, Head of News and Documentaries at Grampian TV, and I were filming Mary Sandeman for a music series called *Aite Mo Ghaoil* and where Calum Kennedy was her chosen guest artiste. The second time was in 1996 at the National Mod in Blairgowrie, where I was launching my first novel, *Cùmhnantan*.

I didn't have much to say to him.

When I re-read the above paragraphs I feel like giving myself a good skelp on the arse. OK, Calum's actions were discreditable to him. But I, and others, owe Calum Kennedy a deep debt of gratitude. He was the pioneer who successfully negotiated the gulf between Gaelic folk singer and mainstream Scottish Variety.

With eyes closed, I address silently the words "Thank you" to the computer screen, in tribute to the best singing voice ever to come out of the Highlands.

25

Zihuatanejo

In January, 1991, I was seated at a glass-topped table in the Club Garibaldi in Zihuatanejo in the state of Guerrero, Mexico, when the alcohol began to take hold. I distinctly remember ordering a posse of aggressive, near-naked women to desist from stroking my thighs and shoulders. Although places like the Garibaldi encouraged in me the heightening of the party mood and a lowering of decorum, I'd had a ration of these gorgeous creatures and I had decided to let my hair grow out that evening – "To hang up my kilt and my bagpipe" was the way I put it mentally. Sure, I'd been having the odd blow on the Great Highland Bagpipe in the courtyard of my modest hotel in the foothills of the Sierra Madre, but tonight I was giving myself over to unadulterated boozing. *Gritaré por todo el mundo*, I was going to cry for the entire world, and I didn't feature dusky young *chicas* in my immediate future.

Despite my chaste resolve, I found myself being aroused by the erotic atmosphere of the Club Garibaldi. No, I was not immune. I responded to the beating pulse and screaming trumpets of the Ranchero band up on the platform ahead. This was not greed, but hunger. For flesh, alcohol and smoke, naked hunger, oozing, obsessive, and overpowering. This was a place where female breasts came out to play. All this flesh, I thought. Put a man like me in a room full of sweet chillies, sooner or later I was going to take a bite.

On the Pacific coastline, Ixtapa-Zihuatanejo were twin resort towns, four miles apart, yet had totally different characters. Ixtapa was the modern half, its beach front lined with high-rise hotels squeezed along the long white sand of Playa de Palmar. The wide bay dotted with tiny islands was good for boat trips but bad for swimming. Zihua-tanejo, a former fishing village with forested headlands plunging into secluded bays, was preferable to me. It offered good-value restaurants, cheap, older hotels and a much more authentic Mexican atmosphere.

In the travel brochure of my mind, the prose description of this louche nightclub read something like this . . . Ear-splittingly loud instrumental music, soaring ruined male voices wailing about drunken nights in the cantina . . . smoke from foul-smelling cigars filling the dance floor and surrounding tables and chairs . . . rickety old chairs and tables painted in lurid primary colours . . . prints of Emilio Zapata and Pancho Villa on hessian-covered walls . . . diminutive men, with a decided Indian cast to their features, dressed in white three-piece suits with flyaway lapels and outrageously flared trousers, dancing smoothly with drop-dead gorgeous chicas . . . I loved it.

(Incidentally, big Duncan 'Husky Bill' McLean, my geography teacher at Bellahouston Academy, showed us pictures of Central and South American Indian women and described them as 'shapeless puddings wearing a *ruana*, a traditional poncho, topped by a bowler hat'. He lied. The Indian women I saw in Zihuatanejo were veritable knockouts, exceedingly well put together. Most of them were lean and lithe and had skin the colour of amber, with eyes, dark pools of mystery, promising adventure and sin.)

The club was a tidal pool of male and female hormones. Despite my over-indulgence in Tequila, it took about thirty minutes before the iron fist of anxiety loosened its grip and a wave of relief passed through my body. What was wrong was that my life had become increasingly marginalized. I'd move from one place to another prompted by the most nebulous promise of work or money. I lacked continuity. In my view I had been travelling to find myself, rather as if I was a packet of cigarettes that had been displaced. (Nowadays, after bopping around four continents with the vigour of a Mexican jumping bean, I associate 'travel' with 'travail'.)

I gazed at the beautiful deadpan dancers and sensed that theirs was a world of display and laughter, joy in life. I and the other handful of gringos there were shut off from all of this.

Suddenly, I became aware of the lead singer in the mariachi group onstage. He was fat and middle-aged. He was accompanied by three guitars, two violins, a double bass, and two piercing trumpets. The musicians were all dressed in skin-tight black trousers and short waist-coats, both garments dripping with silver. The voice of the fat man soared above the accompanying instruments. I drowned in the sound and the sentiment.

Que me entierran en la sierra,
Let me be buried in the mountain,
Al pie de los magueyales,
At the foot of the maguelyales,
Y que me cubra esta tierra
And this soil may cover me
Que es cuna de hombres cabales.
That is the cradle of horsemen,
Mexico lindo y querido,
Beautiful and beloved Mexico,
Si muero lejos de ti,
If I should die far away from you,
Que digan que estoy dormido.
Let them say I am only sleeping,
Y que me traigan aqui.
And that they should convey me here.

To my horror, the fat lead singer of the group was making his way towards my table. He glanced down at me and broke into a wide maniacal grin, his pink tongue slithering behind tobacco-stained teeth. I suddenly became alert. I had never clapped eyes on this vertically challenged matador in my life. I tried to ignore him as he drew closer. Do the backstroke, I thought, maybe he caught my act in Kinlochewe and he's looking for my autograph . . . Then I felt his hand on my shoulder and I heard his hoarse shout:

"¿Eres de Escocia, verdad? You're from Scotland, aren't you?" he enquired.

"Yeah," I said.

"¿Toca la gaita? You play the bagpipe?" he said.

"Yeah," I said.

He asked me what I was drinking. *"¿Que tomas?"*

"Scotch." Pause. "Beer." Pause. "Anything," I muttered.

Like a magician, he produced a bottle from the sash that surrounded his ample waist and plonked it down on the table.

This was my introduction to Mescal, a powerful cortical depressant. The first glass of this poison tasted so bad that I immediately gulped down another one. A pleasant feeling of alcoholic decrepitude fought with vague alarm inside me.

"¿Tiene la gaita aqui? Have you got the bagpipe with you?" he asked.

I nodded.

"*Bueno*," he said, removing his Tonton Macoute sunglasses. "*Puede tocarla con nosotros*, You can play with us." There was a sudden bully-ing·note in his voice.

I looked into Ricardo's eyes – yes, that was his name – and what I saw there raised a lump in my throat. Life on the road as a Mariachi was tough, Ricardo was a very tough character, and eye to eye with him now, I suspected that despite his corpulent frame he was a lot stronger than he looked. His eyes looked like the points of jacketed nine-millemetre rounds. It was clear to me that this was a man who was not accustomed to grapple with moral problems. He had never used anything more than his trigger-finger, it appeared to me, to resolve dodgy interpersonal relationships. People did things his way. "The group is my passion," he told me. "I want you, gringo, to join us. I would hate it if you refused." He spelled it out for me, confessing that to turn my back on Ricardo, 'the man' in this town, would be a terrible insult. "This would be baaad, *señor*," he said.

"I'll think about it," I said, nodding my head as he turned and headed back to the bandstand. I took another swig of spirits and pon-dered upon the silent but powerful metaphysical communication that had taken place. I knew with the suddenness of a kick in the shins that I was going to join this group of *ceàrdannan*, vagabonds, and that I'd play the Highland Bagpipe with them. ¿*Como no*? Why not? It seemed like a good idea at the time. I had started by taking a reckless position, and very quickly elevated it to the arrantly ridiculous. My rating as a Mariachi singer was – well, call it fanciful.

My musings were interrupted by a query from a short Canadian gentleman in his late fifties. He was lean and balding, wearing gold wire-rimmed spectacles and dressed in a pink cotton shirt with a but-ton-down collar, casual slacks, and expensive slip-on shoes. Leaning forward from an adjoining table to speak to me, he never relinquished the tight grip he had on the hand of his young, strikingly handsome male companion whose smooth skin was the colour of honey and whose jet-black hair and high cheekbones betrayed Indian blood.

"You gonna do it, Mac?" he said.

"What?" I said, playing Mickey the Dunce.

"You gonna enlist with that scumbag?" he said excitedly.

"Maybe," I said, though I had all but made my mind up to join the Mariachis of Jalisco.

"Don't do it, man," the sugar-daddy said. "That guy's bad news. I dunno how many pies he's got his fingers in – you know, marijuana, cocaine, shake-downs of restaurants and cantinas, all that illegal stuff – and he's got a hair-trigger temper. You take my advice, you'll get in the breeze, man."

"I'm not worried by that little squirt," I said confidently. "I can handle him. No problem."

"You're one stupid Scotsman," the Canadian told me.

"Thank you, *sir*," I said winking at his companion. "That's what my mother says. My wives, they're pretty sure as well."

"You're poking the snake, man," the older man hissed. "*Buena suerte*, Good luck." This was said with patent insincerity as he turned to his companion and resumed stroking the back of his hand.

"I have to get on that stage with the pipes," I protested, "or I'll get on the wrong side of Ricardo."

As it turned out, I managed to do both.

I can recall only fragments of that night. I cannot remember anything beyond my initial stumbling walk to the stage, where I gave an uninhibited selection of Mexican tunes. Back in the eighties, Charlie Cochrane of Denny in Stirlingshire had arranged the Mexican Hat Dance, *Alla en el Rancho Grande* and *Cielito Lindo* into an attractive medley for the British Caledonian Pipe Band, who featured in the 1986 Olympic Games in that country. Fortunately, Tom Johnson had given me a copy of this stuff, and I remembered enough of it to bring the cramped house down. I recall shambling down dark, narrow, cobbled streets to various tiny restaurants where I repeated my performance. Drunk with success – yes, and with Mescal, too – I raised my voice along with my new Mariachi companions in choruses like *No Tengo Dinero* and *Ojalá que te vaya bonito*.

> *Cuantas cosas quedaron prendidas*
> How many things have been kept on
> *hasta dentro del fondo de mi alma!*
> in the depth of my soul!
> *cuantas luces dejaste encendidas!*
> How many lights did you leave on!
> *yo no se como voy a apagarlas.*
> I don't know how I'm going to turn them off.

Ricardo succeeded in illuminating the rest of my stay in Zihua-tanejo. The period between hooking up with the Mariachis and my expulsion from the country was a wild and orgiastic time, and I simply adored it. There was a visceral thrill in feeding off the energy of the audience.

Of course, at the start of this series of adventures I had not intended to make my nerve-ends crazy and raw with dissipation. No, when the telephone call came from Sean Connery, or Big Tam as I came to know him, I had actually been sitting on a couch in my cousin's living room in Windsor, Ontario – for quite a few days – sipping beer and seriously considering a return to the UK. My tour of the college circuit in Michigan and Scottish clubs in Southern Ontario was over, and I had a few dollars to show for it.

My cousin, Donald MacKinnon, approached me cautiously with the telephone. He mouthed the words 'Sean Connery' and handed the instrument over to me. I was not surprised. Ever since Christmas Eve 1990, hardly a week went by without the actor – and I'm talking about the most famous screen actor ever to emerge from Scotland: this guy was up there with Eastwood, Hoffman, Pacino and De Niro – badgering me for copies of various comedy albums I'd made over the previous twelve years. I listened with growing irritation to his requests for *everything* I'd ever recorded. Why was this former Edin-burgh milkman and bodybuilder laying siege to my and my poor old mother's mind? The short answer is: I don't know.

Maybe he had some kind of Scottish surprise event lined up for his co-star in his current film, Michelle Pfeiffer. Perhaps he was just looking out for free cassettes. He was phoning from some toney resort in Mexico, he told me, but it was to a dictated Box Number in Orlando, Florida, I was to send *all* the cassettes. I reminded him, rather diffidently as I recall, that I'd be out a fair bit of change for postage. "No problem," he said. "Money'sh no object." And indeed it wasn't. I never saw a suntanned cent. To this day I reckon that Sir Sean owes me four pounds and seventy-three pence. I hung up and faced my cousin and his wife, Jean. "That's our secret agent phoning from Mexico," I said. "He wants more copies of about five additional albums. Says he's lying by a pool with his headphones on, and he's laughing his ass off."

My cousin said nothing for a moment, and then he suddenly came alive in his chair. "Goodness!" or, in his pidgin Gaelic, "*Dia gaw!*" he exclaimed. "You should have asked him for his address down there and delivered the tapes personally. The weather's beautiful in Mexico at this time of the year, and you need a break. He'd reimburse you for your travel expenses and throw in a nice big fat fee."

I shook my head sadly. "I don't think so, Don," I said. "I get the impression that our hero would steal the worm off a blind hen."

Nevertheless, over the succeeding days, the idea of making a trip south of the border at my own expense was taking root. One cold morning in downtown Windsor I gave a travel agent ninety-nine dollars and ninety-nine cents for tickets on a blue-rinse charter flight bound for Ixtapa, the custom-built tourist resort the Mexican government had decided was going to be the next Cancun.

In my memory Zihuatanejo, four miles along the coast from the one long strip of pavement with manicured lawns and clunky hotels that comprises Ixtapa, has become a grid of pastel-coloured buildings whose breath was the soughing of the tide. Pencilled waves fibrillated on a column of moonlight. Beaches of soft white sand were surrounded by jagged rocks. The Paseo del Ocotal, the main street, was crowded with flashily dressed couples, the males swarthy with open-necked shirts exposing medallions and abundant chest hair, the women with dramatically piled hair and livid eye make-up. Indians, bowed under cords of firewood and bags of fertilizer, lumbered through pavement markets. Little children skipped between wooden bins and handcarts. There were wagons selling chorizos, pistachio nuts and ices, steam tables on wheels, thin men and barefoot boys hawking lottery tickets.

One night, after leaving my room on the outskirts of town, I emerged into the streets of this former fishing village around midnight. Two boys, in military uniform and toting rifles, stood in a darkened doorway, yawning as they waved a shy greeting. A fluttering, fiery wind smelling of petrol and rotting fish rolled across my face and clattered through the fronds of the palm trees that lined the pavements.

I sensed that the crowds were in Mardi Gras mood. The orchestra was tuning up, the players had all applied their make-up, and the curtain was about to rise. As I stood there in the Paseo del Ocotal, lighting a cigarette, I smelt the same balmy air that assaults you in the tropics, the same drunk-inducing mix of salt air and romance and mystery. I was aware, however, that a parasite of self-doubt and self-destruction was nibbling at my psyche. Something in me, I was convinced, had warped. I tried to work out what had gone wrong.

Why was I about to endure savage and unnatural pressures for the umpteenth time? How had I ended up as the black sheep grazing on the lower slopes of the Sierra Madre Mountains in Guererro? How had I skidded off the Monopoly board into the darker regions of the liberal dream? The short and all-embracing answer was booze, and its pernicious effect on me. Already, I had been in rehabilitation programmes so many times that I had lost count of the number of wee white beds I had occupied in places as far apart as Aberdeen and New York. My take on things, that night, was that my addiction was a low-maintenance one. At a deeper level, I knew that if I entered the neon-lit doorway of Club Garibaldi, a considerable sum of dollars in my pocket, the after-shock would most certainly come. And when it did, its manifestation would be harsh and weird. Sunk in some thought tangle I couldn't penetrate, I took the Celtic method of dealing with perplexity. I was heading for a stiff drink. As I veered across the street, I knew that something was seriously wrong with this film clip.

Now, it wasn't like this in the beginning. I was a happy child. I was secure and I was confident. In the darkness of this evening, as an adult, I was once more caressing the self-destruct button. A faint awareness was born that the bright mornings of childhood would have to be examined later. I had no idea that in fifteen years' time I would be following my own Camino Real. This journey would not take place in a foreign country, but in Glasgow back in Scotland, territory that for me carried a lot of freight. In Mexico I was not prepared for the consequences of a personal inventory.

26

Los Mariachis

The voice of Colin Robertson, my short, fat, bespectacled manager in the Nineties – an extremely tough former bouncer at nightclubs in the city of Glasgow – boomed through the telephone speakers on the reception desk of the Hotel Suzy.

"So how's Mexico treating you?" he asked.

"Great," I replied. "Terrific. You know, I joined a gang."

"Really?" he said in the tone one employs when dealing with a drunk or a lunatic.

"Yeah, I'm a member of the Mariachis de Calisco," I bellowed drunkenly into the mouthpiece.

"Louder, Norrie," Colin said. "Linda's sleeping upstairs. She's in a coma compounded of equal parts of Vat 69 and Mogadon, and she didn't quite hear you. You're in a gang? That's magic, Norrie."

"It's marvellous," I gushed. "I did some research into the Mariachis de Guadalajara, listened to their rap, but the Calisco mob had a better health plan and a really generous superannuation scheme, so I went with them."

Colin laughed. "What do you need?" he asked.

"Three hundred quid, US dollars," I replied quickly.

"Give me your address," he rapped out, "and I'll get an International Money Order off to you this afternoon."

I could imagine Colin back in Glasgow, circling his temple with a forefinger.

I gave him the address. He started to say something, but I was gone.

I was in a good mood, which always precedes a bad one. As usual, my mood changed abruptly within the hour. If my chat with Colin had been the meal, my involvement with Conchita, the female lead singer in our band, was the bill. You look at an attractive female, and the next thing you know you're in your own private Iraq. Not a good move, Norrie.

An inch or two taller than me, Conchita carried herself like a queen. Her long limbs were crowned with a swell of lips and flared nostrils beneath prominent cheekbones. You bet I'd noticed her. All during the tour, whenever she was fronting the band, I was like Saint Paul on the road to Damascus, blind to everything but her light. With her bright eyes and hair the colour of mahogany, she was fetching in a way that was electrifying. Radiating cool composure at the same time as an almost angelic innocence, she held a powerful appeal for someone like me. Here, in a vessel of surpassing beauty, was the promise of an attribute very highly prized by Hebridean men: subservience. The Mexican men favoured blondes. Their ideal of beauty was pale Anglo-Saxons. They had not to be too skinny. That suggested poverty.

Los Mariachis de Calisco, with the Teuchter tagging along, had been touring on the route between Chilpancingo and Acapulco playing in various zocalos and plazas. The most prestigious gig we played was in the aptly named Plazuela de los Mariachis in Guadalajara, the country's second-largest city. It was also considered one of its more beautiful. Situated a mile high in the Sierra Madre, the capital of Jalisco state, it was a city of narrow streets and intimate plazas.

The Plazuela, just off the city's central square, was surrounded by cantinas and open-air cafes, and resplendent with different groups of the street musicians for which the plaza was named, as many as six bands at a time, all strolling the cobblestones, playing requests simultaneously.

The sun fell, and the stars came out. It was a clear, balmy night, and I was overcome with what I remember as an enchanted glow. There were kids round the café tables and pulling on their mothers' skirts: there was singing and the rat-tat-tat of loud conversations. These were human beings warmed by one another's company. I realized the Great Highland Bagpipe was drawing a lot of heavy water with the members of the other Mariachi bands. Seizing my pipes, I made my way to the centre of the plaza and struck up. The tune I played was the haunting 'Dark Island' composed by *An Gille Dubh MacLachlainn*, Iain MacLachlan, who came from Creagorry in Benbecula. When the music, echoing in the darkness, stopped, and the song drifted off into silence, somewhere in the distance, a saxophone could be heard replicating the Hebridean melody. I responded by reprising the last four bars of the tune. Again came the sound of the horn. And now it was moving closer to where I stood. A sigh went up from the

257

crowd. The music of the bagpipe, saxophone and by now trumpets, seeking each other, steadily converged. The Mexican musicians, playing counterpoint solos, advanced slowly across the cobblestones, and together four of us stood side by side, and began playing as one. The boozers in the cantinas went crazy. It just does not get any better than this, especially if you're out of your face with drink.

My performance did me some good with Conchita as well. Throughout the marathon tour I was to be seen, like Apollo, lumbering after my Daphne. She took the pipes from me when I rejoined our group, and carefully packed them in the case. When she rose, she did a thing that stole my heart away. Addressing me as a hero, she smiled at me and, touching my face lightly, she whispered in my ear: "*Que tu vaya con suerte*, May you go with good fortune," and left to go back to Ricardo's table. I detected within myself something close to happiness. Oh, yes, I felt certain that the world should belong to singers and musicians. As I watched Conchita, some strange sensation of discovery grasped me. I was rescued, finally free. I knew that I would be describing this tour for the rest of my life, still recollecting shadowy images on a computer screen, far into the night.

During the tour we made enough pesos to be able to afford the strong drink that made me weak, and to sleep in hammocks in cheap uninspiring rooms reminiscent of prison cells with bathrooms that were on the far side of clean. (I've been trying valiantly to recall all the various pueblos, towns and cities in which I played my bagpipes and sang with Los Mariachis de Calisco, but I stagger up against the fact that I used to get so stavin' drunk with them, my head is still leaking and I can't remember half of them.) A bottle of Caña and a couple of glasses of ice-cold Sol in a bucket in the sink would be broached and consumed by me in double-quick time. I'd probably tan another bottle of rum after smoking a pack of domestic cigarettes. That was how I started my day.

If you happened to be drinking along with me, it indicated the end of the day. Miguel, Paco, Ernesto, Gilberto and others in our crew, a rag-tag assemblage of musicians, were all big drinkers themselves, and they noticed nothing untoward in my abuse of alcohol. They all loved to hear me sing Glasgow street songs. A nonsense song used by girls, as they bounced two rubber balls against the pavement and an adjacent tenement wall while they twirled and retrieved the balls with either hand, was called 'Ma Maw's a Millionaire'.

> *Ma maw's a millionaire,*
> *Blue eyes and curly hair,*
> *Down among the Eskimos*
> *Playing a game of Dominoes,*
> *Ma maw's a millionaire.*

Another favourite with the boys was 'Haw, maw'.

> *Haw, maw, will ye buy me a . . .*
> *Will ye buy me a . . . will ye buy me a . . .*
> *Haw, maw, will ye buy me a . . .*
> *Will ye buy me a banana?*

Girls (and, very occasionally, the odd boy) had been playing these ball games for generations. The school playground was the arena where crowds gathered to watch the 'champions' who were the most agile and physically fit, had the best hand-eye co-ordination, and who could play the longest without dropping the balls. At home during weekends and holidays, however, individuals would perfect their skills to return to school hoping to travel up the unwritten league tables. In a rickety old Mexican bus filled with reek of diesel, tobacco and alcohol, I had an inexplicable flashback.

I am back at the corner of Midlock Street and Brand Street; I am smoking a cinnamon stick and gazing at these young lassies playing 'balls'. I marvel at this mysterious game, where a girl uses two hands, two legs and all sorts of gymnastic positions to continue in play until one of the balls misses her grasp. There she is. Audrey Bambrick. Playing a game while a small crowd of spectators and competitors fix their gazes upon her 'match' to watch out for any mistakes. Audrey is feeling good, and rather than using the two new sets of balls her aunt had given her for her birthday, she plays with her old 'faithfuls'. These are heavy, worn, multicoloured rubber balls, but hit where she wants to hit on the wall after bouncing off the ground. She controls them without thinking, along to the rhythm of the song. She goes through each 'level' of First Leggy, Second Leggy, Splitsies, Backbridge, Jibby, Wee Burlie, Big Burlie, Stookie, Dummy, Wan Hauny. Audrey catches the ball with her left hand by raising her arm and grabbing it before it bounces. Other girls wait for this ball with their left hand close to their chest, letting the ball come to them. I wonder if this tells us something about the player.

*Reaching out confidently and taking the ball or cautiously waiting for it to
nestle in the bosom and the cupped hand, afraid the ball will drop if they
try to grab it . . .*

Where did they learn the rules, songs and the immutable choreography of the game? It certainly wasn't from a worksheet or Care in the Community.

"Indifference upon you", as Seumas Mòr would render his native Gaelic, "*Coma leat co dhiù*". Here we were back in our home base in Zihua, and the boys and girls were whooping it up in Club Garibaldi. I was half in the bag, as I had been every night since joining the gang, and was vaguely aware that I was sinking deeper and deeper into a dangerously hedonistic lifestyle.

During this wild and orgiastic time I had even considered (gasp!) going teetotal. *Mas Tequila,* More Tequila, soon routed these heretical thoughts, and inevitably, given the close contact I made with scores of half-naked women, I was put on a constant sexual high. Most nights I gave in to this massive temptation.

On the evening of our homecoming, Club Garibaldi was crowded. This was the kind of place where, in about ten minutes, you could round up a score of desperados who'd be up for committing all sorts of mayhem. Taped Ranchero music blared from four-hundred-watt speakers. A frosted glass of Tequila stood on the table before me. I took a sip and looked towards the tiny dance floor. Ricardo was dancing with the statuesque, dark-haired Conchita, whose full breasts were squirming out of her bikini top. With a straight back, motionless from the waist up, wriggling violently below, she allowed Ricardo to pursue her across the dance floor. Her expression was one of acute boredom; her movements were entirely abandoned. Ricardo pursued her, inclining forward from the waist, shuffling like Michael Jackson, an eager grin on his face. They never touched.

Suddenly, Ricardo went down on one knee like Elvis Presley. The crowd roared. Conchita looked straight at me and tilted her chin up in invitation. "¿*Quieres bailar*? You wanna dance?" she asked.

"*No, gracias*, No, thanks," I responded. Within, I recoiled.

"*Viene, amor*, Come on, honey," she said, skipping over to my table and tugging at my arm. I realized that everyone in the place, particularly Ricardo, was watching, but it would have taken greater willpower than I possessed to refuse her offer, much as I wanted to.

The people of Mexico are religious, courteous and prone to extreme violence. Yes, they are an intelligent and charming people. The one weakness among the males is an affection for the *revólver*. As I joined my temptress on the dance floor I knew in my bones that I had entered dangerous territory. The other couples dispersed. Ricardo sat in a distant corner watching us impassively. A new *Corrido*, fast and upbeat, kicked in. For what seemed half an hour I pranced before a laughing audience, while I wiggled my hips in a grotesque imitation of the Twist. The muffled whomp of the amplified music entered my bloodstream and I found myself attempting a modified James Brown kind of quickstep. As Conchita's movements became increasingly complicated, however, my confidence evaporated, until finally I tripped and fell headlong to the floor. It was fun being in the fast lane. My partner helped to my feet. My face was burning. We breaststroked our way through the smoky murk towards the door. I turned round to look at my fellow revellers, to see how they were taking my enforced exit.

I should not have done that . . .

Everyone in the place was looking at Ricardo, their faces filled with fear. He was not exactly ordinary-looking. Though not tall, he stood straighter than anyone else, with more self-awareness. He wore his matador's outfit with a sense of theatrical style.

Once outside, Conchita kissed me wetly and ran her hand between my legs. Although I attempted to receive this gesture like a Stoic, I found myself stepping backwards. I was truly afraid – of her, of sex, of the mysterious chasm between my own race and one where homicide was the most frequent consequence of slighted male honour.

Fortunately I had retreated before her determined advance; unfortunately, my back hit the side of our battered bus, and Conchita pinned me against it.

"*¿Viene a mi cuarto?* You come to my room?" she breathed wetly in my ear.

"*¿Como no?* Why not?" I said. Great idea, eh? Yeah, right up there with Kennedy deciding to take a trip to Dallas.

She gripped my left wrist with her right hand and hauled me across the dusty road past the mocking taxi drivers in front of the Club Garibaldi, who hooted their horns at the audacity of Conchita and my own woeful submission. A raucous cheer went up from a group of youths who were loitering outside a Laundromat. Tugging and sporadically yanking me into a faster pace, she led me to an intersection about a hundred yards down the main road. She turned left here and dragged me down an alley until we reached a burnt-orange-coloured two-storey building. She fumbled with a key, all the time keeping an iron grip on my wrist. The stench of recently cooked fajitas was strong. Pushing the door open, she bundled me into what appeared to be a kind of kitchen with a single bed in a corner. Female undergarments were ranged over a bathtub. A phalanx of ointments, pills and creams were set against a full-length mirror in a corner. An older memory of sin slipped into focus. It started with a flogging . . .

My father has discovered his twelve-year-old first-born in the company of his best friend, Francis Aloysius Carrabine, smoking Woodbine cigarettes in the rafters of our close. What we called 'the rafters' was a trellis of rough-hewn beams that criss-crossed the entrance to our close: they were designed to protect our building from German bombs. He easily reaches up, seizes me roughly by the forearm and hauls me up the stairs to our home, where, I know, he will administer physical punishment. The weird thing about Big Neil's flogging is the completely dispassionate way he disciplines me. He orders me to take all my clothes off. He then invites me to come to the kitchen table – without a stitch of clothing on my shivering frame – and eat perhaps a bowl of porridge or a soft-boiled egg. I choke down as much as I can, and Big Neil informs me in cold, impersonal language that I have brought disgrace upon the family and will have to suffer the consequences. I am then placed firmly, but with a curious kind of . . . well, tenderness, over the seat of an old wooden kitchen chair. He tells me to grasp the front leg of the chair with one hand and a rear leg with the other. A tin basin is placed on the linoleum below my drooping head: to catch the vomit. Big Neil then, without haste, lashes his son's bare buttocks with the razor-strop. Howling, gagging, the boy endures this humiliating torture in full view of his weeping mother and terrified sister.

Then comes the kindness. As soon as Big Neil considers that his errant son has had enough, he dresses the bloody wounds on the boy's back and buttocks with gauze bandages dripping with a thick, yellow, viscous solution. Next, he carries the boy through to the recessed bed in the back bedroom and leaves him there to weep in the twilight for an hour or two . . .

After a while, something mind-blowing happens. The father returns to his son and treats him with unexpected solicitude. It is always in the aftermath of physical abuse that Neil teaches his son phrases in Spanish, a language he acquired during his stay on the Argentinian pampas, where my grandfather,

Iain Eòghain Ruaidh, John son of red-headed Ewan, broke horses for a living. Neil reads to the boy from a book of classical myths some hack has published under the title Tansy and Bubbles in Fable Island, *or simply regales the boy with accounts of the superb horsemanship of the Argentinian gauchos or the physical features of Hottentots in South West Africa. God, so much weirdness!*

Talk about contradictions! The day after the brutal flogging he purchased a second-hand 'fairy cycle' for me. I obviously wasn't the only member of our family ricocheting between opposites.

The beating from my father did not deter me from smoking. The serpent had, and still has, its fangs in me.

In her room, Conchita kicked off her high-heeled shoes, drew her skirt off, then her panties. Languidly, she shrugged off her bikini top. She wet her fingers with spit and stroked her large nipples slowly and with care until they become darkly erect. She cupped a breast in one hand, its nipple surrounded by dusky gooseflesh, and with her other hand forced my head downwards to meet it. Without hurrying at all, she used the swollen tip to trace the outline of my lips. In sweet humiliation my knees buckled and I bit, sucked, licked her breasts, belly, moved my mouth over hips, along the inside of her thighs, until at last my face was buried in her black, abundant pubic hair. She used both her hands to force my head up, her fingers clutching fiercely at my hair, and I saw in the dim light her conical breasts, and my head swam. She thrust her hands between my arms and rib-cage and hauled me upright.

"*¿Que pasa?* What are you doing?" I said.

"*Tranquillo, hombre*, Take it easy, man," she said. With tiny steps she backed me up to the bed. Carefully she laid me down, face upward, on the cotton sheets. She sat beside me, one leg crossed over the other, and gazed down at me for some time with affection suffusing her face. Without giving any impression of haste she placed her hand on the bulge in my trousers, and slowly, lazily even, began to squeeze and stroke it. I asked her to stop and she said she didn't believe I wanted her to stop.

I surrendered. I was worried, though, that if she stripped me she'd see my ugly, misshapen feet. As far back as I can remember I have been deeply ashamed of the lumps of hard, dead skin that disfigured my heels and toes – something to do with old shoes my mother used to get for me from Solly, the Jewish owner of a dress shop she worked in over at Charing Cross. The shoes, invariably of excellent quality, were the cast-offs of Solly's son David and were always too tight for me – and I have always been reluctant to expose my deformity to others.

And now:

. . . My father, on his knees before me, anoints my feet with Archangel tar. How in the name of God did he get his hands on this acrid-smelling stuff?

"That's not painful, is it?" I hear a voice say. I do not know if it is Big Neil speaking.

"It's – it's very nice," I say.

"Keep this on. Two hours. Three hours," my father says. Turning to my mother, he speaks harshly: "Peggy, it's those bloody shoes, right? I see that Jewish trash in this house again I'm going over to show Solly what he can do with them. What size does this dwarf David take anyway?" I feel a knot of emotion move within me. Niall Mòr truly cares about me. That is to stay with me for six months. It has never really uncoiled. And it has never gone away either . . .

Under the sweeping caresses of Conchita's hand I entered a ductile state. I allowed myself to be swayed, or rather, I allowed myself to attribute to drunkenness my eventual acquiescence. Conchita made it easy. "*No tendras que hacer nada*, You don't have to do anything," she repeated. "*Haz el favor de echarse*, Just lie there." And she was as good as her word. I felt her strong fingers tugging on the buckle of my belt, and two wings of pitch-black hair shrouded my cheeks as she lowered her head to bestow a kiss.

But her lips did not make contact with my mouth.

The hinges on the door were squeaking.

I clenched my fists, nails almost piercing my palms, as I realized a third person was in the room. When I heard a soft cough coming from the direction of the door I was petrified by fear. I ignored the lover who was so anxious to serve me. I was no longer aroused by Conchita's big breasts, though I observed their gentle sway as she breathed deeply and rapidly. My partner was now a long, long way from my consciousness, though her flesh was only inches removed from me. Mortal fear overwhelmed me and left me paralyzed. I was poised for flight, but lacked the strength to flee. I was certain of only one thing. Another baleful eye, a wild eye in the skull of a male, was observing me closely, and it would not be long before I heard the accusation of my unknown enemy.

27
Fear

"*¿Ricardo?*" said Conchita. I heard the click of a light switch, and then – lo, there was light. The fat singer stood by the door of her room.

"*Si*," said Ricardo as he swaggered over to the bed. "*La puerta estaba abierta*, The door was open," he said, baring his stained teeth in a rictus of grim cordiality. "*¿No tienes la llave para la cerradura?* Don't you have a key for the lock?"

I myself was attempting a kind of ingratiating smile. But I was certainly not happy. When he sensed my fear he drew a revolver.

Now you knew this strutting bantam just must have a body covered in knife wounds. Here was a guy who was so downright macho, and sure of it, that he could afford to dress like a *clown*.

Ricardo walked round the bed and twirled the revolver, occasionally resting the barrel against Conchita's head. Replacing the sexual arousal in me was dread.

"*Ricardo, por favor no pegues a un gringo*, Ricardo, please, don't fight with the gringo," Conchita said plaintively, and she began to cry.

An ugly laugh came from somewhere above my head. I received a rough kick in the ankle from a stout boot.

"*O no, Conchita*, Oh, no, Conchita," Ricardo said. "*No voy a ir a pegarme con el gringo. Yo voy a haceros a bosotros otra cosa*, I'm not going to *fight* with the gringo. I'm going to do something else to the pair of you." Five seconds passed like a yacht changing course in a stiff breeze. Ricardo sniggered, or, more accurately, hissed through his broken teeth. "*Voy a ir a mataros*, I'm going to kill you." he announced evilly. His words clanked like chains about me.

My terror was stark and immediate. I was overcome by a surge of adrenalin. My heart raced, my pulse quickened, my breathing grew rapid, and my palms began to sweat. I was totally and absolutely immersed in fear. Despite having been subjected to massive injections of sensory input my nerves had already started to fray. I could see the quivering of my fingers in my lap. This was not a common or garden dose of the shakes. This was terror. Fear was blank. My brain was dazzled, my body frozen, like a hind caught in the headlights of a car.

Ricardo, with an over-large hooked nose and his thick, slobbery lips, was one of the most ill-favoured human beings I have ever met. His appearance was not what films and fiction had led me to expect. It was significantly worse. This dyed-in-the wool psychotic embodied all the visual attributes of the stereotypical Mexican outlaw. About forty-five years old, he had the broad face and thick moustache that were familiar from archive photographs of the legendary *bandido*, Pancho Villa.

Clearly outraged, he began to wave his arms about as he punctuated his soliloquy on betrayal. Finally, the accumulating energy with which he was charged had achieved critical mass. "Here, gringo, when a man steals from you, he has to kill you," he said, casting a sidelong glance at the naked Conchita. "If he does not kill you, he will live forever with a scorpion on his back. He knows that some d you will find him, and on that day he will take your life. In Mexic we call it *justicia*."

"Not revenge?" I managed to gargle.

"Justice," he said firmly. "Yes. It is v hat must be done."

I was in a condition of barely controlled hysteria. My adrenalin was pumping at the red line. What was I going to do? I was reminded of every cowboy and gangster film I had ever seen, and envisioned myself, lying face-down in a squalid shack, leaking vital fluids through my cheap T-shirt.

Here I was, face to face with a killer on the verge of apoplexy. Terrific. My senses were on high alert. I wasn't sure how long I had been sitting there. I was aware of the danger but was unable to move or react, helpless to stop what was happening to me. Man has a dreadful adaptability. Within a few minutes I got used to the idea of living or dying in the most sordid surroundings.

Suddenly a ray of hope penetrated my current apathy. Ricardo gripped the butt of the revolver in his right hand and with his left he seized Conchita's hair and hauled her to her feet. Fully six inches shorter than the woman, Ricardo stood in front of her with his entire being oozing insolence. His face exuded malevolence.

Conchita had stopped crying and was not smiling. Naked, she smoothly spread her arms wide. Her body was entirely motionless.

Ricardo watched her carefully, his teeth grinding together – a warning sign that he was brimming with anger. The scent of the oil he smothered his hair with was strong, the smell of unhealthy yearnings. His thick lips were constantly in motion, twisting, pouting, compressing and being gnawed by blackened teeth.

Conchita took a step closer to him. Ricardo raised his gun arm and pulled the trigger. It was just a brief moment, but it felt so long. After the deafening bang I seemed to be transported to a mountain top looking down upon a mist-covered lake. Slowly my vision cleared and my hearing was restored. With his left hand Ricardo fingered the tips of one of Conchita's breasts. Most unprofessional, *amigo*.

Conchita looked down at the thick fingers that were groping her flesh like hungry worms. The couple were playing some kind of game of chicken, and both tried to steel themselves not to blink.

My insides turned to water; fear dried my mouth and caused me to think more clearly. My arms and legs were coming to life again. Other ideas were invading my consciousness, none of which involved being a spectator at a live sex show. Given my upbringing and education, it was difficult to disguise the fact that I abhorred violence. If I was not ashamed of my fear of physical violence – and in some hidden subconscious corner I was loath to dredge, I was sure this was the case – I simply had to act and get out of here. It was now or never. I bounded out of bed and head-butted Conchita with all the strength I could muster on the base of her spine. She crashed forward into Ricardo, sending him sprawling on his back. I leaped over the gasping bodies, seized my bagpipe case where I had abandoned it on the floor, and ran through the open doorway. The catarrh of an idling diesel engine caught my attention. The hundred and fifty yards to the taxi rank outside Club Garibaldi was a fast walk through eternity. I made it to a gigantic, battered old Oldsmobile and yelled, "*Vamos*! Get going! Ixtapa."

Within twenty minutes, bare-chested, but at least wearing jeans, I was booked into 'Chico and Antonio's' on the north-west end of the Ixtapa hotel strip. This did not come cheap. Fortunately I still had some dollars, pesos and, most importantly, an Amex card. "*No hay un problema*, No problem," said the attractive receptionist. Accordingly, I registered for a couple of nights and, temporarily at least, my bagpipe and I were safe within the walls of Room 346.

I caught sight of myself in the bathroom mirror. As though on a dimmer switch, my eyes brightened. The corners of my mouth rose slightly. My brow miraculously smoothed. Swinging between elation and relief, I was not sure what to think. I knew I felt a lot better than I had half an hour ago. I threw up a clenched fist and silently applauded myself. Idiot. I was fighting unconsciousness. All the booze I had consumed that night was pulling me down. I threw myself on to the bed, closed my eyes and fell asleep.

This then: I am lying on a hammock in a beach shack in Goa looking down on my emaciated body, my skin in folds. The beaded curtains part, and in comes a mocha-coloured Singhalese youth. He snatches up a carrier bag and informs me that he has been summoned to Colombo on urgent business. Somehow I know that he has been sharing my quarters for some time, and that he has been worried by my physical decline. With a wave of his hand he is gone. A few seconds later, I realize he has taken the wrong bag. He has taken mine, stuffed with books. I open his almost identical bag some time later and discover it is stuffed with banknotes: rupees, dollars, pounds and deutschmarks. I am too weak to get up and pursue my lodger. And I leave the open bag on the earth floor . . .

Abruptly, I am back in the cursed schoolhouse in Lochaber. There is an old, waxy map of the world hanging on a wall. I am scrutinizing carefully the red portions, that to me represent freedom. I walk on stilts to the teacher's desk, raise the lid and gaze at the bundles of paper inside. This is a world I know well – a world full of sheets of paper which tell people who was present on a particular day, how well or how badly children had performed in examinations. I understand immediately that my life resembles an old ragged coat made from the remnants of other people's lives. My eyes are caught by a calendar on another wall. There is an image of a Royal Navy warship on top of it. With astonishment I read the inscription below the ship – SS Holderness! I fire up my disposable lighter and, hurrying over to the open teacher's desk, I set alight the bundles of papers. When I am sure that the fire has started, I scurry over to the calendar and tear the thing off the wall. It too is consigned to the flames. I seem to be destroying my past in the fire of my vengeance. I retreat to the open doorway and stand with my back to it, as the smoke from the desk swirls past me. My eyes are smarting. A stab of fear wounds my stomach: Cha bhuin mi dhan àite seo, *I don't belong here, and* Tha rudeigin ceàrr, *Something is wrong. My heart beats faster and I am bathed in sweat . . .*

I awoke with a pounding headache. I felt my armpit. Wet and slippery and smelling bad. I needed a bath. I needed a lot of things, but right now I needed another dram. Thirty minutes and two miniatures of spirits from the mini-bar later, I closed my eyes for a full three seconds, and savoured the warm sensation that seemed to rise from the base of my stomach and fill my entire being. Within minutes the euphoria was frayed at the edges by inchoate anguish and self-pity. Why me, God? The only remedy was another dram.

Just to sit in that admittedly swish hotel room in Ixtapa thinking of Conchita and Ricardo depressed me, so I went out to the terrace and paced up and down until I attracted the attention of a white-jacketed *mesero*, waiter, to order a beer. The place was buzzing. The staff and visitors came from every region of Central and North America: exotic Indians, black-haired *mestizos*, blond Canadians and Americans, and their varied languages and dialects gave the place the feel of Babel. But I was restless. While I enjoyed the creature comforts of Ixtapa, I hankered after the woodsmoke and rugged excitement of Zihuatanejo. Was this another manifestation of my dislocation from my rural roots?

Later that night, much later, I became increasingly convinced that I could talk my way out of any trouble I might find on the other side of the bay. This gratuitous measure of confidence was actually attributable to the contents of the mini-bar, which I had methodically emptied, and the ice-cold beers I had drunk in my posh hotel. Suddenly my sordid little flight from reality was rudely interrupted. A waiter whose moist pink lips and shiny white teeth looked terrifying from six feet away had entered my arc of vision. I assumed he must have been observing me for some time. He spoke: "*Amigo, creo que tu tienes un problema*, I hear you are in trouble, my friend."

"*¿Quien*, Who?" I said in pretended bafflement. " *¿Yo*, Me?"

"*Si. Tu*. Yeah. You." he replied confidently. He lowered his voice like a conspirator. "*Conozco un hombre que viene de Zihuatanejo*, I know a man who's from Zihuatanejo. *El te puede alludar . . . por un precio*. He can help you . . . at a price." The waiter rubbed forefinger and thumb together. "*Emos encontrado un restaurante en la planta baja*, He'll meet us in the restaurant downstairs," he whispered.

Fifteen minutes later, the waiter and I were sitting on bar stools.

"*Cuando el benga, abla con el*, When he comes in, talk to him," the waiter was saying.

"*¿Como lo reconocere?* How will I recognize him?" I asked.

"*Lo reconoceras*, You'll recognise him," the waiter said, with all the confidence in the world.

"*¿Seguro?* Really?" I said, doubt in my voice.

"*Seguro*, Really," the waiter said.

Sure, I recognized him. He walked right by our stools. He passed us without saying a word, and then took a table in the rear. This guy was 'Don't Watch Alone' material. I had never seen before my two eyes anyone who looked any more evil, threatening or dangerous than this man. In addition he was really *huge*.

The waiter said: "*Bien, bete para alli y abla con el*, Okay, go back and talk to him."

I took a deep breath. I went back.

"*Buenas Noches*," I squeaked.

"*Buenas*," he growled.

No smile.

The man waited for me to sit down. He narrowed his eyes. Then, slowly, he spoke: "*Señor Maclean, estoy aqui para alludarte con el problema de Ricardo, Señor Maclean*, I'm here to help you with the Ricardo problem." This was a searing blast of heat from the depths of hell. "*Si Ricardo abusa de ti, le cogere*, If Ricardo abused you, I'll get him. *Pero si tu desonras a Ricardo, nadie volvera a verte nunca mas, por que no me gusta perder el tiempo*, But if *you* dishonoured him, nobody will ever see you again, because I don't like to waste my time."

That was all. I said: "*Tengo que ir al bater*, I have to go to the toilet." God be round about me, this was certainly the truth. My bowels were in an uproar.

After spending a very long time in the toilet stall, I crept back to the waiter and the very welcoming bar stools. No sale. I gulped my whisky, opened my eyes and found myself wishing I'd wake up from this terrifying nightmare. Petrifying. My blood on the deck somewhere in Guerrero and 'Lochaber No More' for you, Norrie.

The drunken days and nights rolled along like less than perfect waves, and my preoccupation during my waking hours was money and where I could get more of it. Asleep I was tormented by vaguely erotic dreams . . .

The pair of us, Liz and I, are pushing our way into a wood, and once sheltered from the main road, we stand and begin to kiss passionately in a clearing. I am thinking that we should lie down, but no words come to my tongue but the shy nonsense that comes to a teenager. So, I continue kissing her and fondling her breasts.

The thought comes to me that she is in heat as she licks, sucks and nibbles at my lips, all the while a low humming noise coming from her throat. I push her backwards until her back strikes the trunk of a fir tree. She takes off her high-heeled shoes. Carefully I lay her down on her back, and start to take off her jeans, then her panties.

Standing, I take off my own clothes. I kneel down between her thighs, and as I slide upward, my mouth searching for hers, my hands searching for her breasts beneath her blouse, I get a glimpse of arms stretched out in welcome.

'Norman,' she says, breathless, and turns me over effortlessly and straddles my thighs swiftly. 'Do you want me to take this off?' She indicates her blouse.

'Yes,' I reply.

'You sure?' she asks teasingly.

In one fluid motion she divests herself of the blouse, and with a wiggle of her shoulders she shrugs off her brassiere. She ferries one breast to her mouth and her darting tongue licks the nipple feverishly. With her free hand she kneads her other breast. She is proud of her body and the power it has over me. She smiles. She glows. She is hungry. 'Put your head back, love,' she says. 'I know a trick that'll bring you pleasure.' She quickly moves her entire weight backwards, places her hands on my knees and forces them apart. Her own knees are nudging my private parts, and when I squirm to resist this slow torture, she spreads my upper legs still further apart and lowers her body until her breasts, full, soft and heavy, are caressing my open mouth, from one corner of which a lucent string of drool spreads. 'Worship me, Norman,' she whispers. Like well-prepared actors, we move carefully and smoothly. She turns gracefully and stretches her long body lazily on the forest floor by my side. I raise myself up on one elbow. I wet my fingers with spit and slide my hand downwards and start to rub her lightly with my fingertips. She arches her back.

'That's it, Norman,' she gasps. 'Don't stop. Please don't stop.'

I would emerge from this tantalizing trip on my time machine utterly exhausted. This could not go on. I decided that I was unable to take any more of the horror that was Ixtapa. Knowing that Ricardo and Conchita were in each other's arms over on the other side, I was battered with longing. I laid my head back against the pillow, certain that I would never understand one single thing about myself.

28
Mamacita

Although my memory is cluttered with the debris of my last two days in Ixtapa/Zihuatanejo, I still remember my very last day in the place. Well, sort of.

I opened my eyes. Dawn had broken, cicadas and frogs from a nearby creek began to call. Birds of prey I took to be buzzards were hovering above the market. I was lying on my back on the soft white sand of Playa La Ropa, back in Zihuatanejo. That's right. I had left the comparative safety of Ixtapa and somehow made my way back to a very dangerous place. My left arm cradled my pipe case on my chest, while my right hand was wrapped round a bottle of rum. I didn't have a map or a watch – I'd sold my Tag Heuer to a Canadian traveller in a bar twenty-four hours previously – to tell me I was in the wrong place at the wrong time again. My breath grew shallow, and quickened as I stumbled to my feet. The sunlight seemed to rush up suddenly against my face, palpitating rapidly like the wings of a butterfly. My heart pounded in my temples and in my chest. My leg muscles flexed nervously. Though my hands were wet with sweat, I kept a firm grip of both bagpipe-case and bottle. My face felt hot, and my lips were starting to stick to each other. Putting the bottle's mouth to my lips, I allowed the lukewarm rum to bathe my tongue.

Here I was, swaying like a caber cradled by some brute at Braemar Highland Gathering, wobbling, and almost tipping over onto my face as I tottered off with stoic, knock-kneed baby-steps up towards the Malecón. I was barefoot because I'd sold my trainers to a young guy in a bar the previous evening for eight bottles of *Sol* lager. With pipe-case in fist, I wandered through the loamy fragrances of an open-air market, through mounds of cheese, haphazard piles of vegetables, and past butcher stalls where the fetid odour of dried blood enveloped slabs of goat, rabbit and horse meat. At last I found what I was looking for: a tiny stall decorated by a canvas awning. The proprietor was selling booze. I persuaded him to fill my almost empty rum bottle with *Caña*, a poisonous sugar-cane-based concoction, for the equivalent of eighteen pence. I immediately took a jumbo-sized swallow from my new comforter in order to drown the rambunctious nest of wasps in my belly. I stood under the awning long enough for the alcohol to conduct its usual pogrom on my brain cells. Then, in jeans and a singlet bearing the legend *Argentina es el lugar* that I'd borrowed over in Ixtapa, with a waterproof Berghaus jacket over my shoulders, I hit the road. Carrying a pipe-case and a bottle I was going to *walk* to *Aeropuerto Internacional Ixtapa/Zihuatanejo*, seven miles outside the market where I had been indulging in my usual form of self-medication! Should I have been allowed out on the streets without medical supervision?

No.

Of course I never completed the course. Once I left the shady streets of Zihuatanejo with its shop awnings, the heat struck me, almost bowled me over as if the doors of a blast furnace had been thrown open. I stopped frequently for small sips of the fiery spirit. I considered going back, could not decide, and then went on. The *Caña* fuelled me for about two miles, before exhaustion overcame me and my eyeballs began to feel like boiling rocks. The heat was melting me down. I was tired, dusty and sweating. The paucity of traffic on the hot and sticky road to the airport was depressing. Occasionally, rickety old lorries with wildly waving bare-chested youths on board would lumber past me.

No private cars. The sky was clear, not a cloud to be seen, only the cruel sun which beat relentlessly against my sodden Berghaus jacket. I was too fatigued, too appalled to move any distance further. I was exhausted, dirty and sweating: my bare feet hurt.

I heard marimba music in the distance. A vision then came to me like a slide passing through a projector. It was a tiny shack with a thatched roof. I could see a long table flanked by benches. More importantly, there were people there. More accurately, there was an old woman with long, grey hair stirring something in a pot on some kind of hob, and two little girls pecking at typewriters on one of the benches. I approached them slowly. With my hands jammed in my pockets, which contained only damp travel tickets and my passport, I glided into the welcome shade of the shack. I had run out of ideas.

"*Buenos dias, Señora,*" I said, in what I hoped were sober tones. The old woman – I had already identified her as *mamacita*, old mother, in my mind – invited me to sit on the bench opposite the giggling little girls, who were obviously sisters. One would be about six and the other eight. The *mamacita* then asked me how she could be of service.

"*Estoy mareado*, I feel dizzy," I croaked. "*Quisiera una cerveza*, I'd like a beer."

"*El gusto es mio*, with pleasure," she replied. This was a response from heaven.

Within seconds I was gulping *cerveza morena* from a frosted glass.

Now came the difficult bit.

"*Senora, hay un problema*, There's a problem," I whispered.

"*¿Esta todo bien*? Is everything all right?" she solicitously enquired

"*No tengo suficiente dinero*, I don't have enough money," I said.

"*No hay problema*, No problem," the *mamacita* said. "*Puedes pagarme mas tarde*, You can pay me later." She looked at my jeans. "*Me gustan tus pantalones*, I like your jeans. *Me gustaria comprartelos*, I'd like to buy them. *¿Cuanto pides por ellos*? How much do you want for them?"

"*Quince dolares*, Fifteen dollars," I quickly replied.

"*Vale*, Okay," she murmured calmly.

I stood up, took off the jeans and handed them to the *mamacita*. In return, she gave me a twenty dollar bill.

"How much will you give me for this jacket?" I said, drunk with the acquisition of much needed money.

"*El selbe*, The same," she said.

I quickly peeled off the sweat-soaked garment and received another twenty dollar bill.

Despite being down to boxer shorts and singlet, I had an afternoon that ranked as one of the most enjoyable of my life. I helped the sisters improve their typing skills, and I played the bagpipe for them: I sang Gaelic and Mexican songs. I twinkled like a little star. The reason for all my spurious bonhomie was the seemingly endless supply of chilled beer and packets of cigarettes that were regularly dumped in front of me on the table. Every so often the *mamacita* would send the girls scurrying off into the surrounding jungle with a few dollar bills. I asked the old lady once or twice where they were going. "*La tienda*, The store," she would explain to me, as though addressing a retard. Could I believe it? Somewhere out in the great uncut there was a *store*? After a while, though, the fact that there existed a commercial retail enterprise in the middle of nowhere ceased to bother me.

When drinking I always wanted to get to the line without going across, and then, some hours later, I'd look back and see that the line was a mile behind me. I let the love pour through me over the world. At one point I commandeered one of the typewriters and tried to write home. It was no good. I just sat there on the bench, my mind as empty as the cloudless blue sky above, but knowing that someday all this would have to be described, and grateful that the little girls' demands for further instruction from me kept me from doing anything creative at that time.

The *mamacita* washed my hair in a tin basin. In halting English she said with gratitude: "You learn *las chicas* real good."

It was the word 'learn' that did it for me . . .

Our entire family – mother, father, my young sister, Lorna Flora, and myself – are together in the kitchen of the flat in Ibrox. It is noon on a Sunday, the last day in the life of Niall Mòr. In a flash, I am back in the mean streets of Govan and Ibrox. When I recall my sour, priggish words to my father, I puzzle over what strikes me as a nasty truth. I miss Neil Maclean more than anyone else in the world, Peigi included.

The harsh clatter of the *mamacita's* broken English catapulted me back from my dream. She had discovered that the check-in time for my flight to Detroit was seven-thirty that evening. "There ees some possibleness that my daughter, Maria, may be be able to get you out to the *aeropuerto*," she said.

"Oh," I said – white. What, I wondered, would I do instead?

The girl would collect me around six in her Toyota pick-up and take me to the airport. Tears of gratitude, or perhaps guilt, poured down my cheeks. If my co-ordination had been better I'd have been turning cartwheels. It really didn't get much better than this. Of course, as we used to say during some of our blistering Socratic seminars when we were smart sophisticates at the university, '*This is physics, man . . . what goes up must come down, Jack.*'

And I was about to come down very soon. With a bang.

And so it came to pass that it was Maria who ran me to the airport. She was only a teenager with huge black eyes, olive skin and an alabaster smile. After stopping at the entrance to the concourse she did a really sweet thing. Through the open door of the truck she leaned forward, kissed me on the cheek and pressed a twenty dollar bill into my free hand. I was still, it goes almost without saying, gripping my pipe case in my other hand.

"*Es usted muy amable*, You're very kind," I stammered.

"*De nada*! You're welcome!" was her gracious response.

Revving the engine in preparation for a fast trap, she must have been assailed by a sudden thought. She turned off the ignition, applied the handbrake and leaped out.

"*Tu no puedes entrar al aereopuerto sin zapatas*, You will not be allowed to enter the airport barefoot," she said.

"*Pero no tengo zapatas*, But I don't *have* any shoes," I said.

"Not to worry," she said, flashing that gleaming smile. "I'll give you mine."

And she did. Swiftly she took off her own high-heeled sling backs – they must have been the equivalent of a British size four – and urged me to crush my bare feet into them.

"*Espero verte otra vez*, I hope to see you again," she said, smiling sweetly.

"*Adios*, Good-bye," was all I could muster in reply.

Well, I did my best to get my feet crammed into her shoes and I suppose, technically, I was shod when I teetered into the airport building. There's no denying, however, that dressed in singlet, shorts and high-heeled shoes five sizes too small for me, I was bad to look at. But I was cool. I stood up straight, walking like a man again, though my feet were a couple of burdens causing me excruciating pain, and entered one of the circular little bars which were numerous in this place.

"*Una cerveza morena*, A dark beer," I said to the smart young bartender.

He quickly obliged. When I later asked for and received four packets of Marlboro, the gratitude of the survivor lit every follicle from within me. That emotion didn't last long. As I guzzled my beer and smoked cigarette after cigarette, I wasn't able to delude myself into thinking I was anything other than a drunken, befuddled man. No, I thought, you are without a chance, Norman. All my decisions had been made a long time ago.

To make myself feel better, I decided to play my bagpipe. In my usual state of inebriation I played very fast. I played no marches. There's no way you can march like a member of Strathclyde Police Pipe Band in size four high-heeled shoes. No, I regaled the growing crowd with little Hebridean reels and jigs. Tunes like '*Mo Shuirgheach Laghach*, My Amiable Suitor', '*Cailleach nan Cearc*, The Old Woman of the Hens', '*Anna BheagMhurchaidh*, Little Annie Murdoch's Daughter', '*Nighean na Caillich*, The Old Woman's Daughter' and '*An Deoch Làidir*, The Strong Drink' burbled from my pipe chanter. I was flying.

A crowd formed a circle around me and the people began to dance. Some moved gracefully; others ridiculously. Couples jogged and swayed. They jerked together and apart. Occasionally some couples would swirl apart, and through my drink-crazed eyes I would catch a glimpse of the thighs and calves of some attractive woman, and I would feel shame.

At the conclusion of my impromptu little recital my entire body was bathed in sweat. As I stooped to place my bagpipe on the floor, I felt a heavy hand on my shoulder. Two thugs in silly uniforms, like bellboys, stood behind me. They carried holstered guns on their belts. *La Policía*! They led me away to a kind of four-sided glass cell measuring about twelve feet by ten.

"*¿Pasaporte, por favor?*" the younger policeman snapped.

I handed over my passport.

The older policeman looked like Jack Palance, only swarthier. He cast dark eyes on my passport, raised them to look at me, looked back at the document, and once again at me. What he saw seemed to make him very sad.

"What was the purpose of your visit?" he asked in a low, pained voice.

"*Vacaciones*," I said in my best pseudo-Mexican accent. I told him I was going back to Canada.

Then things started to go wrong. Two grim-looking faces confronted me. The elder of the two policemen said: "*¿Visa?*"

What the devil was this mouth-breather talking about? I didn't have a visa. Then, suddenly, I experienced a flashback. On my arrival in the country, I vaguely recollected, I had signed a flimsy piece of paper, the kind of thing you might be given as a receipt at your local off-licence for a bag of booze. In my mind's eye the vision crystallized. Yeah, I *used* to have a visa. It had turned into papier mache in the humidity and I had long ago slung it.

"*He perdido mi visa*, I've lost my visa," I lisped pathetically.

The senior man had a smile on his face like that of Lawrence of Arabia after the capture of Khartoum. Without saying a word, both turned about and exited the glass cell, locking the sliding door that led to the concourse. I gazed forlornly through this door and could see clearly my precious bagpipe and carrying case at the booth where I had so recently been such a knockout entertainer.

A couple of times in the past I'd reached this absolute zero of the truth, but I knew that this time I'd never be able to guess what move I could make to become another person. I could feel a vibration running up my body through my legs.

Just then the glass door slid open and two snowbirds, male and female, entered the enclosed space, unaccompanied by policemen. I saw the triumphant grins on the faces of the pair who had arrested me, however, as they locked the door again. I was no longer alone. The presence of these North American vacationers was as welcome as the mail steamer arriving in Loch Carnan a hundred years ago.

"What's going to happen to us?" I squealed in panic.

"Nothing much," said Hank, a car salesman from Ohio. "They're just holding out for, you know, the bribe?"

"How much?" I asked.

"Twenty bucks a head, I reckon," said Lou, his wife, nonchalantly.

"But I don't *have* twenty bucks," I exclaimed. (This was an alcohol-induced lie. I had about eighteen dollars stuffed down the front of my shorts, but I just knew I'd need them later.)

"That's okay, dude," Hank said, eyeing me from high-heeled shoes to sweat-stained singlet. "We believe you. Stay cool. We'll pay the twenty dollars for you."

Melting, almost feminine gratitude overwhelmed me.

Suddenly, I saw the two policemen had returned. They stood outside the glass door and talked rapidly. They nodded to each other like consulting surgeons. They entered our place of confinement with outstretched hands. I rushed forward to find out when we would get out. I was gently pushed back against the far wall of the glass case. It was all beginning to feel like a genteel kidnapping. Hank slapped the sixty dollars into the palm of the senior cop. The younger guy opened the sliding door and we were free. In my case, not quite.

I was trotting over to where my bagpipe still lay when the senior policeman bellowed: "*Senor Maclean, necesitas esto,* You'll need this." He was waving my passport. He walked briskly over to where I stood frozen with apprehension and handed me my passport. With an admonitory index finger waggling in my face, he spoke sternly:

"*Norman Hector MacKinnon Maclean, te advierto*, Norman Hector MacKinnon Maclean, I'm warning you." He was enjoying this. "*Tu nunca has entrado a la Republica Mejicano*, You are never to enter the Republic of Mexico again."

I didn't care. Not then I didn't. I do now. I'd love to repay the kindness shown to me by the *mamacita* and Maria. After my unjust incarceration I grabbed my bagpipe and carrying case and ran to the check-in line. Whoops! That was a scene that'd make your nipples hard. Ye Gods! I don't know how I boarded that plane to Detroit, but I did, and, after purchasing two or three overpriced miniatures of whisky, I enjoyed what I considered the most wonderful flight of my life. I reclined in the back of the plane, occasionally ordering an over-priced miniature of whisky with the last of my money. I offered a cigarette to one of my fellow addicts in the rear of the plane, whose obvious distress at flying at all I began, rather pompously, to pooh-pooh.

Eventually I drifted off to sleep.

My troubles weren't over yet, though.

29
Motown

I'll never forget Detroit. At first, I felt like some hero who had survived a brutal time without complaining once . . . aloud. I was wrong.
A couple of hours later I was sure I was dying. When I wobbled off
the plane at Motown City airport in my singlet, shorts and high-
heeled shoes, a flashing clock and thermometer informed me that
it was 21.35 and the outside temperature was -12C. They're pretty
fascist in their anti-smoking approach in America, and if I wanted a
cigarette – and, oh, I did, I did – I had to stand outside the terminal
building. This was as cold as I had ever been, and on the two or three
times a nicotine fit overcame me, I could endure the cold only for
about a minute or so. Even inside the terminal building, where I sat
with my bagpipe case between my trembling knees on a plastic bucket
seat, all it required to make any butcher feel right at home was a side
of beef hanging on a hook. Captain Scott or Amundsen might have
endured these temperatures, but I doubt it. Not in the gear I was
wearing.

I sat shivering there and looked enviously at returning vacationers
being welcomed back to God's own country by friends and relatives, and being whisked off in snug, warm cars to homes in Michigan
and Southern Ontario. I didn't have enough money to take the little
shuttle bus that goes back and forth through the tunnel connecting
Detroit and Windsor, Ontario. I had finally, irreversibly lost the plot.

As it got later, the faces in the terminal building were gradually
all black. The descendants of thousands of African-American families
who poured into the motor plants of Detroit just after the First World
War were not living, financially and socially, on a parallel plane with
white people. This had led to an inordinate number of people getting
shot in Detroit. A booming underground economy, based primarily
on cocaine money, fuelled the demand among young black males for

guns. Guns for these young men became status items. They signified power, safety, glamour, excitement and manhood.

As I sat there drowning in melancholy funk, I saw something alarming. A lithe black man in his late thirties in a yellow velvet suit, standing two yards away, seemed to be taking an unhealthy interest in me. I didn't want any hassle, but that's what he'd get if he tried to hassle me, I thought. I glanced down at my feet and legs, and had to admit that indeed I must have looked like I was of the transvestite persuasion. The man's brown silk shirt was open at the neck, its collar overlapping the lapels of his jacket. His coke spoon was platinum. He was wearing tan alligator shoes and an apple green felt hat. His gold watchband and chunky gold bracelets screamed one word: drugs.

He approached me.

"Good evening, bro'," he said.

"I'm too tired to talk to you, man," I intoned wearily.

"Ah just thought I could prolly help you," he said, sitting down on the plastic seat next to me. "What's your story, slick, and why are you dressed like that?"

"I lost my clothes in Mexico," I said, "and I'm running on empty."

"If you like," he said, "I can take you to a party downtown. You like to party, blood?"

Think, Norman, think! The suggestion appalled me. I'd sooner enter the Killing Fields accompanied by Pol Pot than go with you, I thought.

What I finally said was: "Maybe I'll take a chance."

"Yeah. Yeah, take a chance," he drawled. "We'll do a couple of lines, have a few drinks and I'll introduce you to some real foxy chicks, right?"

"Well, my brain seems to have completely shut down," I said. This was true. The only words I heard clearly were 'a few drinks'.

"Let's do it, nigger," he said, rising quickly and motioning for me to follow him. I grabbed my bagpipe case and the little plastic pouch containing my cigarettes and walked behind him to a car-park some considerable distance away from the terminal building. By the time we reached his white Dorado with sculptured rear window, white sidewalls, blue interior lighting and leopard upholstery, the intense cold had turned my arms and legs a rather attractive shade of purple. I allowed the pimp – for I was sure that was his trade – to bundle me into his car. At least it was warm, I thought, as I squeezed myself into the luxurious leather seats, but once we set off, the radio playing progressive jazz, it was hard not to feel that greater challenges lay ahead.

I used to think of Detroit as a scabrous, peeling cluster of tenements. Not at all. The downtown area presented a magnificent skyline of handsome buildings with thousands of winking lights. As we swung down on the Edsel Ford Expressway, heading for downtown, I basked in the waves of heat that blasted from the dashboard.

"Getting comfortable now, dude?" my chauffeur asked.

"You bet," I said. "Mind if I smoke?"

"Go ahead, bro'," he said with a casual wave of his bejewelled hand.

In truth, for the first time in weeks I felt the fever had broken. My host turned tuned the radio to his favourite station, and some smarmy disk-jockey introduced a rapper who barked out a riff of rhyming couplets that were almost completely unintelligible to me. I knew, however, that this was a recitative of violence. This was boom-boom music for slick urban hustlers and bored teenage males who resented the fact that God had given them faces full of pimples. My attention was caught by a plastic bottle containing liquid lodged in a cup holder on the dash. It had a label that proclaimed 'LeRoy's Pimp Oil'. This was presumably '*to perfume yo' pimpmobile, y'unnerstand, nigger?*'

"Where's the party?" I asked.

"Place called 'Treasure Chests'," he replied.

"Where's that?" I asked.

"The Cass Corridor," he said mockingly.

"The Cass Corridor?" I said with a quiver in my voice.

"Yeah, the Cass," he confirmed proudly. "You heard about it?"'

Of course I had heard of it. Back in Canada I had been warned by my cousin Donnie MacKinnon dozens of times about the dangers of Detroit in general and the Cass Corridor in particular. "If you go to the Big Ugly, Norman, be sure to arrive in daylight, and forget about any nightlife," he used to say. "The Cass Corridor, Norman," he'd frequently intone, "is a very bad neighbourhood in America's most deprived city."

"Sure," I said easily to Isaac – we had exchanged names back at the airport – "that's where the people are all . . . uh, black, and where snipers on overpasses shoot at cars passing on the Freeway below them."

"We don't roll that way no more, brother. We use this," Isaac said, tapping the side of his head with a long forefinger.

"Will there be any drink at this place?" I asked.

"Say what?" Isaac said, his voice rising in pitch.

"Can I get a drink of whisky at this *thing*?" I said in exasperation.

He patted my left thigh with his right hand. "Sure, baby," he said airily. "You know what, bro'? Isaac here be thinking that whitey's got a little booze habit. Am I right?"

"Yeah," I said with a heavy sigh, watching the cigarette twitch between my trembling fingers.

"Don't worry, homey," he said, "we'll soon fix you up." He glanced down at the thigh he had so recently touched. "Hey – that outfit is maybe just the thing to get you out of the Cass alive – 'specially the shoes," he said, giggling. "You is one *weird* mutha'. Wish I'd a camera."

"What do you mean?" I said, though I knew what he meant, alright.

"For whitey," he rasped, "the Cass means 'one way in, one way out'. Yo' is a long way from Brigadoon now, Jack."

As we got closer to the city centre, the area got seedier, and the snow-covered streets had been left to the blacks. On the right hand side of what I thought was Woodward, there were scores of whores wandering in and out of severely lowlife bars with names like 'The Frisky Pussy', 'Purple Lips' or 'The Tender Trap'. At the end of a strip of topless bars, I asked him if we had far to go.

"Nearly there, Norm," he said soothingly.

'Pleasure Chests' turns out not to be the kind of dive I've been expecting. Instead it is a swish bar and restaurant packed with black people whose prevailing mode is flamboyance. Extravagance. In corners away from the flashing lights above the dance floor, couples are canoodling.

Within an hour, on either side of me, grinning drunk, two intoxicating, statuesque black women in satin evening gowns are squeezed into a velour banquette against one of the walls. Hair, legs, thighs, breasts come together in the crush. These girls look good. If they are hookers, they are not cheap. I am not seriously listening to Ofelia – she is the really tall one: six four, at least – and her younger companion Stella, who has a smile full of tease and a shapely, firm body, as they chatter across me. My eyes are closing.

"Norm, honey? Man up, dude. Come on, man up," Ofelia said. "Norm, you still with us? This is Ofelia and Stella here. Hey, Norm!"

I blinked rapidly, trying to focus on my companions. They told me my accent was cute. I told them I thought their accents were cute too. We toasted each other's accents. I had become quietly unsober.

At that moment, Isaac, the pimp or dealer who had brought me here, returned to the table in front of us. He smiled with evident pleasure on the trio before him, as he placed a bottle of white rum and some packets of Camel cigarettes on the table. "Enjoy, children," he said, and strutted, with an air of territoriality that I regarded with awe, over to the bar.

I was fully awake now, and young Stella poured drinks for the three of us. "It's time to get yo' swerve on, honey," she said, as she raised her glass. My chest, a lot warmer now, was decorated with the bejeweled hand of Ofelia, who had slung a long arm round my shoulder. "Sugar," she purred, caressing my nipple, "why don't you give us a blast of that Scotch horn thing you was talking about before?"

"Yeah, Norm," Stella squealed. "Show us yo' Scotch horn, babe." The girls shrieked with laughter and I joined in because . . . well, I was always a gentleman. You could ask any of my wives.

I gulped the remainder of my drink and eased myself off my seat real slow, wrenched the pipe from the case and, with Maria's broken-backed stilettos on my feet, lurched towards the low podium where the disk-jockey was plying his trade. After an apologetic nod in his direction, I struck up the pipe and sailed into a ten-minute recital. God, I was hurtling straight up to the moon then. Reels, jigs, hornpipes, Gaelic airs, Cajun quicksteps, even 'You're the One that I Want', all flowed from controlled but relaxed digits. I was a guy who knew how to put on a show. Not a show you'd necessarily want to see, but a show all the same. Here was a guy who understood that no performance was complete without him taking his bottom hand off the chanter and pressing the flesh of some woman.

I was a guy who liked to dance while playing the bagpipe, not that after all these years I had learned to dance. For the fast stuff I had two basic moves. The first one consisted of a series of heel-toe shuffles: for the second one I just jumped up and down on the spot to the pulse. It looked like a kind of Celtic hopscotch. For the slow stuff, even in high heels, I went all Scots Guardsman. When I played '*Mo Nionag Dhonn Og*, My Young, Brown-haired Girl', or '*Gruagach Og an Fhuilt Bhàin*, Fair Maid of the Golden Tresses' or '*Bealach a' Mhorbhairn*, The Pass of Morven', just before the pulse, I thrust a stiff leg before me, keeping my foot absolutely parallel to and about six inches above the floor. On the beat, I gently placed the outstretched leg on the floor and allowed it to *slide* forward for about eight inches or so before jerking the other leg forward, pausing for a split second at the ankle of the now stationary first leg, and repeating the manoeuvre. Michael Flatley met Adolf Hitler. Man, did some *cac* go down that night!

I fought my way through a crowd who were giving me a standing ovation. I made it to where the girls were. Stella kissed me on the mouth and did some exciting things with her tongue. "Norm, cupcake," she said, "I'd like to put you in my pocket and munch on you all day." Ofelia merely embraced me and *lifted* me off my feet. She whispered wetly in my ear as I dangled helplessly with my feet almost a foot off the floor: "You got the magic hands, baby," she said. "Yo' strut yo' stuff wit' that plaid skirt thing on yo' skinny white ass, you gonna do a lot of damage to the chicks down on the Cass and I'm gonna be busy, busy, busy, you know, slappin' a few of these ladies alongside the head?"

"Let me down, please, Ofelia," I whimpered. She slowly allowed me to regain my footing. I took a large swallow of rum. I lit a cigarette and puffed deeply. "Look, girls," I gasped between coughs, "I've got . . . I've got to get over to Windsor. My cousin's expecting me."

Ofelia towered above me, smiling broadly, and I was drowning in her big, brown eyes that were flecked with amber, and imagined that her generous mouth was about to devour me.

"No problemo, sugar,' she said, ungrammatically. "Mah pleasure to get you to the Canadian border, at least."

"Don't go anywhere wit' that bitch, Norm," screamed Stella, feigning alarm. "She snatch the nuts off you-all and use them like dice." This warning was accompanied by a rapid shaking movement of her loosely clenched fist.

But I did. All Ofelia did was put her arm round my waist and, giving me plenty of her soft breast against my cheek, gently escorted me to the door. Isaac was standing, glass in hand, at the bar. He raised his drink to his mouth, and with his free hand waved me goodbye. And thus I bade farewell to Detroit, the city where they kill the weak and *eat* them.

The ride was a rocket. I was born to be treated like this, I thought, as I lolled in the passenger seat of a two-tone Lincoln. A gorgeous woman was driving; deep soul and down-home blues were playing on the CD machine. All too soon we came to the end of the Detroit-Windsor tunnel, and I could see the glass-walled Immigration booth thirty yards ahead. I scrambled out of the car, and Ofelia leaned over to kiss me lightly on the cheek. "Yo' is mah *ma–an*, Norm," she drawled, as she engaged gear and executed a neat three-pointer. She reversed until she was level with me about twenty yards into No Man's Land and shouted through the open window, with a wave of her hand: "Yo' is mah ace number one *brother*." The moment she took off I felt tears pricking my eyes. I turned towards a glass structure thirty yards or so ahead and waved her goodbye without looking.

I trudged towards the Immigration booth. My head was hurting. I wanted to be tucked up in a warm bed. I wanted be with Ofelia. No, I really wanted my mammy. When I got to the booth I just dropped the pipe case at my feet and slunk up to the bullet-proof, perforated window like an evil thing exposed in sunlight. At the booth, an old white guy with a belly out to here stared at me.

"Help you, sir?" he said.

Wordlessly, I slipped my passport into the metal at the base of the window. He flipped through it and pushed it back towards me. I lifted it and turned away.

Before I reached my pipe case, I heard the fat old geezer with the hair growing out of his ears yelling: "Hey, you!" I ignored this because it couldn't be happening.

"You! Hey!" he was shouting. "You get back over here!"

Now what the *fuck*? I turned and glared. *Cia fhad' a bhios do chorraich ort, a Dhè?* How long, Lord, will your wrath be upon me?

"What have you got in that case?" he enquired belligerently.

I drew closer to the window, and sniffling with weariness, said: "Just bagpipes, sir." I saw the officer's eyes widen and he offered a crooked smile.

"You play bagpipes?" he said, showing some interest in this alien drooping in front of him.

"Yes," I said quietly.

The Immigration guy's face went aneurysm red.

"That's great," he exclaimed excitedly. "You Scotch?"

"Yes," I admitted.

"Our family's Scotch-Irish," he blurted out.

"Where did your people come from?" I enquired, not really wanting to know; but I did want to prolong this exchange. Perhaps I could hit him for the taxi fare.

"Right on the border," he exclaimed proudly. Great. The guy obviously went to school on a short bus. I'd go for it.

"I'd dearly love to hear the pipes again," he said wistfully.

"Listen, sir," I said, pissed at myself at the pleading whine that issued from my throat.

"What?" he said, with more than a hint of suspicion in the query.

"Could you possibly lend me my taxi fare so that I can get to my cousin's house on Ribberdy Road?" I pleaded in a 'greeting' voice.

"You can't telephone him?" said the Immigration guy. Little note of contempt here for a man who didn't even have loose change to make a call.

"Tell you what," he said as though hit by a burst of sudden inspiration. "You play for me 'The Pap of Glencoe', 'Delvinside' and 'The Little Cascade', and I'll give you . . . oh, twenty dollars. What do you say?"

I didn't say: I played. Never in my life have I played as well as I did then on the concrete floor of the tunnel at three o'clock in the morning. At the conclusion of the requested tunes, the officer extracted a limp twenty dollar note from his wallet. He smiled beatifically and slipped it into the trough. "Thank you, Scotty," he said, and he sounded sincere.

This penchant of mine for playing the Great Highland Bagpipe in inappropriate places and at odd times was a kind of infectious neurosis – the poison ivy was recurrent – that had never paid off to the extent it had done in that cold cave. I snatched the bill and wheeled away into the snow-covered street of downtown Windsor. I saw a plume of smoke coming from the exhaust of a parked car about fifty yards ahead of me. I hauled my pipe case and plastic bag into the back seat of what turned out to be a taxi and told the driver my destination: 1439 Ribberdy Road. I paid the guy. There was some change to be pocketed. Slowly, slowly I walked towards my cousin's house. I placed my hands on the panels of the front door, bowed my head and offered a prayer of gratitude for the tuition I had received from Pipe Major John Macdonald.

The wind, whooshing along noisily and steadily, but from ever-shifting directions, brings me back to my vigil in front of my computer in Bellahouston for an instant. But it is only for a brief interval. My not-to-be-denied home movie restarts almost immediately.

30
Cameras

I had a fairly long trajectory as a front-of-camera person – from the days of *'Se Ur Beatha* in the mid-Sixties, through *Tormod air Telly* in the late Seventies, right up to a cameo role as a shopkeeper in an episode of *P.C. Stewart*, a television comedy drama directed by Robbie Fraser a couple of years ago.

I have written in some detail about the disappointment felt by me at the failure of *It's Himself, Norman*, broadcast by BBC Scotland in 1980, to engage an audience. I am convinced that if only I had been more vocal in my dealings with the production staff in this venture, the outcome might have been much different. The filming of Iain MacFadyen's attempt to find a successor to Billy Connolly had a disappointing result. The pilot programme he produced bombed. Technically, it was well directed and the sketches were polished and swift. Sad to relate, there were few laugh-provoking moments. Though I myself acted like a deranged Kenneth Williams in the sketches and strove to present myself as a kind of Steve Martin wild and crazy guy in the monologues, I had holes in my stomach at the end of every taping as the invited audience stampeded for the exits. It was like the fall of Saigon.

The problem was the writer, Eddie Boyd. Though famed as an accomplished creator of gritty, back-street thrillers set in the underbelly of Glasgow, a comedy writer he was not. The thing was that, unlike my involvement with Neil Fraser some years previously, this time round I had no clout at all. At script meetings I'd boldly express my opinion of some piece of writing. "This is awesomely unfunny, gentlemen," I might announce. "*Unfunny?*" the production team would exclaim in unison, as if I had asked them where was the nearest place I could acquire a sexually transmitted disease. It was all too clear that the English-speaking production team did not take too kindly to freely expressed opinions from an upstart Teuchter entertainer.

I can't blame poor Eddie for the sketch that almost cost me my life. I wrote it, and on paper it promised hilarity. The premise was that Bonnie Prince Charlie, all ponced up in velvet knickerbocker suit, lace cuffs, silk stockings and slippers, was about to be rowed over to Skye by Flora Macdonald. To the strains of 'Speed, bonnie boat, like a bird on the wing . . .' I swanned down a wooden jetty on the shore of Hogganfield Loch, north of Glasgow, to the waiting dinghy and Flora. The prince was to extend a foppish, languid hand to his faithful follower. She would roughly seize his wrist and over-enthusiastically give it a strong pull, with the result that he would topple in slow motion into the water. As a visual gag, it conformed to my comedy reality theory that embarrassment, a sense of injustice and actual pain give a comic result. What I had forgotten about was the concept of stunt doubles, and how perishingly cold fresh water can be in February. As the icy water closed over my bewigged head, the shock caused my heart to boom alarmingly.

I was hauled out promptly by some heavies and swiftly transported to the Crowwood House Hotel, where I was dumped in a hot bath while girls from the Wardrobe Department attempted to dry out my near-ruined costume on radiators. "What . . . why . . . what on earth are you doing, girls?" I croaked. "I'm so sorry, Norman," somebody replied, "but the cameraman didn't get the shot. You're going to have to do that scene again." They might as well have said, "You've got amytrophic lateral sclerosis, Norman. You are on a certain downward path to total paralysis, and, eventually, death." Diving into Hogganfield Loch for a second time in damp clothing was the hardest thing I have ever done. I thought I was a goner. Needless to say, the scene ended up on the cutting room floor.

A concluding vignette from an outside broadcast in the Kelvin Hall proved to be quite amusing. MacFadyen had been greatly taken by my playing of popular songs on the Highland Pipe. He arranged for me to play 'You're the One that I Want', accompanied by Brian Fahey and the BBC Radio Orchestra, at a massive variety show. A sprinkling of stardust was provided by a scantily dressed group of lithe professional dancers called 'Pan's People'. They had an enormous following among male viewers because of their frequent appearances on 'Top of the Pops'.

Now, I've mentioned before that I always found the maintenance of the bagpipe a tedious chore. Shortly before my long-anticipated Travolta impression with the lovelies, I discovered that the top joint of my outside tenor drone was secured to the tuning pin by about three millimetres of hemp. What I ought to have done was re-hemp the pin, lower the bridle on the cane reed to sharpen the pitch of the drone and Patrick MacCrimmon's your uncle. I took the easy way out, and contented myself with slavering over the pin and gingerly fixing the joint to the three millimetres of hemp that was all that remained to secure the two pieces of the drone together.

'And a one, two, three, four . . .' I silently counted my intro, and proudly marched onto the stage to join the beautiful girls who were already gyrating to the James Last-type sound of the orchestra. The four-four time signature was admirably suited to a flashy entrance. I'm belting out *'da-da-daa, da-da-da da-da, and I'm losing con-tro-ol'* when I really did lose control. The top joint of the outside drone detached itself from the tuning pin and, suspended by a silk cord, landed with a soft plop on the right breast of a gorgeous young dancer who was shuffling energetically on a spot immediately to my left! She glared at me indignantly, and, ever the gent, I edged a few inches to my right. She, it seemed, could not depart from the prescribed routine of her choreographer and had to remain where she was. My jerky movement to terminate this grope, at one remove as it were, only made matters worse. The top joint started to swing like a pendulum, and all through the interminable routine, every phrase of the song was punctuated by the percussion provided by the soft plop of wood on female flesh. *'you're the one that I want* PLOP *oo-oo-oo, baby* PLOP *the one that I want* PLOP . . . '

An alert cameraman spotted this embarrassing activity and zoomed in. Members of the orchestra and the house band were watching the images on suspended monitors and corpsing all over the place. I've often mused that this sordid experience must have turned the young dancer off bagpipes for life. I imagine her nowadays, a handsome middle-aged lady who still retains her figure, living in a cottage in rural Hertfordshire. Suddenly, while viewing television, she glimpses a shot of pipers of the Dragoon Guards advertising their latest CD. In an instant she becomes the victim of a vicious panic attack as she remembers being molested by a set of bagpipes in Glasgow back in 1981. If breathing into brown paper bags doesn't work, she'll have to seek counselling.

Snap, darling! I suffer the same symptoms at present in my decrepit physical state when I hear *any* one of the Macdonald brothers from Glenuig – Dr Angus, Iain and my favourite, Allan – playing the pipes. In Moidart they're known as *clann a' 'Whaler'*, offspring of the 'Whaler': in South Uist where their mother came from they have a different *sloinneadh* or patronymic. They are *na gillean aig Mairead Ailig*, the sons of Maggie daughter of Alex. Pipe-Major Johnny MacKenzie, an excellent player and composer, may have put their hands on the chanter when they attended the Queen Victoria School at Dunblane, but the music was in their genes, probably on the paternal *and* maternal sides of the family. I listened to Dr Angus and Allan at a recital held in the College of Piping at the beginning of last November, and afterwards I felt as I do when I view clips of Stuart Cassells and The Red Hot Chili Pipers or Fred Morrison playing on the television screen. These guys belong to a different species. They're not the same as 'manufactured' pipers like myself. Like my Hertforshire lady, I too, perhaps, would benefit from psychiatric treatment.

Feature films wouldn't be needing me, I used to think. One might say that my future feature film career was stillborn. One would be wrong. Nine years on from the ignominy of *Comfort and Joy*, Timothy Neat, teacher, art historian, film-maker and writer, was directing a film, from a script by John Berger, on location on Hamburg, and wanted me to take part in it. I had the time of my life on that shoot. Firstly, I couldn't make sense of the script. It seemed to be a kind of metaphor for the fall of the Soviet Union and the human displacement and suffering caused by this event, but maybe it was about something else completely. Who knows? *I* didn't know. The PA, a Mongolian called, believe it or not, Ghengis, didn't know. The Russian camera crew hadn't a clue. The lowly German scene-shifters just did as the haughty Russian cinematographer ordered. I don't think Tim, whose films include *Hallaig*, which won the Pascoe MacFarlane Award, and *Play me Something*, which received the Europa Prize at the Barcelona Film Festival, had a coherent overview of the story. In one scene, shot in a railway carriage in one of Hamburg's railway stations, the set-up was an absurdity: twelve strangers are crammed into a carriage with lights, mikes and single portable cameras to the accompaniment of babble in at least seven different languages. The Russians, who were huddled round a stationary camera, spoke no German, and the barked commands of the old man to the Germans were never carried out to his satisfaction. "*Nyet! Nyet! Nyet!*" he'd grumble, and the hapless German crew scuttled to readjust equipment.

The motley cast was from all over Europe – Poland, Italy, France and Germany – and the language barriers proved frustrating and caused many delays. It bothered me that I might not be able to improvise with these established film actors. And yet I was grateful that I was being paid handsomely to sample different cultures.

I went a few hard rounds with that particular conundrum. A nibble at one scene which took a couple of days to film involved yours truly improvising in Gaelic, a Pole who understood Russian and German but spoke no English, an Italian leading lady who spoke French but no German or English, and poor Tim on his hands and knees in the middle of the compartment imploring me with hand gestures against the noise of everybody talking. "Whatever are they trying to say, Norman?" he'd ask plaintively, obviously attributing to me linguistic abilities I didn't possess. I'd make something up, like, "I think the Russian's of the opinion that he should go with an 80 mil. lens, followed by a quick zoom or perhaps a slow pan to my ecstatic face as I rest my head on Helena's bosom." Tim would throw his hands up in a gesture of resignation, and nod without quite understanding. Sustained by regular sips of Kornlikor I kept in a cigar holder, I would have liked the filming to have gone on for ever. All too soon, however, Hans, my minder and chauffeur, would arrive at the set in his big Mercedes and whisk me off to my lodgings, the brothel.

Yes, that's right, my accommodation was provided in a brothel! On the evening of my arrival in Germany – I had been delayed in the Grosvenor Hotel in London at the Sony Radio Award ceremonies, where I was up for a prize in the Short Feature category under the aegis of Moray Firth Radio – the chauffeur, Hans, apologised profusely in slightly accented English for the fact that I would not be housed along with the rest of the crew, but would have to sleep in a house of ill-repute in the St Georgi district of the city. "Iss very bad place, St Georgi," he announced sadly. "Many, many drug addicts and . . . how you say? . . . prostitutes. I'm sorry, Herr Doctor Maclean." I pretended to be sorry too, clucking my tongue in feigned irritation.

The arrangement was ideal. Delivered to the hotel around four in the afternoon, I'd greet the working girls with smiles and many pouting, kissy 'mwaahs', and retire to my mirrored bedroom for forty winks. Ursula, a big-boned welterweight from Dresden, who would have made a good signing for Rangers as a defender, would come in at eight with a plate of sausages and potatoes. No, nothing untoward ever happened between me and the professionals. They sensed that I was an eccentric, and took pleasure in spoiling me by seeing to my laundry and making sure I had plenty of salami, cold cuts, cheese and pumpernickel bread when I returned from cruising the mean streets and inns with Hans in the early hours. The majority of these athletic, blonde girls were from the East. After the unification of Germany, these easterners found it hard to get work commensurate with their qualifications in the West. The street photographer who invited you to have your photograph taken with a strapping female glamour model might well have been a paediatric surgeon back home. It made you think, there but for the grace of good luck go I.

I don't know if the film ever saw the light of day. Probably it didn't, is what I think. What did see the light of day, or at least a shimmer of Celtic twilight at the Celtic Film Festival in Tralee in the late Nineties, was my own film, *Keino*. I wrote this with financial assistance from the CCG, the Gaelic Broadcasting Council, and – dry my perspiration! – acted in it as the psychotic tinker, Ailidh. The log-line reads: '*A lovers' tryst in a derelict Highland schoolhouse turns into a savage nightmare when a terrorised young folklorist, his adulterous married mistress and her psychotic tinker husband engage in a vicious board game . . . for truly bizarre stakes.*' The BBC transmitted this flawed effort one night towards the turn of the century. It probably went out late and I didn't see it. As everybody knows, you come home after a lock-in in your local pub, and there's a nervous youth on screen reading what purports to be Gaelic from the autocue with all the flickering eye movement of, say, Clive James, then it's time to make for your pram. That means it's *really* late.

The only time I appeared in front of cameras with a good bucket in me was entirely my fault. Perhaps I was influenced by the professional manner in which old friend and manager David Burns discharged his duties back in 1997. Resplendent in full Highland dress, he made introductions, arranged gigs, collected monies for admissions, CDs and one VHS video. Most importantly, at the end of each ceilidh he presented the cast with buff-coloured envelopes stuffed with greasy banknotes. He came up with the idea of hosing down an entire show, getting the footage edited professionally and releasing another video cassette. Profits from the sale of this proposed project would be split, after a one-off payment to the participants, between us on a fifty-fifty basis. I approved. I too wanted to go beyond my current experience of stand-up, to examine it, as it were, a proper discipline. I wanted to assess the audience reaction to each one-liner and gag and allocate to each of them a mark out of ten. Anything below seven was ruthlessly extirpated. This process took some time and effort – a new running order for every new gig. Those bursts of frenetic activity on the laptop made me feel virtuous for not having anything to drink. I refrained from joining the others at the post-ceilidh ceilidhs, locking myself in my hotel bedroom and assigning comedic weight to the evening's programme. Obviously I had abandoned spontaneity and improvisation in favour of effectiveness. The results were gratifying. Work and cash poured in.

It wasn't to last. The combination of monastic application, and guilt and worry about my mother's deteriorating mental and physical condition, added to my stress. I'd leave her alone in the flat we shared in Bellahouston – the cancer had got Wee Colin in 1995 – with stabbing pains of guilt in my stomach to perform in the far north somewhere and, although she had carers coming to look after her three times a day, I never knew what would confront me when I'd return. On at least half a dozen occasions I'd discover that in an attempt to tidy up the flat she had stuffed newspapers and magazines into the oven compartment of the cooker, switched it on for some reason, and had forgotten all about it. I would come home to be confronted by a smashed outside door and a quartet of firemen wearing respirators and wielding axes in the smoke-filled kitchen. Sleep for me was hard to come by. Almost every night I'd hear the drag of my mother's zimmer as she slowly made her tortuous way to the toilet. I'd be instantly awake, waiting with racing heart for the dull thud of her body hitting the deck. This would result, I imagined, in another broken femur or tibia and a fast trip to the A & E. Of course, most of the time she didn't fall, would shuffle back to the single bed in the living room and in a short while emit soft snores. I, on the other hand, would be wide awake, and would spend the rest of the night drinking espresso coffee and smoking cigarette after cigarette.

Two days before a scheduled gig in Caithness, I cracked and went to the pub for a drink. Feeling bad about drinking, I drank more. For two days before David Burns called to take me to Wick I certainly wasn't doing anything to extend my life expectancy.

This trip gave me the answer to a frequent query from friends and enemies alike. 'Norman,' they'd say, 'did you ever go onstage under the influence?' I would avoid the temptation to lie and deny any such thing. 'Yes,' I'd reply. 'But only one time.' The truth has much to recommend it: you don't have to think too hard, and it slips out easily.

The venue was Wick Town Hall, and the disaster took place about ten years ago. The setting was a low-ceilinged pub next door. I hadn't bothered to attend the sound-check in the late afternoon, and I was revving up for the performance by downing a bottle or two of Chilean Merlot.

David and the rest of the members of the back line came into the pub, saw that I was fraying at the edges, and everybody frowned in irritation.

"Are you fit to go on?" he asked.

I parsed my predicament for some time. To hell with this slavish reliance on scripts, I thought. I'd go in bareback and wing it. My order of a double Glenmorangie malt whisky harmonised with the array of wine and beer glasses on the table before me.

"You bet I'm fit," I announced boldly.

After the introductory announcement by David that the crowd were to be entertained by 'The King of Highland Comedy, Norman Maclean', I piped myself to the microphone and, throwing all my cards in the air and hopeful of catching some of them in mid-flight randomly, I launched myself into my shtick. It went quite well at first. My rejection of the crutch provided by a written and memorised script, however, had its downside. Despite myself, whenever I strayed from the script that, for me, had been engraved on the tablets of Moses, I began to berate myself mentally and quickly grew increasingly cross and confused.

I was in the middle of a rambling conceit where I postulated that the notorious outlaw Jesse James had been slain by a cunning Harrisman called Black Angus Morrison. On this night the killing took place beside Wick harbour. Suddenly it occurred to me that I had no idea of the punchline. How this mumbling monologue might end had been erased from my memory. I rambled on with increasingly convoluted asides – 'Yes, ladies and gentlemen, Black Angus was so ugly that his entire body was covered in bruises where women had been poking him with ten-foot poles' – but I hadn't a clue as to which point in this goofy tale I had reached. My speech degenerated into Japanese. '*Kam sa ham ni da* . . . er, *noi wiki wiki*,' I bleated. My narration ground to a halt. To my alarm my eyesight was going too. Very quickly I was enveloped in darkness – blind as well as dumb. I did manage to get off in a quivery voice the deathless line, 'Is there a doctor in the house?'

There was. Someone vaulted onto the stage, exerting considerable effort to go by the gasps and grunts coming from in front of me. A warm hand seized my elbow, and I was escorted to the rear of the stage and down some steps to the corridor which led to the dressing room. There the doctor sponged my eyes and dried them.

"Conjunctivitis," he pronounced confidently.

"What's that?" I whimpered pathetically.

"Attacks the muscles behind the eyes," he said airily.

"Will I ever get my sight back again?" I asked. I had internal visions of getting the wrong change from my good friends, the publicans, and of me clumsily sweeping brimming glasses of precious drink, for which I'd paid dearly, off the counter and onto the floor of the pub.

"Oh, yes," he declared firmly. "A few applications of Golden Eye Ointment – this stuff I'm now going to rub into your occipital sockets – and you'll no longer be blind drunk. You'll still be drunk, but not blind."

True enough, my eyesight and, a little later, my sobriety were restored. That night, my short-lived career as a drunken performer came to an end. Never again would I appear onstage with a drink in me. I have been zealous over this principle. If I ever had drink taken before a gig, I just didn't turn up.

It was around this time that I teamed up with Mick Macneil, ex-Simple Minds, and his brother Donnie. They were the sons of *Uilleam Beag*, Little William, of Nask in Barra, and *nighean Dhòchain*, Dunky's daughter, from South Uist. Mick's departure from the most successful Scottish band to have conquered the USA was marked by him receiving a vast sum of money, which allowed him to live in luxury. Among his many acquisitions were a town house in Glasgow's West End, a mansion in Dumbreck, a crofthouse on the island of Vatersay and a luxurious recording studio in Berkeley Street. I took many a midnight taxi ride to this place, where on a diet of curries, pizzas and unlabelled cigarettes, I sang and played a lot of instruments. Eventually, we came up with a beautifully produced compact disc which, because it had no comedic elements on it, I refused to release.

The strange thing is that I chanced upon this instrumental and vocal collection about a month ago, and, to my astonishment, there was material there which I consider still stands up. Perhaps when my ship comes in I'll launch it as a kind of legacy album.

¿Quién sabe?, who knows?

31

The Suit and the Road Rat

I knew by the mid-Nineties that what I'd *not* be doing, as I'd done in the past, was donning the Chartered Accountant's boiler suit and spinning my wheels in schools. Under pressure from my mother and wife to 'get a proper job', I had served an eighteen-month sentence in Oban High School as a teacher of Gaelic and hated almost every minute of it. Not altogether true: I formed a little piping club in Room 29, where I, Angus MacColl, who turned out to be the greatest piper of his generation, Iain (Buffy) Donaldson, a brace of young pipers from Bunessan in Mull and a young guy from Iona, skirled away each lunchtime. It was marvellous. In addition, I was to have among my pupils Karen Matheson and Donald Shaw, who even at that time had formed Capercaillie, which is now firmly established as one of the world's top contemporary Celtic acts. I cherish to this day my friendship with Karen of the sublime singing voice, and with the barnstorming accordion player, Donald, who is now Artistic Director of the annual cultural festival, Celtic Connections.

Nor would I be encased with polyfilla and reeking of 'Ram' aftershave, sitting before a computer screen in the offices of television companies like SMG, BBC and the various little independent production units like Bees Nees, Media nan Eilean and Zebo Productions. Gaelic television seemed determined – how does the locution go? – 'to try it without me'. I had attempted to be a 'suit' before, with no great success.

It was at the 1991 Celtic Film Festival in Inverness that I became aware that people other than myself were assiduously attempting to breach the thorns of Gaelic television. Ted Brocklebank, a Big Player in Grampian Television, had invited me up to this lavish junket as a kind of reward for my allowing him to make a documentary film of my life and sordid times.

THE LEPER'S BELL

We were having a power breakfast, the tab for which would keep an Ethiopian village in food for a week. The Big Player, a native of St Andrews in Fife, was used to dining in the best restaurants. His tailor was so good he had cut Ted's suit so that you couldn't even see the outline of the dorsal fin. The guy was tall, fair of hair and beautifully dressed. After a stint in print journalism in Dundee he had been recruited as a newsreader by Grampian Television. He was fluent and articulate, an energiser. He quickly progressed up the corporate ladder to become Head of News and Documentaries. At the age of forty, he had accumulated the traditional icons of success: town houses in St Andrews and Majorca, a *pied-a-terre* in Aberdeen, a flashy state-of-the-art company car and a nubile young P.A., a very efficient girl called Hazel Deans. It was small wonder that when Grampian was taken over by the Scottish Media Group apparatchiks from every political party in Holyrood invited him to become a 'list' MP. That is what he did, and now he represents East Fife for the Conservative Party in the Scottish Government.

At this time, such 'Media Persons' – particularly those who had invested heavily in shares in their respective companies – were generally so well-off they didn't know what particular car they were driving on any given day. Whenever they started to wonder if it was the Porsche or the Range Rover they'd brought to work, all they had to do was to go down to the car-park and look for their vehicle. They tended to say to themselves, "Of course, of course. It was raining this morning, and I brought the blue one."

Ted's voice, well-modulated RP, had grown evangelical. "Norman," he intoned, "join us as a Gaelic consultant – allow us to put your name and academic qualifications on our bid for the north of Scotland franchise, and, above all, introduce us to your muse, Highland comedy, and before you will lie a veritable . . . um . . . Aladdin's . . . er, cave." What a silver-tongued devil that man was!

Hey, I was vaguely aware that a whole lot of people were making a whole lot of money in Gaelic television and that I wasn't one of them. I say 'vaguely', because I had just been discharged from an alcohol rehabilitation clinic, Castle Craig in Peebles, where, for about fourteen weeks, I had been denied access to newspapers, radio and television. Accordingly, I was unaware that the three Scottish television broadcasters had been offering short-term contracts to anyone who had even a smattering of Gaelic. Scottish, it was rumoured, were

300

placing sheep dogs in Harris on stand-by. The Beeb were recruiting young graduates from the degree factories who were fluent in five languages but intelligible in none. Grampian, for God's sake, were after me!

That week, at the Celtic Film Festival in Inverness, I used my eyes and ears to check out those who attended this bash. Investors everywhere were making great leaps of faith. Few were the voices of doom, and many were the believers that the world, the Gaelic world, had entered a new, golden age of prosperity.

The primary decision-makers, to a man (though there were a few male-impersonators in skirts around), were monoglot English-speakers. Like weightlifters, they seemed to have sore wrists, because they were constantly gripping them tightly. Or maybe they were merely apprehensive about being mugged for their Rolexes. In the wake of these heavy-hitters trailed swarms of 'independent producers'. This is a contradiction in terms. Like 'holy war'. There is no such beast as an independent Gaelic producer. All independent Gaelic television producers are dependent on the broadcasters. They didn't look like much, those Gaelic-speaking hopefuls. Heavy on facial hair and soft tweeds. Either they resembled little Teuchter chess champions, or little Jewish crofters. They all had the adenoidal whine and the hollow volubility, in both languages, of the superannuated disk-jockey.

Predictably, I took Grampian's shilling. In addition to the pleasures of power there was to be money, fame, sex, a stake in creating Gaelic popular culture, and the opportunity to have a great deal of fun in the pursuit of these pleasures.

Afterwards, when I washed out of Grampian, I took Scottish Television's shilling as well. Once ensconced in Alistair Moffat's 'Think Tank' as a 'Programme Consultant', my long-term career outlook was seized by a violent fit of sneezing. The job, admittedly well-paid, was pure nerve gas. Because of my assorted addictions, I was like Carreras competing in the traditional singing contests at the National Mod. I just didn't fit in. I still liked salty, fatty foods. I still smoked cigarettes. I didn't jog, nor did I do step-aerobics, nor work out on formidable machines of gleaming metal. I was used to hearing the chimes at midnight, and cared not a jot about the whales. I was about to find out at first hand about merriment in Gaelic television.

Every Wednesday I had to report to what employees of Scottish Television unblushingly referred to as 'The Cutting Edge' in

Cowcaddens. A disaster. I spent a year and a bit floundering around between my lap-top in the Gaelic Department and the smokers' cage next to the canteen, where I over-smoked, avoided Moffat, and socialised with a clutch of unrepentant pleasure-seekers who went clubbing or partying in their leisure time.

Oh, I knocked off some proposals right enough. One was a game-show called *Biodh Agad*, Take That, where friendship counted for nothing and everyone ended up, to some degree, embarrassed and occasionally humiliated. Its virtues were that it would have been funny, didn't require tremendous intellectual skills on the part of participants or audiences, and was studio-based. Another was an instructional series for the Great Highland Bagpipe. Among the many ideas I had for documentary and drama programmes were *Pipe Dreams in Pontevedra* – cameras following Fred Morrison, known in Galicia as 'El Rey de la Gaita', from his home in South Uist to a final concert in Pontevedra or Santiago where he would strut his stuff in front of a crowd of five thousand young, hot and sexy Spaniards. The story of *Dòmhnall mac Mhurchaidh*, Donald Morrison, a period drama set in the Eastern Townships of Quebec in 1880s, would have been a very fast and exciting one. It was culturally specific. It revealed universal truths. In this distillation of one person's life we had the opportunity to reveal that rare thing: a story which, as well as being insightful for the rest of the race, gave expression to what it was like to be a Gael in a world where ancient values have not been surrendered and modern ways have not yet conquered. Here, in the Eastern Townships, ironically almost entirely Francophone today, two worlds collided, and in their coming together vivid contrasts emerged. A pictorial expression of this process of dilution of old ways would surely resonate in the Gaelic community today. This was a true tale of a proud, stubborn man of Lewis descent who fought a courageous battle against injustice – and lost.

I lost too. Not even my treatment of the fantastic, incredible tale of the flamboyant conman, Gregor, Prince of Poyais, found favour with Scottish Enterprises. I had had enough of the entrenched conserva-tism of the Scottish moguls and I left the company. (To be honest, though I have said in the past that I'd sooner rub cow dung on my head than be involved in Gaelic television broadcasting, I was just grandstanding. Of course I'd jump at the opportunity to write for or even appear in telly. And I wouldn't knock back a commission from Gaelic radio, either.)

Wearing a suit and being spoiled by young females promised a life that some residual self had always wanted. Every Wednesday, for about two years, I had been reporting to the Gaelic Department of STV, where, instead of writing scintillating proposals for television programmes, I hung out with the lively young underlings of the boss, Rhoda Macdonald. Rhoda, who got on well with the males in her department – guys like Duncan Macneil from Barra, Donald Cameron from North Uist and me – was hard and demanding with her female staff. The only female she didn't dominate was Anne Lorne Gillies, who was ensconced in an enclosed office writing scripts for a children's programme. For around a year and a half I was living in a swamp of intrigue fuelled by long smoking and coffee sessions with the likes of Lloyd Quinan, the weather man, who because of his daily appearances on the tube became well-known to almost everybody in the south-central belt. He too became an MSP. Sandra MacIver, *Nighean a' Chaiptein*, from Back in Lewis, was Rhoda's personal assistant, and she supplied me with endless cups of coffee. Another beautiful girl called Kathleen MacInnes, a graphic designer in the department, was a good companion at lunchtime breaks in McDonald's. She was very funny, with a gift for mimicry and impeccable South Uist Gaelic. (She has since blossomed as an actress and a Gaelic recording star. Her smoky voice wraps itself round the lyrics of old and modern songs, and her version of *Òganaich an Òr-fhuilt Bhuidhe* invariably leaves me enraptured. Speaking of songs of loss and sorrow, the song *O Thug Iad Bhuam Thu* is made real to me by the way Margaret Stewart imbues it with longing. These two tracks to which I can relate are the most valuable in my newly acquired iPod.)

This pleasant but unproductive spell in Cowcaddens lasted too long. After only about a month into it I wasn't sure that manipulating paper would turn out to be beneficial as a career move. One day I had a moment. There just came flowing over me the certainty that only when I was what Connolly called a road-rat did I feel any good. I quickly gathered up my lap-top, on which I had been writing my second Gaelic novel, *Keino*, and without a glance backwards went AWOL.

Round about the autumn of 1995 I hooked up with an old friend, David Burns of Haddington, East Lothian. David's parents owned the Golf View Hotel in Golspie when I first met them. The son and heir was a big, burly party boy who worked for Esso offshore and was making plenty of money. Together we made plenty of money too. With my son Martin on drums, Angus MacColl on guitar and mostly Ross MacPherson on accordion we were 'Norman Maclean, Highland King of Comedy, and the Clansmen.' David took care of business. With access to free phone calls from the oil rig he was indefatigable in finding work for us.

Up and down, back and forward, we travelled across the country. David made up posters, took the money at the door and did the introductory voice-over at the start of the show. As usual, I fed on the energy of the charged-up audiences. David was responsible for selling VHS videos and cassettes and did very well out of this activity too.

We were looking for ways to fritter away our earnings. Dog racing at the 'flapping', unlicensed track in Armadale, Midlothian, was our passion for a while. Then we discovered Thailand. Provided one appreciated that these nubile Asian females were all consummate actresses with the same drama coaches working from unvarying scripts – *Me be bestest wife in world to you, give you Thai massage, sleep with you, everything* – you could be diverted for a while from your everyday world at home.

As usual, I pushed the boundaries of this fantasy world to their limit. I got married . . . well, I attended some kind of Buddhist ceremony where saffron-clad monks tootled on nose flutes and heaped garlands of flowers on me and my bride, a much younger Thai lady who had the interesting name of *Porn*. She had sleekly muscled legs, I remember. I don't recall much more about her or the festive occasion, because I was very much the worse for drink and marijuana. I was in a fugue state, and remained so for the rest of the vacation. Something about the roar of the jet engines and the smell of their fuel at Bangkok Airport made time stop for me.

As soon as we landed back at Glasgow International Airport, David rushed me to the Priory in Langside, an over-priced private clinic where a regime based on the precepts of Alcoholics Anonymous was strictly enforced. At the preliminary interview with the Director, who kept saying, "It's high time you came aboard, Norman. Come aboard, please," I was so out of it that I imagined he was inviting me to embark on a voyage in a ship. This was to my mind an opportunity to fulfill an adolescent fantasy. I told him I'd be delighted to join him and his crew, and promised to return later when I had fortified myself with more whisky.

I have no recollection of my return to Mansionhouse Road, but awoke there in an extremely sumptuous cabin which far exceeded my expectations for a merchant freighter. I quickly rose, donned a fluffy housecoat and presented myself at what I took to be the Purser's office.

To the smart young girl, dressed in navy trouser suit and white blouse, who stood smiling behind the solid oak counter I said: "I'll have a double rum with pep, my dear."

"Name?" she inquired.

"A.B. Seaman Maclean," I replied smartly. "I'm in cabin number . . . er, I forget. It's at the far end of the alleyway, starboard side."

The young officer smiled. "Mr Maclean," she said, "you're not on a ship. You're in the Priory."

Visions of Catholic monks, or nuns even, drifting around the place and singing plainsong, came to my mind's eye. "The Priory?" I said. "What's that?"

Here, Mr Maclean," she said still smiling, "take this pill and go back to your room."

"What's this?" I demanded.

"It's Librium," she said. "It'll help calm you down. And you can come back for more if you need it. You're written up for more."

"There's a hidden camera here, right?" I hollered. "This is a commercial, isn't it?"

"Go back to your room and rest," she said, always smiling.

I toddled back to my quarters and found that the pill took the edge of my withdrawal symptoms. Indeed, I slept soundly in the comfortable bed, and in the morning felt considerably better than I had done the previous evening.

After a very tasty breakfast of kippers, toast and coffee, a guy of about fifty in a cheap off-the-peg suit entered the room and presented me with a bill for over nine hundred pounds. This was the terrible terminus of a journey splattered by fiscal irresponsibility.

That night, David Burns came to visit. He expressed some astonishment at how well I was looking. "Listen, David," I pleaded, "you've got to do something for me."

"What?" he said flatly.

"You'll have to help me pay this horrible bill they've given me," I said plaintively, as I proffered the offending slip. "I thought . . . you might want to take the cash out of our joint account . . ."

But David said, "Let's have it."

"I'd hoped there might be sufficient funds . . ." I said in a small, faint voice. "Surely there must be some way you could pay this fucking nine hundred pounds."

"You tanned the account in Pattaya, Norman," David said evenly. "Tell you what I'll do. I'll cover your bill on my credit card."

"Thank you, David," I said, and I felt immense gratitude towards him for helping me out of this financial jam.

"It's a loan, Norman," he said. "I want the money back. If you don't pay me, you'll have to watch your back. I mean it."

"You'll get it," I promised.

Of course, I didn't pay my debt, and decided on my discharge to go it alone. I did so at great inconvenience for a couple of years. But my heart wasn't in it anymore.

It is a source of regret that I haven't been able, since the millennium, to generate enough money to give David the money he was due. We haven't spoken since 1999.

Why, after a month undergoing a supervised dry-out, did I relapse again and again? I had been wrestling for a long time with the habit or addiction debate. Briefly, some addicts believe that for genetic, psychological and environmental reasons they are afflicted with a disease. Others who abuse alcohol, or for that matter who indulge in behaviours which have a detrimental effect on themselves and others, are convinced that they have a choice. They do what they do because their drug of choice gives them pleasure. I've been going backwards and forwards between these two places all my adult life, and suspect that I'll be doing so for as long as I retain my health. If on occasion I incline towards the bad habit, self-indulgent, irresponsible model, at the same time I have no wish to denigrate the work of self-help groups like AA. The one-size-fits-all prescriptive treatment followed by these people in their quest for lifelong abstinence can be repetitive and boring, however.

32
Lochaber No More

On a bitterly cold evening in February 2007, I paid my last visit to the little schoolhouse at Srathan. For reasons that bewildered me beyond speculation, I was unable to resist the siren song that drew me once again to this remote spot. Perhaps I was attempting to divert the flow of images that have presented themselves to my mind's eye ever since I began to write this memoir. Maybe it was to impose some order into the review of my almost used-up life that I leaned against the front wall of the building and allowed myself to glide into a stationary Zen state, my brain, like a child's balloon tethered by string, chock-full of images, accompanying but not part of the body below.

There was something deeply dispiriting about the endless, strangely amplified patter of rain on the corrugated-iron roof of the schoolhouse. Despite myself, I found myself anchored to the spot. I recognized that some kind of chronology was forcing itself into my consciousness.

I was smiling at the absurdity of my balloon simile when suddenly a terrible roaring assaulted my ears. Connolly's master puppeteer was now exacting cruel revenge for the manipulations to which I'd subjected myself. I had been crouched in a severe hunch for some time. I knew that the presence who had been compelling me to witness wave after wave of recollections, who forced me into this life-changing experience, was not finished yet. Pain brutally attacked my head, shoulders and legs. My vision had become blurred, I swayed from side to side, my feet rooted to the spot in front of the schoolhouse porch – all connection between body and brain had been severed. Oddly, I could watch myself behaving in this terrifying way. I made a layman's crass diagnosis. The sheer volume of reconstituted memories had overwhelmed what was left of my brain.

My mind recoiled in horror, drifted away from the cripple I had become. It was like some weird decapitation . . . A strange scene was before my eyes. A man lunged away from the doorway of the school. With mounting terror I realized I was watching myself. God, look upon me! How long could the body and brain tolerate this craziness? Garbled laughter issued from the mouth of the apparition. How long had I been in my reverie? – seconds, minutes? "Jesus!" the other Norman Maclean groaned, "I must hurry." It was Bruce Springsteen time. *Gotta get outta here.* Already I was heading for my car. I broke into a zig-zagging run. Ram-bam-bam, up the little path towards the main road, right to the door of the little Daihatsu.

I muttered the blasphemy learned so long ago from Catholic neighbours in Benbecula: "*Mhoire Mhàthair, 's a Dhia, m' anam!* Holy Mother, God, my soul!" Seated in my car, I jammed the key into the ignition. The engine screamed. I squealed into a three-point turn and roared off down the glen. In the grip of nameless dread, I did not know why I was trying to escape the long-running movie of my life. In a hurry, I pressed the 'play' button of the basic cassette unit mounted beneath the radio, and the drumming of the car wheels on the gravel as I fought with the wheel round a bend in the road provided a percussive introduction to the familiar Gaelic song. The words wounded my brain:

> *Three things come without seeking,*
> *I mean fear, jealousy, love,*
> *and it's no cause of shame*
> *that I was ensnared for one,*
>
> *for many fine ladies*
> *were guilty of this like me,*
> *giving love that proved fleeting,*
> *with little reward at the end.*

"Go! Go! Go!" I shouted, driving up an incline in low gear. Once on level ground again, I had calmed down sufficiently for me to drive using all my concentration. I fancied that some kind of emotional explosion had taken place within me, and hands and feet worked with the silent desperation of one who acts under the domination of some as yet unleashed power. I was breathing in gasps, in sobs.

I was at Mùrlagan before I realized what I was going to do: I was going to make for Roy Bridge. I would get to the hotel there and hide myself in a room until morning. It would be fine. Everything would be all right as soon as I got home to my little studio flat in Glasgow. The truth was – and I knew this with certainty – what started off as an impulsive trip to the head of the glen had become a lifelong process. I knew that I now had a vivid vision of who I was, of how my weaknesses outweighed my strengths and what relationships and family really meant. I was glad I had taken a risk. "This is the hour of my birth!" I cried out loudly.

Seven o'clock at night, and the tar on the narrow road that wound down the side of the loch was shining wetly. Despite cold and rain I kept the car windows open, for I knew that tiredness was not far off, and I tasted wood-smoke in the wind. At least one of the holiday cottages had to be occupied. Trees, rocks and brief glimpses of the lives of strangers in sun-drenched lands all lashed out at me through the windows of my mind as the little car sailed eastward to Achnacarry. My fevered imagination witnessed dark-skinned gentlemen in white suits, beautiful dusky girls with scarlet, knowing mouths who danced and drank . . .

Here was Cùinnich now. I stopped on the bridge and came out of the car. Though the house was in darkness, the sound of some kind of music, I swore, could be heard coming from the building. I listened for a moment, and extraordinary, high-pitched voices rose above the harsh rasp of trumpets, *Ai! Si, si, Senor – Ai! Ai! Ai!* Instantly every neurone in my brain was awake.

Although part of my mind denied that this was happening, the Spanish-flavoured music, which gradually became more faint, was not altogether a source of astonishment to me. It was beside this house I witnessed the greatest strangeness that ever befell me. The following injection of Celtic mysticism had just popped unbidden into my brain. What was this vivid recollection? Was it to do with *bòcain* or ghosts? Did I really believe in such things? Despite my surface scepticism, a shiver went through my spine. It was only the pitch-dark landscape and my manic outburst up at Srathan, I explained to myself. To follow the narrow path from the bridge to the front door of Cùinnich house was to journey from the immediate into the haunted past.

It is the beginning of winter, and Seumas Mòr and I are returning home to Srathan under a frozen-blue sky, with the wind from the loch making our eyes water, when the old boy announces that he is going to get something to warm him up in Cùinnich, inhabited at that time by Jimmy Henderson, a Lochaber native, and his wife.

The old fellow is inside the main house, enjoying a dram, I suppose, and I am seated on a stool in the byre watching a bitch called Chance and her pups which had been born two days previously. I look up at the rafters. Someone or something is sitting up there. I know this is impossible, because Henderson and his wife have no children. Yet it is clear that someone is perched on the cross-beam. The figure waves to me, and though I can discern tears on wrinkled cheeks, I cannot tell if the thing is male or female. I get up and walk until I am directly below the figure. It is muttering in a language I don't recognize. I hear the words 'hombre' and 'sincero' when, suddenly, the interior of the byre becomes dark. The bitch begins to whimper. I turn round and see a tall man dressed in a cloak and a soft, wide-brimmed hat standing in the doorway. He speaks to me in Gaelic: "Bury me not on the moor," he says. He looks at me with a smile on his face and points to the stool with a silver-tipped stick he is carrying in his hand. I go back to my seat, very excited. My heart is pounding, but not through fear. The most powerful feeling I have is regret that I am ignoring something important.

I could not ignore the strong feeling that assailed me at that moment. I could not explain this, but a conviction that was strangely powerful and inescapable overwhelmed me. The apparition of the benign Spaniard whom my memory had dredged up, and who did not want to be buried on the moor, was connected somehow to my own father, Niall Mòr. I was unable to provide a rational explanation for the appearance of the ghost. Though I tried to make a connection between my father and the Latino props, the attempt was like trying to catch the brown trout I guddled for in the burn below me all these years ago. I made a silent vow to visit his grave in Craigton when I got home. Perhaps I should make peace with the man, so full of contradictions, whom I really didn't know.

The dutiful son returned to his car and resumed his journey. I proceeded more slowly that time. I realised that from the day my father died, my life had changed. From that moment, however I conducted my life did not matter. Something within me had withered. The plaintive melody of the love-song reached my ears.

Air fàilirinn, ilirinn,
Ùilirinn, o-ho-ro laoi,

> *Cruel fortune, unknowing,*
> *Set me in the yoke of your love.*

I considered the horrendous price that Flora, Sandra, Maeve, Audrey, Mary Catherine, Ella, Liz, Margo, Greta, Sylvie, Porn, the two Peigis, and dozens of other girls with whom I coupled, paid for their love. These women, who penetrated my soul with their lascivious gestures, with the scent of their skin, with their absolute command that aroused in me unthinking acceptance, they would be able, I had thought, to resolve all the confusions and failures that might come my way. It was indeed cruel fortune that set those unfortunate women in the yoke. In my present depressed mood, I wondered if perhaps I had met them when it was already too late – at a time when I no longer had the capacity to appreciate the life-giving joy they had to offer. Any suitable response I could have made to dalliance or even to fleshly lust had died beside the casket of Niall Mòr.

Some events come too soon, and others come too late, and by the time a man finds out about them there is nothing to be done . . .

Later, someone was pounding on a door.

"Norman," he shouted, "it's me, George."

I did not answer. I covered my head with a pillow. All I could hear was the fast beat of my own heart.

"Norman," came the voice, much fainter, "are you all right?" Knuckles rapped on the door. The door handle was tried again and again. Footsteps retreated and a door banged.

I drew a breath. What to do? This was the first time since I got sober I had wakened up with no clear idea of where I was and how I got there. But I knew it would not be the last.

I shuddered and tried to wake up. My heart was pounding and my limbs were paralyzed. Locked in a stupor – not sleep, but not full wakefulness either – my right arm was trapped beneath my body and had no sensation in it. The pillow was bloodstained.

Quickly, I swung my bare legs off the bed and struggled to sit up in this darkened room. I caught sight of my watch on the bedside table. Jesus Christ, it was 5.20! In the morning? Or was it night? A packet of Camel cigarettes – Camel, my father's favourite brand – together with a box of Swan Vestas matches lay on the table too.

To find out where I was, I walked over to the dressing table. Pain in my lower back hit me like lightening. 'Claremont Hotel Oban', said the key-tab.

I sat once more on the edge of the bed and tried not to think about the previous night. Everything after reaching Achnacarry was woozy – a series of dim images without sound. I did remember drifting up to the filling station at Onich and deciding to fill up. Sound was restored as the door of the shop opened and the owner, Angus, emerged. He was a Skyeman, and had the typical characteristics of a communicant in the Free Presbyterian Church: a tight thin-lipped mouth when silent, the wrath of God in his voice when speaking and pure hysteria in his eyes at all times. Without offering a greeting, he walked slowly over to the old pump, and with deliberate movements started to fill the tank. I was becoming increasingly irritated at his slowness.

"*Dhia, Aonghais, beiridh a' Bhliadhn' Ur oirnn mum bi thu deiseil*, God, Angus, it'll be New Year before you finish," I snarled in exasperation.

"This way," he responded in Gaelic, "there's more time to yarn to people."

"Not everyone," I said, "has the time or inclination for chat nowadays."

Angus holstered the muzzle and screwed the petrol cap on. "More's the pity, Norman," he said.

I tossed my head impatiently and turned away. "How much is that I owe you?" I said.

"Four," he said.

I stood in the middle of the forecourt, hands on hips, glaring. Abruptly I decided to smile. "Hey, that's all right, Angus," I said, trying to hide my desire to flee.

He stared at me, giving me a full taste of his hysterical eyes.

I groped for my wallet and extracted four banknotes. I offered them to Angus, but made no move to join him.

At last he spoke: "You'll have been performing at a concert then?"

I began to babble. "No," I said. ". . . Well, yes, I was . . . in a way. Up in Golspie . . . a wedding reception – you know that guitar player . . . ah, in the band Montana?"

"No," Angus said.

"Well," I said, "his father's got married to some American heiress, and the old man's a fan of mine . . . It was a kind of last-minute thing."

There was a kind of awkward silence. Angus strolled round the car and looked closely at it. "No gear?" he said.

"What?" I shouted.

"I don't see any instruments – pipes or guitar," he said. "Come over here. I want to talk to you."

I walked slowly over to the car. "What do you want?" I said.

Angus spoke quietly and rapidly. "I hope to God," he said, "you didn't stop off in Lochaber. Your car has been seen a lot there over the past years, and people are talking. They're saying, 'He must be searching for something . . . or someone.' Do you understand?"

"No, Angus," I said, smiling all the time, "I had no stops anywhere."

The two of us looked at one another for a while.

Angus pointed to the money I was still clutching. "Keep that," he said. "Buy a meal on the road south."

"Thanks, Angus," I said. "One thing I'll not be doing is drinking your health . . . no disrespect . . . I'm TT now."

"That's good, Norman," he said. "Look after your own health."

And Angus turned and walked away, back to the shop.

Now, in an unfamiliar hotel room, I was on my way, coughing uncontrollably; head down, into the bathroom. I looked at my face in the mirror above the washbasin. My skin was flushed, a black bruise coated with dried blood flourished on my right temple, and my eyes, above the swollen nose and bruised mouth, were truly the eyes of an eighty-year-old. I ran cold water and splashed it on my face. I poured handfuls of water into my parched damaged mouth. There was a metallic taste at the back of my throat. I had been violently sick sometime recently and there was a dull ache in my stomach. Whenever I remembered recent events I became coloured from the same palette of murky feelings – regret, envy and the ever-present conviction that I am a phoney and maybe I'll become the real thing in the future.

Back in the bedroom, my cigarettes were waiting for me. I lit a cigarette and puffed deeply. Within half a minute my entire body received the welcome message, *You're going to be fine, Norman*. At least, I hadn't had any alcohol. I took another deep drag and sighed . . .

A sudden memory from last night engulfed me: voices – female voices.

"Hey, Norman," a young girl said. "Tell us one of your Benbecula stories."

"No, Sandra," another female voice said. "The poor guy's knack-ered." She proffered a half-pint glass full of dark, fizzy liquid. "Here, darling, drink this. It's only Coca-Cola."

Faint impressions gelled into crisp images.

On either side of Norman Maclean, a soppy grin on his face, in the lounge of the Claremont Hotel, two young girls were squeezed into a red leather banquette against one of the walls. Our bodies were squashed together in sensual abandon. This was Detroit all over again. I was not seriously listening to the back and forth of Lynn and Sandra.

Who were these females? Were they young mothers out on the town? Were they on the staff of the Claremont and enjoying an after-hours drink? As they traded inconsequential chit-chat, my eyes were growing heavier and heavier.

"Norman, pet? – don't peg out on us," Lynn, the tall dark-haired one, said. "Don't be rude to Lynn and Sandra. Hey, Norman – get with it."

I turned towards Sandra, whose soft breast was pressed against my arm and said, "Honey, I've had it . . . got to . . . crash." Lynn giggled and said huskily, "Well, Norman, maybe you should go up and take a shower." Sandra took this up, showing teeth as she smiled mockingly. "Yes, maybe you should take a shower, Norman," she said. "Lynn and I will come up and give you a hand." The girls shrieked with laughter and I joined in . . . until I remembered something.

In an instant I was reminded of my ugly, misshapen feet.

"Look, girls," I said desperately. "I've got . . . I've got to . . ."

In a taunting singsong voice, one of the girls chanted, "*Norman* doesn't want us, and *we* don't want Norman."

I heard this through a buzzing haze. I heard words but I was not sure I was hearing them. Then I was walking. I was in motion.

"You OK, Norman?" a man's voice asked.

Turning, in motion, my legs gave out, the tiles beneath me pitched suddenly, and I fell. The sharp edge of a table flew up to meet my right temple. Norman Maclean entered the realm of the seven clouds . . .

Much later, I came to, seated in a chair overlooking a window in the hotel room. On unsteady feet, my breath rasping in my throat, I proceeded to the window and looked out. The hotel was facing the bay, and in the orange glow of the street lights the dark current of the sea slid lazily against a handful of fishing boats moored over by the pier. Further out, though I could not see them clearly in the wet dawn, were the mountains of Mull, a place so like the country I had left. I realized, though my brain was befogged by the injury to my head, that my true home was not up there beside the hills. I derived my identity from the islands, where beaches of soft, white coral sand were kissed or battered by the sea, where geese and black clouds of starlings flew above close-cropped, orderly machair-land, and where every chimney sent smoke rich with the smell of peat up to the great, wide canopy of the sky. I knew then that Uist was the place that had been allotted to me on God's earth to conduct my business. Certainly, I had left it in the past, and doubtless I should leave it again and again, and in whatever place I'd find death I should wish that the people would only think that I was asleep and that they might transport me across the blessed sea so that I should have my burial in *Baile nan Cailleach*, the Township of the Nuns, Cemetery in Benbecula.

I had been shuffling between the toilet and the cigarette packet for over two hours, remembering, thinking about and rebuilding the events that happened up the glen and long after that. I had learned lessons that would leave a mark on me for the rest of my life. Perhaps I should have to carry the burden of guilt for my treatment of Niall Mòr and the rest of my lovers like some tumour for all future time. Perhaps my own death was approaching. I did not know. As Peigi used to say, 'tomorrow is not promised to any of us.' It did not matter. I was sure of only one thing: it is bad enough to be an actor in the wrong play, but it is immeasurably worse when you find this out and you no longer have the strength to fight that you may get back what you have lost.

Epilogue

I was tempted to pull the pin on these tidal waves of memories with that final plangent note about being an actor in the wrong play. I envisioned a film, perhaps, featuring someone whose measurements corresponded to my own, with a marked resemblance to Samuel Beckett, standing at a window and declaiming these lines in a faux-sincere voice. Pretty slick, eh? In a novel, this metaphor would have sounded a deliberately bathetic chord to end a sad, occasionally funny trawl through a talent to abuse. Yet . . . and yet . . . I feel these endings would be shallow and leave me unfulfilled.

In January this year I had a session with a psychic in a scruffy room off Leith Walk in Edinburgh. I had just recorded the narrative for my fourth novel, *Slaightearan*, with big Al George, ably assisted by Mairead Ross, the Gaelic policewoman, in Canongate Studios, and was feeling pretty pleased with myself. Walking up Leith Walk, I saw a crudely painted sign with a directional arrow bearing the information: MADAME ROSA, CLAIRVOYANT, WALK RIGHT IN, NO APPT. NECESSARY. "She *knows*," I managed to gasp before entering the dimly-lit cubicle.

Madame Rosa, whom I took to be some gypsy crone from Romania or Eastern Europe, demanded the twenty pound fee up front, which I promptly paid with a flourish. Then she took my right hand in hers and turned it over, palm upward. She used her middle finger lightly to trace a line along my palm to the wrist.

"I can read the future in your palm," she said.

"What do you see?" I asked.

"You have a very long life-line," she said. "Your love-line is broken, I'm sorry to say."

"You sure?" I said.

"Definitely," she said.

"I can also see that you have had a passionate affair with alcohol," she said.

I yanked my hand away. "What the hell is this?" I exclaimed.

Madame Rosa raised her own hands in surrender. "Easy," she crooned. "Okay? It is all clear to me. You have just broken up with a woman with three children. She was much younger than you."

I sighed and rose from the table. "Thank you, Madame Rosa," I said. "You're right about the love line and the break-up. I hope you're right about the life-line too." I left the room and made my way to Waverley Station to catch the 18.30 train to Queen Street. It was probably then that I decided to commit my thoughts about my variegated life to paper.

The old gypsy was dead right about the broken love-line. I had just terminated a relationship with a woman half my age in Acharacle. I have changed the name of this individual because she is so young that if this work is ever published it will cause needless embarrassment to her and her three children. Lila, as I will call her, was the single unmarried mother of a girl and two boys, ranging in age from ten to five, who looked after her demented granny. When she offered me her young flesh in the drunken aftermath of a gig in the village hall, she looked to my crippled receptors just the ticket. What was to have been a guilt-free routine stretch of bed fun turned into a dark and quarrel-laden time. The kids ran thumping around the house at all hours of the day and night.

I seemed darkly exhausted, except when I was tending to the more salacious aspects of courtship, and my days were largely unhopeful. I would be snapping at everybody, then apologising. On one visit I had been drinking quite heavily, and was seated with Lila at the kitchen table awaiting the arrival of granny from the community centre she attended. In fairness I have to relate that Lila herself was an uncontrolled binge drinker. We were bad for each other.

She slowly placed the beer can she had been drinking from on the table and smiled at me in a manner I'd learned to be wary of. I creaked up to my feet. Suddenly we heard the rumble of the bus from the community centre as the carers returned with granny. We both headed for the living-room, where I had left a litre bottle of vodka on my return from the Shiel Lodge Hotel the previous night. We collided and both staggered back, screaming, "Crabbit old drunk" and "Violent bitch" respectively.

I remained in the kitchen while Lila made for the living-room and the vodka. While preparing a ready-meal for granny in the microwave,

I had a brief glimpse of how dishearteningly long this could go on, how time-wasting and inconclusive this protracted affair would turn out to be. A slow understanding spread through me, a long cringe, a loss of spirit. I'm too *old* for this garbage, I thought. Eventually, I wheeled the old woman to her room at the far end of a long corridor, and decided to confront my young lover.

When I entered the living room she was sprawled on a couch, babbling away with no clear idea of what she was saying. There was about an inch of vodka left in the bottle.

"*Gaahhh*," she said by way of greeting.

"You've finished the booze," I said accusingly. My fun quota for the year of 2007 hadn't even been approached.

"*Aaamhh humh kraaas odk shluck*," she said in high, strangled slurring.

"Easy for you to say," I snapped. "Fucking impossible for me to understand." Oh, boy! I'm an assertive man at last! The thought came to me with some force, I loved it.

"Mmwahh," I said, blowing her a departing kiss.

The dysfunction between us had worsened after the death of my mother, Peigi Bheag, in January 2005. The guilt I felt for burdening her with my presence in her well-run home after the parting from my wife in 1995 was bad enough. There was something unnatural, I thought, about a middle-aged man who had been married twice – at least twice – being dependent on his aged mother. When she was admitted to Florence House in Govan, a residential nursing home, five years later, suffering from dementia, there was an additional layer of mixed emotions blanketing me.

I used to visit her every day, and I knew how to press her buttons, to have her ramble on about schooldays in Carinish and in Kinning Park. I bought her a tape recorder and chose a rake of Gaelic cassettes from my own large collection. Her choice of song should have been banned by Brussels. Night after night she'd ask me to set up and play *Òran an Anchor Bar* sung by Murdani Mast. This was a picaresque ballad by the singer-composer about the night he and his shipmates fell foul of a gang of Glasgow Teddy Boys in Finnieston.

> *Gur ann air oidhche Haoine bh' ann,*
> *Chaidh sinne sìos Corunna Street.*
> *Gun deach' sinne gun smaointeachadh*
> *A-steach dhan Anchor Bar.*

> It was on a Friday night,
> We went down Corunna Street,
> And went, without thinking,
> Into the Anchor Bar.

If truth be told, I enjoyed singing along with this number myself. It reinforced my belief that there existed a powerful antagonism on the part of Lowlanders against Gaelic speakers. Oh, yes, I'd think, when Murdo Daniel Matheson concluded his Bacchanalian ditty, this is another example of '*mì-rùn mòr nan Gall*, the great ill-will of the Lowlanders'. But it wasn't difficult to lose track of where I came from and where my own catharsis began.

Although the staff at Florence House were good to her and tried hard to accommodate an often querulous old woman, this was a place where spent people went to die. I tried to force the memories of this once pretty woman, who had become a husk in the days after her ninety-eighth birthday, out of my head. I used to hold her hand as she grew weaker and weaker.

I remember vividly one conversation we shared some days before my mother lost the light. I peered at her face as she lay propped up by pillows. Something was wrong. She began to pop and roll her eyes, which had a moist glow.

"*Dè tha ceàrr, a mhàthair*? What's wrong, mother?" I said.

"You knew your father was unfaithful to me, didn't you?" she said.

"I suppose so," I said.

"I didn't mean, you know . . ." she said.

"What?" I asked.

This was a thin-ice special for Peigi Bheag. Her unlooked-for broaching of the subject of my late father left me with my eyes turned down, away, never meeting the glittering eyes of my confessor.

"He was soft," she said in a plaintive little-girl voice.

"How?" I said.

"He always felt he could *help* women," she said. "Especially good-looking blondes."

"Uh-huh," I muttered, on some internal delay.

"I should have taken a blade to his private parts, eh?" she hissed.

In the clarity of my dying mother's admission, something I had known about for over sixty years, I had nailed the kernel of our relationship. My driving emotion had always been resentment more than love. My mother had always reminded me of Gus Matheson, the predatory, pleasure-seeking pal of my youth. She presented herself as a hard-working, soft-spoken woman who was firmly grounded in the reality of the now, but underneath, all the time, there had been a desire to wreak revenge on her philandering husband, and to enact fantasies of onrushing trains with his lovers as bound female victims. I wondered if my own unsatisfactory relationships with women had their origins in the hidden anger I felt at the bitterness she had always exhibited towards Niall Mòr when he was alive, and indeed to all men after he died.

My mother inhaled another shuddering breath. "Norman?" she gasped.

"What is it?" I said, without much solicitude.

"I want to tell you something," she said.

"What?" I asked, suddenly fearful of what might come next.

"I've seen you so often," she sighed, "stretched out on the couch, blind drunk, you know?"

"And?" I blustered.

"When I looked down on your wasted body," she said, "I was afraid."

"Why?" I asked, my curiosity aroused.

"Your face was so ugly," she said. "So often you had the face of an old man, all wrinkled and bony."

"Is that right?" I said softly.

"*Shaoilinn-sa nach b' ann leam fhèin a bha thu*, I'd be thinking you didn't really belong to me," she said, reverting to her native Gaelic.

"*Dè thuirt thu, a mhàthair*, What did you say, mother?" I said in puzzled tones.

"*Is còir dhut clag lobhair a chur mud amhach*, You should have a leper's bell round your neck," she said.

"*Carson*, Why?" I asked.

"*A chionn 's gu bheil thu neòghlan . . . neòghlan . . . neòghlan*, Because you are unclean . . . unclean . . . unclean," she croaked.

"*Dè tha sibh a' ciallachadh*, What do you mean?" I said anxiously.

"*Chan eil annad ach tàcharan, a Thormoid*, You're but a changeling, Norman," she said with as much vehemence as she could summon, as she struggled to draw oxygen into her wasted lungs.

I didn't think she was referring to the old Scottish superstition of fairies kidnapping infants from their cradles and leaving sickly, wizened creatures in their place. My interpretation of 'changeling' was that my industrious old mother had secretly observed all the masks and false personae I had assumed over the years. Her deathbed words were perhaps a lot closer to the truth of things than my own lame rationalisations for my bizarre behaviour had been.

After I received the long awaited telephone call from Florence House, I was sent spinning into an alcoholic stupor that cost me two years of my life. When my mother finally slipped away, my niece, Elizabeth, was a tower of strength. Sorting through her grandmother's possessions in the home and being a model hostess in my flat after the burial, she relieved me of many potentially painful experiences.

Earth and pebbles rattle on the lid of mother's coffin as Willie Parke, standing twenty yards from the graveside, plays 'The Flowers o' the Forest' on a resonant bagpipe in a fine smirr of rain.

The strange thing is: I haven't communicated with Liz for three years.

From 2005 right through to my accident in the summer of 2007 I was steadily drinking myself into deadness. Frequently, the bed-time story I narrated in my mind before drifting off into restless sleep was that I would die and be buried in the same lair as Niall Mòr, Lorna and Peigi Bheag. This was a conclusion to my ruined life I devoutly wished for. My friends had all peeled away from me, one by one. My mother, however, had never gone away from me. Inside, in my head, she still talked to me in the soft, lilting cadences of North Uist. She guided me. There still existed an umbilical cord that connected and never disappeared.

So, rebelling against my dark fall, I sought help from Gordon Lawrie, father of Griogair, from Duncan Nicholson and Allan Henderson, two musician friends, and Seòras Phàdraig Chaluim Ruairidh, a former Washington DC cop who came originally from South Uist. I'm afraid my idea of therapy was to start complaining about my own life, debts and unpaid bills and physical decrepitude. These guys persevered, Gordon and his wife Morag helped me greatly, and with the encouragement of young Brian McGeachan, a freelance journalist, I put history on pause for a while and started work on this present memoir.

Life cannot always be lived in the past. I have to think in the present and have some consideration for the future. Really, things at present aren't too bad. They're not great, but they're different. I'm not doing as many live gigs, but I am doing a lot of writing. Being crouched rather uncomfortably over the word processor on a daily basis has been my salvation. It always was. I started off with a Gaelic language novel called *Cùmhnantan*. This is a snigger at the cupidity of media types involved in Gaelic television. The next effusion, *Keino*, is a darker novella dealing with subjects like guilt, suffering, sex and redemption. It's not surprising really that this book didn't sell all that well, as the truth is that the majority of the bilingual population is non-literate. Even a broadcasting star like Cathy Macdonald confessed to me that she found it difficult to read Gaelic prose. We are inundated with English language radio, television, film, novels and newspapers, and it's small wonder that we prefer to be presented with English.

Next out was *Dacha Mo Ghaoil*, *Dearest Dacha*, a comedy romp involving ostriches, Russian 'working girls', a trio of rural scallywags and a capable female lawyer from North Uist who attempts to sort things out. I had a fourth novel, *Slaightearan*, *Tricksters*, launched in March 2008. This is another jokey story about two semi-professional thespians from the islands whose attempts to become financially whole provide many comic scenes. I have been diverted, enlightened and made to feel virtuous by my rattling attacks on the computer keyboard. I intend to continue with this rewarding activity as I have a notion to send up the jiggery-pokery indulged in by some of our MSPs in Holyrood.

On the live stand-up comedy front, I'm in two minds. On one hand, I'm considering a well-chosen comeback. I favour gigs where I don't have to sell myself. Favourite venues would be Inverness, Dingwall, Lairg, Lochaber, Moidart, Kyle of Lochalsh, the Western Isles and the Tarbert, Ardrishaig, Lochgilphead axis in mid-Argyll. As they were in the past, these places could still provide forgiving audiences. On the other hand, I don't know if I'll be able to endure the travelling and sheer physical effort I'd have to expend on a high-energy act.

I suspect that I'll embark next year on truncated mini-tours with shortened routines because of physical infirmities. Any instrument requiring digital dexterity is forbidden to me. Bagpipe, clarinet, flute, guitar and saxophone are all no-nos in the foreseeable future. Accordingly, if I want to make instrumental music, I am confined to Donald

Black's 'Highlander Mouthorgan'. Of course, I can always expand the singing elements in the proposed mélange. Sure, I can still carry a tune, though not very far nowadays.

Recently, on Saturday, 3 May 2008, I did a sit-down Dave Allen-type gig in Lairg, Sutherland. Granted that I clearly looked like the old wreck I am, the two spots of about thirty minutes duration went surprisingly well. The members of Lodge Scotia were a jolly crowd. They comprised, together with a score of local masons, the kind of audience I like. They hooted, laughed uproariously, stamped their feet in approval and clapped enthusiastically. My kind of folk – fond of a drink. A caveat: look at the example of poor Calum Kennedy.

I am purged of the lust for fame. I'm not even all that interested in Queen Cash. I have enough money. But I don't have *all* the money. I've had to establish limits. I no longer seek the stardust balm that I spread on my wounded soul in my more affluent days. For a short while in the Seventies and Eighties, when I hit it, if not big but palpably, all of sudden there were no more rules. I didn't have interior values to guide me. *Scoosh* – off I went. No stability. No brakes. No nothing. I was Mr Open Shirt, Chains and Sovereign Rings, and Mr Check Out My Sternum at that time.

I admit that I still have a hankering to stand in front of people who have been saying 'He's past it, I thought he died in 2007,' and proudly announce, 'Two tears in a bucket, and I'm still here!'

I've often mused on the motivation of performers. I hazard a guess that most people who are driven to show off in public are basically shy folk. 'What?' I hear the astonished cry. 'Why would a shy person tell jokes to strangers, teach esoteric subjects like Mathematics, produce and present television programmes, write and play music, sing songs, and write books, stage and radio plays?' My response would be that the majority of creative people, and I include poets, painters, punters of soccer free-kicks in this subset, do what they do not because they think they're marvellous, but because they want to prove to themselves that they are. This little perception may not apply to everyone, but it certainly does to me.

I don't think that education will require my services ever again either. A year ago I had the altogether altruistic idea that I would like to put something back into Gaelic culture. After completing a formidable obstacle course of questionnaires to determine that I wasn't a bra-pinger or a 'stoat the ba' – "Come over here, wee boy, and you can get a shot of my ball" – I discovered there was no demand for the skills of an Honours graduate who had experience of presenting candidates in Gaelic at Higher grade.

Of course, part of me rejoices that there obviously exists a deep reservoir of teaching talent to service increasing numbers of students who wish to learn the language. I even offered to take creative writing workshops in *Sabhal Mòr Ostaig*, the Gaelic College in Skye, free of charge, after a rewarding afternoon encouraging and stimulating some very talented students: the 'high heid yins' didn't even acknowledge my follow-up letter. I suppose I'll just have to accept that in classrooms and lecture rooms I'm slowly losing profile. This is a phenomenon familiar to anyone with experience of show business. Everybody gets the elbow some time.

Yet another activity that has been stifled for me is travelling in Europe with the Clan Wallace Pipes and Drums. This was undoubtedly the worst pipe band in the world, but somehow in the millennium they received invitations to perform in Spain, Italy and France. And what memorable experiences these trips were! Deliberately ignoring the unflattering dress code – 'bovver' boots, thick mountaineering socks, dull, dun-coloured checked plaids and shapeless Hessian skirts in the *Braveheart* style – and, more importantly, turning a deaf ear to the squawks and squeals of ill-matching chanters and untuned drones as with waggling fingers we raced through, at breakneck speed, tunes like 'Men of Kilmaurs' (really, 'The High Road to Gairloch') and 'The Battle of Stirling Bridge' (really, 'Paddy's Leather Breeches'), I used to close my eyes during the thrice-daily recitals and think of Scotland.

The most exciting feature of these continental trips for me, however, was the opportunity to visit places in France, Spain and Italy I'd never be able to afford were I to consider going to them under my own steam. I'll be sorry to give up these jaunts, but I have my suspicions that the Clan Wallace are now moribund and that Seòras, the self-proclaimed chieftain, has been rumbled by the foreign agents who booked him. I'm not too worried. If I want to go back, I can if I'm solvent. I no longer believe that happiness lies in another place as I did when I confused freedom with hedonism. Taking 'free' as far as you can probably equals 'dead'.

The feeling is approaching of a clear break just ahead of everything I have known. It may not be the 'end' but a 'transition' is definitely on its way. If I'm not headed for a better life, at least I'm advancing towards something unexpressed in the life I've had to date. Maybe it's a good thing that I'm being forced to curb the excessive workload my unrelenting work ethic forces upon me. At my age – my seventy-first birthday has just passed – my outlook has to be tempered by moderation. It's hard, but I've had to face some truths. I recall the words of Bob Christie of Grampian Television at a disciplinary hearing, after another little box-up on my part. "Norman," he said waspishly, "all your life you've been encouraged to think of yourself as special. You're *not* special." I've accepted this. After all, I never quite made it out of the minor showbusiness leagues.

It is prudent, I think, to stage-manage my activities so that I do not place myself in jeopardy. For example, unless a friend is picking me up by car, I don't go into town at night. Go into town? On my own? At night? In the homicide capital of Europe? Good God, have I taken leave of what is left of my senses? I must desist from coming up with those suicidal suggestions. Slow down, Norrie! In case I meet some young, fit psychopath with a snout full of Buckfast and a blade in his pocket, I'll stay in the groove I occupy at present.

Oh, yes, it looks as if my life will be devoid of unnecessary excitement from now on. It'll be devoted to keeping stress at bay. Something has shifted within me. I look forward to continuing with my scribbling.

I'm convinced that I'll no longer pretend to be in charge of my own destiny, for I know that vagary of fortune has as much to do with destiny as any exercise of free will. At the risk of tempting Providence, I am confident that I am ready for anything that is going to come to me. A boon of growing and feeling old is that I expect very little and really value things as they arrive. Unfortunately, as I've said, I'll have to manage this without Peigi. About thirteen years ago she announced that she could no longer live with me. Her song was always the same: 'I Hate To See You Killing Yourself'. I packed up and left to live with my aged mother. There was no acrimony in this separation. Peigi comes down to my wee flat in Bellahouston at least once a month, wrinkles her nose with disdain at the untidiness of the place and sets to cleaning, hoovering and making enough food to keep me going for a week or two. Once every six weeks or so we dine in an upmarket restaurant, linen service, dimmed lighting and soft, middle-of-the-road music. We've even been known to indulge in a spot of cheek to cheek, smoochy dancing on the odd occasion. It's just, as the old joke says, I do it in Glasgow: she does it in Oban.

Enough foolishness, already. *Is mithich a bhith a' bogadh nan gad*, it is time to be steeping the withes. What the hell are withes? This is a native Gaelic saying meaning 'it is time to be going'. It comes from a time when withes of birch were used for halters and all the fastenings of horse-harness. These withes would become stiff and brittle if laid by for some time, and would therefore be steeped for a while before taking to horse.

Drink? I honestly don't know. While abstinence is suiting me just now, I know that I will be presented with circumstances in the future that will demand that I elevate or depress my mood by taking drink. That's why they invented the stuff in the first place. *'S iomadh rud a chì am fear as fhaide beò*, Many a thing will be seen by the man who lives longest, as the old Gaelic proverb says. I suspect that like most addicts I don't profoundly want to give up. After all, you're highly unlikely to become addicted to something you dislike or which doesn't give you a modicum of pleasure. I shall always remember my weaknesses are stronger than I am and that I have a choice.

I choose now to bring this history to a halt.

Con amistad, a chàirdean, Ciaoito!

I am coming out.